9x10/08 v 10/08

A GIFT FROM THE
FRIENDS OF THE
LA JOLLA LIBRARY

D0122930

MAR 2 5 2008

ALSO BY JUDITH THURMAN

Isak Dinesen: The Life of a Storyteller
Secrets of the Flesh: A Life of Colette

CLEOPATRA'S
NOSE

CLEOPATRA'S

NOSE

39 Varieties of Desire

JUDITH THURMAN

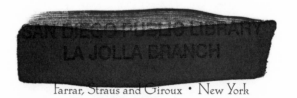
SAN DIEGO PUBLIC LIBRARY
LA JOLLA BRANCH

Farrar, Straus and Giroux • New York

Farrar, Straus and Giroux
19 Union Square West, New York 10003

Copyright © 2007 by Judith Thurman
All rights reserved
Distributed in Canada by Douglas & McIntyre Ltd.
Printed in the United States of America
First edition, 2007

With the exception of "Hidden Women," these essays previously
appeared, in slightly different form, in *The New Yorker.*

Library of Congress Cataloging-in-Publication Data
Thurman, Judith.
    Cleopatra's nose : 39 varieties of desire / Judith
Thurman.— 1st ed.
        p.   cm.
    ISBN-13: 978-0-374-12651-3 (hardcover : alk. paper)
    ISBN-10: 0-374-12651-8
    I. Title.

PS3620.H88C57 2007
814'.54—dc22
                                                    2007005092

Designed by Jonathan D. Lippincott

www.fsgbooks.com

1   3   5   7   9   10   8   6   4   2

In memory of Hayat Mathews

Contents

Hide and Seek

The essays in this collection were, with one exception, written for *The New Yorker* between 1987 and 2007. My editors proposed certain assignments, which I was free to decline, and I came to them with others. But the nature of my affinity with a good subject reveals itself only when it is ready to—never before. Tofu and Flaubert; a fashion show and an election; pornography and hair; kimonos and bulimia—all have at least one trait in common: they put up a dogged struggle with my presumptions as a stranger trying to do them justice.

The title of this collection revealed itself to me, too. It comes from a musing on carnal attachments by Blaise Pascal that was found after his death in 1662 and included, with other fragmentary thoughts, in his *Pensées*: "Anyone who wants to know the full extent of human vanity has only to consider the causes and effects of love," he wrote: "Cleopatra's nose: had it been shorter, the whole face of the world would have been changed." "Had it been shorter" is a charming twist. Pascal himself had a classical thinker's aquiline beak with a slight bump at the bridge. The nubile buttons and ski jumps currently in vogue would have been considered common by his contemporaries. There are no extant images of the actual Cleopatra, and the iconic depictions don't agree, but a Frenchman of Pascal's erudition certainly knew that the Ptolemies were Greek, and he seems to have imagined the Egyptian queen as she saw herself: an avatar of Aphrodite, whose profile is generally represented as a fine though virile shaft—a Grecian arrow, with a slightly pointed tip—like that of her twin, Apollo.

Though Pascal might have chosen a less farcical body part as a synedoche for Cleopatra's beauty, it wouldn't have advanced the audacious premise of the *Pensées*: that proof of God exists. The arguments are aimed at an intelligent skeptic, and Pascal—not only an evangelist, and the greatest abstract thinker of his age, but a practical genius who designed the world's first streetcar system (for Paris)—savors the challenge of outsmarting him. Each maxim is engineered as a deceptively humane trap baited with allusions that a sophisticated reader will find disarming: to gambling and dress; to sport and seduction; to the sensual appetites. Sensing, tasting, feeling, smacking of, being conscious, and smelling are all represented by the same verb in French, *sentir*, and one needed a fine nose to cut a proper figure at the Bourbon court. But you can't smell, either transitively or intransitively, without being reminded of your kinship with the lowliest creatures who root and rut, or that the ripeness of the flesh—the bait in Pascal's trap—precedes its corruption. Thus is the moral of a Christian philosopher craftily embodied in the organ of a mythic voluptuary.

A mutual interest in corruption is part of what draws me to Pascal, an otherwise unlikely lodestar for a critic whose beats at a secular journal tend to fall under the heading of "human vanity." The author of the *Pensées* was an ascetic Jansenist who lost his mother at four, never married, and seems to have died a virgin. "The sweetness of love," he writes, even at its most innocent—a maternal caress—is a fatal temptation and a false comfort that he urges men of conscience to abjure. Yet there are few shrewder students of worldly life than this cerebral zealot repulsed and fascinated by rankness, and if he can't persuade me that his God exists, his style is proof that a work of literature can be a form of redemption.

Thirty-nine pieces from twenty years of a journalist's career are, in a way, the chapters of a biography. Whatever social or literary history they distill, each one takes place at the moment in my own life that it was written. It still surprises me that I chose, or fell into, the genre of nonfiction. Its rigors require a focused mind that I don't naturally possess, and as a young woman I set my inner metronome to tick more idly: one line of poetry at a time. In the early 1970s, a small press in London published a chapbook of my work. After college, I had moved abroad to live and travel on my savings from a summer job writing ad copy for a company that owned beauty salons ("A wig of beauty is a joy for weather"), and I might have stayed there enjoying a marginal though amusing life immersed in foreignness had it not begun to affect my accent and therefore my ear. Eventually—though probably not soon enough—I was embarrassed to be asked by fellow English speakers, "What country are you from?"

Back in New York, I found occasional jobs using the three languages I had acquired. A shady German who imported porn films hired me to write dubbing scripts and a friend of ours—a Swiss actress who, at the time, was also playing Ophelia—to do the moaning. Without any sense of incongruity, I began contributing to the newly launched *Ms.* magazine. My first profiles—of the poets Louise Labé and Sor Juana Inés de la Cruz (a courtesan and a nun)—were published under the rubric "Lost Women," and in 1974, at the behest of Gloria Steinem, the editor in chief, I tried a portrait of Isak Dinesen. Perhaps my experiences in the cutting room—of anonymity and ventriloquism—had something to do with its conceit. I framed it as a conversation with an elderly Danish countess living in Tuscany who had supposedly been one of Dinesen's childhood friends. The countess was an invention, but the interview wasn't labeled imaginary by the magazine, and more than one reader was fooled, including Dinesen's executor, a custodian wary of unlicensed trespassers, who wrote me an alarmed letter. She believed that she had recognized my phantom confidante by certain telling details—the breed of her dogs, a fondness for unsugared lemonade—as a widow whom I later had the pleasure of meeting in the course of my research on Dinesen's biography.

I can't explain how I came to endow my countess with a kennel of Dandie Dinmonts, or with a tone of worldly dispassion that I didn't possess, but which lent a certain authority to the imposture. Nor can I explain the uncensored ease with which I produced it, and which I have never been able to recapture. But while I was culling these essays from a much larger body of work, I had a mildly uncanny revelation. In 1974, I was hearing a staticky broadcast of my own mature voice speaking from the future.

There are many ways for a woman to be lost, or to lose herself, and the subject has become one of my specialties. The first of my lost women was my mother, Alice, who was born two blocks from the Yorkville brownstone where I have raised my son. She was generally as unconfiding about herself as a fugitive, which in a way she was— the fugitive from a life she might have lived. But there was one episode in her youth that she liked to recall, particularly when I had poured her a second glass of sweet sherry and we were sitting at her immaculate kitchen table in Queens under the fluorescent light. Quite apart from the story, the pleasure that it gave her (her pleasures were rare enough) left a potent impression.

Alice had an unlikely family connection to *The New Yorker* that was, in a way, seeded long before Raoul Fleischmann, the magazine's publisher until his death in 1969, bankrolled its first editor in chief, Harold Ross. Fleischmann was the son of a German immigrant who made his fortune in the yeast business and who, in 1907—the year my mother was born—decided to open the replica of a Viennese bakery and café on Broadway and East Tenth Street. The Vienna Model Bakery became a New York institution, not only because of its gemütlich charm and the excellence of its baked goods but because, at the end of the business day, the management gave away whatever merchandise hadn't been sold. Sometimes as many as five hundred hungry and indigent men and women waited for a handout at the back door on what Fleischmann, who coined the concept and the term, called "a bread line." His son Raoul received a gentlemanly education and, as a young man, lived with his family in princely style, but his father wanted him to learn the business of making dough (and not just the green variety) from the ground up. He entrusted Raoul's apprenticeship to the bakery's foreman, himself a master pastry chef who had learned his trade at Vienna's Hotel Sacher. This wiry Hungarian—my grandfather Leo Meisner—had immigrated to New York in the late 1880s after a childhood of vagabondage in cen-

tral Europe that eventually beached him, at thirteen, savage and penniless in the imperial capital. He was one of twenty-one children—
twenty sons and a daughter—by his father's two wives, and he had
escaped from the care of a "wicked" grandmother at the age of eight,
with his younger brother. A bout of typhoid contracted, he said,
from drinking the water and living on the frogs in a fetid pond somewhere in Herzegovina had left him bald, and with his polished skull,
high cheekbones, and lashless Tartar eyes, he somehow looked both
infantile and ferocious. He was, however, an incorrigible bon vivant
who spent his salary in the dance halls of Eighty-sixth Street, and on
flashy plus fours, and a canary-yellow Packard with a jump seat that
was, for years, the only vehicle besides his bakery van parked on his
block of tenements, east of the old El.

Though I can't see Raoul Fleischmann stoking the ovens, I like to
imagine that my grandfather taught his protégé something about
schnapps, pinochle, and floozies—his other fields of expertise. They
became friends, and Fleischmann took an interest in the Meisner
children. He arranged for the eldest, my uncle Wesley, to attend his
own alma mater, Williams College. Wesley was a muscular blond, and
his German was pure. In the late thirties, he did some freelance spy-
ing for the FBI by infiltrating Nazi Bund meetings in the local beer
gardens. Fleischmann, I suppose, wishfully reckoned that my uncle's
Teutonic features, passion for Heine and the Romantics, and prowess
as an athlete (he and Johnny Weissmuller trained at the same Y and
swam together in the East River) would compensate for the chasm of
class between a tough working-class Jew and his privileged classmates. It was a short-lived experiment. But when my mother needed
a summer job, Meisner asked his friend if there wasn't something for
her at his magazine. Fleischmann had only one question: "Is she still
so fat?"

Alice was the dormouse in a family that loved drama. A Catholic
daughter with the same temperament might have dreamed of the
convent; Alice put her faith in the efficacy of silent worry on everyone's behalf. She devoured her father's *kipfel*—a Viennese croissant—
as voraciously as she read her brother's books, and mutely retreated
to the fire escape from household storms. Her younger sister, Charlotte, a tomboy with Titian hair, once bashed Alice over the head

with a violin. "I just got fed up with her goodness," my aunt told me, seventy years later.

At sixteen, however, Alice sloughed her cocoon of flesh and emerged as a shapely girl whose loveliness was both sensuous and fragile. There is something about her enigmatic smile in old photographs—behind dark glasses, or at the beach in a jersey bathing suit and a striped turban—which suggests that she enjoyed her effect on men. Her decorative stint as a temporary receptionist in *The New Yorker*'s hallowed premises on West Forty-third Street led, after she graduated from Hunter, to her employment as a "fashion forecaster" at Condé Nast. She could never explain exactly what she did beyond spending a fortune on hats and going to the theater and the opera (during intermissions), where she made notes on whatever "trends" in fashion she could discern, which were transferred to color-coded punch cards and analyzed by a mechanical sorting machine at the office. This fantastical interlude—Rube Goldberg meets Dorothy Parker—ended with the Depression, when Alice was rather less glamorously employed teaching English and Latin to the rowdy boys in a South Boston high school.

By the time I was old enough to take stock of my mother's character, she had reverted to the habits—the furtive eating and daydreaming—of her girlhood. Having once been vain of her complexion, she showed a vain indifference to its ravages, which gave her a resemblance to the old Auden. After one of her periodic bouts of starvation dieting, she bought some pretty clothes, and a rich sister-in-law gave her a Dior hand-me-down that she wore to PTA meetings, but eventually it went the way of her resolve. I knew her mainly as a semi-recluse in a shabby housedress who read with a pencil in one hand and a cigarette in the other. Smoking was probably her greatest indulgence, followed by order, solitude, lists, foul weather, crosswords, and grammar, and the grammarian was a martinet. Alice told me proudly that when *Ulysses* was first published, she had punctuated Molly Bloom's soliloquy. Until I left for college, my compositions got the same treatment. "You have to admit that it reads better this way," she would say, having mutilated some piece of homework with a pair of scissors. The first time that I received a galley (the essay on Nadine Gordimer in this volume) corrected by the late Eleanor

Gould, *The New Yorker*'s formidable chief copy editor, it felt as though my maternal nemesis had come back to haunt me. The margins were almost a work of art, every inch finely tattooed with wispy hieroglyphs, like the feet of a Moroccan bride. So I took out my mother's old primers—Longmans', Fowler, Strunk and White—and vowed to make Miss Gould pay Alice, if not me, her most grudging compliment: a clean proof.

Alice was over forty when I was born, and, as she needed to become invisible for long stretches, she was fortunate to have produced a placid only daughter who could distract herself. When I was eight, the age that my grandfather escaped from home, I began to write verse. These singsong ditties, Alice believed, might one day be of interest to posterity, so she recopied them in her schoolmarm's penmanship into a looseleaf binder. But then she did something I still can't explain. She wrote half a dozen poems of her own and, like a crooked cardsharp, shuffled them into the pack. They parroted my diction, but their artful lightness couldn't have been that of a child, who blurts out the little she knows rather than shedding the ballast of too much knowledge to achieve simplicity. "Of course they're yours," she insisted when I questioned their provenance. "You just forgot about them." She may have thought that by producing a false miracle she could inspire me to perform a true one, though she was, of course, also showing me up, denying it, confounding our identities, and—to the degree that I connived in this perverse act of inverted plagiarism—stoking my grandiosity. Young children may be harder to fool than their parents like to think, but they often don't have the courage of their disbeliefs.

Disbelief is essential to good writing, which, in my experience, is a line-by-line combat with self-forgery. In that respect, it is a humble version of Pascal's bet: Can I or can't I, through a feat of style, prove my existence to intelligent skeptics, none more skeptical than I am? But I also write to discover the nature of my affinity with an elusive subject who was only rarely real to herself. Alice's guises continue to surprise me, and some of them, like a chameleon on a leaf, are hiding in these pages.

I

THE WOLF AT
THE DOOR

· ONE ·

The Wolf at the Door

The Italian performance artist Vanessa Beecroft lives with her American husband, Greg Durkin, and their seventeen-month-old son, Dean, in an isolated house off a dirt road on Long Island's North Shore. Durkin, who has worked in the movie industry as a financial analyst but is currently a graduate student in sociology, found the place by searching the Internet for properties that were within commuting distance of Manhattan and had an indoor pool. Beecroft suffers from exercise bulimia—a compulsion to burn off calories that she considers excessive—and until recently she liked to swim a hundred laps every day. She also used to take ten-hour hikes, and she still goes for vigorous long walks through the nature reserve that surrounds her house. Before the baby started to toddle, she sometimes carried him along, slung on the ledge of a bony hip. "When I was pregnant, I didn't allow myself to relax for a minute," she says. "I spent all day swimming, training, and doing aerobics. I've since slacked off a bit, because I find that yoga is the only workout that doesn't make me too hungry."

Bulimia is an eating disorder epidemic among young women. (Beecroft is thirty-three.) In its most common form, a ravenous binge—equivalent to several meals, or even to several days' worth of food—is closely followed by a session of self-induced reverse peristalsis. The practice is both psychologically addictive and socially contagious. According to an unscientific survey of my friends under thirty, there isn't a dormitory bathroom in the country that doesn't reek of vomit. Older women suffer from bulimia, too, probably in smaller numbers, although treatment statistics do not, obviously, provide a reliable head count. Actors, dancers, and models are particularly susceptible, and so are young male athletes, like wrestlers and jockeys, who have weight goals to meet. There is an extensive clinical and self-help literature devoted to the disorder (which is commonly medicated with antidepressants), along with dozens of websites and chat rooms, some of them clandestine trysting places for defiant anorexics and bulimics, who fondly call themselves by the dollish names "ana" and "mia," and who warn intruders seeking to cure them or girls "in recovery" not to enter. Members of the sisterhood trade pictures of their idols (Calista Flockhart and Lara Flynn Boyle are especially admired), proud accounts of their sometimes lethally ascetic practices, and advice on concealing them.

It is hard to think of a human stain—an addiction, sin, perversion, or taboo—that doesn't, in a shame-free age, have its bard. Bulimia, however, is one of the most intractably unglamorous of dirty secrets, as humiliating as incontinence. Bulimics transcend their own threshold of disgust, although not easily the repulsion of others: they are a stealthy tribe. Clogged plumbing or rotten teeth sometimes give them away, but I have known women who have managed to conceal their daily rituals for years without getting caught by a parent or spouse. This interesting subject, one of propriety's last frontiers, has been largely neglected by creative artists, with a few exceptions, Beecroft being among the most notable. She has been working since her adolescence on a project called *XXX Book of Food*: 360 watercolors and drawings that she intends to publish in the form of a cube-shaped book divided into colored sections. (Bulimics often separate the courses of a binge with markers of taste and texture so that each stratum is visibly discrete and, during gluttony interruptus, can be carefully ticked off the elimination manifest.) "I used to eat by color," she explains, "all orange one day, all green, yellow, or red the next. I wanted my obsession made formally explicit." She started the book as a diary in the early 1980s with the intention of showing it, one day, to a doctor. The first four years of entries were lost by a typist, but the remaining six (1987–93) make up a log of every morsel (or nearly) that she consumed, and a journal in words and pictures of the feelings—predominantly self-loathing—that her struggle with a recalcitrant appetite aroused, and still does. I found the cumulative tedium of this strange artifact poignant and compelling. So, perhaps, will anyone who, like Beecroft, has "wished demonically for something horrible to happen to me just to make me thin," and who has "weighed every one of my life's experiences on the scale of how many kilos I have gained or lost from it. In the end, I don't even care if people say I'm a good artist. I only care about whether or not I'm fat."

Beecroft's self-discipline is Spartan, though she told me that she "has to have something very bad every day, like a piece of cake or a drink." Most of the bulimics I have known or read about aren't so abstemious. They, too, gauge goodness and badness on a kitchen scale, and they may diet as strenuously as she does, but they relieve themselves of the tension inherent in long-term deprivation with vast quantities of delicious, forbidden junk. A woman in her seventies who has been a compulsive eater for most of her "petty, claustrophobic life" once told me that her daily "sprees" were its only source of "spontaneity and free choice," and while she knew they were "sick" and "wasteful," she couldn't bear to give them up for that reason. Beecroft's diary, however, covers a period when she lived on a monotonous regimen of the same health foods day after day: a bowl of unseasoned brown rice, an apple, a serving of raw carrots or homebaked bread. "I tried to throw them up," she recalls, "but I couldn't, and when I started retching blood, I had to stop"—which is why she switched to extreme exercise as a purgative. "In my diary, I use the word 'vomit' metaphorically. It stands for the violence of the intention." Not merely, however. Once, as a teenager, she smashed a bag of walnuts with a hammer and ate the contents shell and all, winding up in an emergency room with acute peritonitis. The doctor told her that she needed a psychiatrist. She found one who had belonged to the Red Brigades. "I got really fascinated by his politics," she recalled. "Unfortunately, he was too expensive." (Eating disorders and Maoism seem to share a common ground: they are a form of utopian moral extremism—a belief that, with enough ruthlessness, it is possible to achieve perfection.)

Beecroft plans to exhibit the book at a major retrospective of her work that opens in October at Italy's leading museum of modern art, the Castello di Rivoli, outside Turin. She is also willing to discuss her enthrallment to food with passionate candor, and to describe its role in the tableaux vivants—some fifty to date—that have made her a controversial star of the performance-art world. These spectacles, the initial ones produced on a shoestring, the later ones expensively staged, have been widely admired by curators and critics (but also frequently condemned as voyeuristic and exploitative). They feature large groupings of nude or undressed "girls" who stand mutely for several hours in a gallery or museum, occasionally breaking ranks to stretch or to sprawl, but remaining, in principle, strictly impassive to an audience that is, of course, fully clothed. In the earliest works, Beecroft assembled an eloquently motley collection of fleshy and slim bodies. Emboldened and enriched by her success, she hired scores of uniformly thin, depilated beauties and arranged them as human colonnades. ("I think of them as architecture," she says.) On different occasions, their trappings have included white bras, black body paint, Heidi wigs, control-top briefs, G-strings, gladiator sandals, panty hose, fedoras, faux-mink chubbies, and four-inch stilettoes. A percentage of the women, especially at the beginning, suffered from eating disorders, and they were all volunteers—friends, fellow art students, or interesting-looking female specimens whom she picked up on the street. Yet even when she started recruiting professional models and paying them their going rate, they had to be willing to undergo a painful (if boastworthy) trial of extreme discomfort and exposure. Beecroft herself doesn't participate in a performance once she has given her instructions to the troops: she's a general rather than a first lieutenant. Her charisma, however, has increased with her visibility, and women gladly, one might even say hungrily, do her bidding and become her tools. Designers—among them Miuccia Prada, Tom Ford, and Manolo Blahnik—have been eager to contribute props. A photographer and video crews document the pieces (Beecroft used to do the photography herself), and those images are the commodity that Beecroft's dealers market to collectors. "Reproduction glamorizes the experience and leaches it of ambiguity and emotion," she says flatly. "I'm sorry it's necessary. Pictures of the girls out of context make the work look too sexy. To me, the actual performances aren't sexy at all. They're about shame: the shame of the audience and, to a lesser extent, of the girls, but most of all my own."

Beecroft had doubted that a local taxi driver could find her hideout in the woods, so when I arranged to visit her for the first time, she offered to meet my train from the city. She pulled up in a silver BMW and apologized profusely for arriving a little late. With Dean in tow, she looked like the stressed Madonna in a moody, cinematic parable about suburban anomie. (Her mother, she says, was pregnant with her when her parents first saw Antonioni's *Blowup*, which starred Vanessa Redgrave, and they liked the name.) Being lovely to look at and extremely photogenic has not hurt a career that bridges the worlds of art and fashion. Beecroft has a patrician forehead—smooth and high—and prominent cheekbones. Huge, thickly fringed brown eyes are set in a pale face dusted with freckles that was framed, when I met her last spring, by unruly russet curls. (She has since shaved her head. "I saw one too many Holocaust movies," she told me.) Her strong features have a fragile aura of hectic radiance. A tattoo artist in Milan with an upper-class clientele decorated one forearm from the elbow to the wrist with a lurid Vargas-style pinup, and the other arm with a merchant seaman's anchor and eagle. Elsewhere on her body there are fish and a Japanese dragon. These tough-guy badges of bad-girlhood are at odds with her ladylike appearance, and particularly with the enormous diamond engagement ring on her left hand. She and Durkin, who is seven years her junior, met on the street outside the Williamsburg loft she used to rent. He was looking for an apartment in the neighborhood, where bohemians mingle with recent immigrants from Eastern Europe, and Beecroft mistook him for a Russian. He has the dark-haired beauty of an Attic swain, a lifetime of experience with overbearing older women, and he proposed impulsively after a three-month courtship. "When Greg gave me the ring, I said, 'Oh, thanks,' and tossed it across the bed," she says. "I assumed it came from a vending machine at the mall." (It came from his maternal great-grandmother, although the fortune it represented has since diminished.) Yet Durkin's courage—or foolhardiness—impressed her. "Vanessa is an extreme feminist," her photographer,

Dusan Reljin, says, "except that she looks for a strong man to control her." She struck me more like the wild girl in a folktale, bewitched as a punishment for her temper, who turns into a howling wolf and devours her prospective liberators. Her wedding in Portofino became a "project," with costumes by Prada, Trussardi, and Alessandro Dell'Acqua—the entire bridal party and all the guests wore white—and a reception on a soccer field hosted by the editor of Italian *Vogue*.

The fame and shock value of Beecroft's work have made her a public figure, so she is never unconscious of being on display. She moves with a dancer's litheness and poses for photographs with the aplomb of a mannequin. Her voice is seductive and a little fey: the feather clapper in an iron bell. One sometimes has the impression of a lonely virago doing a wishful though also slightly contemptuous impersonation—almost a takeoff—of a baby doll. Beecroft's father is English, and she speaks his language fluently with a lilting, percussive accent. Her Italian is exceptionally cultivated and formal, even old-fashioned (her mother taught classics and literature)—pure of slang and rich in subjunctives. Most people change character when they switch in and out of their mother tongue, but there is very little discontinuity between Beecroft's English and Italian personas, perhaps because the uncensored stream of her confidences seems, in contrast to its grammatical precision, so primal.

Fashion and the acquisition of clothes "obsess" Beecroft, she admits, almost as much as eating does, for similar reasons. She claims to shop in "a ravenous and stupid frenzy—everything I buy is a mistake," yet she dresses in the height of style, even in the country, almost invariably in a minimalist white or black designer outfit and the kind of Capezio pumps worn by tango dancers. Beecroft is about five foot seven, but people often perceive her as Amazonian or statuesque, perhaps because of her outsize vitality, or perhaps because she is rarely without heels. (The platforms and spikes that the girls wear in her performances are, she says, their "pedestals.") The afternoon we first met, her own pedestals were red and her Prada ensemble immaculately white. I expected a wraith, but her weight usually hovers around sixty kilos, she says—132 pounds, most of it muscle. It is not uncommon for a runway model of six feet to weigh fifteen or even twenty pounds less than Beecroft does, so, even at her thinnest, she is never emaciated. "I aspired to be as thin as an anorexic," she admits. "I loved fasting once I got past the pain of the first few days, which I did with the help of amphetamines, but I never went too far." It was partly a lack of nerve. Anorexics are more aggressive and bulimics are lazier, she says, "but ultimately I didn't want to waste myself. Bulimia is, among other things, a form of research for my work: a source of information about what's going on inside me."

When we reached the house, which Beecroft bought for the family when they outgrew the Brooklyn loft (her art has been lucrative), she led me through a series of monochromatic, sparsely furnished rooms. The architecture is mid-century Nassau County modern: cedar siding, low ceilings, track lighting, sliding glass doors that open to a series of decks, and a rec room on the lower level, off the garage, that she said she planned to use as an office. The previous owner tacked a tower onto the house, a lighthouse-style bedroom suite where, in another era, swinging or pot parties might have taken place. Beecroft retreats to it when she wants to escape her tempestuous marriage, or to "hide" from Dean's nanny, who has a "bossy attitude" and a big appetite, and whose eating habits she finds "oppressive." "I think the tower could be great for a writer. Come do a book there," she said. When I asked why she didn't commandeer this aerie for her own work instead of holing up in a sunless tomb that was dank even on a hot June day, she admitted that the thought hadn't occurred to her. "I gravitate to the shadows." But the funkiness of the decor and its *Blair Witch*-y setting in the deep woods (she chose the isolation in part to be far from the temptations of grocery or convenience shops) are, in fact, eminently chic, and one can imagine Steven Meisel shooting a Versace layout in the kitchen or by the pool. "I didn't touch anything," Beecroft says, "not even to paint the walls white, because if I start I'll have to tear the place completely apart, and I despair beforehand of getting it perfect enough. I need everything to be perfect." Bulimia is also a demented form of perfectionism.

Beecroft may resent having to fill her refrigerator with fattening treats for the nanny ("She doesn't understand that if she leaves half an egg bagel on the counter it's hard for me not to finish it"), and she generally tries to fast until dinnertime, but she graciously offered me yogurt and a selection of fruit, which I declined (I had picnicked on the train, since, under the circumstances, I could hardly expect solid refreshment at my destination), and we sat at a table in the sun with bottles of water. I was relieved to see that her baby, who was then nine months old, had a healthy appetite, and whenever he started to fuss, Beecroft nursed him, though throughout the afternoon I noticed that she always proffered him the same breast. At one point, this imbalance began to feel almost physically painful to me, and, more out of politeness than for her own comfort, she shifted him to the other side. I also worried that Dean, who was crawling around the deck naked except for a diaper and a sun hat, would get splinters. He did, but his mother tweezed them out of his pudgy knees so tenderly and expertly that there was barely a whimper. Like an adolescent, Beecroft seems to lack any foresight for disaster—indeed, any sense of mortality. (Discretion, a form of prudence, is equally alien to her.) When she fights with Greg, she told me, she sometimes takes the car out on the expressway late at night and floors the accelerator. "I'm sure nothing will happen," she says with nonchalance, although she conceded that she should probably get a driver's license. (She since has, though after failing the test twice, both times for recklessness.) In the course of our talks, which took place intermittently over ten months, she revealed a dazzling capacity for elation that was expressed in sudden, beatific bursts, like solar storms. Yet she seemed to possess not the slightest imagination for ordinary happiness.

When Beecroft describes her life's dramatis personae, the word "mean" recurs as a leitmotif. She uses it of her mother, who raised her on a macrobiotic diet; of her angelic-looking half sister; and of her "grave" and "soulful" young husband. He can sometimes be "as mean as possible, but I'm meaner to him—I tear men to pieces, so it is probably my fault." (After an explosive row this autumn, in a Los Angeles airport hotel, the police were called to intervene, and they handcuffed Beecroft, with polite apologies, until she calmed down.) Durkin's eighty-three-year-old maternal grandmother, Eunice Carrigan Schneck, with whom Beecroft feels a kinship, "is considered the meanest member of the family," especially toward her long-suffering daughter, Greg's mother, Sheril—a registered dietician. Sheril Durkin is a sinewy woman in her mid-fifties with a yearbook smile and a confiding manner that belie a hard life. She gave me her professional opinion that eating disorders are usually caused by "crazy mothers."

Sometimes, however, these difficult relatives are as inspiring to Beecroft as the protagonists of a Greek myth or tragedy. (I suppose that devouring one's children qualifies as bulimia.) She is flooded with compassion for their fatal flaws and respect for their powers of endurance. I also came to understand that she uses "meanness"—*cattiveria*—as a perverse compliment: the snarl of the beast defending the carcass of its prey, or of the prey that will not let itself be taken without a fight; the mordant pissiness of the unbowed, of all those who struggle and prevail. Asked to name the sentiment most foreign to her, Beecroft responds, without hesitation, *clemenza*—pity. Among the gods, as a classical scholar I knew once pointed out, Eros is the most willful, and he carries the day in Olympian contests because desire is the principle of change. To which one might add, voracity is the motor of desire.

Sheril, Eunice, and Eunice's ninety-year-old sister, Ruby Keller—the blithe spirit of the family—were the central figures in a curious documentary that Beecroft shot just before Christmas in a suite at the Plaza Hotel, a performance that she described to me ahead of time as "Euripides meets *Grey Gardens*." It was supposed to be "like a little trial at which we interrogate the truth of their lives—the truth of lost youth, lost dreams and love, and of approaching death." At times, it seemed more like a session of fashion therapy for seniors. Beecroft raided her own closet for evening wear of sentimental value, including a lamé sheath of her mother's and a white Saint Laurent wedding dress that she bought for a potential ceremony "long before I had a man." She also designed some striking futuristic costumes in polyester jersey. Her elfin friend Tara Subkoff ("a miniature Catherine Deneuve," as Beecroft accurately put it) acted as the stylist and wardrobe mistress. Subkoff is the designer behind Imitation of Christ, an exclusive line of one-of-a-kind garments that could be described as mutant vintage. "I don't like my work to be pigeonholed either as fashion or as art—I'd love it to be considered science," Sub-koff said. "Vanessa's work is also hard to categorize. She has a very visual relationship with her relatives and their clothing. They're like her paper dolls."

The piece consisted of three vignettes, each lasting about thirty minutes. The first two went off smoothly. Beecroft dressed the old ladies in shocking pink and red long dresses, and a makeup artist touched up their faces and hair. They seemed to enjoy being painted and fussed over. Then they were told to stretch out side by side on the queen-size faux-Empire *lit à la polonaise*. The composition had a macabre charm: two well-rouged if lumpy bodies lying in state on a plush bier, in a powder-blue room, with the snowy park bouncing wintry sunlight through the window. Any embalmer would have been proud to present a grieving family with such a deluxe memento mori. Ruby fell asleep and snored softly, and Eunice cracked testy jokes from her rigid, supine position.

In the second vignette, Sheril entered in a red chiffon cocktail dress from Rive Gauche and sat on the bed. "Vanessa loves to make people happy," she observed. "She's the best mother in the world, but she'll find out about sons and mothers. I spoiled Greg rotten be-cause he had such a tough childhood. His father abandoned us, then his sister died. Now his wife's the one paying the price." Between takes, the three women made an amiable effort to address the themes of lost youth, dreams, and love, although Ruby and Eunice had nothing but "happy memories." Eunice once owned a shop that sold women's bathing suits in the Hamptons. "You'd be amazed at how many men wanted to try them on," she said. She also recalled that her wedding guests had, during the war, chipped in their gas coupons to send her on a honeymoon. On a vacation with her husband, Ruby met the pope. Sheril's marriage was, she said, "blissful" for the first seven years. But Eunice rolled her eyes with withering scorn when Sheril confessed that she had forgiven her husband, a Vietnam vet, for running off with another woman.

During the lunch break, I was surprised to see Beecroft eat several chocolate bars in quick succession. She had told me that she was go-ing on "an anti-yeast diet." She had a heated discussion over the phone with her mother in Italy, then "broke up" with her husband, who was home with the baby. (They quarrel and reconcile regularly.) "Greg thinks I turn everything into an opera," she said sadly. Eunice read her favorite gossip column through a lorgnette and complained about her "disgustingly large" room-service pastrami sandwich. Sheril polished off a platter of roast beef and a plate of cookies. Ruby, in the meantime, was playing solitaire. But when it was time for the actors to dress for the third vignette—"approach of death"—trouble erupted. Eunice got huffy, and refused "to play along with this hysterical nonsense any longer." She specifically objected to lying like a corpse next to her sister in the costumes that Beecroft had laid out for them: white bridal outfits cut like christening gowns, with head-hugging cowls and, over the cowls, billowing tulle veils. "You can't make a fool out of me," Eunice said, scowling and shaking her blond flip.

"No one will ever recognize us without our double chins," Ruby suggested brightly. She had already obediently donned her cowl, and she looked like the freshly hatched newborn of a wrinkly alien species.

I thought that things were finally going rather well, or at least adhering more closely to the Euripidean scenario, but Beecroft was distraught. She told Eunice that she had spent $10,000 of her own money to mount the production, and now she stood to lose her investment. "There are some things you can't buy, and I'm one of them," Eunice retorted. "I'll give you the money back." She disappeared into the walk-in closet, ostensibly to look for her checkbook, but returned with a glass of amber liquid that Sheril brusquely snatched away. Subkoff, who is about sixty years younger than Eunice, had gamely volunteered to take her place on the bed, and was suiting up. "This whole thing is very *The Handmaid's Tale*," she sighed as she fluffed her veil and prepared to salvage the scene. "I wish my own old aunt could see me. She's a nun."

Beecroft has been accused of staging "sex shows" in the name of feminism, of "objectifying women," and of "pandering to the male gaze." Critics have also signaled the "sadomasochistic" subtext of performances that are heavily influenced, as the artist readily admits, by the work of Helmut Newton—who photographed Beecroft for *Vogue*, two years ago, in a minuscule leather bikini. Surely these terms of judgment are too blunt with overuse and sanctimony to be penetrating. A refined appetite, however, demands fresh stimulation. The gourmets of the art world are especially picky. And fifty productions based on the same formula—their impact inversely proportional to their glamour—inevitably begin to pall. Beecroft knows, she told me, that she needs to move on.

But Subkoff's casual reference to Margaret Atwood's 1986 novel offers a shrewder insight into Beecroft and her oeuvre than much of the academic debate about them in the art press. *The Handmaid's Tale* describes a totalitarian future in a fundamentalist America, where young women are kept as reproductive slaves by aging patriarchs of the religious right and their barren wives, and ritually raped by both spouses. (The conceit seemed flimsy to me when the book was first published. Recent history has given it a faintly prophetic glimmer.) I still find the novel more persuasive as a work of erotic fiction—a fantasy of incest and bondage—than as an Orwellian dystopia. Atwood the artist had a lot to say about the pathology of desire, but Atwood the militant wouldn't let it be said. She wasn't willing to tell the truth about women's anarchic feelings—particularly their voracity. Beecroft is.

Human beings of both sexes eroticize their primal bonds with those who feed them. When they are starved for nurture at an early age, their character builds not upon a solid core but upon a void. To others, they may seem sturdy and accomplished, but they know that at any moment, like a house built over a sinkhole, they can vanish into it. They comfort themselves with the image of a magical Provider whose perfect love will satisfy them once and for all. Bingeing on sex or food tantalizes them with a fleeting taste of completeness. (So does bulimic shopping. The closet is a maw, and clothes, like our infantile selves, are full of promise, though vacant of life until we inflate them.) But the insatiably hungry revert to blaming their partners or their appetites—and to handing out punishment accordingly—for their inevitable relapse into the void. Their lives are a quest for relief from want in which the strong take the offensive. They attempt to recover an illusion of wholeness through domination, and they become the sadists and the predatory seducers of both sexes. The weak experiment, perhaps no less aggressively, with some form of defensive self-starvation. Their voluntary privations feel superior to the despair of the famished child, which was suffered helplessly. In Beecroft's art and life, those two strategies converge. Most hollow souls dissemble the shame of their emptiness. She has turned hers inside out.

Beecroft's parents separated when she was two. She moved with her mother to a farmhouse in an olive forest near the town of Malcesine, on the slopes above Lake Garda, where they lived, she says, "without men, a telephone, or a car." Her younger brother was raised by their grandparents. He grew up to be a lawyer. Her father stayed in London, where he sold classic Bentleys, dabbled in philosophy, and studied the Cabala. He eventually had another son and daughter. Beecroft has been painting a series of portraits that depict her younger sister, Jennifer, as a dangerously beautiful and sullen-looking punk Lolita with clumpy mascara and a greasy tan. "I paid her a lot of money to pose," she adds, "because it made us more equal. I didn't exploit her."

The younger daughter knew their father as the elder one never did, and perhaps for that reason, Beecroft speculates, "he doesn't interest her, while I idealized him." Andrew Beecroft, she says, "is a smoker, a drinker, a dandy, and a decadent—very lean and pale, with pinkish-yellow hair." He loves the company of "old noblewomen broken at heart." For years they had no contact. "I went looking for him when I was fifteen, but he dismissed my energy as being 'too negative,' " Beecroft says. "So I returned to London the next year, hoping to impress him with my 'positivity,' but I couldn't. I thought he was the most beautiful man in the world. Our encounter left me with a deep sense of failure. Now we have an intellectual relationship."

Her parents, Beecroft says, were children of the sixties. "My mother is strange and big-boned, with strong, even mannish features, but still beautiful and womanly." She sees her as "huge," with a body "like a piece of sculpture." (In photographs, she looks to me like the matron from the lid of an Etruscan sarcophagus, though not so benign.) "She never cared about the girlie stuff. I had to hide my first copy of *Vogue* from her—she disapproved." They lived "in chaos," Beecroft says, "but we followed a strict macrobiotic diet. The neighbors called us 'the foreigners.' They ate pasta with rabbit sauce, and we never had scheduled meals: just home-baked bread, whole grains, and vegetables, most of them raw." On the day her mother did the baking, when the loaves were still warm from the oven, "I sometimes ate all of them, and then I would pass out." Bread, she says, makes her "crazy," and if she eats bread she doesn't want to be touched. "My mother would scream at me that it wasn't the bread that had made me sick, it was hatred for her." Now that she is a grown woman, Beecroft and her mother have become friends. Her mother, she says, doesn't remember the tempests between them: not "tearing the house apart," not "expecting autonomy of a six-year-old," not "crying for two days in a row and counting on me to take care of her—she has amnesia." At the same time, "she could be extremely loving and playful. She is well-bred and a serious reader. She adores the cinema. I had probably seen every Bergman film by the time I was five. But I struck back at her when I was older, and I used to throw her clothes out if I didn't like them—they went right into the trash. I've always been very opinionated about how people should dress. My father, for example, dresses to perfection. I like clothes that are more photogenic and impractical than real. I own closets full of things to wear, but they're all the wrong size. I was never any good at shopping."

In 1980, when Beecroft was eleven, she and her mother moved to a village on the Ligurian coast, near Portofino. "My girlfriends there were anorexic," she recalls. "Three of them were the daughters of a rich, aristocratic family, and when I met them they were plump. Then they refused to eat anything but apples, and turned into skin and bones. I was so impressed. Their little brother was anorexic, too. I remember that he used to tear up thousand-lira notes and chew them one little piece at a time. My mother sent me to a gynecologist when I was thirteen or fourteen, because my puberty was delayed. He gave me hormones, and I gained ten kilos. My breasts mushroomed—they became enormous. I felt Kafkaesque, and fell into a depression. About then, I read that Fassbinder made movies to feel real. I started drawing for the same reason."

At eighteen, Beecroft met a thirty-five-year-old Sicilian duke who, she says, "introduced me to a melancholic world of aristocrats right out of *The Leopard*. I never slept with him—I slept with a friend of his who wasn't so noble—but we tooled around Palermo in a white Triumph. He gave me some lovely presents and he asked my mother formally for my hand. She didn't care one way or the other. As perhaps I've told you, we're a contemptuous family. Our problem is that we are too good for everybody but never good enough for ourselves. My clearest recollection about that period, however, is of gorging on grapes and cheese. When I came back from Palermo, I started keeping the food diary systematically, but I never intended to make it public. Then I changed my mind."

In 1988, Beecroft enrolled in art school, at the Brera, in Milan. "I needed a job," she claims, "because my mother wouldn't give me any money. So I became an au pair. Everybody in the family I worked for had red hair, like the dolls in the drawings I did as a child in Malcesine. It's my favorite color." (In her first American performance, staged in New York at P.S. 1, in 1994, the girls wore red Raggedy Ann wigs.) "I don't remember anything else about them—if, for example, they were happy or not—but they loved food. I never remember places or situations, just how my body looked in a mirror at the time." It was about then that she ate the bag of walnuts in their shells.

"I became a performance artist by mistake," Beecroft says. "There is something vulgar about the genre: its human reality. In high school, they told me my drawings looked like Schiele or Pontormo. But I never felt they were good or important enough to be taken seriously. I preferred the purity of minimalist art, which reminds me of that great epigram about mathematics: 'It fixes with an abstract formula the infinite variety of the world.' I still try to make each of my performances more abstract, harder, more artificial, more photogenic, less embodied than the one before. My career started because one of my professors invited me to participate in the annual school show. I wanted to call up all the girls I had been staring at for four years—girls who had something wrong or crazy about them but were still beautiful—and confine them in a room, and give each of them a piece of my underwear. So the girls became the work. I like to know that each of them has a weakness. Seeing other women's bodies is a relief, because even the most desirable body bears the scars of an imperfect life." Perfection, in its way, is an invisible scar. "There is nothing erotic about the way I look at women. I play on the girls' sexuality to offend the audience. I don't mind being irritating—rubbing people against their grain. My shrink tells me that I'm a bully. You could also say that I behave like the man of the family. I pay the bills, and I've punched Greg in the face." I asked her if she thinks of herself as a wife-beater. She considered the notion with respect. "I know that I am violent," she concluded, "and I'm not proud of it. But I need catharsis. My worst fear is to be held captive by niceness."

Last August, Beecroft staged what she said was to be her final tableau vivant, "but then I always say it's the last one and it never is," she added. (The film made at the Plaza in December was the first in a new series of tableaux morts that will feature members of her family, including her father, or his "surrogate," posing on hotel beds.) "VB51" took place over two days at a castle near Hanover, in Germany—Schloss Vinsebeck—that belongs to Count Wolff-Metternich. Beecroft had told me that the piece would feature "old" women, and evoke the mood of Resnais's *Last Year at Marienbad*, but by mid-July she was still vague about the details. We poked around a thrift shop in Williamsburg together, and she bought a white chiffon prom dress that she thought she might use as a costume. I wondered how she would ever organize the logistics of a complex foreign production in a month's time. "I always improvise at the last minute," she explained. "I need the anxiety of imminent failure."

The performance featured an atypically mixed cast—diverse in age and type—including Beecroft's mother, mother-in-law, and sister; the actresses Hanna Schygulla and Irm Hermann; a contingent of the "decadent" local aristocracy, fine-boned Meissen sylphs; and an "anorexic" Italian art critic. All but two of the participants (Schygulla and Hermann) wore white. Beecroft's mother consented to appear with her eyes blackened like a raccoon's, and the makeup accentuated the heaviness of her features and the feral panic of her gaze. Sheril

Durkin, with her shag haircut and martyred smile, seemed out of place. Schygulla has become a chanteuse, and she had agreed to perform only if she could sing, Beecroft said. "OK, I thought, let her: we'll edit it out." (But she didn't.) Fassbinder's sex goddess will be sixty next Christmas. Age has blurred her beauty, but it hasn't extinguished her raspy smolder. Robed ecclesiastically in black, she buzzed among the human statuary intoning, in three languages, snatches of the lyrics from Schubert's *Winterreise*.

A tape of "VB51," edited to about ninety minutes, premieres early in April in Paris, at the Cosmic Galerie. A Beecroft piece, however, is worth watching in its entirety. The work may seem frivolous initially, but the fashion and nudity prove to be a distraction. If bulimia is contagious, so is stoicism. As hours pass in silence and boredom—time slowing to a creep, the way it does on a long flight, for the duration of a fast, or in minding a baby—one becomes aware, viscerally, of all the cravings, pangs, chills, yawns, oozings, aches, itches, yearnings, blushes, and impatience that the women are braving and suppressing, and of one's own. Beecroft may belabor an idea or exalt a whim, but her art conspires with your nerves to hold you captive of everything unbearable that you have to contain.

—March 17, 2003

TWO

Siren Songs

E dna St. Vincent Millay must surely be the only poet loved by both Thomas Hardy and Dave Garroway. In Hardy's view, America had produced two cultural artifacts that could be considered great—the skyscraper and Millay's verse. When Garroway was the host of *Wide Wide World,* one of television's first magazine shows (1955 to 1958), he signed off after every broadcast by reciting four lines from the last stanza of "Renascence," a poem written by Millay when she was nineteen:

> The world stands out on either side
> No wider than the heart is wide;
> Above the world is stretched the sky—
> No higher than the soul is high.

The audience of *Wide Wide World* probably knew where the lines came from. Millay had been hugely popular between the two world wars. A volume of her sonnets sold fifty thousand copies in the depths of the Depression. Hardy and Garroway weren't her only unlikely fans. Arthur Symons compared her to Keats and Poe; Kenneth Tynan loved her dramatic verse; and Edmund Wilson called her "one of the only poets writing in English . . . who have attained to anything like the stature of great literary figures." But rarely has an idol so widely revered suffered such a drastic devaluation in her own lifetime. Millay received what the French call a *coup de vieux*—a brutal and sudden blow of age—and it fell at about the same moment on her beauty and her reputation.

For more than a decade, 1935 to 1946, Millay was a serious junkie. At the peak of her addiction, the "elfin" poet, five foot one and a hundred pounds, was dosing herself around the clock with nearly two hundred milligrams of morphine a day (ten is the standard dose for a terminal cancer patient). By the time she died, at fifty-eight, in October of 1950, she had reduced her abject dependence on narcotics, though even after several hospitalizations for alcohol- and drug-related nervous breakdowns, she defined sobriety as restricting her daily liquor intake to a liter and a half of wine. While there were no witnesses to her death (Millay had been widowed for a year and was living alone on her country estate, Steepletop, near Austerlitz, New York), the scene, like many from her life and work, seems overplayed, as if fate had resorted to an old screenwriter's cliché. Working late and drinking hard, Millay pitched down a dark flight of stairs and broke her neck. The next day, a hired man found the corpse in a silk dressing gown on the bloodstained landing. Millay's head was resting beside a notebook that contained the draft of a poem. She had circled its last three lines:

> I will control myself, or go inside.
> I will not flaw perfection with my grief.
> Handsome, this day: no matter who has died.

Millay and her husband, Eugen Boissevain, had no children and had wanted none. "I have never settled down," she once told an interviewer. "I could never have married the kind of person with whom I would have had to settle down . . . My husband is responsive to my every mood. That's the only way in which I can live and be what I am." Her estate passed to a younger sister, Norma Millay Ellis. There had been another sister, Kathleen, a minor poet, novelist, and paranoid who died in 1943, and a formidable, self-sacrificing mother, Cora, who also wrote poetry but had supported her girls (she was divorced from their hapless father) as an itinerant practical nurse and weaver of hairpieces. All the Millays sewed, swept, cooked, laundered, sang, acted, and were lovely. If the poet's hardscrabble but artistic New England girlhood reads like *Little Women*, by the time her sisters and mother joined her in the seething Greenwich Village of its glory days, just after the First World War, their family life had become a bohemian takeoff of that Puritan morality tale, with Vincent, as she was called, hogging the roles of both Amy and Jo, and Marmee-Cora rolling the cigarettes, slugging back the gin, and telling the shockable Edmund Wilson that she "had been a slut herself so why shouldn't her girls be?" The Millay "theater piece"—as Nancy Milford observes in *Savage Beauty: The Life of Edna St. Vincent Millay* (Random House, 2001), which will be published this fall—was "their story of triumph over adversity, one of the best women's stories there is in America: hopeful, enduring, centered in family, and fraudulent . . . because it was built on so much unadmitted pain."

It's striking how many writers of both sexes have been offspring of mothers like Cora Millay, exceptional women disappointed in marriage and thwarted in ambition and desire who give all and ask for nothing except that the special child live gloriously enough for two. It's also striking how often their children, though they may be self-serving and rebellious in other respects and relations, shoulder the burden of making such mothers complete—giving them an enhanced reality—and perhaps that task, inherently impossible to finish, is fundamental to art. The farewell letter that Cora wrote to Edna as her daughter was about to sail from New York for Paris, in 1921, to become a foreign correspondent for *Vanity Fair*, suggests the archetypal bond from the mother's point of view: "There can be no real separation for two like us." A stanza that Edna wrote after Cora's death, in 1931, captures it from the child's:

> In this mound, and what's beneath,
> Is my cure, if cure there be;
> I must starve, or eat your death
> Till it nourish me.

After Edna's death, her sister Norma moved into Steepletop, where she slept in the poet's bed and left the dead woman's clothes hanging in the closet. Norma published an edition of the *Collected*

Poems but, rudely or coyly depending upon the suitor, blocked access to the juicy papers, intending one day to write what she called "The Biography." In 1972, when she was seventy-eight, Norma finally decided that this task might better be entrusted to a sympathetic professional, and her choice fell upon Milford, whose life of Zelda Fitzgerald, Edna St. Vincent Millay's contemporary, was one of the big literary events of the feminist new wave—the first liberation of a madwoman from the attic—selling more than a million copies. When Norma died in 1986, Milford was fourteen years along and only halfway to her last page. In 1999, another potential biographer, Daniel Mark Epstein, himself a poet, discovered that the unpublished diaries, journals, and letters Milford had been working with—some twenty thousand documents—were now at the Library of Congress, and he soon secured permission from a new executor to consult them. Epstein's life, *What Lips My Lips Have Kissed: The Loves and Love Poems of Edna St. Vincent Millay* (Henry Holt, 2001), will also be published this fall, along with *The Selected Poetry of Edna St. Vincent Millay* (Modern Library, 2001), edited and introduced by Milford.

Savage Beauty is a five-hundred-page distillation that was nearly thirty years in the making. *What Lips My Lips Have Kissed*, half the size, was researched and written in about eighteen months. But haste can sometimes, paradoxically, work to a biographer's advantage. It spares one from the fatigue, introspection, disillusionment, eclipse of an overview, corrosion of confidence, and mixed emotions attendant upon any long and troubled intimacy (but also essential to understanding it). There is something to be said in art as in love for the week of living dangerously, and Millay kept saying it. A life as messy as hers and an oeuvre as uneven can benefit from compression. Epstein's chronicle is well researched and briskly narrated, without an iota of wit but with intelligence, and his ear is often keener than Milford's for the telling quote. He makes at least two revelations she seems to have missed—of Millay's first homosexual experience, with a girl in Maine, and of her late, ruinous obsession with horse racing. If only his style were not so perfervid, so riddled with italics, so defensive—even surly—about his status, in relation to Milford, as the tenacious underdog. While Epstein is eager to rehabilitate Millay's "genius" and to restore her to what he believes is her rightful place as one of the great love poets of all time, he does little to convince the reader of his claims beyond using adjectives like "immortal." He is more persuasive in establishing Millay's bona fides as a "sex goddess," frothing over her "red integuments" and "secret circles and folds"; her petite "34-22-34" figure with its "surprisingly large" breasts; and the "crimson flame of her hair—not carrot-colored, let no one call it that." He adds that there is "a beautiful switch of the poet's hair still kept in her bureau drawer in tissue, eerily as fresh and vivid as the day it was harvested . . . I have heard that a man before me fainted at the sight of it." According to Epstein, "poetry is the exercise of hyperbole." But biography isn't.

The authorized life is an ample, sober book in which Milford, without losing her senses, accounts for most of the integuments Millay once kissed. But she doesn't persuade me any more than Epstein does that her subject is a great poet. Nothing can shake my conviction that a great poet would never, under any circumstances, publish lines such as "Down, you mongrel, Death! / Back into your kennel! / I have stolen breath / In a stalk of fennel!" (Curiously, the Modern Library anthology that Milford edited includes nothing Millay wrote after 1923, thus omitting her fine late sonnets and giving no sense of her trajectory as a writer.)

At times, Savage Beauty seems like a collage, or a garment much altered—let out and taken in—whose new seams don't quite match up. Milford punctuates the narrative with frequent asides in the form of an ongoing dialogue—a tug-of-war—with her patron and primary source, Norma, the poet's vestal and the biographer's Nemesis, who dropped cryptic hints about deeper mysteries that remained unsolved and let slip that she had destroyed certain overly revealing or unseemly materials, including pornographic photographs. These encounters, usually over drinks, which sometimes included Norma's husband, Charlie, who enjoyed deflating the Millay hype, are not well enough developed to be more than a distraction, and one senses a competing story—Milford's—straining for expression. Yet Milford understands something fundamental that Epstein doesn't, which is that to tackle a siren you have to resist her seductions. With patience and guile, she has done so and survived. So has what's most affectingly human about Millay.

Millay, whose genteel-sounding middle name pays homage to the eponymous Greenwich Village hospital where an uncle had received lifesaving care, was a great literary rake in the Romantic tradition. Her affairs with men and women were the fresh wood she fed to the fire of her poetry, often several logs at a time. In any affair, one person loves more than the other, but Millay was almost invariably the better loved. In his memoir *The Shores of Light*, Edmund Wilson claims that she could show "invincible magnanimity" to those she had cast off (he was himself a castoff), and lavishness is certainly one of her finest qualities. But the compulsive seducer is often a man or woman who suffers from a morbid fear of being abandoned and takes pleasure in inflicting abandonment. This was true of Millay, who could be spectacularly cavalier. The bite of her best love poetry comes from its heartlessness and the swagger of its virtuosity.

A Maine Yankee with Irish blood (and Irish wit, coloring, and propensity for high drama and strong drink), Millay was born in 1892, which places her in the fin de siècle generation of Pound, Eliot, Marianne Moore, H.D., and William Carlos Williams. Her antipathy to the modernist revolution, about which neither of her biographers has any comment, was that of a Papist at the time of the Reformation. Epstein does compare "Renascence," fantastically, to Eliot's late poems: "There can be no more precise account of the psychic burden of the great poet, the *moral* poet." But Millay loathed Eliot (along with Pound and Auden), and wrote a satire of *The Waste Land*, priding herself that it wasn't "abusive . . . merely murderous." In this regard, it's interesting to consider the lines from which Milford, apparently without irony, takes her bodice ripper's title:

> I am waylaid by Beauty. Who will walk
> Between me and the crying of the frogs?
> Oh, savage Beauty, suffer me to pass,

> That am a timid woman, on her way
> From one house to another!

One of Pound's best dicta was "No metaphors that won't permit examination." Millay's modest contribution to modernity was not as a Little Red Riding Hood in a dark wood; it was to write—on her wolfish way from one bed to another—with supreme boldness about her lust and to live her woman's life with supreme disregard for anything but her art and pleasure. By adolescence, she had done enough housework and child care for a lifetime. She treated suitors for her hand as she later, laughingly, claimed to treat her publishers: "Although I reject their proposals, I welcome their advances." Her style of bardic charisma vanished from poetry with the Beats, but it survives in the world of rock music.

If Millay was a "genius," it was as a diva, and in her odd mixture of venality and idealism she resembles the nineteenth-century actress who is the heroine of Susan Sontag's novel *In America*. To the crowds who came to hear them recite in provincial halls across the country, American high culture meant a double bill of Elizabethan drama and French boudoir farce performed in Victorian costume with a British accent. The verse Millay declaimed in her mesmerizing voice—

> Nay learnèd doctor, these fine leeches fresh
> From the pond's edge my cause cannot remove:
> Alas, the sick disorder in my flesh
> Is deeper than your skill, is very love.

—now seems as ersatz as the high-flown pastiche that A. S. Byatt supplies in wholesale quantities for her imaginary Pre-Raphaelites. A great poem of any age and in whatever style restores the unmediated innocence of experience and sensation, while a dated poem merely reminds one of how innocent one used to be. Where Millay's work is still alive on the page, it's as a form of musical notation that preserves the allure of a subversive personality, or in a handful of lyrics that transcend her false distinction between the poetic and the mundane—which was the same line she drew between her own priestly entitlements and those of laymen.

The hundred and seven couplets of tightly rhymed tetrameter about cosmic sorrow and ecstatic rebirth that constitute "Renascence" were composed by the teenage Millay in 1911 and published in a widely reviewed anthology called *The Lyric Year*, an event that made the precocious girl a minor literary celebrity. The attack of claustrophobia she describes—the narrator is buried alive by the sins of the world ("Ah, awful weight! Infinity / Pressed down upon the finite Me!")— had much to do with the privations of Millay's childhood. But at a recital in her confining hometown, Camden, Maine, she impressed a rich and well-connected bluestocking—Caroline Dow, the dean of the YWCA Training School in New York—who rescued her. Miss Dow invited Millay to stay at the Y, bought her some decent clothes, introduced her to the grandees at the Poetry Society of America and the MacDowell Club, and arranged for her to attend Vassar. Epstein and Milford disagree about the extent of Millay's sexual experience at this point, but she had already begun to smoke and drink, to flirt expertly with older men in a position to advance her career, and to sleep with girls. In the dorms at Vassar, she lorded it over a harem of smitten younger classmates, who revered her as their Sappho.

Between scripting and starring in virginal college pageants, Millay misbehaved so egregiously, at least by the standards of propriety then in effect for female undergraduates, that she was nearly banned from her commencement. In Greenwich Village, though, the proper thing was to be as disreputable as possible. Once on her own there, she consorted with radicals like John Reed, Floyd Dell, and Max Eastman, editors of *The Masses*, who were then on trial for sedition. Millay herself was never a leftist, but she liked cutting a heroic figure in the service of a good cause. In 1927, she was jailed for marching in a demonstration against the death sentences of Sacco and Vanzetti, and her poem on their execution, "Justice Denied in Massachusetts," became as famous as "Renascence." In the thirties, she pitted her celebrity against the Lindberghs' to publicize the evils of isolationism. In the forties, she spoke out against Hitler—bravely and in anguish—in radio broadcasts, interviews, and verse "lamentations." But guests invited to Steepletop were always reminded to bring their evening clothes, for the Boissevains liked, as she said, to "live in grand style," and Millay treated her help as badly as her lovers: "The only people I really hate are servants. They are not really human beings at all."

In the beginning, of course, Millay couldn't afford servant problems. The chances of living in grand style on a poet's wages were as dim in 1917 as they have always been, and, hoping for a lucrative stage career, she studied acting with the Broadway star Edith Wynne Matthison, from whom she acquired a vaguely British accent, though she also practiced cursing while darning socks in her "hell hole" on Waverly Place: "Needle in, shit. Needle out, piss. Needle in, fuck. Needle out, cunt." Floyd Dell, one of her lovers, recruited her talents as an actor, dramatist, and director for the Provincetown Players, where her greatest triumph was *Aria da Capo* (1919), an antiwar play in the style of the commedia dell'arte, with Norma Millay in the starring role. "You should see this bitterly ironic little fantasy by Edna St. Vincent Millay," Alexander Woollcott wrote in the *Times*. "This is the most beautiful and most interesting play in the English language now to be seen in New York." It was also during these buoyant Village years that Millay promoted her marquee name as a femme fatale with impious little jingles—advertisements for wantonness—that everyone recited:

> My candle burns at both ends;
> It will not last the night;
> But ah, my foes, and oh, my friends—
> It gives a lovely light!

When *Vanity Fair* sent Millay to Europe in 1921, to be its first foreign correspondent, she landed in Paris, as she had arrived in the Village, at the height of its glamour as a haven for refugees from convention. She caroused with the expatriates at the Rotonde, including Fitzgerald, with whom she was not impressed. She described him to Wilson as being like "a stupid old woman with whom someone has left a diamond." She traveled with admirers to Italy, Hungary, and—on horseback—through the wilds of Albania. She made some desultory passes at a novel for which she had received a big advance, but ran through the money and got into debt. Her editor at the magazine offered to double her stipend if she would drop the pseudonym she used for her dispatches ("Nancy Boyd"), but she refused: the inviolate name was reserved for literature. Yet, in two years abroad, "The Ballad of the Harp-Weaver" was her only work of distinction. This dark fairy tale in twenty-nine singsong verses is narrated by an orphan whose destitute mother weaves him a prince's wardrobe on her magic instrument, then dies of the exertion. Milford relates the central metaphor to the maternal sacrifices of Cora Millay, and describes the unstated drama succinctly as "matricide cloaked in sentiment." But how could the fantasy of a sumptuous fashion windfall not appeal to a fanatic clotheshorse living on the cheap in Paris? When Wilson came to see Millay, he found her "better dressed" than she had ever been, and better "cared for," by which he seems to imply "kept." The "girl poet," now thirty, was eminently resourceful. She continued to rack up conquests, specializing in attached men and fragile youths, and leaving behind a wake, as she puts it in a poem, of "fresh wreckage." Eventually, she suffered one of her "extravagant" depressions, accompanied by a mysterious intestinal blockage for which she blamed the rich food, but which Epstein diagnoses as a case of Crohn's disease, and retreated from the Continent—pregnant—to a cottage in the English countryside, where her mother, who had come for a visit, induced an abortion with a brew of herbs.

In May of 1923, on the basis of "The Ballad of the Harp-Weaver," "A Few Figs from Thistles," and eight sonnets, Millay received the Pulitzer Prize for poetry. She had just met Boissevain, the housemate of Max Eastman, at a party in Croton-on-Hudson, which was then a colony of artists and intellectuals who had left the Village to escape the tourists. Fellow guests watched the couple fall in love "violently and in public," as Floyd Dell put it, and they were married that July. Boissevain was a Dutch-born widower twelve years her senior, the scion of a distinguished liberal family in the newspaper business. As a young man, he had rowed in the Olympics and been analyzed by Carl Jung. When he met Millay, he earned his living as an importer in the East India trade, and though his fortunes were unstable, he had the means to install her in a "dollhouse" on Bedford Street in New York and to buy her a diamond bracelet, an emerald ring worth $40,000, a lavish wardrobe, and the four-hundred-acre farm upstate.

Perhaps Boissevain's generous and sunny character speaks well for Jung's gifts as a therapist. No knight (or governess) from a romance novel has ever possessed such a collection of improbably paired virtues as did this paragon, who was handsome without being vain, virile yet tender, solid but never dull, and a tireless though unjealous protector: the ideal mate and perfect foil for a fragile monomaniac like Millay. One of their cattier acquaintances likened Boissevain to a "cruise director," and for the next twenty-five years he directed their life as smoothly as the storms of Millay's nature would permit. He kept their house, farmed their land, entertained their friends, and stage-managed her career, which, after he lost his money, supported them in the style to which they had both become accustomed: "pigs in clover."

In 1926, Millay wrote the libretto for an opera by Deems Taylor, *The King's Henchman*, set in tenth-century England, which was one of the most successful productions ever mounted at the Metropolitan Opera. (It has never been revived.) She published eight more books of verse, including one for children, and a translation of Baudelaire's *Les Fleurs du mal*, a joint venture with her last great love, the poet George Dillon, who was fourteen years her junior and the only man to break her heart. Even when her work received cool reviews, as in the mid-thirties it began to, with critics complaining, Milford notes, "that her celebrity had outstripped her poetry and that the younger generation was moving on," Millay remained wildly popular. A reporter predicted that she would become "a bookseller's staple, like Shakespeare and ink and two-cent stamps." Her strenuous cross-country reading tours still attracted rapt crowds, high fees, and fawning publicity. According to Milford, "It was the . . . emotional vibrance of her voice that held her audiences to her. Yet it was odd that this . . . woman would still alternate her serious lyrics with her girlish kiddie poems." It wasn't odd: Millay was a consummate performer, but her motor ran on adulation, and, like alcohol, it warped her judgment of how much she could take before she embarrassed herself.

The Romantics of the 1920s had a lot in common with their counterparts of the early nineteenth century, and, as Wilson observed, it was difficult for those among them who survived their wars, vices, and breakdowns—their "scorn for safe living and expediency"—to "slow down and slough off their youth, when . . . they had been able to treat their genius as an unlimited checking account." Boissevain, robust himself but complacent, did nothing to temper or contain Millay's reckless voracity. His "child" missed the sea? They bought an island. She needed the stimulus of a young man's passion? He left her to him. Her nerves craved an anodyne? He supplied it. Toward the end, he was shooting her up, and himself, too. Milford belatedly allows that their relationship "had turned into a destructive dependence," while Epstein continues to see this service in an Orphic light: "He would follow her into hell to be with her and to lead her out . . . or they would both die there together."

In 1940, Hitler overran the Low Countries and Boissevain lost contact with his family. Millay, a year into menopause, was getting fat and blowsy. She had never recovered from Dillon's rejection, which confirmed the tragic news announced by her mirror—and her reviews—that she had lost her erotic power. When she published her last book of poems, *Make Bright the Arrows*—a quixotic and grandiose but just and heartfelt work of anti-Nazi propaganda—she was accused of prostituting her talent and tarnishing her name. (No one had lodged any such protests when she was writing propaganda for free love.) By now, she was smoking hash to calm down, popping speed to wake up, drinking to pass out, and hiding her syringes. She stopped writing except for her drug log and an excruciating journal. ("Things I *must* do for Eugen if I truly love him . . . Even if I am suffering TORMENT, speak in a voice with *no hint* of pain.")

In 1949, Boissevain died of lung cancer. Two weeks later, Millay was admitted to Doctors Hospital suffering from "acute neurasthenia" aggravated by malnutrition and cirrhosis of the liver. After her discharge, she returned to Steepletop with a nurse, and the local postmistress handled her correspondence. Then that spring she announced, "It's time I stopped being such a baby." She had never lived alone, but in the months before her fatal fall she was planning a solitary trip to Ragged Island, her retreat off the coast of Maine.

Millay's poetry, wrote her old flame Edmund Wilson, "will always be there to make the casualties of her life seem unimportant," but he was wrong. It is as a resplendent casualty of sex, drugs, and fame that she lives on.

—September 3, 2001

THREE

Doing It in the Road

I spent part of every summer until I was ten with my grandmother, who lived in a working-class suburb of Boston. The neighbors were devoutly Catholic, and they occasionally took me to Mass at their parish church up the hill. On sultry August afternoons in that era before vernacular prayers and air-conditioning, my friends and I used the sanctuary as a place to cool off and to play the confession game. One girl would tell her sins and the others would invent her chastisement. We were fond of the word "flagellation." Peggy, who was pale and fat, entertained the fantasy of scourging herself for a mystic bridegroom. I considered converting, so as to be eligible for sainthood. In the late 1950s, there were still not many avenues of glory open to ambitious virgins who couldn't tap-dance. Heroic self-abnegation was, as it has been for two millennia, one of the few.

Marie scornfully rejected any thought of taking the veil. She had already tried smoking and had no intention of practicing any romantic austerities. It was she who pointed out that there was a cavity between our thighs, and that boys would want to put their "thing" there, and that if we let them "it would hurt like hell the first time, but you do it for love." I must have read about St. Catherine of Siena (1347–80) that summer, because her hagiography left an indelible impression that I associate with the secrets Marie thrust upon us in the purple-tinted gloom of Our Lady's. As a young novice of the Sisters of Penance, Catherine had nursed a woman with breast cancer. The lesions were suppurating and gave off a nauseating smell. Because she aspired to dominate her physical sensations—attractions and repulsions—in the name of submission to a higher power, the future Doctor of the Church drained some of the pus into a ladle and drank it. That night, Jesus came to her in a vision and invited her to drink the blood spurting from His wounds. A few years later, she wrote, "I, Catherine . . . turn to and lean upon the tree of the most holy cross of Christ crucified and there I wish to be nailed; and do not doubt that I will be pierced through and nailed with him for love and with deep humility."

In a working-class suburb of Paris, another Catherine, surnamed Millet—a devoutly Catholic schoolgirl of my generation—dreamed of becoming a missionary nun. Her large family lived in a small apartment. The parents' marriage was unhappy, but they were too poor or too conventional to separate. Catherine once glimpsed her mother and an admirer stealing a kiss, and she describes this memory as a "primal scene." She and her mother shared a bed. Curled up on her side of it, the daughter masturbated resentfully and inexpertly—she says that she had not yet located her clitoris and wouldn't for a long while. Young girls often indulge in violent fantasizing even as they stopper their nascent lust with an excess of prudery. Catherine abandoned her reading of a Hemingway novel when she discovered that the heroine has multiple lovers, and she reacted with hostility to an atypical confidence from her mother, who casually remarked one day that she had slept with seven men. It was more intolerable, though quite natural, for Catherine to imagine that her parents might picture *her* in a man's arms. She fled their house soon after she was deflowered—at eighteen ("not particularly early," as she notes). While she never tried to hide her subsequent, hard-driven promiscuity from friends or colleagues, she always concealed it from her mother and father. They are presumably now both safely dead.

Catherine did not become a missionary, or at least not the kind she had once imagined. For several decades, she has edited a journal called *Art Press*, curated exhibitions, and written art criticism. But, with boundless and in many respects conventional female application, she has also pursued her desire to be nailed for love. Last year, Millet published an ostentatiously obscene work of erotobabble in the form of a memoir about her "unreserved abandonment of the self to a way of life." *The Sexual Life of Catherine M.* provoked a predictably heated dialectical response in the European media while selling some 350,000 copies in France alone, and in 2002, it was translated— carelessly and in places incoherently—into English (Grove, 2002).

Millet was born in 1948. Twenty years later, student revolutionaries mounted the barricades, gaily chanting "*Merde au chagrin!*" They piously believed that desire sets one free, and many still do. Catherine M. thinks of herself as a "libertine" philosopher ("My backside is the other side of who I am"); as an evangelist of sexual liberation theology; as a "valiant warrior" waging a class struggle against the "gentrification" of her erotic life; and as a mystic searching for the "grail" of "fornicatory communion," though her more obvious goal seems to be inclusion in the record books for various Olympic feats of endurance and agility. Over the years (her chronology is vague), she has been what the French call a *partouzeuse*—an orgiast. Orgies, mostly of the gourmet, mate-swapping variety, have taken place in luxurious Parisian salons and specialized clubs for centuries, though they were particularly popular in the 1970s, when Millet was young. Within weeks of losing her virginity and running away from home, she discovered group sex, and her gymnastics in the garden and bedrooms of a borrowed villa outside Lyons with a band of contemporaries led to progressively more heterogeneous and less well-upholstered sessions of consensual gangbanging on benches in the Bois de Boulogne, on the games table of a louche swingers' club, on the corrugated-metal slats of a truck parked outside the Soviet embassy, in the cabs of semis, under the stands at a soccer stadium, sitting up in a sauna, supine in the grotto of a mansion, in stairwells, offices, backseats, cemeteries, bathtubs, peep-show cubicles, a three-star restaurant, museum storerooms, and on the hoods of cars in parking lots on the outskirts of Paris, where throngs of frenzied anonymous strangers would, for hours at a go, serially or several at a time, take their pleasure in all of her willingly proffered orifices. "I was completely available," she writes (her favorite orgy being a bragfest), "at all times and in all places, without hesitation or regret . . . and with a totally clear conscience."

The "quality" of an experience, Catherine M. says, was unimportant to her. She preferred to keep the genteel preliminaries—coquetry, foreplay, drinks, a friendly hello—as brief as possible. She didn't mind, and even welcomed, filth, rudeness, haste, uncomeliness, and bumbling in her partners: "To fuck above and beyond any sense of disgust was not just a way of lowering oneself, it was, in a diametrically opposite move, to raise yourself above all prejudice." She prided herself, rather like a sled dog mushing through a blizzard with a vial of lifesaving vaccine, on never begging off, despite a raging migraine or an excruciating case of "the clap . . . the shared fate of those who fuck a lot." (It is striking, though, that Millet ignores that other shared fate of so many who fornicated as recklessly as she did without protection—death. There isn't a single reference to AIDS, not to mention what must have been intensely bothersome chronic cases of herpes and cystitis. One has to wonder if she hasn't exaggerated her exploits or possibly invented some of them. Anal intercourse with forty men in a night calls for an exceptionally hardy constitution.)

One also learns, toward the end of the memoir, though by then without surprise, that Millet first realized she'd never had a proper orgasm when, in her late twenties or early thirties, alone in bed, she finally achieved one with the help of a "Japanese vibrating dildo." Though she alludes to her "vast plain of desire," few women would seem to have learned less about the geography of rapture from its exploration, or derived so little profit from its mining rights: "The teasing I have had for offering my body so easily but not knowing how to make money out of it!" Though Catherine yearned to be "a high-class prostitute"—"a Madame Claude girl"—or, even better, an icy tease like Belle de Jour, slumming in a seedy brothel, her short, slightly bowed legs, artless enthusiasm, and distaste for pillow talk disqualified her. But over the years she did collect, in addition to the dildo, a few tokens of gratitude: a designer bath towel, some costume jewelry, taxi fare, the odd hundred-franc handout, a contribution toward a Saint Laurent dress, and free dental work. Few careers in public service have been as selfless.

Lust is a great and inexhaustible literary subject, but writing graphically about what excites one isn't literature. The same stupid things excite everybody. Pornography is a form of pidgin—a trading tongue without the deep wellspring of nuance that produces clarity. Millet's memoir was greeted abroad as "absolutely staggering" (*Le Monde*) and in some reviews here as a profound contribution to our knowledge of the senses. Italian television staged a debate between Millet and the archbishop of Como—a "courteous" encounter, she recalled in an interview. "He only made two critical observations: that my book was less philosophical than those of de Sade—I don't agree . . . and that he wouldn't like to be my husband."

The Sexual Life of Catherine M. suggests, however, that the mental hymen of the reading public is a membrane capable of miraculous regeneration. Surely, works in which a tough French girl who will do "anything," who has read too much Bataille, and who complacently flaunts her voracious appetite for violation in the name of free agency—aggressively seeking what men like to pretend women must be forced to beg for—aren't subversive anymore, despite the current fashion for them. The dreary films of Catherine Breillat, *Romance* and *Fat Girl*, and the repulsively cynical *Baise-moi*, by Virginie Despentes and Coralie Trinh Thi, belong to the same genre as *The Sexual Life of Catherine M.* It is also now almost fifty years since the distinguished essayist Dominique Aury published *Story of O* under the pseudonym Pauline Réage. Even then, the subject and the imagery were hardly original: the Sadean château; the mysterious, priapic confraternity; the female initiates—temple whores—who reverently acquiesce in the penances imposed by their priestly dominators. Inverted Mariolatry is a trope of the French erotic tradition, which endlessly retells the same story of defilement. She who is without sin is submerged by her Lord in a baptismal river of filth to emerge as She who is without shame. The author's gender gave authority to the novel's premise of absolute carnal surrender as an avenue to divine grace, and Aury was the first woman to write so frankly and unsentimentally about her fantasies of bondage. But what is most thrilling (rather than merely titillating) about *Story of O* is the tension between its radically explicit scenes of torture and fornication and the purity of the sentences that describe them. Aury's reticent virtuosity—her withholding—is the foil for O's abject self-abandon. If this weren't the case, her fable would be not the masterpiece that it is but a clinical case study of masochism, author's and subject's, in the form of a mildly heretical, comically exalted, didactically perverse, and ultimately banal piece of French art porn, like the volume here under review.

Millet's chthonic vulgarity is a provocation. She poses as a combatively uncongenial woman who lives according to an old-fashioned, romantic code that abhors bourgeois prudence. Her asocial persona even wears a faint halo of autism: the idiot savant obsessed with repetition and feats of arithmetic (the first and least awful chapter of the book is called "Numbers"). Given her fascination with scorekeeping, detachment, and anonymity, her sexual ethos seems a little queer—in the style of the seventies—and one sometimes wonders if the narrator is not a woman but a gay female impersonator. Like the denizens of the old West Village trucks, piers, bathhouses, and bars, Catherine M. is addicted to the rush of novelty and controlled menace, to the thrill of sodomy in public places with faceless thugs, and to lightless back rooms full of ambiguous moans where the sudden flare of a match illuminates a grimace. She loves the morphological variety of male members and styles of penetration as much as if not more than coitus itself. She recognizes the rapport between lust and wanderlust, both of which simultaneously dissolve one's bearings and refresh one's keenness of sensation.

Yet the middle-aged swinger who narrates *The Sexual Life of Catherine M.* is also a credentialed intellectual with a nice apartment, an impressive academic bibliography, and an athletic life of the mind. In the name of piety, many a puckish Renaissance painter tested the tolerance of his orthodox patrons with a flamboyant St. Sebastian or a slutty Eve, and Millet, the art historian, plays that game in reverse. In the name of authenticity, she challenges the black-garbed hierarchs of moral relativity to call her bluff. At least one of them did. "Can anyone still believe," Jean Baudrillard wrote in *Libération*, railing against reality TV and Millet's "exhibitionism," "that truth remains when its veil of secrecy is lifted?"

Lazy as most of Millet's prose is, it bears the imprint of her critical training. "I am a formalist," she announces. In ruminative asides,

she wishes to impress us with her life's "antinomies": privacy and exposure; solitude and plurality; confinement and escape; propriety and
transgression—the conflict between the vestal and the bawd who
shape her character. "As far as I can see," she writes, "there is a balance to be sustained between the acquisition of moral and intellectual
qualities which earns the respect of our peers, and a proportional excellence in practices which flout these qualities, brush them aside,
and deny them." The most interesting paradox, however, is that Millet's spectacular hubris in telling this story under her own name is an
act of self-mortification more hard-core than any in the text. She
even seems to be courting, like her namesake, a kind of martyrdom.
The pustulant public ridicule that she drains into a ladle and forces
herself to swallow with such a show of humility must be particularly
galling to a cultivated French palate.

Men and women suffer from grandiosity in different ways. Men tend
toward fantasies of omnipotence, women of uniqueness. Millet wants
her readers to ask themselves the question "How can she?," and one
does. But perhaps her motive, hidden in plain sight, is prodigiously
ordinary: to hold the interest of a man. She has, for thirty years, been
a partner in an intimate union of two who share a bed, a bank account, vacations (they especially like "outdoor fucking"), squabbles,
a workplace—a "couple culture," as she puts it—and who have for a
decade been legally wed. Her husband is a novelist and amateur photographer named Jacques Henric. Though neither of them ever renounced "sleeping with lots of people," his affairs, Millet says, her
voice trembling a little, like any betrayed woman's, filled her "with a
terrible feeling of being supplanted," and Henric's possessiveness was
just as volatile as that of any Latin lover. Was he the enraged brute
who, as she slept, slashed her shoulder with a razor in "revenge" for
"one of my unwisely detailed accounts"?

Henric published a companion volume to *The Sexual Life of
Catherine M.*, called *Légendes de Catherine M.*, and its cover features
the shapely naked "backside" of the young Millet. "A free woman,"
he writes, "without guilt, is a pretty gift for a novelist." The memoir
of a sexual showoff, one might add, makes a pretty gift for a voyeur.

The author's head shot of Henric shows a taurine man of about sixty-five, in a black leather biker's jacket. There are more photographs inside—mostly snaps from their holiday trips over the years—including several taken in Spain of Millet flashing her droopy little breasts, neat pubis, short legs, and "supple" waist at the grave of Walter Benjamin. They are accompanied by a flaccid text of such orgiastic fatuity that it seems like parody. Vaunting his own obscure novels and commingling his blather about reality and appearances with the refined aperçus of poor Benjamin, who deserves to rest in peace, Henric proceeds to drop more august names in a few pages (Rimbaud, Joyce, Baudelaire, Artaud, Genet, Kafka, Proust, Céline, Lacan, and the indispensable Bataille) than there are drunks in a phone booth. The tone of his voice eerily recalls that of the only other French erotomane who is as tedious to read: Colette's first husband, Willy.

Colette probably would have slept with Henric to teach him a lesson while dismissing Millet as one of those women whom she calls "a Madame How-many-times." She also might have chastised her familiarly with the same smart slap that she gave to her friend Radclyffe Hall, who had asked for a critique of *The Well of Loneliness*: "Obscenity is such a narrow domain. One immediately begins to suffocate there, and to feel bored."

—June 10, 2002

FOUR

Night Kitchens

The abbot's garden at the temple of Daisen-in, in Kyoto, is a rectangle of raked gravel bordered by a white wall on one of its long sides, and by the wooden porch of an old pavilion on the other, where the monks meditate. From behind the wall, a camellia bush throws off its scent. The grooves made by the rake run horizontally, like steady but freehand rulings on a blank page, until they eddy around two conical mounds, each about a foot tall. One evening last June, just after the temple had closed, I joined the sitting meditation, the hour-long zazen, held on the porch and open to the public twice a week. There were five other sitters, all Japanese, one a young mother who had her children in tow, two plump boys and a little girl. I could hear them squirming at the end of the row (the wood creaks), and once or twice the presiding monk spoke to them in a low voice, breaking the silence. But after a while, with an impressive show of stoicism, they managed to keep still.

I had been to Daisen-in earlier that week, and at my first sight of the mounds I surprised myself by bursting into tears, perhaps because, for all its austerity, the garden is an image of release: of the moment at which, after an intractable struggle, you get permission from yourself to let the inessential go.

The temples I had come to Japan to visit were of a different sort, though they, too, had a Zen foundation. They were the workshops where tofu is handmade by artisans faithful to the old tradition. Here I should admit that, to a Western palate—mine, at least, unable, despite my best efforts at Daisen-in, to transcend an incorrigible greed for new sensations—even the greatest artisanal tofu didn't produce the kind of epiphany that my first mouthful of white truffle, or of a fruity tomato, or of corn rushed from a field into the pot did. But tofu has been the dietary mainstay of monastic life in Japan for about a millennium—it was imported from China and Korea, along with Buddhism—and it has never lost the soulful, exalted aura of its provenance. In that respect, its relation to the bean curd sold in plastic tubs at American supermarkets is that of a rice cracker to a Communion wafer. Westerners tend to regard tofu as a convenient and perhaps necessary but vaguely pathetic substitute for some less wholesome, more morally dubious carnal indulgence—a rare burger, say. They may even be a bit disdainful of a dish (as they would be of an individual) that, by their standards, lacks an identity, or begs for a disguise. Every tribe, however, has an ancestral food that its exiles yearn for and that its children can't live without: its manna, which is often soft and white. When a tofu master offers you a slice of bean curd he has just unmolded, he is inviting you to partake, insofar as a stranger can, of what it means to be Japanese.

Okutan is a place congenial to such reflections. It is the oldest tofu *riyori* in Kyoto. The original restaurant was established almost four hundred years ago within the walls of the Nazenji temple, and the current proprietor, Yasuie Ishii, is the fifteenth generation of his family to preside there. He is now in his sixties, but as a young man he bought a villa and its outbuildings—a cluster of thatched pavilions—near the temple of Kiyomizu-dera, with the idea of one day opening a second Okutan. This newer branch sits on the hilly site of a village once owned by the temple's lord. Guests eat at low tables in a tatami room cantilevered over the garden—a lush glade of cherry, cedar, and maple trees. *Mukashi dofu* is the first course on the set menu: a dish from the monastic repertoire. A kneeling waitress prepares it at your table. She sets a clay crock on a charcoal brazier, adds two or three small bricks of *momengoshi* ("cotton" tofu—well drained of moisture and firm in consistency), pours some hot water over them from a kettle, and, after they have simmered for a few minutes (they are not supposed to steep, as they do in the classic hot pot, *yudofu*), she ladles them into a bowl. You then help yourself to a sprinkling of scallions and seven hand-ground spices, and a spoonful of enriched fish stock that contains algae from Hokkaido. The courses that follow observe the principle set by the first: exquisitely bland bean curd, devoid of the bitter or metallic aftertaste that, in the commercial product or its milk, is masked by additives, and served with a refined sauce or paste that sets off its plainness the way a fanciful bijou sets off the elegance of a couture dress. Yet nothing else at Okutan, or perhaps in Japan, rivals the purity of *shima dofu*—an ivory-colored attar of bean curd that arrives on a turquoise plate, with a coral drop of sea-urchin (*uni*) purée, and whose creation is an almost mystical rite.

I was having lunch with a Japanese friend—a native of Kyoto—and after the meal Mr. Ishii introduced himself to us. We chatted briefly about a mutual acquaintance, Hiroko Tanaka, who had arranged the interview. Madam Tanaka is a lithe woman of sixty who dresses in kimonos and wears her dark hair swept high off her pale forehead in a classic pompadour. A fan, a cell phone, and a pack of cigarettes are all tucked neatly into her obi. She has a dancer's carriage and the stage presence of a beauty who has spent her life being looked at. Her theater was the world of the geisha house. Like many retired geishas (who are called *geikos* in Kyoto), she opened a bar on one of the cobbled backstreets off the river, in the Gion quarter, and she trains a small troupe of teenage protégées—*maikos*—in the arts and protocol of her former profession.

Though Mr. Ishii is a busy man, he devoted the better part of an afternoon to giving us a course in soybean history and gastronomy. This engaging lesson took place in his tofu kitchens and in his private museum of beans, which is housed in a crypt beneath the restaurant. Beans, he explained, are the seedpods of legumes, which grow on every continent except Antarctica, and *Glycine max* (soya) is one of some twenty thousand species, the majority of which are poisonous. Mr. Ishii has managed to obtain (and, in some cases, to finesse through customs, with the help of airline-pilot friends) about five thousand specimens, along with their flowers, which he displays, mostly for his own enjoyment, in glass bottles and vitrines. He also took us to his studio, in one of the thatched pavilions, where he edits photographs taken on a life of travels to the remote, mostly tropical places where one finds exotic bean stalks like the locust tree and the Calabar. I wondered about this extravagant politesse, until my friend received a cell-phone call from Madam Tanaka. Ishii-san, she said, had once been her admirer. But not even a celebrated geisha could get him off the subject of tofu.

Histories vary, but according to Mr. Ishii the art of extracting a milky liquid from the soybean and turning it into a cheap and versatile solid food by means of a curdling agent—a salt or an acid—was invented in China about two thousand years ago. The Chinese called the dish *dofu* (*do*=curdled; *fu*=bean), a name as basic as the nutrient it described. About seven hundred years later, a delegation of monks studying Chinese Buddhism brought the technique back to Japan with them. Tofu was exclusive to the upper classes (nobles and samurai) and the vegetarian clergy for about five centuries, in part because the labor required to pulverize dried soybeans (*daizu*) by hand, with a mortar and pestle, was too costly. But the advent of the millstone made tofu accessible to common people, and its place in the national diet and psyche has been compared to that of bread in France, or of potatoes in Eastern Europe—a difference being that one cannot live by bread or potatoes alone, whereas tofu (discounting one study, not cited by Mr. Ishii, that links its consumption by middle-aged Japanese American men to an increased incidence of brain atrophy in old age) is an almost uniquely perfect food: low in calories, high in protein, rich in minerals, devoid of cholesterol, eco-friendly, and complete in the amino acids necessary for human sustenance.

The workshop where Okutan's tofu is made occupies a multi-chambered grotto beneath the dining rooms which has the chaste and contemplative atmosphere of a chapel. Apart from the plumbing and electrical fixtures, almost no alloyed metal or industrial materials have been used in the construction of the kitchen, or are used in the cooking process, as if they might profane the tofu with their modernity. Nearly all the accoutrements—even the sink—are handmade of cedar, and the stove is a slab of lava. In the kitchen's inner sanctum— the salt room—the regimen of purism is absolute. Adobe walls of clay mixed with rice straw are sheathed in bamboo; the ceiling is tented in thatch; the floor is cobbled with sea stones; and, though the dim light is electric, the bulbs are disguised by old wrought-iron lanterns. Here, Mr. Ishii explained, he distills his *nigari*—the coagulating agent. Salt from the mountains of China is wrapped in straw and suspended from a wooden tripod over a weathered cypress barrel. It absorbs humidity from the walls, and exudes its moisture in an almost imperceptible drip, filling the barrel at the rate of three centimeters a year. Every six months, he adds more salt to the bundles, and if their hemp bindings break he replaces them. Otherwise, they have been hanging undisturbed since he courted Madam Tanaka, about thirty years ago.

Shima dofu, however, is the one variety of bean curd at Okutan that isn't curdled with *nigari*. It is an exceedingly expensive delicacy (about $50 for a few thin slices), and on special occasions Mr. Ishii delivers a provision to the emperor's palace, molded with the imperial mark, a sixteen-petaled chrysanthemum. A dish of great antiquity, it comes from one of tofu's early landfalls in Japan, Ishigakijima—a small island southwest of Okinawa, a hundred and fifty miles from Korea. Mr. Ishii learned the art of making *shima dofu* in his youth, from two old women there.

If you would like to try whipping up a batch at home, here is the recipe. Negotiate a contract for organic soybeans with a reliable farmer whose fields lie on the slopes of Mount Hira, in the Shiga Prefecture, where the soil and the water are unpolluted. Make sure that the farmer harvests the beans as late as possible—preferably in December. (Green summer soybeans become edamame, and most commercial soybeans are harvested in the fall. The extra time on the stalk intensifies the flavor.) Pick the beans over carefully, throwing out those eaten by worms—a desirable sign that the farmer isn't cheating with a little DDT. Soak them overnight in very cold springwater. The beans will swell. Rinse them in more of the same, and grind them with a granite mortar, using all your strength, for two hours. Drain the pulp in a bamboo colander, and put the white soy juice you obtain—*gojiu*—to cook on a stone hearth. Let it bubble, subside, and bubble again, several times. (Heating *gojiu*, otherwise known as soy milk, is an essential process that deactivates a toxic substance found in most legumes which blocks digestion.)

Sometime well before you reach this point, however—perhaps while you are waiting for the delivery of your soybeans—hire a boat, and locate the tiny island of Hateruma on your charts (it isn't that far from Ishigakijima). The island is inhabited only by several hundred farmers, who raise sugarcane. Off the coast there is a coral reef (perhaps the sugar farmers can tell you where to find it). You will need a depth finder in good working order, because when the tide is at its lowest ebb you are going to moor the boat and gather the seawater—as Mr. Ishii does—that cascades from the reef, which has an exceptionally rich and complex mineral content. This primordial bouillon is your curdling agent. Add some to the strained *gojiu* (time and failure will teach you the precise amount), stirring with a wooden paddle, and turn the thickened curds into the slatted four-by-ten-inch cedar boxes that you have lined with a fine-grained cheesecloth. Cover them, weight the covers with blocks of lava—about ten pounds per box—and leave them to drain. Do not, under any circumstances, cool your *shima dofu*, as you would common tofu, by unmolding it in a tank of water, which slimes the skin and dilutes the flavor. What is that flavor? Sublimely unsensational, like a perfectly clarified consommé—which keeps the spirit but discards the substance of the earthy ingredients and patient toil that have gone into it.

Traditional tofu-making in Japan is a nocturnal occupation. At Okutan, the staff starts at 4 AM, but many artisans show up for work around 2, and it is probably a good guess that behind the only lighted windows blazing in a darkened town, soybeans are being soaked, ground, boiled, strained, reboiled, curdled, pressed, drained, cooled, sliced, and packaged. So at five o'clock one morning, I rolled off my futon in a lovely old *ryokan*, the Yoyokaku, near the beach in Karatsu, ready for research.

Karatsu is a small provincial city in the Saga Prefecture, about four hours by train from Kyoto, on the spectacularly eroded west coast of Kyushu Island. It is a former whaling port known for its pottery—dun-colored vessels used in the tea ceremony, which are a legacy of Japan's invasions of Korea and of the Korean artisans who returned with their samurai conquerors to settle there in the sixteenth century. The city is also famous for a rowdy, picturesque harvest festival, the Kunchi, which features a parade of gigantic floats and a week of revelry and feasting every November. But off-season it is a quiet backwater, rife with the sort of intrigue that makes for an old-fashioned novel of manners.

By the time I had found my shoes at the front door of the Yoyokaku, and had unlocked my bicycle, the sun was up. I pedaled across a bridge linking the beaches to the mainland, and past Karatsu Castle—a fortified seventeenth-century pagoda that is imposing at a distance, though deplorably restored—which guards the entrance to a bay dotted with misty and misshapen islands. The town was still shuttered, although a few fishmongers and flower sellers were setting up their wares. Downtown Karatsu is Kyoto in miniature: a grid of low, mostly ramshackle timber-and-stucco houses which converges on two glass-vaulted pedestrian arcades, Gofukumachi and Kyomachi.

My destination was a tiny restaurant in Kyomachi, which has a ginkgo counter with ten seats, framed by parchment walls decorated in drippy ink by an inebriated artist. You have to reserve well in advance, and be on time for an early meal (breakfast or brunch), because the service ends at noon, when the exhausted workers go home to sleep. The cuisine consists almost entirely of artisanal tofu made nightly, on the premises, by Yoshimasa Kawashima, an oenophile, chef, organic farmer, philosopher of gastronomy, and devotee of flower arranging and the tea ceremony, whose family has been making tofu in Karatsu for nine generations. He, however, has created his own signature product, *zaru dofu*, a melting, ethereal confection with a mousselike consistency which is eaten with a spoon. It starts out like other artisanal tofu, but one of Kawashima's secrets is his *nigari*—magnesium chloride, which is trickier to use though milder than the more common calcium chloride, which leaves a saline aftertaste. As the creamy curds of *zaru dofu* are setting, they are scooped from the vat and mounded softly into shallow bamboo colanders, where they drain, and in which they are packaged for sale. These appealingly rustic receptacles give Kawashima's delicacy its name (*zaru* means "basket"). It is served in some of Tokyo's best restaurants, and exported to New York by air twice a week, where diners unable to make the twenty-hour journey to Karatsu can try some at Megu, in Tribeca.

That morning, the breakfast menu included white, green, and black *zaru dofu* (the green is a pale celery, and the black a mauvish blue, like a berry gelato) served half a dozen ways: with soft rice and wasabi; with pinches of sea salt or sesame seeds and dribbles of olive oil or tamari; and in a bowl of the thick and fragrant house miso. A side dish of homemade plum pickles accompanied a seared bream, which had probably still been alive when I left the inn. The fish course was followed by a square of "silken" tofu, *kinugoshi*, deep-fried but custardy on the inside—a contrast in texture that reminded me of crème brûlée (if you can imagine eating crème brûlée with chopsticks). The soybean lees (*okara*) dissolved on the tongue, like the fine shavings of a mild root or nut. *Okara* is the residue of the separation process—the stage at which the boiled soybean pulp is pressed in cheesecloth. It looks like sawdust or wheat germ, and it is often fed to animals or used as fertilizer, but Kawashima considers it worthy to be savored with a sprinkling of fish powder, minced carrot, and Japanese mushrooms. There were two soy-milk desserts: a gelatinous sweet made with sesame paste, and a pot of quivering blancmange.

Kawashima is a large presence in Karatsu: a local boy made good, whose fame, or at least whose tofu, has reached America. At a smoky café with dark woodwork and a polished bar that seemed to have been modeled vaguely on a Greenwich Village coffeehouse, the customers were happy to tell me what they thought of him. One was a stocky, middle-aged woman who had come in for a jolt of caffeine after her tango lesson. She lit a cigarette, as did the waitress and a white-haired gentleman in a business suit. He fled, however, when another woman arrived and settled down with a cigar. The echo of ribald female laughter in the hazy gloom gave the place the atmosphere of a coven. No one seemed surprised that I had flown seven thousand miles to eat *zaru dofu*, but they gave me to understand that Kawashima was a "character" and "very rich"—he had bought "a big estate," a much envied property in the hills, and a beach house, too. There were forty other tofu-makers in the town, but it was hard work, and none of the others made as much money, they said. I tried to buy them a round of espresso, but they wouldn't hear of it. The tango dancer pressed me to accept her fan.

I had also heard around the Yoyokaku that Kawashima owed at least some of his fame to another local luminary, Takashi Nakazato, one of Japan's greatest potters and the scion of a Karatsu dynasty going back thirteen generations, whose patriarch, Taroumon Nakazato, is a Living National Treasure. Nakazato is a noted gastronome who has helped to make a number of reputations, particularly those of sushi chefs and sake brewers. His original enthusiasm for Kawashima's *zaru dofu* piqued the interest of the press. But the two men had quarreled, it was said, over some matter of etiquette, and their falling-out seemed to enthrall the town. When I met Nakazato, he was at work on a huge urn in a serene, barnlike studio with high rafters and mullioned windows. The light was streaming in, and his assistants were silently prepping a rack of pots for firing. Their master is a slight man of sixty-eight, with a noble head, and his intense containment—a stillness of eye and body while his deft hands move—gives him a sagelike aura. When I asked Nakazato about Kawashima, he slowly looked up from his wheel. "I love food," he said laconically. "I know a young sushi chef in the pine forest. Do you know the pine forest? You should go there." There was a long pause. "There is lots of great tofu in Japan."

Kawashima bounded into the restaurant at about eight, as his pretty wife, Keiko, was clearing away the Nakazato pottery on which breakfast is served—rust-and-ash-colored vessels with a dark underglaze and a primal beauty. Tofu-making may have a Zen gestalt, but Kawashima—a sporty fifty-eight-year-old with a goatee and a crew cut—doesn't make a monklike impression. He is the sort of character the French call a *gaillard*—a bon vivant bristling with rakish vigor. One keeps up with him at a fast trot. His cottage-scale factory and offices occupy a warren of rooms in a somber two-hundred-year-old house, with blackened beams, which survived demolition when the arcade was built, and seems out of synch with its festive swags of plastic wisteria. At the back of a rather cramped, unlovely industrial kitchen, baskets of *zaru dofu* were moving down a conveyor belt, getting wrapped and labeled. (The tofu is handmade, and strictly organic, but the packaging is mechanized, and a small fleet of white delivery vans was waiting at the loading dock.) Kawashima's younger brother was dressed in kitchen whites, stirring soy milk in a metal vat. It was warm but hadn't been curdled yet, and he offered me some from the ladle. Its taste was slightly beany, yet elemental, with an ineffable sweetness, as if it came not from a plant but from a breast.

"I've started showing up late," Kawashima told me. "At around three, to give my brother some breathing room. He's learning the ropes, and the only way you do that is by yourself." Kawashima's elder son has also decided to become a tofu-maker, after a brief stint at Gateway Computers. "I didn't oblige him," Kawashima says. "I told him, on the contrary, to get away from home, the way I did. In my late teens, I left Karatsu for Fukuoka"—the nearest large city— "and worked at another tofu place, to see how they did things. I studied *chabana*, flower arranging, and learned to make tea— my business for ten years. When I came home, I wanted to create something new with tofu." A sudden loud clatter made me start: Kawashima had just pulled down a steel trapdoor in the ceiling, and he shooed me up the ladder. Under the eaves, he has built a tearoom for himself.

In the next two hours, making the rounds with Kawashima, I got to see quite a bit of his enterprise and its fruits. Having asked me if I liked dogs, he took me to his beach house—a Hamptons-style bungalow in an upscale enclave near the castle—where we played with his St. Bernard. Then we drove ten miles out of town, through strawberry fields, and up into the hills, where Kawashima owns several acres. We fed the fat koi in his pond, and tramped through the woods to admire his Shinto shrine, an altar guarded by two gaping stone dogs, one of which catches evil intentions, while the other spits out good luck. I helped him open the elaborately engineered stone sluices that irrigate his kitchen garden, where he stopped to do a little puttering. His wife doesn't like the country, he confided, so this is his bachelor kingdom, and he bought it with his "pocket money," because she also wouldn't like him spending the profits of their business on it. All his crops—tomatoes, melons, eggplants, cherries, a few beans (for edamame), and some white lettuce—are organically grown, as is the rice that he is seeding, experimentally, in a blanket of cotton, to keep down the weeds.

Though I normally don't start drinking at ten in the morning, I had the excuse that it was nine in the evening (of the night before) by my body clock, and Kawashima is a persuasive host. "I think I was born to make people happy," he said. So, having tasted some of his homemade plum wine, we sat at the kitchen table of his farmhouse, chasing our aperitif with a bottle of excellent Chapelle-Chambertin '96, while Kawashima reminisced, as oenophiles do, about the great vintages he has owned and drunk—an '81 Pétrus, some venerable Lafites—and what he ate with them. His memory stirred, he ducked into a walk-in wine cellar, the size of a bank vault, and came back, looking very pleased, with a Château d'Yquem '21. I wrestled with my conscience before insisting, with feigned conviction, that he shouldn't open it.

The farmhouse is built in the traditional style, with shoji windows and a tiled roof curling up at the edges, though its amenities are from a glossy shelter magazine. It sits on a rise overlooking a valley of terraced rice paddies that were simmering under an opaque sky and waiting for the spring rains—a timeless scene only somewhat spoiled by a fretwork of electric pylons. A little farther up the slope, Kawashima has added a luxurious bath pavilion that, like his kitchen, is a sybaritic gadgeteer's paradise. (The plumbing responds to voice commands.) The tub is in a sort of turret penthouse with glass walls that faces a deep forest furrowed by ravines and inhabited by wild boar and monkeys. When Kawashima is soaking there, he says, he sometimes sees a constellation of impudent simian eyes staring at him through the glass.

I doubted that *zaru dofu*, or any other sort of tofu, not even *shima dofu*, would have enough character to hold its own with a great Burgundy like the one we were drinking. But wine and bean curd, Kawashima's twin passions, are more compatible than you might think. To prove the point, he served us a little *amuse-gueule* that he devised for wine tastings: a wedge of dense and pungent saffron-colored *miso zuke dofu*, which is a block of *momengoshi* steeped in fermented miso, wrapped in *konbu* (a form of kelp with a thick, ridged leaf that, in its dried form, resembles a slice of rubber tire tread), and aged for months. At last, some tofu with bite: an alarming, even macho one, like that of a Roquefort at the limit of ripeness.

If you don't speak Japanese, traveling alone in provincial Japan is not for the timid: the lingua franca is pantomime. I mastered the greetings, which change according to the time of day; a few adjectives (though I got into trouble with *oishii*—delicious—which may have a lewd connotation in the wrong context); and I learned to count. So finding the Yoyokaku had been a stroke of luck. The motherly proprietress, Harumi Okochi, whose husband's family have been innkeepers in Karatsu for more than a century, is a former English teacher with a nuanced command of the language, and of the local society and folklore. Her library overlooks a rock garden and a waterfall, and, after I had bathed in the *ryokan*'s communal tub and wrapped myself in a blue-and-white *yukata*, she poured me some tea and we sat reading poetry—paeans to tofu. She asked me if I knew the *Manyoshu* (*Assembly of Ten Thousand Leaves*), an anthology of literary treasures collected in the eighth century. "Some of its earliest verse," she said, "was written on Kashiwajima, an island you can see from the tower of the castle, and the fishermen there may have been among the first Japanese to make bean curd. According to legend, their tofu was so hard that it could break stones. That is what they still call it: *ishiwari*—stone-breaking—*dofu*. Though I have lived here all my life, I have never tasted it."

Kashiwajima is a worn, whale-shaped lump of volcanic rock boiling with greenery. Its love poets were the soldiers of a lonely garrison, watching the sea for Korean war galleys thirteen hundred years ago, and pining for their wives. One afternoon, I hired a launch from a pier near the castle. It bounced across the swell while I clung to the guardrail with white knuckles. Mrs. Okochi, who had changed from a kimono into a pair of cotton trousers, sat primly unperturbed in the cabin, watching for flying fish, and holding a beautifully wrapped box of sweets from the inn, which she'd thought to bring as a gift for the chief tofu-maker, Hiromi Takahira, who had agreed to reopen her workshop for us at an ungodly hour: 3 PM.

The little marina was deserted, though from somewhere nearby we heard the sounds of karaoke. There wasn't a teahouse or a store in sight, so we meandered around the waterfront until we found the workshop, in a corrugated shed on one of the piers. Pampas grass, wild hollyhocks, and thistle were growing by the front door, and the place, like the island generally, had a melancholy air. Kashiwajima has always been dependent on the sea, but in recent times it has lost many of its young people to jobs on the mainland. The elders who remain, however, are a hardy lot. An *uni* fisherman with white hair and a deep tan, who squatted in a doorway on sinewy haunches while mending his nets, was looking for a wife, he told Mrs. Okochi, eyeing her hopefully. "You should meet my sister," he added, waving down an elderly cyclist laden with buoys and baskets—Kashiwajima's last female abalone diver. She was pedaling home in a ratty wet suit and a faded bonnet, toothless and cheerful, though also a little embarrassed, she told Mrs. Okochi, to be seen with such a puffy face. That, she explained, is what happens when you plug your ears and hold your breath long enough to catch a snap-jawed mollusk clinging to a reef thirty feet down.

At the workshop, Mrs. Takahira, a seventy-one-year-old fisherman's widow with a round face and a radiant complexion (tofu and hard labor are her beauty secrets, she said), welcomed us with a deep bow. The windows of the shed were open, and the sea breeze carried a scent of rain, wildflowers, and algae. Before her marriage, she told us, she worked on her parents' farm, growing soybeans, and then she became a nurse in Karatsu. After her husband died, and her two sons left home, they told her to stop making tofu for herself—it was too much trouble. But about five years ago she decided that the island should exert "more of an effort to show the world that we exist," she said. "In the olden days, we were known for our *ishiwari dofu*. People made it for funerals and weddings, and it was eaten in a fish broth. Now they're too busy. I started thinking that maybe it could be revived. A few friends said they would help, and the Karatsu town council gave us some marketing advice. There are sixteen of us, and we take shifts."

Stone-breaking tofu got its name, according to Mrs. Takahira, because one day an islander walking home dropped her basket and spilled her tofu. "It didn't crumble, but the stone it fell on did," she said. "You can believe that or not, but it's very concentrated. We use five times as many soybeans for the same amount of tofu as other makers do, and organic Japanese *daizu* is three times as expensive as American beans, so we don't make much profit. They passed a law saying you can't use the local ocean water as a *nigari* anymore—because of the pollution—so we buy evaporated natural sea salt from O-Shima, and that's what makes it so hard. But too much salt turns your tofu bitter, and if you overcook it, it stinks."

The only concession Mrs. Takahira makes to convenience, or age, is to pulverize the soybeans in an electric grinder. Otherwise, her tofu-making is powered entirely by muscle. She presses the *okara* with wooden rolling pins, then squeezes it like an Old World washer-woman wringing linen sheets. Each of the molds is compressed for forty minutes with a twenty-pound weight that she slings about with one hand as if it were a can of tuna fish. When she turns out the bricks of bean curd, their surface is crackled, like parched desert clay. Their texture is a bit grainy, and they offer some faint resistance to a knife. They are thoroughly *oishii*, though, with an intense soy flavor and the definitive, though unplaceable, sweetness that artisanal tofu seems to share, and which, like the scent of lotus blossoms in a folk-tale, signals the presence of an unseen divinity.

—September 5, 2005

FIVE

Exposure Time

The woman who will stop at nothing was a Fury, a bacchante, and a saint courting martyrdom long before she was a self-immolating modern artist. But she became a heroine in and of the 1960s, and by going too far she raised the bar of audacity for imagining how far a woman can go. The legends of Sylvia Plath, Janis Joplin, and Diane Arbus all had their roots in that decade. They fed a hunger for narratives of suicidal transcendence that were particularly seductive to the young, perhaps because it takes a lifetime to accept that we have, and are confined to, the solitude of one body.

Idolatry is a form of vandalism that often inspires a violent counterreaction of antipathy to the idol. Even before her death, in 1971, Arbus was exalted as a genius and reviled as a predator who conned her subjects out of their dignity. The judicious books that accompany two new shows give perspective to her intentions and, in the process, to her character. *Diane Arbus: Family Albums* (Yale, 2003) is the catalog of an exhibit curated by Anthony W. Lee and John Pultz at the Mount Holyoke College Art Museum in South Hadley, Massachusetts. An informative short essay by Pultz focuses on specific work, and an erudite, longer one by Lee reconsiders Arbus's portraiture in the context of social and art history. The show takes its premise from a letter that Arbus wrote to Peter Crookston, an editor of the London *Sunday Times Magazine*, in 1968, announcing that she was embarking on a project whose working title was *Family Album*. "All I have is . . . a sort of sweet lust for things I want in it," she told him.

"Like picking flowers. Or Noah's ark. I can hardly bear to leave any animal out." The pictures she took for the album, which was never published, were commissioned by magazines or by private clients, and some were made for art's sake. Like all her work, they explored the nature of closeness and disaffection, sameness and anomaly, belonging and exclusion: the tension between our sentimental expectations of what is supposed to be and the debacle of what is. Arbus put it more simply to Crookston: "I think all families are creepy in a way."

Freud thought families were creepy, too, and his essay "The Uncanny," from *On Creativity and the Unconscious*, suggests why Arbus's portraits still have the power to disquiet, repel, fixate, or even enrage the beholder out of proportion to their formal content. The German for "uncanny"—the adjective used for horror stories—is *unheimlich*, the grammatical negation of *heimlich*, which is the word for "secret," while *heim* means "home." Freud concludes that a sensation of something uncanny occurs in civilized people when they are suddenly surprised by a home truth they have repressed—a primal fear or desire. Looking at Arbus's work, one has that visceral shock of the forbidden. It's creepy not because her subjects are handicapped, loony, hideous, bizarre, sad, or perverse (though most of them are) but because there is something fundamentally taboo about the way she bares their primitive substance without their seeming to know it. The beholder's shudder relates to the memory, conscious or not, of that ancient nightmare in which one walks through the school cafeteria in a stained shirt or trousers while thinking one is safely clothed. Our dignity depends upon continence in the broadest sense of the word, and Arbus's subjects leak their souls.

The other, much more ambitious Arbus show is a long-awaited retrospective at the San Francisco Museum of Modern Art. It is accompanied by an aptly titled compendium, *Diane Arbus: Revelations* (Random House, 2003), which contains a critical appreciation by one of the curators, Sandra S. Phillips, and a technical discussion by the photographer Neil Selkirk, who has been the official printer of Arbus's work since her death. *Revelations* has a number of pictures, and variants of pictures, that have never been seen before, though none of the new material significantly alters one's impression of the oeuvre. The real revelation is contained in a chronology compiled by the curator Elisabeth Sussman and Doon Arbus, the artist's eldest daughter and her executor. Their narrative punctuates an eloquent assemblage of previously unpublished writings and images: notebook entries, snapshots, contact sheets, passages from letters to family members and friends.

The only previous Arbus retrospective took place in 1972, a year after she committed suicide at forty-eight. It was a landmark event for its host institution, the Museum of Modern Art, setting an attendance record for a solo photography exhibition and for sales of the accompanying monograph (one of the best-selling art books in history), while roiling a tempest of controversy, moral and critical, not only about Arbus's working methods and subject matter but about her life. Doon Arbus, who was twenty-six when her mother died, and who was revolted by what she describes in an afterword to *Revelations* as an "onslaught of theory and interpretation," not to speak of scabrous anecdote, that engulfed her mother's legacy, effectively shut down the reactor of the estate.

"Much of modern art is devoted to lowering the threshold of what is terrible," Susan Sontag wrote in her penetrating excoriation of Arbus in *On Photography*, which was first published as a series as essays in *The New York Review of Books* in 1973. With the passage of time, the fresh horrors fabricated like daily bread by art and by history muted the hostility to Arbus's transgressions—her exploration of what Sontag described as "an appalling underworld" of the "deformed and mutilated." Doon Arbus, however, held fast to the high ground of her reticence. She zealously—even perversely, in the estimation of many scholars—refused virtually every outside request to reproduce the photographs or study the papers. The judgment was hers to make, and one can respect it without approving it. But Arbus's lasting contribution to modern art is as a portraitist, and the great questions that portraiture—of which biography is an offshoot—puts to both subject and beholder are "Who are you?" and "How did you become what you are?" It seems fair to interrogate an artist in the same spirit—particularly, perhaps, in the case of a photographer like Arbus, whose problematic intimacy with troubling subjects (or subjects that she renders troubling) and unseen yet palpable presence in the frame generate so much of the mystery that draws one to the images.

This summer, without much notice, five members of the Arbus family collaborated on a play that was performed at the Cherry Lane Theatre as part of the New York International Fringe Festival. Doon Arbus wrote the play, *Third Floor, Second Door on the Right*, some thirty years ago, and, like the material in *Revelations*, it had been sleeping in a drawer. Her younger sister, Amy, acted as the artistic adviser for the production; their half sister, Arin, directed it; their stepmother, Mariclare Costello, designed the costumes; and their eighty-five-year-old father, Allan—who gave up photography in 1969 to become a full-time actor, and whose move (with Costello) to Los Angeles to pursue a movie and television career jolted Diane Arbus profoundly, for better and for worse—played the central role. In a rambling monologue prompted by a young reporter, an old man living alone, in physical and emotional disarray, whose best friend—a famous figure—has recently committed suicide, examines the impact on his life of the friend and his death. Arin Arbus told a reporter that the drama wasn't "autobiographical," but perhaps it helped, like a communal meditation, to steel the family's nerves for an anticipated blaze of scrutiny fueled by the retrospective, and perhaps it represented a willingness to expose their private feelings of abandonment to their own scrutiny. Or perhaps the timing is a coincidence.

Doon Arbus insists in her afterword that the new book and show "do not signal a change of heart"—she isn't cured of her ambivalence—"but one of strategy." That strategy is to provide the public with a "surfeit" of documents as an antidote to the junk of myth and gossip, and *Revelations* is, by design, daunting to the idly curious or to the accidental tourist. Anyone serious (and the test of commitment seems a bit imperious) is invited to lose herself in the luxuriant labyrinth of material and encounter Arbus privately, unmediated by a "tour guide." Jay Leyda pioneered the genre of biography as montage in his out-of-print masterpiece, *The Years and Hours of Emily Dickinson*, in which he abdicates the authority of a narrator and transfers the burden (and privilege) of discovering meaning to the reader. The rewards of this approach become apparent when one compares the beguiling, humane, and self-observant character whose poetic wryness reverberates throughout *Revelations* to the stock tragic figure of the tortured artist enshrined in the only biography of Arbus that existed until this autumn.

Nineteen years ago, Patricia Bosworth—with a stubbornness one can admire—dodged the obstacles set in her path by the Arbus estate, including the refusal of any cooperation by Doon, Amy, Allan, and Arbus's former lover and most intimate confidant, Marvin Israel, and published an unauthorized life. Bosworth, who knew Arbus slightly—she had once modeled for her and Allan when they were employed as fashion photographers—was diligent about filling, or circumventing, the gaps in her research, and she managed to construct a detailed narrative, basing its architecture on published sources and on candid, indeed often mind-bogglingly indiscreet, conversations with other friends and family members, including Arbus's older brother, the distinguished poet Howard Nemerov; her younger sister, Renée Sparkia, a sculptor; her garrulous, elderly mother; her sometime lover and patron, Peter Crookston; and her mentor, the mystical, eccentric Lisette Model. But the biographer ultimately couldn't resist the luridness or the pathology of the material, and her informants apparently couldn't resist playing it up for her. Too many quotes and facts were unattributed, and the biography was widely condemned as gratuitously sensational. I would have said that its main failing was Bosworth's determination to read the work as a symptom. "Many of Diane's photographs," she observes, "had to be taken in order to relieve her mind of the faces and night worlds that were haunting it." The haunted artist embraces her demons and is destroyed by them. This is the view that *Revelations* seems designed to rebut. "Her suicide seems neither inevitable nor spontaneous, neither perplexing nor intelligible," Doon and Sussman write.

One should beware of a biography that follows a too familiar plot. On the other hand, one should probably also beware of a daughter's protective impulse to rehabilitate the image of an artist whose work still has the power to appall, and of a mother who apparently despaired of her life so profoundly that she took it.

Diane Arbus (her preferred pronunciation of her first name was Dee-Ann) was born in 1923 to David Nemerov and his wife, Gertrude, whose wealthy family owned Russek's, the now defunct New York department store. She and her siblings grew up in sprawling apartments on Central Park West and on Park Avenue. For the first seven years of her life, Diane was raised by a "sad" and "lovely" French governess whom she adored. Maids, nannies, cooks, and drivers came and went. The parents chain-smoked, dressed glamorously, entertained in style, collected art, and took frequent first-class trips to Europe, sometimes with their courteous children, of whom much (though nothing not well groomed) was expected. David Nemerov worked long hours. His wife told Bosworth that she suffered from paralyzing bouts of depression. There were rumors that he philandered. The milieu of the elder Nemerovs was classically nouveau riche without being cartoonishly crass. "Our bourgeois heritage seems to me glorious as any stigma," Arbus wrote gaily to Marvin Israel—a stigma, she added, that was "just perhaps more hilarious than to have been Negro or midget." The amusement was ephemeral, like the ebullience, which fluctuated, for Arbus, with periods of tenacious gloom that she understood were "goddamn chemical," and for which she sought therapy and medication. Her heritage was, in fact, that of most artistic children of privilege, who feel that their true selves are invisible, while resenting the dutiful, false selves for which they are loved: a dilemma that inspires the quest, in whatever medium, for a reflection.

The Jewish princess burdened by her "immunity" from common suffering sought a quality that she called "aristocracy" in her damaged subjects—the caste consciousness of the changeling and the misfit. The friends of Arbus's youth were always impressed by how "different" she seemed, and part of the difference, particularly as she aged, was her disregard for prudence (a form of immunization) in matters of sex, money, friendship, maternity, personal hygiene, love, and, of course, art. The sense of being a special case, which Arbus cherished, albeit guiltily, was probably what fed her self-regard until, in what would have naturally been middle age, she found her calling. But it must have been thin gruel for a hungry woman of exceptional intelligence who skipped college and became a mother before she'd had a chance to establish her identity as an adult, much less as an artist. Arbus's greed was never, like her parents', for possessions and status, though she couldn't help treating experience as an acquisition, the more prestigious the higher the price her nerves had to pay for it. The notes she makes in her appointment books for projects and pictures—"ethnic beauties," "racial pinups," teenagers, the decrepit, diaper-derby contestants, female impersonators, gangsters, dwarfs, homosexuals, debutantes, pimps, Boy Scouts, groupies, nudists, strippers, widows, fetishists, ballroom dancers, beggars, rock-and-roll groups, triplets—resemble the lists of a shopper obsessed with multiples who is on an insatiable spree.

There is an interesting link between Arbus's work and the family business. The advent of the department store and the fashion magazine coincide, historically, with the rise of the middle class, but also with the heyday of Romanticism, and its repudiation of everything that the bourgeoisie embodied. The sixties were a neo-romantic era that equated intensity of sensation with authenticity of feeling, and Arbus's photographs spoke powerfully to members of the generation then coming to maturity. How many of them longed—and tried—to do what Arbus did, to act out the scenario of the coddled child who divests herself of her hollow patrimony and descends into the gutter seeking life's harsh and arduous but vibrant truth? The Arbus photograph that perhaps best captures this alienation, and that of the time, is, ironically, one of the few without any human figures. It shows a barren living room in Levittown, Long Island, dominated by an immaculate expanse of textured carpet and a Christmas tree dripping with tinsel that brushes the low ceiling. Like bickering spouses, two clocks, one on the television, the other on the wall, split hairs about the hour. It's impossible to imagine that the bright jumble of presents on the floor—items on someone's gift list ticked off methodically and wrapped by an underpaid stranger—will provide the recipients with anything but a brief moment of distraction: that sugar high of Christmas morning which, in joyless families, only exacerbates each member's sense of emptiness and futility.

Diane was an exceptionally pretty child, with luminous green eyes, fine bones, and thick hair. She never lost her doelike fragility or her dreaminess, and even in her forties, ravaged by depression and hepatitis, she still had a nubile aura. The coincidence of bleak glamour and waifish loveliness with ferocious drive was a powerful element of her allure. Her creative gifts were encouraged by her mercurial father and well-meaning private-school teachers, but the austere pride of the artist expressed itself precociously as a revolt against being doted on—which is to say, patronized—by her inferiors.

In an age when girls of her background "saved" themselves for their wedding night, Arbus (never, in later life, a sexual economizer) married very young. She met Allan Arbus, whom she regarded as a kind of twin, when she was thirteen and he a college dropout five years her senior who was working in the advertising department at Russek's. They married in 1941, less than a month after her eighteenth birthday. Allan gave his bride her first camera, and Diane subsequently enrolled in a photography course taught by Berenice Abbott. The newlyweds began taking advertising photographs for Russek's, and a few years later, after Doon's birth and Allan's discharge from the army, they formally went into business together, developing a strenuous, improvisational style of treating fashion that earned them commissions from *Vogue*, *Harper's Bazaar*, *Time*, and the *Times Magazine*, among other glossies. Diane was the stylist on the shoots, and Allan operated the camera. An advertising executive interviewed by Bosworth fondly recalled Arbus's work on the "Modess . . . because" ads, and noted that she "did some terrific documentary stuff on a no-shrink shirt."

As a beautiful couple with a taste for experiment, the Arbuses belonged to a bohemia of young artists who were planting the charges that exploded in the visual culture of the next decade. It was common, though, for an avant-garde woman to be trapped by an Eisenhower-era notion of her destiny as a female. Allan Arbus was generous about helping his wife cultivate her creative freedom, and the alliance survived their eventual separation. But after years as a helpmate, Arbus rebelled, at least professionally, against the claustrophobia of a cocoon she had outgrown. Her *mezzo del cammin* came in 1956. She was thirty-three, furiously frustrated with her subordinate role in the studio—attending to the models' hair, makeup, and clothes—and chronically dissatisfied with her own pictures, which represented a different kind of woman's work. Many of them were idyllic portraits of parents and children, similar to the photograph of a father and son, commissioned from the Arbus studio by *Vogue*, that Edward Steichen had, the previous year, selected for inclusion in his mammoth exhibition at the Museum of Modern Art, "The Family of Man." It was a show, Steichen wrote, conceived to mirror "the essential oneness" of humanity, a premise to which much of Arbus's mature work is a violent rebuke.

Leaving the business to her husband, Arbus enrolled in a course at the New School taught by Lisette Model. A nonconformist born in 1901 into a rich and cultivated Viennese family of which the Nemerovs were, in a way, a slightly degraded, second-generation image, Model moved to Paris when she was in her late twenties and, a decade later—outrunning Hitler—immigrated to New York. She photographed bathers at Coney Island, Harlem delinquents, the drunks and peddlers of the Lower East Side, and the human oddities at Hubert's Dime Museum and Flea Circus in Times Square—turf that Arbus was shortly to explore, and in a sense to appropriate, though apparently with Model's blessing. She "pushed" Arbus, she told Bosworth, to confront her inhibitions. She criticized her infatuation with grainy images. She helped her to master the mechanics of a camera, conquering what Arbus referred to as her guilt about being a woman. And she urged her to search for the wellspring of urgency that every artist has to tap.

Arbus's friends agree that she had some mysterious conversion in Model's class, and that her style was dramatically purified and focused after their encounter. Model shrewdly described Arbus as "not listening to me but suddenly listening to herself." Yet I also suspect that for an impractical woman "confirmed," she admitted, "in a sense of unreality," who had never outgrown a childish dependency on her parents and husband, the example of an older female artist—a survivor both of privilege and of adversity—who had channeled what compelled her into a camera without fear or apology was as galvanizing to Arbus as anything that Model said.

The radical turn that Arbus took in the late 1950s wasn't political, although in 1968, that year of revolutions, she spent several days in Beaufort County, South Carolina, on assignment for *Esquire*, photographing the patients of the civil-rights activist and rural doctor Donald Gatch. "I had never seen poverty like that," Arbus said later. The accompanying text, by Bynum Shaw, was entitled "Let Us Now Praise Dr. Gatch," and it was, Anthony Lee writes in *Family Album*, "meant to liken Shaw's reportage and Arbus's photos to the famous project by Agee and Evans." But the pitiless formal symmetry with which Arbus composes her photograph of the elegant Dr. Gatch, wearing a three-piece business suit with a white shirt and tie, and Addie Taylor, an ageless crone and the epitome of misery standing in the doorway of her windowless shack, is more suggestive of their hopeless inequality than of his compassion. Nor is there any doubt about who is the aristocrat. The picture seems to represent a critique of liberal idealism by a woman without much faith in a better world.

Arbus had met Walker Evans in 1961, counted him a friend, was "whammied" by his 1971 retrospective (though "by the third time I saw it I realized how it really bores me," she confessed), and he cited her in his survey of the eighteen most important photographers in history. While they had qualities in common, including what the curator John Szarkowski, writing of Evans, calls a "willful act of protest against polite society," and the tension that Lee discerns in both bodies of work between modernist rigor and documentary grittiness, their likeness was probably less to each other than to the great German portraitist August Sander (1876–1964). "Everyone today looked remarkable just like out of August Sander pictures," Arbus reported to Israel in the spring of 1960, "so absolute and immutable down to the last button feather tassel or stripe. All odd and splendid as freaks and nobody able to see himself, all of us victims of the especial shape we come in."

The respect and sympathy for her freaks that Arbus expresses in her letters—particularly those to her children—and her apparently solicitous, ongoing engagement with them, is at odds with the view that she was exploiting their credulity. Some subjects seem to have used her in their own way, and their portraits were, in part, souvenirs of initiation and trophies of acceptance. Doon Arbus was, she once wrote, "often frightened by" her mother's "capacity to be enthralled, by her power to give herself over to something or to someone, to submit." At times—perhaps usually—Arbus was cunning and aggressive, but so are many photographers. Photography was then, and still is, a macho profession, and if she took its machismo to greater extremes than her peers of either sex, it was in part to scourge her native timidity and to prove that she had the balls to join her subjects' orgies, share their nudity, endure their stench, revel in their squalor, and break down their resistance with a seductively disarming or fierce and often sexualized persistence until she "got" a certain expression: defeat, fatigue, slackness, anomie, or demented joy. Richard Avedon has described how he, too, outwits the vigilance of his sitters or waits for their moment of surrender, although the contest hinted at in his portraiture seems fairer. Arbus, it must be said, picked on the helpless and the obscure. But if her pictures make one wonder how she got them, and why her subjects consented to pose as they did, everyone with a true and false self secretly knows the answer. The yearning for love is, in part, a desire to become visible as one really is to the Other, though every time one dares to let oneself be seen, one risks being seen through.

Arbus's freaks may have been the objects of her "sweet lust," but she doesn't fetishize them, and they were never a cabinet of specimens to her the way Sander's pageant of anonymous German types was to him. On the other hand, Sander was concerned with class distinctions and social roles, while Arbus harrowed the more subjective, unstable terrain of eroticism and gender. Some of her sitters—in a way, all of them—seem not to have noticed how far their forms have strayed from those of the creatures they were supposed to be. They are members of a transitional species who inhabit a limbo where young girls wear the blasted look of menopausal women; middle-aged homosexuals pass themselves off as femmes fatales; dyspeptic infants grimace with the bloated rage of old men; and bodies are mortified with pins, fire, hormones, needles, knives, razors, makeup, surgery, and strobe lights.

Perhaps Arbus seems ruthless because she exposes her subjects' naïve faith in their connection with and resemblance to the rest of humanity even as she cuts them from the herd. While they may pose with a lover or in family groups (the Jewish giant and his parents; the dominatrix and her client; the blasé suburbanites on their chaises longues; the blind couple in bed; the Russian midget and his friends; the bespectacled, obese nudists; the woman with her baby monkey), their illusion of belonging is belied by her exposé of their isolation. The depth that Arbus gives to that isolation both as a social fact and as a psychological predicament distinguishes her style from the superficial flamboyance of other photographers (now legion) who specialize, fashionably and forgettably, in the grotesque. It also sinks her subjects into a well so deep that one feels they will never be able to emerge.

The last years of Arbus's life, 1969 to 1971, were the greatest period of her work. She had begun seeing a psychiatrist, Dr. Boigon, and "one fascinating thing I am beginning to get through my thick head," she wrote ambiguously to Allan and Mariclare about her therapy sessions, "is that it doesn't matter what you do . . . except to yourself." She seems to have meant that no one cares what you do except yourself, though in the context—her death was a few months away—the very lightness of the remark becomes ominous. Her artistic progress, however, elated her. "I took the most terrific pictures," she wrote to Allan at the end of November 1969, about a series of portraits made in homes for the mentally retarded: "FINALLY what I've been searching for. And I seem to have discovered sunlight, late afternoon early winter sun light. It's just marvelous." In one of her masterpieces, *Untitled* (7), the rural landscape seems bathed in the lowering and eerie radiance of an eclipse, and the misshapen figures of her brain-damaged subjects—descendants of Goya's gargoyles— march across the frame with unsteady steps as if to the music of a piper one can't hear. A grave child of indeterminate sex with a painted mustache and averted gaze holds hands with a masked old woman in a white shift. They are oblivious of—and, in a way, liberated from—Arbus's gaze. After years of posing her subjects frontally, she had begun to prefer that they did not look at her. "I think I will see them more clearly," she wrote to Amy, "if they are not watching me watching them."

In the weeks before her death, Arbus was working steadily on new projects and seeing friends. Crookston was excited about a photographic essay that she had proposed to him on "Loss of Power"—portraits of defeated world leaders like Johnson, Khrushchev, Nkrumah, and de Gaulle. On July 26, *Apollo 15* was launched to the moon. Doon was in Paris, Amy at summer school, Allan on a film set in Santa Fe, and Marvin Israel at Avedon's house on Fire Island. Alone in her apartment in Westbeth, the artists' housing complex in Greenwich Village, Arbus took an overdose of barbiturates and slit her wrists in the bathtub. The medical examiner's report mentioned a diary entry that it referred to as the "Last Supper" note, but the page in question and two succeeding ones, according to *Revelations*, were "meticulously excised" from her appointment book "and have never been recovered." The chronology ends with the coroner's flat yet gruesome description of the half-decomposed corpse. No orifice is spared. The inclusion of this document by Doon Arbus at first strikes one not only as unseemly but, given her writerly tact and filial protectiveness, incomprehensible. Perhaps one should read it, though, not as the kind of Judas-like betrayal that Arbus was often accused of but as a savage gesture of poetic justice, as blind to propriety as was the art of the woman it lays bare, and as the final payment, by an honorable executor, of her mother's outstanding debt—a debt of self-revelation—to her subjects.

—October 13, 2003

II

RULES OF

ENGAGEMENT

ONE

Choosing a Place

Intelligent people who confess that they haven't yet got around to reading Nadine Gordimer often protest that they "must," and her fans are rarely willing to qualify their awe and admiration by telling you what they love about her. Great writers deserve better.

Why is Gordimer intimidating? She asserts that it is possible to do something about evil. There is no harangue, just a challenge in the form of a narrative. The challenge is to imagine with her what shape, obstacles, limits, and value the doing of something might really have. We aren't used to such cool practicality in a modern writer, to such nonchalance of instinct. Gordimer understands necessity as something apparent, though not simple; her art is in many ways like the spider's. No wonder, then, that she mocks those foreign reviewers who, in projecting their own "morbid symptoms" onto her situation, have created "courageous" as a literary value for South African writers. It isn't courage that builds webs.

The awe that readers express for Gordimer may also reflect their perception, useful though poignant, that vital assurance is different from anxious drive. It is rare to find the combination of destructive and healing powers under control in one sensibility. Her fury is as shameless as her lyrical eroticism. Her penetration into her characters sometimes makes you feel she has expropriated rather than invented them. She homes in on their tics of speech and thought with a precision that would be cruel if it were not, like the mynah bird's, so impartial. The voice that speaks to us in this manner, in our own language, comes from a distance greater than that which separates our continents, although it is, perhaps, only the distance that we so meekly accept as inevitable between life and art.

A Sport of Nature (Knopf, 1987) is Gordimer's ninth novel, and the first since she published *July's People*, in 1981. That was a much shorter book, almost a novella. It had the claustrophobia of a theater piece, and it was written for a tight ensemble of characters—a white family and its black servant (July), who were isolated in his native village. Their confrontations were immediate and centered on concrete things: keys, a gun, remembered grudges, fears bred in the bush by the rain and heat and by languages not understood. The continuous pressure exerted on every surface by a distant revolution and its history held the novel's perfect shape together. *A Sport of Nature* is a much more unrestrained piece of writing: in its form; in the time and ground it covers (forty years and three continents); and in the author's unabashed fascination with her central character. The lifetime of this slippery girl is that of apartheid, and her function is that of all picaros: to infiltrate a society at every level, though without any forethought.

What we have here, then, is a guided tour, and our guide, as is so often the case, is the kind of young woman to whom no one can deny a favor, and who is equally generous with her own. She takes us home first: to the suburbs of Johannesburg, where her family lives; then she smuggles us across the border, to a country that has achieved its independence, and where, in shabby lodgings and offices, and in villas abandoned by former colonists, a group of exiles, black and white, is organizing the Azanian revolution. The horizon broadens as we follow our young woman to Eastern Europe, lobbying for guns and butter; to London, seeking column space and cachet in the best leftist drawing rooms; to the East Coast of this country, where any red dust clinging to the revolution's threadbare business suit has to be brushed off; and, finally, back to Africa—but now to visit the rebels' bush camps, safe houses, and strategic-planning sessions in Hilton bars. Gordimer writes about each of these milieus, and its inhabitants, with a relish that is sometimes wicked and an authority that seems absolute. If she hasn't made the tour herself, she has a lot of flies reporting to her. Sometimes, in fact, there's almost too much detail for the reader to absorb. (A glossary of acronyms—which are as much the litter of a revolution as its spent cartridges—would have been useful.)

When we meet our heroine for the first time, she is in the act of shedding one name and emerging under another. This is the kind of opening scene Gordimer often writes, composed of small, expertly focused, pleasurable sensations that relax a reader, and of flashes of mystery that draw one into a story. A schoolgirl is going somewhere. Her train is crossing an African landscape. She throws the name Kim "up to the rack with her school panama" and becomes Hillela.

It is worth paying attention to these names. A name never pushes an individual toward the idea of his fate more dramatically than in wartime: it is a password, an incitement; it recovers, under fire, some of its original incantatory power and economy. For example, the names that are chanted by the spectators in the courtroom at the trial of Hillela's cousin—"*woza Luthuli, woza Mandela, woza Tambo, woza Sisulu . . . woza Kgomani*"—are the essence of what both sides recognize cannot be negotiated. The feeling of solidarity they arouse is inspiration as the old poets understood it, which was to permit yourself to be visited by the dead and charged by the outcome of their lives.

The name Kim has served Hillela as a kind of unmarked skin, deflecting questions and permitting her to pass as a girl like any other. But it disappears after the first few pages, and it was, for all we know, something her mother picked up from a paperback novel or a movie magazine. But Gordimer never wastes a detail: it also makes her the namesake of Kipling's orphan. Hillel was the girl's great-grandfather, a Zionist peddler. She is embarrassed to admit the connection, yet she turns out to be the heir both to his displacement and to his faith in the divine right to a homeland. And, for those interested enough to pursue the reference, it leads us to that Rabbi Hillel who was the president of the Sanhedrin at the time of Christ, when the Jews were facing dispersion and struggling to preserve their identity under the Romans. "If I act not for myself," Hillel asked them, "who shall act for me? And if I act for myself alone, what then am I? And if not now, when?" Finally, Hillela is a one-off, pretty sort of name, easy to remember. Its combination of sounds, in English, suggests the landscape of a woman's body—a body that will prove to be this novel's liberated territory.

Gordimer's territory has always been morality, in the roomier Greek sense of the word. In Greek, morality is *ethos*, which means, literally, "choice of a place." All moral action in her fiction—and I think one can say all its dramatic action—has to do for her black characters with the anguish of displacement and their response to it, and for the whites with their choice of a place, of a moral relation, to that injustice. The counterpoints of her narrative mirror the laws that govern the movement of people under apartheid, as they reflect each other in two so nearly matching words—passport and passbook. How you pass is the question: freely, with your own name; furtively, with the forged identity of another; or as something objectively accounted for and transported, like the pieces of equipment on a manifest. Sometimes, as in *The Conservationist*, apartheid is just the corpse no one wants to take responsibility for burying or not burying, so it stinks out in the veld somewhere while the life of the story moves around it.

In her new book, as in *Burger's Daughter*, that corpse is the guest of honor. The other guests are Gordimer's familiars—the whites who consider themselves politically engaged, who take on deserving cases to defend or educate, who instill a social conscience in their children and go on cheap camping trips instead of real vacations as a kind of penance. Hillela's tireless, outspoken, and to some degree admirable aunt Pauline is their epitome. But when she is asked to shelter an unknown fugitive and thus break a law, she hesitates, accuses herself of cowardice, and decides that the risk to her family is not worth incurring for someone who is "just a name" to her.

Gordimer is never not writing about the larger moral issue of sanctuary: the sanctuary of the white family. Whatever high-minded discussions take place within its walls, however many envelopes are stuffed with protest literature while servants are given instruction for leadership roles in a new society, the white parents still command a privilege exclusive to their race: protecting their children and, by their example, empowering them with that sense of self-worth which is inextricable from a sense of middle-class entitlement. That has been one of our own literary themes at least since James: the economics of being a somebody or a nobody. In South Africa, however, the concept of identity loses its slack to the tensions between black and white, and, finally, between life and death.

Consider how, in American fiction, one class of character asks the question "Who am I?" and another class "How much am I worth?" Gordimer forces the heroine of *Burger's Daughter*, Rosa (who plays a cameo role in *A Sport of Nature*), to conclude that there is only one class of answer to both questions, only one she can live with—that she is a child whose father would orphan her for his ideals. And who are *July's People*? The answer for one of them, Maureen Smales, is that unless you are autonomous, your worth, like your self, is defined by whatever figure of authority provides it for you. The husband who has provided hers is now a displaced person—an architect lying on a box spring in a hut, and suddenly nothing more than "a man without a vehicle."

Strip one of Gordimer's schemas of its details and you lose the subtlety, but you are then faced with the starkness and ubiquity of the moral: every black is a fugitive under apartheid, and no white can claim the sanctuary of conscience—which for Gordimer is self *and* worth, indivisible—without sharing his fate.

That harshness of hers toward the decent whites, which has on us the cooling effect we call our admiration, and which has increased a little with every novel, approaching intolerance in *A Sport of Nature*, needs some perspective. In a lecture she gave five years ago in New York, Gordimer told her audience that there were two "absolutes" in her life: that racism is "damnation in the Old Testament sense" and "no compromises as well as sacrifices should be too great in the fight against it"; and that "a writer is a being in whose sensibility is fused what Lukács calls 'the duality of inwardness and outside world' and he must never be asked to sunder this union." It is too easy to assume—and I think some writers do, with a kind of perverse envy—that these absolutes, one positive and one negative, create a force field, and that Gordimer's career simply flows between them; or that her vigor and longevity, like those of centenarians in some mountain village, have been conditioned by a simple diet of pure principles and the affirmation that, as an elder yet a producer, she continues to be needed. What she said, however, was that the existence of those absolutes "often seems irreconcilable within one life, for me." And she imagined, not without a note of wistfulness, how "in another country, another time, they would present no conflict." The compromise—the sacrifice—that Gordimer makes in her novels is, I think, with her own freedom to do the kind of literary beachcombing, the poking into and savoring of timeless subjects, that she occasionally permits herself in her short stories.

The longing for a vacation from the forty-year-old state of emergency in South Africa may be what has driven Gordimer to write *A Sport of Nature*. It is something between a novel and a vision, just as its heroine, Hillela, who has the shimmer of a mirage, is something between a fata morgana and a character. She belongs to the future, to a country that has not yet come into being, and she moves through the story with an aura that is a bit like the blurry surface of a Polaroid snapshot as it emerges from the camera, and which gives you the same primitive, voyeuristic pleasure in relation to time.

The title refers us to the dictionary's definition of a sport of nature (*lusus naturae*) as "a plant, animal, etc., which exhibits abnormal variation or a departure from the parent stock or type . . . a spontaneous mutation." It also refers to the fact that Hillela is another something new out of Africa, a singular creature, who will not perpetuate the strain "of madness" in her race, and will therefore be fit to stay on once the old order has been brought down.

This is a loaded proposition on several counts. The mutants of myth and fiction have a creepy propensity for turning on their creators, and among the modern writers who have treated the subject, there seems to be a consensus that the impulse to purify the race constitutes its single most monstrous genetic flaw. But to all our unstated objections Gordimer replies:

> Utopia is unattainable; without aiming for it—taking a chance!—you can never hope even to fall far short of it . . .
>   Don't you see? It's all got to come down, mother. Without utopia—the idea of utopia—there's a failure of the imagina-

tion—and that's a failure to know how to go on living. It will take another kind of being to stay on, here. A new white person. Not us. The chance is a wild chance—like falling in love.

If the use of dashes seems reckless, it may be excused by the fact that this is a letter addressed to Hillela's aunt Pauline by Pauline's young son, Sasha. He leaves it around rather than deliver it—one of those gestures which betray the rational half-grown child's magic wish for a mother to "understand what she couldn't, ever." That is precisely his predicament: he is half in and half out of manhood, independence, conviction, desire; his gradual and tortured emergence runs parallel to Hillela's more facile, though less sheltered, one, and to reach his apotheosis he must descend to it, while she will be Assumed to hers. But the burden of doubt in the novel rests on Sasha's shoulders, and that, I think, defines him as its true hero—a modern hero: one whose solitude makes us weep for him. Sasha, though, is also a hero in the Greek sense: he to whom the gods offer a choice between the place of love and the place of duty. What he doubts most heroically is his ability to sever the bond to his mother, and to dispose of his own "worth" without regard for his preciousness as a white child.

Hillela may be the new white person, but she is also the type of malleable waif who has always attracted art students, guerrilla poets, mad scientists—the more conventional kinds of Pygmalion. One of her revolutionary intimates attempts to sum up her qualities with the word "innocent." She is innocent of prejudice, vanity, shame, scruples, possessiveness, inhibition, nostalgia, fear, frigidity, and the *sachel* you pick up in a middle-class Jewish family, which consists of knowing, when you have a good thing, how not to spoil it. Her mother's one distinction was to lack that *sachel*, too. She bolted when Hillela was two or three, leaving a box of photos and a pornographic love letter—addressed to the Portuguese gigolo she defected with, not the traveling salesman she left behind, who sends Hillela to a Rhodesian boarding school when he remarries. Both she and Gordimer have an obscure soft spot for this oaf. Perhaps it's simply that he's a man.

Gordimer has rarely bestowed her affection on a *female* who has
so little ethical tension to her character. There would be none at all if
Hillela didn't have some of the white child's choice of a place. She
gets this from her two maternal aunts—first, Olga, who offers her the
advantages of orthodontia and "a dress-sense," and then Pauline,
who holds up the mirror of her own social conscience. Neither of
their efforts takes hold, however, nor could it: show me a romantic
heroine who has not grown up motherless and she is sure to have had
a mother who was a nonentity. (The successful daughter of a *woman*
learns to cultivate resemblance and gratitude, not risk-taking and singularity.) Hillela betrays the expectations of both of her surrogate
mothers with versions of a single transgression: blithely crossing a
boundary—of race in one instance, of kinship in the other (she se-
duces her cousin Sasha). Both Olga and Pauline suffer for their deci-
sions to expel her, but, I think, suffer not so much because she has
behaved badly as because she has behaved incomprehensibly—which
frightens them. Mothers abhor a stranger.

Hillela, for her part, seems relieved to have been sprung from
"the house of their lives," where it wasn't "possible to move about."
She is now free to embark on her years of living marginally—as a
"tramp," a "beach-girl," sleeping her way into and out of indigence
and into the liaison that lands her in exile, among the revolutionaries.
She marries one of them, and marries well. Her husband, whom she
sees for the first time as an "obsidian god" swimming toward her in
the ocean, is a key figure in the banned African National Congress.
Before Whaila Kgomani is assassinated on their kitchen floor, she
gives birth to their daughter.

This nativity is one of the crucial scenes of the novel, and it is lit
for drama and contrast, like a bare stage. There is a shadowy hospital
room, brightness at a window, a somber white nurse, a laughing
black one, a pale mother, and her first incandescent thought: "She
wanted, above all consideration of life and death, to tell Whaila how
the baby had come out: like him, like him." How should we understand this? Gordimer continues to engage something in us deeper
than curiosity and more volatile than resistance until, several pages
later, she is ready to give her answer:

Satisfaction sank deep as the cool moisture that existed under the parched sand: not to have reproduced herself, not to have produced a third generation of the mother who danced away into the dark of a nightclub, the child before whom certain advantages lay like the shadow of a palm tree, the aunts who offered what they had to offer.

The language here is provocative, despite the bland image of Madonna and child. (The only figures missing are the three wise men, and perhaps they are the aunts and the mother, spurned because their gifts are too bourgeois.) But if Gordimer is asking for an act of faith, and promising redemption in exchange for it, she has put up insufficient writerly collateral for her favorite character. Hillela has been conceived by Gordimer as without sin—or at least the cardinal sin, which is the narcissism of mothers.

Not to have reproduced herself. That is the quick of every utopian idea. Of course, it applies to more than biological reproduction; it is also about the reproduction of race or class privileges and enmities. But Gordimer neglects to acknowledge the oppressive aspect of such narcissim. It, too, is a form of displacement. It occurs in anyone who nurtures the autonomy and prestige of others without having, except in fantasy, a claim to her own. One finds it in the hauteur of the old retainer who wears his livery as if it were the ermine robes of his lord as much as in the mother who wears her son's Phi Beta Kappa key as a lucky charm. (The word "vicarious" was early used to describe suffering.)

Narcissism is a disorder that deprives a character or a society of its depth; it's not just a synonym for shallowness. When Gordimer permits us to see this irony playing itself out, as she does, at its most profound level, in the struggle between Pauline and Sasha, and in the form of its most typical fantasy—the modeling career of Hillela's beautiful black daughter—she gets to us under our own skin. But when she flashes Hillela's sinlessness at us, as an example we can worship but not follow, she reproduces the experience of narcissism itself.

The precision and delight with which Gordimer describes Hillela's body—taut cheekbones, full breasts, skin that constantly tingles with intelligence and pleasure—suggest that it is just the kind of place a moralist might choose for her vacation. And what is a vacation if you can't relax your ethical tensions for a while?

Her art never relaxes, but the beach girl vanishes, the martyr's grieving widow pulls herself together and some years later, Aunt Pauline hears that her niece has been lecturing on the black-liberation movement at MIT, among other places, and is considered an expert in her field. She can't resist the observation that Hillela's field used to be, at any rate, men. It hasn't quite ceased to be that now: men for the woman warrior's delight. But Gordimer employs the succession of Hillela's exotic lovers and milieus as a guerrilla leader employs his layovers in bush camps: to give the troops an education in the history, tactics, weapons, and geography of their revolution.

By the time that revolution comes, Hillela has acquired her third name, and with it she sloughs off her individuality and slips away into her public role. The name is a wedding present from her second husband, the African general who returns from exile to liberate his country and become its president. That smiling woman with the high cheekbones whom her aunt Olga barely recognizes—sitting right there next to Yasir Arafat in the photograph—is now called Chiemeka, which is the feminine version of the president's own tribal name. It means "God has done very well."

How satisfying it would be to say amen. If I can't, it isn't that I disliked Kim/Hillela/Chiemeka: she is one of the more engaging opportunists in fiction since Fabrice del Dongo. Nor can one fault her rise to power on the strength of her instincts, though I wish that they had not always been "unerring." And I don't begrudge Gordimer her rapture over this new creature of hers. She has taken "a wild chance—like falling in love." But her authorial infatuation turns into a pride as regressive, in the end, as any mother's doting:

> The President has seen her in a light other than that of perpetuator of a bloodline. Any woman could be that. In fact, no man wanted Hillela to be like any other woman, would allow her to be even if it had been possible for her, herself.

The president is not unique: Gordimer has taught all the men in her new world, white and black, to want Hillelas. And however fully she breathes life into her other women characters, it is so that they may serve the heroine as better foils. In this respect, the novel is itself an "abnormal variation" from its parent stock: alive in its contradictions but static in its ideal.

—June 29, 1987

TWO

Rules of Engagement

Success has always been the greatest liar," Nietzsche wrote. " 'Great men' as they are venerated are subsequent pieces of wretched minor fiction." André Malraux tended to venerate, often uncritically, the colossi he met in the course of a glorious career as a writer and statesman (de Gaulle, Mao, Trotsky, Nehru, Senghor, Kennedy, Le Corbusier, Picasso—his enthusiasms were catholic), and, while he is best known for his Byronic exploits and his epic novels *Man's Fate* and *Man's Hope* (about the Chinese Revolution and the Spanish Civil War), one of his specialties was the funeral oration, preferably declaimed in a stirring tremolo from a podium at the Panthéon, where he, too, is interred.

One could hardly call Malraux's life wretched or his fiction minor, but his latest biographer, Olivier Todd, whose previous subject was Camus, focuses on the pretenses, embroideries, and outright lies— the mythomania—that, in his view, compromise his subject's achievements. *Malraux: A Life*, translated from the French by Joseph West (Knopf, 2005), is the product of assiduous new archival research into the history that its subject made and lived (or fudged). The author, an alumnus of Cambridge, describes himself as an empiricist of the English school, and his book is what the French like to call "an Anglo-Saxon biography," which seems to mean an unfashionably fat tome frilled with footnotes. But, despite his cool Anglophilic rigor and his regard for fair play—an expression that has no French translation—Todd's portrait suffers from a tone of snide and at times vulgar contempt ("Hitler and Mussolini are not Malraux's style") that has the paradoxical effect of heightening Malraux's stature, and the reader's partiality to him, despite his flamboyant self-aggrandizing. Milton's Satan is the same sort of character.

Malraux was born in 1901 to ill-matched parents, who separated shortly thereafter. His father, Fernand, was an amateur inventor and a ladies' man who cut a handsome figure in his officer's uniform but served without distinction as a tanker in the First World War, dabbled in the stock market, and sired two sons by a mistress, Roland and Claude. His melancholy wife, Berthe, moved in with her mother, who lived above a confectioner's shop that she owned in a Paris suburb, and a spinster sister—André's beloved aunt Marie—who helped raise him. He was an intense and precocious boy, afflicted all his life with tics, twitches, and grunts, which Todd diagnoses as Tourette's syndrome. André's pious mother "apparently found him ugly" (photographs of a sweet-faced youth don't agree), and "a sensual component," Todd writes, "was missing" in their relationship. Yet André was the sun around whom a household of maternal satellites revolved, and, growing up coddled, he sought the antidote of virile company wherever he could find it, joining a Scout troop and reveling in the affection of Fernand's father, a grizzled ship owner with a big house near the port in Dunkirk. Malraux, despite his many incarnations, essentially spent his life working at one job: trying to discover—and idealizing—what it means to be a man.

A mediocre school record is often the first possession that the self-invented upgrade, and Malraux claimed to be a graduate of the Institute of Oriental Languages, in Paris, when, given his breadth of culture, he was something infinitely more remarkable: an autodidact whose formal education ended at sixteen, without a baccalaureate. Adolescence is an age of compulsive posing that coincides with a quest for authenticity, and Malraux never outgrew either. Jean Grosjean, an erudite priest who became Malraux's bosom friend in 1940, when they were fellow soldiers captured by the Germans and assigned to cut wood in a village near Sens, wrote that his "strength and weakness [were] to have triumphed over childhood without succumbing to the slightest maturity." The footloose dropout haunted the museums that he later beautified, as de Gaulle's minister of culture, and he supported himself by trolling the quais for rare books and reselling them profitably to an antiquarian. He launched the first of his many deluxe art-publishing ventures; edited some erotica; styled himself an aesthete; frequented a bohemia of poets and gallerists; and contributed essays on Cubist poetry and other esoteric themes to *Action*, a review of avant-garde literature.

One of his colleagues was the homely but smart and impetuous Clara Goldschmidt, a polyglot of German Jewish origin three years his senior, who worked at *Action* as a translator. "She talks almost as much as he does," Todd writes, "and with the same self-assurance." (Todd's own tic is the grating use of the Malrucian historical present, for five hundred pages.) Though Clara already had a lover and a refreshingly low opinion of monogamy, and André, at twenty, was legally still a minor, they eloped on a lark to Italy. A Goldschmidt family friend discovered them sharing a compartment on the Paris-to-Florence express, and her parents' outrage was only slightly mollified by the announcement—telegraphed on the way to Venice—of their engagement. Fernand, who thought that "for a Jew, Clara dresses pretty well," promptly helped his son squander her dowry—the equivalent of $800,000—on the stock market.

Broke but undaunted, the newlyweds set off in 1923 on an intrepid journey to Indochina, in the mode, or so they fancied, of T. E. Lawrence and Rimbaud. The "stench of the alleyways" and "the social reality of colonialism" made a deep impression, Todd writes. But so did the charm of native bazaars and Chinese violins; of grand hotels and boat trips up the Mekong; of lakeside temples of pink sandstone and a camp in the dappled foliage at Banteay Srei, where—with chisels and picks—Malraux and an old schoolmate surreptitiously pried loose some tenth-century Khmer sculptures that they hoped to sell at the attractive going rates ($12,000 for an *apsara*) in London or New York. They were arrested by the colonial police, who made an example of the feckless vandals with a show trial in Phnom Penh. Clara had a breakdown and sailed home to Paris (exercising her convictions about free love by sleeping with a fellow passenger), where she organized a campaign to pressure the court for an acquittal. An imposing roster of Big Pens—Gide, Mauriac, and Breton, among others—signed a petition attesting to Malraux's literary promise, as if one sort of national treasure shouldn't be punished for pillaging another. ("The undersigned . . . have confidence in the consideration that justice is wont to show to all those who help increase the intellectual wealth of our country.") A three-year prison term was suspended, though an aura of shadiness lingered; Malraux wasn't finished dealing in antiquities of dubious provenance or denouncing the injustice of a colonial regime, and throughout his life, his opportunism was as enterprising as his conscientiousness.

In Saigon, he launched a feisty, progressive newspaper, *L'Indochine enchaînée*, that earned some modest fame for exposés of colonial land grabs and other chicanery, along with the gratifying enmity of the local authorities and, for Malraux, his first laurels as a champion of the people. He and Clara spent two "rewarding years" in Cambodia and Cochin China (contemporary Vietnam), which Todd describes as a political incubation period, and they informed Malraux's prescient grasp of Asia's incubating geopolitical importance. The couple returned to Paris, where Malraux took a prestigious editorial job at Gallimard (which he kept until his death, in 1976) and began writing in earnest, while continuing to accumulate capital and credentials as an adventurer. He visited the Soviet Union, Persia, Afghanistan, Burma, Malaysia, and America, and later claimed to have located the queen of Sheba's ruined capital while flying over the Yemeni desert. Mainland China wasn't on his itinerary until the early thirties, yet for decades he floated the fiction that he'd fought the hand-to-hand battle for Canton in 1927 while serving as a commissioner of propaganda for the Kuomintang. He drew upon this "experience" for his novel *The Conquerors* (1928), whose revolutionary hero, the Marxist Garine, is the first of many glamorous alter egos. "Malraux's oeuvre reveals less of what the author is . . . and more of what he wants to be," as the French critic Gaëtan Picon remarked.

In 1933, Clara gave birth to a daughter, Florence. Malraux was happy for a girl; "I couldn't bear a caricature of myself," he said— though his impostures are often just that. The same year, he published *Man's Fate* (*La Condition humaine*), the last volume of an Asian trilogy. In a sequence of lushly violent, staccato scenes whose cinematic potential appealed to Eisenstein, the novel recounts the Communist uprising in Shanghai, its brutal repression by Chiang

Kai-shek, and its expedient betrayal by the Soviets. The punch and poignance of the prose are still fresh, as in the famous opening scene, in which the insurgent Ch'en assassinates a businessman:

> Through the great gash in the mosquito-netting, he could see very clearly; the eyelids open—had he been able to wake up?— the eyeballs white. Around the dagger the blood was beginning to flow, black in that deceptive light. In its balanced weight the body still held life. Ch'en could not let go the handle. A current of unbearable anguish passed between the corpse and himself, through the dagger, his stiffened arm, his aching shoulder, to the very depth of his chest, to his convulsive heart—the only moving thing in the room.

Over the years, *Man's Fate* has served as an inspiration for countless would-be changers of the world. Few of them, I think, can easily have forgotten the "atrocious whistle" of the train into whose boiler captive partisans are thrown alive. But Malraux's metaphysics— ruminations on love, solitude, and sacrifice by men facing annihilation—now have a quaint accent. They remind us that a mere eighty years ago "the death of God" wasn't a graduate-school conceit but a viscerally felt void of authority and grandeur that ideology rushed to fill. Action is Malraux's cure for the "absurdity" of life in a universe without salvation. Its price is martyrdom; its solace is brotherhood; its hope lies in transcendence; and its immediate reward for the author was the Prix Goncourt, which anointed him at thirty-two as the voice of his generation.

Malraux's apotheosis also reminds us that French literature is, or used to be, a kind of priesthood responsible for administering the religion of a secular state—the sanctity of Frenchness—and that the Knights Templar of fiction, the writers who fight and the warriors who write, have always been an elite fraternity. The rise of Hitler offered Malraux a worthy crusade, and he opposed Nazism earlier, and with more vigor, than many of his contemporaries, denouncing anti-Semitism strenuously at a time when it was rife in French politics on both the left and the right. "You can say a lot of things about Malraux," Clara later said, "but not that he is anti-Semitic. And goodness knows I gave him enough cause." Malraux's anti-Fascism took the form of a high-profile solidarity with the Soviet regime, with Communist intellectuals, and with the militant German proletariat. He never joined the Party, and briefly entertained a quixotic scheme for organizing a Left Bank rescue party to liberate Trotsky from Stalin's prison in Kazakhstan. He also dissented from "the extremist evangelists of socialist realism," as Todd puts it. "It's not passion that destroys the work of art," he wrote. "It's the will to prove." On the other side of the ledger, he was prepared to overlook the murder of dissent, extolling the lethal utopianism of Russian "democracy," and he was still starstruck by Mao in the early seventies. Like so many of his contemporaries, he practiced what the political historian Tony Judt calls a system of "double-entry moral bookkeeping": "an insistence upon certain normative values" combined with "the subsequent refusal to recognize their application in selected cases."

The theater of combat was a metaphor for Malraux until the start of the Spanish Civil War, in 1936, which gave his heroic persona its first live exercise on a stage. He was by then struggling to get away from Clara, but he was still partially dependent on her, and on her sensitive reading of his work. Despite increasingly vicious rows, they attended a writers' conference together in Madrid that spring. Josette Clotis, Malraux's pretty paramour—an aspiring writer and a Gallimard minion—also turned up, and he shuttled between a wife and a mistress who were the embodiments of his divided existence: one a *pasionaria*, the other a bourgeoise. Woman's fate or hope, however, was never of much interest to Malraux. Once Josette got him to herself, which is to say, lost his attention, she suffered from "the strange Asian manners of this famously cold man, this edgy, sanguinary fiend, of whom," she wrote in her diary, "there is no proof that he was not slightly homosexual."

The right-wing generals, led by Franco, staged their coup in July of that year, and Malraux hastened to offer his unhumble services to a country whose art, blood sport, and machismo he had always found congenial. A reconnaissance trip to Madrid on behalf of the French aviation minister persuaded Malraux that the government's most urgent strategic need was for planes. He set about procuring aircraft and recruiting pilots, and was rewarded with the rank of lieutenant colonel in the republican air force and command of the España squadron (later renamed for Malraux), a colorful unit of volunteers and mercenaries who kitted themselves out in Mexican cowboy gear—neckerchiefs and sombreros. They flew some twenty-three valiant though futile missions, and on an unspecified number of them their debonair colonel manned the gun bay, supposedly reciting Corneille above the din of ordnance and propellers.

The squadron was based at an airfield near Madrid, and nearly every afternoon Malraux made a well-groomed cocktail-hour appearance at the Hotel Florida—the watering hole of choice for spies, politicos, the foreign press, black marketeers, and anti-Fascist luminaries like John Dos Passos (still a leftist at the time) and Pablo Neruda. He was mobbed by the smitten of both sexes, but at least one barfly wasn't among the spellbound. Jean Lacouture, in an admiring biography of Malraux, published in 1973, observes that Hemingway respected him without affection and listened morosely to the windy monologues on literature and politics while staring at his glass and waiting to get a word in. *Man's Hope*, he cracked later, was a "materpisse." Malraux's egregious vanity made him an irresistible target for a cool shot like Hemingway to take down, and his courage seems to have come in spasms, like his tics. But he spent 1938 in besieged Catalonia, directing a searing feature, *L'Espoir*—adapted from his novel—that was filmed as the bombs rained down.

Malraux lived high and lay low for most of the Second World War. As he said to various recruiters, he was tired of fighting "for lost causes," a telling remark from an inveterately shrewd and lucky gambler who won, for the most part, betting long odds. In February of 1940, Josette announced that she was pregnant (their first son was born that November, and their second in 1943), and two months later Malraux was drafted into the army. As a thirty-nine-year-old reservist, he could easily have avoided active duty, but he pulled strings to get himself mustered in as a foot soldier under the pseudonym Georges André, hoping eventually to join a tank division, like his father. The rout and surrender of the French forces that June ended his eventless career as a regular soldier, and he spent the succeeding months in the rustic cocoon of captivity, with Grosjean. There was plenty to eat, the warmth of comradeship, and his fellow prisoners took over his share of the manual labor so that he could write. Josette managed to visit him, and so did his half brother Roland, who was active in the Maquis, and who urged him to escape while he could because the Germans were looking for anti-Fascist literary celebrities.

Having broken definitively with Clara, Malraux made his way to the Riviera, and for the next two and a half years he lived a domesticated life in the free zone with Josette. When Jean-Paul Sartre and Simone de Beauvoir came to visit, she was shocked by the luxury of the appointments (a manservant in white gloves served a "lavish" chicken dinner). If Malraux took pride in being one of the few writers who, unlike Sartre, refused to publish a word in the Occupation or Vichy press, he was also one of the few who could afford not to. Until the Germans occupied the free zone, Malraux's American publisher was able to send him dollars, and Gaston Gallimard took charge of liquidating pieces from Malraux's art collection—some ancient, some contemporary, provenance unspecified. On a clandestine trip to a ravenous, freezing Paris in the winter of 1943, Malraux managed to dine with Josette at both Prunier and La Tour d'Argent, arriving "incognito" in a noirish overcoat. According to Todd, he had asked Clara for a divorce, but—odiously, under the circumstances—refused her bargain to give him one if he let her leave for America with the half-Jewish daughter whom he never went to visit. Lacouture suggests that he consented to stay married, despite Josette's nagging, in order to help protect his wife and child, though it isn't clear why the resourceful Clara needed his permission to flee. Like Malraux's two half brothers, she joined the Resistance. But it was only in March of 1944, after Claude and Roland were both arrested, that Malraux decided to become a partisan, assuming his favorite starting position: the inside rail. Though no superior had promoted him, he called himself Colonel Berger, and announced, as if the war had just begun—or he had declared it—"When one has written what I've written, one fights."

Malraux's subsequent accounts of his "years" (eleven months) of living dangerously—the clandestine missions, parachute drops, prison escapes, high-level contacts with London, unification of the Maquis, feats of morale-building, ambush and capture by the Germans, rescue by a commando squad, retrieval of bazookas stashed in the Lascaux caves, and of his adoring men chanting "Berger! Berger!"—belong to a genre that didn't yet exist: docudrama. Some scenes had a basis in reality, and many were fabricated or embroidered, but in all of them Mme. Malraux's ugly little boy, dashingly costumed, got to play the *beau rôle*. One would love to know if Malraux felt any shame or scruple about his mendacity, but Todd—a superlative detective—doesn't pose the question. He is keen on Malraux's secrets and incurious about his mystery. The Resistance chapters have an archetypal ending, however, as adventure stories for boys—their version of "Cinderella"—often do: the pretender becomes the hero he impersonates. In the final stages of the war, Colonel Berger took command of some seventeen hundred men in the improvised Alsace-Lorraine Brigade and helped lead them to victory against crack German troops in some of the last actions against the Nazis, including the battle for Strasbourg.

Malraux emerged from the war wreathed in glory—he received the Croix de Guerre—but Death seems to have rebuffed his showing off by maliciously choosing nearly anyone else named Malraux for the team. His grandfather had fallen down the stairs, perhaps drunk. His father, embroiled in romantic and financial intrigues, had committed suicide. Claude was captured by the Germans, and presumably tortured before he was shot. Roland was captured and died on a German prison ship that was strafed by the RAF. Josette, who had started using her lover's name, took her mother to a train station while Malraux was fighting in Alsace, and was run over by a locomotive. And, seventeen years later, Malraux's two sons, Gauthier and Vincent, were killed together in a car accident—the cruelest of ironic twists to their father's ideal of brotherhood *hasta la muerte*.

Malraux had several consorts after Josette: his second wife, Madeleine, a pianist, and the widow of his brother Roland; the aristocratic woman of letters Louise de Vilmorin, an old flame; and, finally, Sophie, Louise's self-effacing niece. Sophie devoted her life to the private needs of a public man in his waning years, who, according to Todd, suffered from depression and alcoholism, and was dependent on amphetamines and sleeping pills. Fatherhood was not Malraux's forte, and his grandiosity never appears so monstrous as in his relations with his children and his nephew/stepson, Alain. When Florence, a beauty, was eighteen, her father warned her that "all the men who court you will just be trying to get to me." Alain was mysteriously banished from the presence of the uncle he called his papa one day after lunch with no warning and, apparently, no provocation.

In August of 1945, Charles de Gaulle summoned Malraux for an interview, and, in thirty minutes of lofty discussion about history, philosophy, and literature, he discreetly confessed the apostate of his Marxist sins. Malraux repented and was reborn. He served his new god with the fidelity of a convert through two administrations (1945–46 and 1958–69), in successively august capacities: adviser on cultural affairs, minister of information, and minister of culture. With Malraux at his right, the place of honor at the cabinet table, the general felt "shielded from the commonplace," he wrote. Malraux took stock of his country's aesthetic patrimony, and his ministry both conserved and enriched it. He left a legacy of meticulously restored historic monuments; founded the Orchestre de Paris; installed Maillol's sculptures in the Jardin du Carrousel; revitalized the Marais; and embarked on an ambitious project, only partially realized, to establish regional arts centers in every department. French republicanism has flourished by assimilating aspects of the religion it overthrew, and Malraux's *maisons de la culture* had an evangelical mission: to propagate among the people what Malraux called his true faith, the religion of art, and "to get the geniuses of mankind, and particularly those of France, loved."

Malraux's ministry, though, sometimes subsidized unlovably subversive work. When Genet's play *Les Paravents* was attacked by conservatives as "anti-French," Malraux rose to its defense by pointing out that it was—far less objectionably, from a Gaullist point of view— "anti-human" and "anti-everything." His attitude to Genet, like de Gaulle's to him, was rooted in the transcendent value that he and de Gaulle attached to national glory, a value tacitly shared by the signers of the petition that had certified the promise of a convicted tomb raider. A genius working in his mother tongue simply couldn't be anti-French; it didn't much matter what he said.

Todd is knowledgeable and amusing about the palace intrigues of the Fifth Republic, and about Malraux's travels as "a multiclient sales rep in literature, action, and politics for the firm of Gaullism, Inc." It was in that capacity that Malraux went to Washington in 1962, where he was feted by an infatuated Jacqueline Kennedy. He repaid her hospitality with a rash, princely promise that horrified the curators of the Louvre but proved to be one of his great publicity coups: the unprecedented loan of the *Mona Lisa*.

The Algerian crisis tested Malraux's Gaullism, and he found himself, in some discomfort, on the other side of colonial issues that he had espoused passionately in his youth. The right mistrusted his conversion and the left considered him a turncoat, yet his writing continued to be widely admired. (Having ceased to produce fiction, perhaps because he wasn't living any, he had turned to memoir and art history.) Malraux may have nursed an ambition to succeed de Gaulle—he spread the rumor that, in a secret will, the general had designated him a successor—but the victors of the world are able to appraise themselves through their opponents' eyes, and Malraux's were finally too avid for approval, innocent of discretion, and clouded by self-regard. Yet there is something about him for which only the word "noble" will do. Malraux was the hero of a tragicomic battle that nearly all of us know and most of us lose: "man's struggle," as he calls it, "against humiliation."

—May 2, 2005

THREE

Not Even a Nice Girl

Like Joan of Arc, Anne Frank is a name that translates easily into every European language, and always manages to sound both humble and powerful. Unlike Saint Joan, Anne was a child of privilege. One of her greatest privileges, as she saw it, was knowing "what it feels like to make other people happy"—particularly her father, whom she called Pim, and who was her first great love and confidant. Those daughters who escape seduction of or by their fathers while enjoying a complicity with them often seem to become the women who are most at ease with their desires. One longs to know what more Anne Frank would have made of that expressive and sensual freedom which is already so striking in her prose.

Pim—Otto Frank—was a man who inspired devotion in a variety of people. He came from the kind of rich German Jewish family that Walter Benjamin describes in his *Berlin Chronicle*, whose furniture was "so wholly convinced of itself and its permanence that it took no account of wear, inheritance, or moves." While Otto Frank lacked Benjamin's erudition, he had something of his tenderness, and, at night, in hiding, he would read his daughter Dickens in English and Goethe in German to keep up her morale.

Frank had studied retailing in America with his school friend Nathan Straus but had gone into his family's bank. By 1934, he and his wife and their two daughters had emigrated to the Netherlands from Frankfurt, his native city, hoping to escape the Nazis. In Amsterdam, he embarked on a career of selling pectin—an ingredient in jam-making—and spices to Dutch housewives. He took on two Dutch partners and a Jewish herb specialist named Hermann van Pels. The new company leased a warehouse and offices on the Prinsengracht, in the old part of the city, which was something of a trek from the Franks' home, in a modern suburb.

Above the warehouse was an empty garret apartment, occupying three floors. In 1942, as everyone knows, eight people went into hiding there: Otto and Edith Frank and their daughters, then aged thirteen and sixteen; the van Pelses and their fifteen-year-old son, Peter; and a prissy, uxorious dentist named Friedrich Pfeffer, who had been wrenched away from his Christian wife, and who shared Anne's room, barging in on her evening ablutions with a certain suspect regularity.

For the next two years, the fugitives inhabited this secret annex (*achterhuis*, Anne called it) under increasing stress but in relative comfort, protected gallantly by their former employees, who kept them supplied with as much food as could be bought with forged ration coupons, and with books, clothing, writing paper, toothpaste, cigarettes, news, and even birthday cakes and Christmas presents. After the war, one of those protectors, Miep Gies, recalled how, one afternoon, she had surprised Anne at her desk:

> She was writing in an account book like those we had in the office. I recognized it. She promptly closed the book and put it away, blushing. At that moment, Mrs. Frank came into the room and said: "Yes, we have a daughter who writes. Did you know that?" She said it in a tone that held pride—and at the same time loneliness and sadness that this child withdrew from her by writing.

In August of 1944, the fugitives were betrayed to the security police, probably by a warehouseman. Two of their protectors were arrested and interned in Holland. Miep Gies was questioned by the Gestapo but let go, and it was she who retrieved the scattered pages of Anne's diary from the annex floor, where the police, searching for valuables, had strewn them. The Frank family, the van Pels family, and Pfeffer were held in a Dutch transit camp for a month and then shipped to Auschwitz. There their paths to death diverged. Otto Frank was the only one to survive. The girls held out until the early spring. A Dutch woman who had seen them before they were moved to Bergen-Belsen later told an interviewer, "Anne still had her face, up to the last." She was nearly sixteen when she died, in a typhus epidemic that decimated the camp, a few months before the liberation of Holland.

Last June, Anne Frank would have been sixty. On her birthday, Doubleday published the Netherlands State Institute for War Documentation's seven-hundred-page *Critical Edition* of her diary, translated by Arnold J. Pomerans and B. M. Mooyaart. The introduction to this tome is a masterpiece of pedantry, written with a deadpan flatness out of Thomas Mann's *Doctor Faustus*. There is, for example, a section devoted to the "microcharacteristics" of Anne's handwriting, which also establishes that her fountain-pen ink smudged because it was slow to dry, and that the leaves of her first diary—an autograph album with a red-and-white-checked cover—were bound to the spine with glue that contained bone.

Nearly two hundred pages later, a reader embarks on three "diplomatically" printed (contiguous but not precisely consecutive) versions of the diary itself: a scrupulous transcription of Anne's original; the manuscript she began revising for posterity in 1944 but didn't get to finish; and the English translation, including material that Otto Frank had cut in the name of discretion and propriety ("My vagina is getting wider all the time, but I could also be imagining it").

The restored passages are in this vein: charming in their candor or their vehemence. They add roundness to Anne's self-portrait, but not substance. What a comparison of the texts does reveal is both how spontaneously the diarist composed her prose and how finely she then tuned it. In order to make such a comparison, however, one needs a certain amount of motivation. The editors' instructions on how to read *The Critical Edition* are more arcane, and harder to follow, than those for a build-it-yourself hang glider. Does every scratched-out comma in the diary deserve a footnote? Are we interested in the financing of Otto's spice business (Frank "had to enter into a licensing agreement with Pomosin which stipulated that he would pay 2½% of all profits for the right to use the Opekta trademark")? Do we care that among the articles rescued from the annex were a shoe bag with the initials A.F. and two Spanish textbooks belonging to the dentist? Are a short etymology of the surname of the Gestapo officer who arrested the Franks, half a chapter on the ineptitude of Anne's German translator, a discourse on the corrections to Anne's Dutch suggested by a family friend (" '*broschjes* [brooch]' became '*broche*,' '*nog* [yet]' became '*noch* [nor]' . . . '*kennen geleerd* [get acquainted with]' became '*leeren kennen* [get to know]' ") illuminating for the casual reader of the diary, or even for the passionate student of history? The answer is yes.

"An edition of the complete diaries was needed for historical reasons," its editors tell us, the primary reason being "the growing number of published slurs, particularly during the second half of the 1970s . . . [that] were intended to cast doubt both on the personal integrity of the author and on the relationship between the original manuscript, the published version, and its many translations." The slurs in question are assertions by former Nazis and neo-Nazis that the Holocaust never took place but was a piece of Zionist propaganda, and that Anne Frank's diary was, in the words of Richard Verrall, a member of the British National Front, "just one more fraud in a whole series of frauds in support of . . . the saga of the Six Million."

Not all the attackers were club-wielding Neanderthals. Some had intellectual credentials. Robert Faurisson, for example, was a professor of literature at the University of Lyons who denied the existence of the gas chambers (his book had a preface by Noam Chomsky, defending Faurisson's freedom of speech). Faurisson argued that Anne Frank's account of life in hiding contains too many descriptions of noisy and rowdy activities—carpentry, vacuuming, sacks of beans bursting, roars of laughter—to be credible. A high-school teacher of English (and former storm trooper) from Lübeck named Lothar Stielau placed Anne's journal in the genre of "the forged diaries of Eva Braun [and] of the Queen of England." Harald Nielsen, a

Danish literary critic, questioned the names Anne and Peter—they weren't convincingly "Jewish." Teressa Hendry, writing in the *American Mercury*, objected to the maturity of the prose—"impossible as the work of a teenager." David Irving, an extreme-right-wing British historian, was one of several critics to charge that the diary had been ghostwritten by Otto Frank with the help of the American novelist Meyer Levin, whose obsession with "the Anne Frank problem," as he called it, is a tragic farce of its own. And an entire book, by a Swede named Ditlieb Felderer, who published it himself, attempted to characterize Anne as a drug addict and a slut (one chapter was titled "Anne's Character—Not Even a Nice Girl"), on the basis of the descriptions of her trysts in the attic with Peter van Pels and her use of valerian for insomnia.

The truth of history is like the ozone layer. An atmosphere of reason depends on its intactness—or, at least, on its repair. On those grounds alone, *The Critical Edition* has a heroic aspect. But, as H.J.J. Hardy, of the Netherlands State Forensic Science Laboratory, observes, with admirable niceness, in his summary of the evidence, "an investigation into the authenticity of the text known as the diary of Anne Frank has many facets"—some, perhaps, stranger than he knows.

The journals of her life in hiding that Anne Frank kept for two years, between the ages of thirteen and fifteen, were published in this country as *The Diary of a Young Girl*. That ingenuous title condescends to what is in fact an epistolary autobiography of exceptional caliber. It takes the full measure of a complex, evolving character. It has the shape and drama of literature. It was scrupulously revised by its author, who intended it to be read. It is certainly not a piece of "found art," as one Dutch critic has suggested—not a collaboration between a child and history, with history doing the lion's share of the work.

Anne was a strong, canny, fluent, truthful writer, who escaped the preciousness that generally mars the work of very young people. She had the usual baggage of ambitions—she wanted to be interesting, she wanted to be great—but they didn't cast their anxious shadows over her page. Here, for example, is what she has to say about Margot, the older sister, who could do no wrong, who wanted to become a midwife in Palestine, and who, Anne imagined, wouldn't kiss a boy until he had proposed to her: "Margot is very sweet, and would like me to trust her, but still, I can't tell her everything . . . she lacks the nonchalance for conducting deep discussions."

Anne's "nonchalance" is a freshness—a gift for detachment—like the young Jane Austen's. Both are comic moralists who take a pitiless view of conventional femininity without renouncing it for themselves. Both have more confidence that men, despite their weaknesses and absurdities, can be redeemed and made worthy of love. Humor is the ballast for their pride and their romanticism, and the leaven for their despair. The frictions and vanities of a narrow world enthrall them. It is, though, a world in which they feel isolated among their familiars—lonely in their depth of feeling and their clarity of perception. Writing is their antidote to claustrophobia, physical and spiritual, yet the claustrophobia seems to heighten their natural gaiety. The young Jane was a famous flirt and lover of "jokes." Anne describes herself as a "frolicsome little goat" whose "cheekiness" drove the adults in the secret annex crazy. One suspects that she must have been constantly confronting them with her mysterious, superior vitality.

That vitality appears in many guises: Anne's schoolyard charisma, her sexual curiosity and daring, a volatile temper, the power to console herself, an animal delight in her body, a certain hubris bred of strength. But its essence—Anne's essence, perhaps—was a sense of self-regard that wasn't spoiled by narcissism or complacency. When the Nazis killed her, they destroyed an intact being.

Anne, of course, didn't feel intact. Like most adolescents, she experienced herself as a "dual personality," whose "real self" was too fragile to expose, and whose false self misrepresented her to the world:

One half embodies my exuberant cheerfulness, making fun of everything, not taking offense at a flirtation, a kiss, an embrace, a dirty joke. This side is usually lying in wait and pushes away the other, which is much better, deeper and purer. You must realize that no one knows Anne's better side and that's why most people find me so insufferable . . . Really, it's just the same as a love film is for deep-thinking people, simply a diversion . . . not bad but certainly not good. I loathe having to tell you this, but why shouldn't I, if I know it's true anyway? My lighter, superficial side will always be too quick for the deeper side of me and that's why it will always win.

The real self had no reflection, and the point of her diary—which is probably the point of most young writers' work, in whatever genre—was to create one. But it was also, under the circumstances, something grotesquely poignant and futile. Barricaded against death and terror by a fake bookcase, Anne went about learning to live, approaching the task with the moral delicacy of an Austen heroine, teaching herself how one reconciles the demands of "honor and conscience" with those of an impious heart.

Ten American publishers rejected the manuscript of Anne Frank's diary before Doubleday bought the United States rights in 1951. The diary eventually would sell some twenty million copies in more than fifty languages, but not until the American stage and film versions, produced in 1955 and 1959, respectively, had helped to create its vast international public, and to turn Anne Frank into a celebrity, leaving her exposed, as celebrities are, to the fixations of idolaters and vandals.

Meyer Levin was something of each. A man of prodigious energy, he wrote more than a dozen works of fiction, of which the most famous is *Compulsion*, a novel about Leopold and Loeb. He also produced several plays, a history of Israel, an anthology of American Jewish literature, a Haggadah, and a collection of Chassidic tales, and still had force left for travels, marriages, lawsuits, psychoanalyses, and polemics; for an active career as a journalist; for a vast, contentious correspondence; for crusades against powers who he believed wished to silence him; and for a twenty-year obsession with Anne Frank.

Levin's second wife, Tereska Torres, introduced him to the diary while they were living in France, and forever regretted having done so. (She came to see Anne, not irrationally, as her principal rival.)

Having read the diary in its French translation, Levin immediately wrote to Otto Frank, offering his services as an intermediary with American publishers. Frank was cordial. When the diary appeared in America two years later, Levin reviewed it "eulogistically" for *The New York Times Book Review*, and, in the words of David Barnouw, one of the editors of *The Critical Edition*, he "argued forcefully that a play and film ought to be made of the book."

Anne's father was sufficiently impressed to appoint Levin his literary agent for a dramatization, and, according to Barnouw, he eventually "gave in to Levin's insistence that Levin himself should write the play." But when a series of producers had declined that play as "unstageworthy," Frank turned to the well-connected impresario Kermit Bloomgarden, who engaged Albert Hackett and Frances Goodrich, a married couple then under contract to MGM, as scriptwriters.

As embittered as a humble but worthy suitor snubbed by an ambitious family, Levin complained that his version of the play had been "suppressed" by a "conspiracy" of "élite" German Jews who controlled access to the media and despised his shtetl origins. This cabal supposedly included Nathan Straus; the Sulzberger family; Lillian Hellman; Bloomgarden; the law firm of Paul, Weiss, Rifkind, Wharton & Garrison; and Otto Frank, whom Levin had turned against. ("You are my Hitler," he told the old man, whom he had once idealized.) What the conspirators had specifically wished to censor, Levin claimed, was any acknowledgment of Anne's "Jewish identity" and religious pride, or her prophetic "message"—that the Jews had been chosen to redeem the world through their suffering.

Sentimentality can be a form of vandalism. (That is perhaps why kitsch, perversely, so often fascinates those with the most iconoclastic taste in art.) The dramatization of Anne Frank's diary by Hackett and Goodrich won a Pulitzer Prize, enjoyed a long run on Broadway, and made the world weep for all the Jewish children whom Anne represents. But the Hacketts (Levin liked to refer to them as "the Hacketts of Hollywood") also stripped Anne's prose of its nuances and reduced her character—which, after all, resides in the prose—to that of a generic Hollywood ingenue. Consider, for example, what they make of Anne's "dual personality":

I have a nicer side, Father . . . a sweeter, nicer side. But I'm
scared to show it. I'm afraid that people are going to laugh at
me if I'm serious. So the mean Anne comes to the outside and
the good Anne stays on the inside and I keep on trying to
switch them around and have the good Anne outside and the
bad Anne inside and be what I'd like to be . . . and might
be . . . if only . . . only . . .

Hackett and Goodrich *had* come to the project from Hollywood
and were steeped in its pieties and simplifications. In their hands,
Anne's diary became the kind of domestic drama in which bad things
happen to good people. A "special" child is often the hero of such a
story, misbehaving just enough to set an example of pluck for the fee-
bler of heart, and looking heavenward at moments of uncertainty. "I
wish you had a religion," the Hacketts' Anne tells her sweetheart, Peter, toward the end of Act II:

Oh, I don't mean you have to be Orthodox . . . or believe in
heaven and hell . . . just to believe in something! When I think
of all that's out there . . . the trees . . . and flowers . . . and
seagulls . . . when I think of the dearness of you, Peter . . . and
the goodness of people we know . . . Mr. Kraler, Miep, Dirk,
the vegetable man, all risking their lives for us every day . . .
When I think of these good things, I'm not afraid any
more . . . I find myself, and God, and I . . .

As a great fan of the movies whose room in the secret annex was
wallpapered with pinups, the real Anne Frank might have been
amazed at her transformation into a perfect little child actress from a
forties film—a kind of tragic, Jewish *National Velvet*. She might also
have agreed with Meyer Levin that to the extent this creature had
usurped her in the popular imagination, she had been betrayed.

The bland "universalism" of the Hacketts' work and its uncritical
reception served only to inflame Levin further. He advertised for justice in *The New York Times*. He importuned major writers to support
his cause. (Many of them did.) He took his version of the play to Tel

Aviv. And he sued Frank and Bloomgarden, claiming that their writers had "plagiarized" his material, and won a judgment for damages of $50,000. That judgment was overturned on appeal, but it turns up in the Nazi attacks on the diary as Levin's "hush money" or as his "royalties" as ghostwriter.

When the hapless but demonic Levin appears on the stage of Anne Frank's life with Stielau, the former storm trooper; Faurisson, the rabid academic; the modish Hacketts; weary, bemused Otto Frank; the heroic handwriting analysts at the Netherlands State Forensic Science Laboratory; and a chorus of prosecutors trading accusations of theft and subversion in English, German, and Dutch, *The Critical Edition* becomes the kind of existential drama that was never made of the diary—one of those labyrinths of modern literature where every truth has a lie for its echo.

"I long for Daddy's real love," Anne Frank wrote, four months into captivity. "Not only as his child but for me—Anne, myself." Otto Frank's love had already begun to fail his daughter, not necessarily because it was faulty but because she was fourteen, and ready to seek "real love" from a boy; and also because she was a writer, and ready to seek love from a reader. Her readiness has a provocative quality to it—a voluptuous openness—and I wonder how many readers have responded to it, perhaps guiltily, with the kind of ardor that Philip Roth displays in *The Ghost Writer*.

The Ghost Writer is a novel about the love of children for their fathers—Jewish patriarchs who don't know how to read their children's prose or love them for what Anne would have called their real selves—and its central characters are a son and a daughter searching for a surrogate. The son is young Nathan Zuckerman. The surrogate is his idol, the ascetic novelist E. I. Lonoff. The daughter is Lonoff's amanuensis, a seductive child-woman named Amy Bellette, whom Nathan chooses to imagine is Anne Frank.

Roth's counter-choice, however, is to imagine that Anne Frank is Amy Bellette. In Amy, Roth can contemplate Anne Frank without the tragedy of her death and the mantle of her fame. She helps him deconsecrate the Jewish saint, the Hollywood ingenue, the Holocaust's most famous victim, and the world's most beloved Jewish writer. But, through Amy, Roth is also able to bring a different kind of reverence to Anne's portrait. What he reveres seems to be precisely what so irritated the two older women in the secret annex, who felt mocked by it; what exasperated the wifeless dentist; what enthralled but also frightened Peter van Pels, and mystified the demure Margot; and what, to a degree, Otto Frank felt that he had to censor in his daughter's diary—the astonishing freedom of Anne's desire.

It should be noted that Roth is no less fixated on Anne Frank than Levin or the neo-Nazis. He appropriates her as his literary property, incorporates her prose into his narrative, and distills her character through the layers of his hero's impudent fantasies. But, in the process, he also reads her with the passionate discernment and the sense of play that she longed for.

In that respect, *The Ghost Writer*, with its heretical presumption, makes an interesting foil for *The Critical Edition*, with its solemn scrupulosity. They both champion Anne's contradictions against those who would make her "pure." And they both remind us that "an investigation into the authenticity of the text known as the diary of Anne Frank" can't be closed. That text is no longer just the writer's version of her real self, but the world's.

—December 18, 1989

A House Divided

If you think about what's most frightening in a horror picture, what gets you, it isn't the images but the soundtrack. The reason, perhaps, is that human beings listen in the womb, and hearing is one of the first sensory experiences—one of trust and connection but also, later, of helpless vigilance. The ear listens for the heartbeat, the footstep, and, in literature, for a certain unwilled cry, to be heard in works as different as the poetry of George Herbert and the stories of Kafka.

The cry resounds from the void in which an infant endures its anguish, rage, yearning, and hunger. A writer can't make a story of that experience, perhaps because language is a relation, and can only describe other relations. But a writer can make a story of the drama of helplessness as it is played out in and perpetrated upon the world, and it is through that drama that the best fiction engages us in history.

Beloved (Knopf, 1987), Toni Morrison's fifth novel, is such a fiction. Her protagonist is a former slave woman named Sethe, living near Cincinnati after the Civil War with the last of her four children—a teenage girl named Denver, with whom she was pregnant at the time of her escape from a Kentucky plantation called Sweet Home. Sethe's two sons have run away from her. Her formidable mother-in-law has just died. Her husband has not been heard from since the day that he and the other slaves attempted to board the "train" of the Underground Railroad. And Sethe's house is haunted by the ghost of her fourth child, a furious infant called Beloved, who died there—her throat cut—eighteen years before.

Despite the richness and authority of its detail, *Beloved* is not primarily a historical novel, and Morrison does not, for the most part, attempt to argue the immorality of slavery on rational grounds, or to make a dramatic case for her heroine's act of violence—the way, for example, Styron does in *The Confessions of Nat Turner*. She treats the past as if it were one of those luminous old scenes painted on dark glass—the scene of a disaster, like the burning of Parliament or the eruption of Krakatoa—and she breaks the glass, and then recomposes it in a disjointed and puzzling modern form. As the reader struggles with its fragments and mysteries, he keeps being startled by flashes of his own reflection in them.

Consider, for a moment, the relation of that fractured scene to the intact, glassed-over family portrait that is beamed into millions of living rooms on a weekly television program called *The Cosby Show*. Bill Cosby has become America's ideal parent, and the household he heads is much the same as the one at which he aims his commercials for automobiles, cameras, computers, stocks and bonds, peppy soft drinks, and Jell-O. What he really pitches, though, is reassurance, and what is most distinctive about him, as a salesman, is his amalgam of maternal and paternal qualities. Cosby is rich and powerful, unlike most mothers; he is tender and present, unlike most fathers. His main role, at least as an actor, is to instill trust in children while disarming their parents' fears of and for them, and he does this so well that he fulfills what must be a vast yearning for the kind of perfect nurturing that almost no one gets, and that would permit the kind of self-mastery that almost no one achieves—most rarely, the children of poor, single-parent families in a ghetto.

Cosby has five children of his own, and he has published his thoughts on raising them in a book called *Fatherhood*, which restates a number of homely truths—basic articles in the implicit social contract of the middle-class family. "Even though your kids may not be paying attention," he advises us, "you have to pay attention to them all the way"; "real fatherhood means total acceptance of the child"; "the most important thing to let them know is simply that you're there"; "kids have one guiding philosophy, and it's greed"; and their "baffling behavior . . . is the same today as it was when Joseph's brothers peddled him to the Egyptians." Cosby's book contains no references to his own past, and there is nothing, except for his picture on the jacket, that identifies him as a black man—nor should there have to be. But his blackness italicizes his message the way a contrasting typeface indicates that a passage has a double, an unconscious, an exotic, or a revealed meaning.

Cosby's assimilated American family lives in a state of grace that he invites his audience to contemplate and envy, if not to share, and it is in many ways an ironic counterpart of Morrison's riven and haunted family. For who were the slaves but the selfless "ideal parents" of their white masters?

As *Beloved* opens, one of the former slaves turns up on Sethe's doorstep near Cincinnati. Paul D. is "the last of the Sweet Home men," and in the score of years since Sethe last saw him, he has been a prisoner on a chain gang, a fugitive living in the wilderness, a laborer for both sides in the Civil War, and a vagabond. Sethe learns from him that his brother, Paul A., was captured and hanged; that their comrade Sixo—"the wild man"—was "crisped" and shot; and that her husband, Halle, was last seen squatting next to a butter churn with expressionless eyes, smearing the clabber on his face:

"Did you speak to him?"
"I couldn't."
"Why!"
"I had a bit in my mouth."

She, in turn, recounts her story. After she put her children safely aboard the "train" and went back to wait for her husband, she was cornered in the barn by the nephews of her master. Inured as he is to the brutality of white men, Paul D. is still astounded that the boys would have "pulped" Sethe's back when she was pregnant. Yet it isn't the beating that she wishes to impress upon him:

"They used cowhide on you?"
"And they took my milk!"

"They beat you and you was pregnant?"
"And they took my milk."

The scene in which the nephews force Sethe to suckle them is one of the most shocking in a novel stocked with savagery of every description, physical and verbal, and the point that it doesn't register as such for Paul D. is an important one. It is not because he lacks compassion—Morrison has endowed him with an almost mystical tenderheartedness. But his experience of slavery has been different from Sethe's, and if his hardships have been more extreme they have also been less damaging to his pride. That pride has been invested in his own attributes: his strength, his mobility, his manhood, his ability to survive. Hers has been invested in her maternity and confused with her maternity, and until that confusion is resolved, which is the real business of the narrative, she is still, and in every sense, a slave/mother.

Sethe and her two daughters, one flesh and one spirit, are trapped in a void at the core of *Beloved*, paralyzed by a powerfully cohesive but potentially annihilating force—maternal love—that scatters and repels the novel's male characters. Paul D. puts it one way when he tells Sethe, "Your love is too thick." Baby Suggs, Sethe's mother-in-law, describes it another way when she says, "A man ain't nothing but a man. But a son? Well now, that's *somebody*." What she also means, in the context of her own life, is that a woman is nothing but a woman. But a mother? That's somebody.

Morrison goes on to amplify Baby's remark, and it is worth pausing at this passage—less for its own sake than because it suggests the kind of impassioned polemic that *Beloved* does not, ultimately, succumb to:

It made sense for a lot of reasons because in all of Baby's life, as well as Sethe's own, men and women were moved around like checkers. Anybody Baby Suggs knew, let alone loved, who hadn't run off or been hanged, got rented out, loaned out, bought up, brought back, stored up, mortgaged, won, stolen or seized. So Baby's eight children had six fathers. What she called the nastiness of life was the shock that she received upon learning that nobody stopped playing checkers just because the pieces included her children. Halle she was able to keep the longest . . . Given to her, no doubt, to make up for *hearing* that her two girls . . . were sold and gone and she had not been able to wave goodbye.

This language is powerful but manipulative. It is meant to awe us, and it does—like the tiny human figure that a model-builder sets next to a pyramid. The abolitionist novels and tracts of the last century aimed for the same effect. They exposed the plight of the Negro as a slave, a victim, a hero, but not as an individual. When Morrison sets Baby Suggs and all her griefs on one tray of the scale, she defies us to supply our own moral counterweight—and, of course, we fail.

The occasional excesses of rhetoric (and sentimentality) in *Beloved* may reflect an anxiety in Morrison that she attributes to her heroine: a need to overfeed and overprotect her children. Paul D. tries to warn Sethe about it, but she won't listen to him, asserting, grandiosely, that she will "protect [Denver] . . . while I'm live and . . . when I ain't." One of the ironies of the novel is, in fact, that its author hovers possessively around her own symbols and intentions, and so determines too much for the reader—flouting her own central moral principle and challenge. For throughout *Beloved*, Morrison asks us to judge all her characters, black and white, according to the risks they take for their own autonomy and in honoring that of others.

Sethe, Paul D., and Denver are a fascinating family unit in part because they are so familiar: a middle-aged single mother, sexually out of practice, whose desire takes her by surprise; a middle-aged man ready to compromise with his own need to wander; and a lonely, secretive adolescent who strains their relationship. Denver is jealous and resentful of Paul D., particularly when he exorcises the ghost of her baby sister, her only companion. She comforts herself with carbohydrates and by daydreaming about the glorious adventure of her own birth, in a rowboat—she was dragged from her mother's womb, prematurely, by a young white girl. But Sethe has, in fact, never fully "delivered" Denver. Fat, dreamy, submissive, fearful of the world, and fixated on her moment of entry into it, Denver will be forced to complete the labor by herself.

Morrison makes this family romance just comfortable and promising enough so that one resents the apparition of a supernatural intruder: a thirsty and beautiful young woman who walks out of the pond behind the house and takes it over. She has no past, or refuses to recall one. There are no lines on her hands and feet, although there are faint scars, like fingernail scratches, on her forehead. She calls herself by the name of the dead baby—Beloved—so there isn't much suspense, either about her identity or about her reasons for coming back. But we are apparently meant to feel that we are actually losing something to Beloved—a story, a family—just as they were becoming real. The family's members are seduced away by her, and forced to serve her, which they do in a trance; and the role of memory in the novel is, at least in part, to inflict enough vivid and specific pain to dispel the trance.

What is most physically striking about Beloved is her smoothness: she's the dark glass of the picture. What is most poignant about her is that, like any vindictive child but unlike most ghosts or vampires, she ("it") is "not evil, just sad," omnipotent but also helpless, like Caliban or Frankenstein. And you finally have to decide between your sympathy with her greed for love and your desire to see the others go on living—the same private choice that one has to make between the claims of past grief and potential happiness.

The slaves in *Beloved* have to make a version of that choice in relation to Sweet Home because the force that drives them from a monstrously familiar place also compels them to resurrect it: the same mixture of homesick love and dread: "Although there was not a leaf on that farm that did not make [Sethe] want to scream, it rolled itself out before her in shameless beauty." They were treated humanely there—insidiously so. Their master, Mr. Garner, was a man who encouraged them to "correct" and "even defy him. To invent ways of doing things . . . to buy [the freedom of] a mother, choose a horse or a wife, handle guns, even learn reading." But the illusion of autonomy, Morrison suggests, is more debilitating, and perhaps, in the long run, crueler, than a full consciousness of servility. The slaves discover when they are turned over to a fiend named Schoolteacher,

Garner's heir, that they have been their master's creatures all along. "How 'bout that?" Paul D. reflects. "Everything rested on Garner being alive. Now ain't that slavery or what is it?"

It's important to the story that one of Paul D.'s first acts when he moves in with Sethe is to break her house up—smash her furniture and dishes—as a way of ridding her of the ghost. But he can't destroy her perverse attachment to the memory, to the idea of Sweet Home—in part because the roles of master and slave, mother and child, have been fused within her. This fusion is what we experience as most sinister, claustrophobic, and uncanny in the novel, and it's what drives home the meaning of slavery.

"I am Beloved and she is mine," the ghost daughter repeats, like a vow or a litany. She means that Sethe is hers—Sethe's body, her attention, her time—and she steals Sethe's "milk" more ruthlessly than the nephews did. "Beloved she my daughter. She mine," Sethe says, claiming a privilege that the law did not accord even the slave owner: he could breed or whip or starve or separate his slaves but not murder them. And in surrendering to each other, in claiming to own each other, Sethe and Beloved create a monster like slavery itself: a greedy infant with a parent's "supernatural" power.

Morrison has a dreamer's gift for choosing names and images, and for the ironic doubling of meanings that gives a dream its cohesiveness and makes it an experience of pure retrospect but pure present. Like a dream, however, the novel is vulnerable to the kind of morning-after synopsis that one critic gave it when, quoting coolly from its steamier passages, he labeled it a "soap opera."

It's worth considering the nature of the objections that people who don't like the better kind of Romantic opera make to those who do. The staging is contrived; the plot heaves; the passions are grandiose and the myths obsolete; no one has a sense of humor. "*Espressivo* at any price," Nietzsche says, scowling, "and music in the service, the slavery, of poses—*that is the end.*"

Morrison is essentially an operatic writer, and as a production, *Beloved* has some of the excesses that Nietzsche objected to in Wagner. She doesn't eschew melodrama in her big, violent scenes, or weeping in her domestic ones. There is a chorus of stock characters— good neighbors, evil prison guards, a messenger of the gods called

Stamp Paid, and even a tree named Brother. The prose is rife with motifs and images that the narration sometimes orchestrates too solemnly. Paul D.'s last speech to Sethe is not the only one that trembles on the edge of pathos: "Me and you, we got more yesterday than anybody. We need some kind of tomorrow."

But if you read *Beloved* with a vigilant eye, you should also listen to it with a vigilant ear. There's something great in it: a play of human voices, consciously exalted, perversely stressed, yet holding true. It gets you.

—November 2, 1987

FIVE

An Unsimple Heart

I once spent a year in the manuscript room of the old French National Library on the rue de Richelieu. Toward the end of my stay, the curator offered to give me a going-away present: a day at my carrel with any manuscript in her archives. I had nearly all of French literature to choose from, but there was no contest. I asked for Flaubert's *The Sentimental Education*. This greatest *bildungsroman*, one of the first modern novels, tells the mock-epic, tragicomic story of Frédéric Moreau, a provincial dilettante who fritters away an inheritance on the wrong women, friends, pleasures, investments, and causes, and whose ambitions are thwarted as methodically as his illusions are demolished. The book was published in 1869, thirteen years after *Madame Bovary*, to excoriating reviews. Writers of an ironic temperament revere it for the qualities that have alienated the larger reading public: its arduous purity of style; its uncompromising pessimism, free of cant; and its refusal to ennoble human nature.

Flaubert wrote a rabidly depressed letter about the novel's reception to his friend George Sand, and she responded with a maternal nudge, typical of their correspondence, for she liked to pretend that his misanthropy was an affectation. "This man who is so kind, so friendly, so cheerful, so simple, so congenial, why does he want to discourage us from living?" she wondered rhetorically. But Sand, who foraged tirelessly for pleasure and companionship, and wrote with complacent fluency, misunderstood the tonic nature of Flaubert's despair. Less of the world is more for him because there can never be enough, and his discouragement with life sets the bar that his pitiless ambition keeps forcing him to transcend.

The draft of *The Sentimental Education* runs to twenty-five hundred shagreen-bound folio pages—a fortune in stationery. The writer so wary of self-indulgence was profligate with ink and paper. He covered his leaves minutely, on both sides, with wiry black script. Almost every line is altered or crossed out, then recopied dozens of times. The manuscript has the aspect of a battlefield on which each inch of forward momentum has been wrested at exorbitant human cost from an implacable enemy. An epitaph for this expense of valor comes to mind: Flaubert's words of mourning and consolation from a scene halfway into *Madame Bovary*, where Emma's romantic effusions begin, fatally, to bore her lover Rodolphe. Here the author inserts a very rare editorial aside: a defense of his heroine's ineloquence, which sounds like a plea to his own conscience for mercy: "As if the soul's fullness didn't sometimes overflow into the emptiest of metaphors, for no one, ever, can give the exact measure of his needs, his apprehensions, or his sorrows; and human speech is like a cracked cauldron on which we bang out tunes that make bears dance, when we want to move the stars to pity."

The best literary biographies give the most exact possible measure of the overflow from a writer's being into his work. In that respect, *Flaubert: A Life* (Farrar, Straus and Giroux, 2002), by Geoffrey Wall, is an admirable if not completely satisfying book. The author—a British university professor—has a penchant for the pastoral "we," and he occasionally succumbs to what, for a Flaubertian, is the fatal pitfall of solemnity. Discussing "Herodias," the last of the *Three Tales* (a late masterpiece that also includes the novellas "A Simple Heart" and "The Legend of Saint Julian"), Wall complains, as might a nineteenth-century cleric writing to the *Journal de Rouen*, that the ending lacks a proper sense of exaltation. Why? Because the disciples of John the Baptist set off for Galilee with his severed head on a dish, and "as it was very heavy, they each carried it in turn." He finds this "a conclusion so inscrutably prosaic that it leaves us yearning for the poetry of the sacred." But only two things are sacred to Flaubert: impiety and perfection.

Anyone foolhardy enough to enter the lists with Flaubert must submit to the ordeal-by-humiliation of sharing a page with his sentences, and Wall survives. His style has flair (if at times too much), and so does his erudition. Citing the famous passage at the end of the *Education*, which must be one of the bleakest elegies ever written—seven telescopic sentences devoid of embellishment that sum up the futility of Frédéric's later life—Wall notes that Flaubert is "showing his successors how to smuggle their old Romantic contraband into a modern realist novel." Wall understands that cunning is necessary, too, when dealing with an obsessive teaser and connoisseur of farce. It is daunting enough to establish a critical beachhead on a character so well defended, in Wall's words, by "lucid comic anguish." But it is practically impossible to ascertain when Flaubert's self-mockery is contrived, and to resist its subversiveness. He was a man who could write of his own violent moods, "I go from exasperation to a state of collapse, then I recover and go from prostration to Fury, so that my average state is one of being annoyed." Two weeks before his death, he told his niece, "Sometimes I think I'm liquefying like an old Camembert."

Wall's condensed portrait is drawn mostly from previously published material, and it doesn't, and perhaps wasn't intended to, enrich Flaubert scholarship. Earlier biographers have mapped the terrain in multiple volumes. Wall is not as dogged as Enid Starkie, as urbane as Francis Steegmuller, or as microscopic as Sartre. No abbreviation of the life may ever match the cranky wit and wry felicity of Julian Barnes's *Flaubert's Parrot* (which, however, enjoys the riffing privileges of fiction). But the author of the *Dictionary of Received Ideas*—the glossary of clichés that Flaubert appended to *Bouvard and Pécuchet*, his "encyclopedia of human stupidity" in novel form— would surely have bellowed with joy at the themes listed after his name in Wall's index. With a few minor omissions, they are as follows:

Flaubert, Gustave: aesthetic mysticism; alleged sadism; artistic intransigence; attitude to marriage; castration complex; celebrity and influence; chevalier de la Légion d'honneur; death; debts; dogs; fatness; hallucinations; interest in history; masturbation; modernity; pleasure taken in books; pleasure taken in travelling; realism; recitations; romanticism; sexual abstinence; sexual initiation; sexual passion; syphilis; use of prostitutes; views on book illustrations.

Flaubert also might have argued against spoiling the effect of such a deliciously incriminating catalog with the clutter of elaboration.

In February of 1848, Flaubert traveled to Paris from his native Rouen to join, or at least to observe, the so-called beautiful revolution. This insurrection of workers and enlightened bourgeois against the aristocracy was fomented by an alliance of socialists, liberals, and Romantic intellectuals (Lamartine was one of its leaders), and, without much bloodshed, it toppled the corrupt regime of King Louis Philippe, instituting the Second Republic—a period of giddy political reform and debate on the Social Contract. Flaubert had just turned twenty-six. He had given up his law studies and had seen something of the world. His father and sister had recently died. He had also embraced his vocation, though its path was obscure. Having scuttled several earlier fictional projects, he was deep into a visionary tale set in the fourth century—*The Temptation of Saint Anthony*. "We think you ought to throw it into the fire and never mention it again," said his friends and lifelong literary confidants Louis Bouilhet and Maxime Du Camp when he read them the manuscript. (Flaubert would always be a frugal recycler. He drafted the saint's history at least three times, and the definitive version—his mature view of martyrdom—was published in 1874.)

The pleasures of Flaubert's intense masculine friendships helped to relieve his periodic fits of boredom and gloom, but he still considered "the great event of his life" to have been his encounter, at fourteen, with the maternally lovely older woman—Elisa Schlésinger—who inspired the character of Mme. Arnoux in *The Sentimental Education*. If meeting her was the high point of his youth, its nadir was the onset, at twenty-two, of a malady that Flaubert would always refer to evasively as "my nervous attacks." His father, a celebrated surgeon, had recognized the symptoms—hallucinations, convulsions, migraines, blackouts, disturbances of vision, and "cerebral congestion"—and had treated Gustave with the only palliatives then known: regular bloodletting and mercury massages bolstered by a regimen of swimming and a restricted diet. Neither the patient nor his family would ever admit the truth: that Flaubert had epilepsy.

He was supposed to avoid violent stimuli, but when news of the republican insurrection reached Rouen, he couldn't resist the chance, as he put it, "to watch the riot 'from the artistic point of view.' " Bouilhet came with him, and they met Du Camp in Paris. There wasn't anything dramatic to see, so they went to dinner at their favorite restaurant. At the door of Du Camp's apartment, they heard gunfire but mistook it for fireworks, and missed the massacre taking place a hundred yards away, on the boulevard des Capucines. They spent the evening listening to Bouilhet recite his poetry. The next morning, they were able to witness a little picturesque street fighting around the Palais-Royal, and Flaubert and Du Camp (they had lost Bouilhet in the melee) were among the first new "citizens" to tour the liberated Tuileries. At this point, Wall says, the royal apartments were still intact, the crowd was in a festive mood, and two stout apostles of the people sat cheerfully at the king's table finishing his breakfast. But, as the palace wine cellars were emptied, their contents fueled a spree of looting and vandalism. "Feeling uncomfortably and identifiably bourgeois," the friends retreated, though they managed to talk a mob out of executing some prisoners. Decades later, Flaubert recalled these scenes from 1848 in the dénouement of the *Education*. He repudiated all parties, right and left, and, with them, the naïveté of his generation. But he reserved his most unbridled contempt for the Jacobin sanctimony of the ideologues and "speechifiers." Du Camp, deeply influenced by the account, remarked in his memoirs that revolution is always "initiated by simpletons, helped along by fools, pushed through by rogues, then taken over by the opportunists."

Their age of disaffections was still remote when Flaubert and Du Camp—who had exchanged friendship rings in a spirit of manly Hellenic devotion—left France, in October of 1849, for eighteen months of vagabondage in the Romantic holy lands of southern Europe and the Middle East. Wall gives the flavor of their journey to the Orient in a gamy little inventory of the souvenirs that Flaubert shipped home:

> All the gazelle skins and the lizard skins had been devoured by worms; the pots of ibis . . . broken in transit; and the Nubian garments (female) were horribly rancid. But many other items . . . had happily survived . . . Hashish, "something special" from Cairo. One small crocodile, Nubian, embalmed. Ten feet of gold-embroidered fabric (wool and silk) from Beirut. Rosaries, eight dozen, from Jerusalem. One rose, ditto, blessed on the Holy Sepulchre . . . Marble from the Temple of Apollo, one piece . . . Flowers, for Louis Bouilhet, picked from just by the door of a brothel in Pompeii.

Sated with sublimity and degradation, the adventurers returned to sit by the fire, dreaming, as Flaubert put it, "about hairless cunts." Or at least that's what he did. He would always suffer, Wall writes, from the indignity of being that absurd creature, "a romantic anarchist with a modest private income," and this costly expedition had depleted his capital. Du Camp, heir to a fortune, repaired to the well-furred lairs of Paris.

The Second Republic was short-lived. In 1851, it fell to the coup d'état of "the people's prince," Louis Bonaparte, who had been democratically elected president of France by five and a half million newly enfranchised (male) citizens, including peasants and workers. He quickly became a reactionary tyrant. "The Second Empire was the ridiculous, Ruritanian outcome of three exhausting, audacious years of political experiment," Wall writes. "Pedantic censorship to crush the disobedient, lavish patronage to reward the compliant—these were the blunt instruments of the state's cultural policy. Flaubert endured the full force of both. He was to be persecuted and patronised in almost equal measure."

Nearly thirty, Flaubert had just begun writing *Madame Bovary*. He spent the next four and a half years living with his widowed mother and orphaned niece in the family manor at Croisset, on the banks of the Seine south of Rouen. The lamp in the window of his study became a beacon to the rivermen. Like Penelope, he worked through the night, mostly unraveling. The book was composed, Flaubert said, at the rate of "five hundred *irreproachable* words a week" and published in six installments in Du Camp's literary journal, the *Revue de Paris*. They were read as avidly by the imperial police of Napoleon III as by the thousands of stifled provincial housewives—*les bovarystes enragées*—who saw themselves as Emma.

In 1857, after much intrigue and publicity—all of it a vile distraction, in Flaubert's view—he was prosecuted by the state for "grossly offending against public morality, religion, and decency." To his lawyer, he declared himself "puzzled as to the nature of my misdeed":

> Sincere books may sometimes have a certain salutary pungency. Personally I deplore . . . those sugary confections which readers swallow without realizing that they are quietly poisoning themselves. It had always been my belief that the novelist, like the traveller, enjoyed the liberty to describe what he saw. Following the example of many others, I could have chosen a subject drawn from the "exceptional" or ignoble ranks of society. I chose, on the contrary, from among the most prosaically ordinary . . . Readers in search of lascivious material . . . will never progress beyond the third page of what I have written. The serious tone will not be to their taste. People do not go to watch surgical operations in a spirit of lubricity.

"The son and brother of famous doctors," Sainte-Beuve wrote in his often quoted review of *Madame Bovary*, "Gustave Flaubert wields the pen like a scalpel." Wall, for his part, is smitten unapologetically by the doctor-father's greatness of character and detects, "beneath the brilliant, educated surface" of his mind, "the same tension, between explicit impersonality and unspoken compassion [that] animates the mature style of his son." Flaubert also happens to have been the child of a surgeon's niece, Caroline Fleuriot, but Wall manifests an odd and hostile incuriosity about her. Except to denigrate

Mme. Flaubert as "glacial," "querulous," and "coldly aristocratic," he treats her as a cipher. Yet Gustave lived with his "Maman" for most of his life. In a certain sense, he inherited her "cult of form," as Sand describes Flaubert's true religion. He respected her advice and depended upon her purse. She provided him with many kinds of comfort and containment. Upon her death, in 1872, Flaubert realized, he told Sand, "that my poor dear mother was the person I have loved most. It feels as though a piece of my guts has been torn out."

Flaubert and his two siblings, Achille and Caroline, spent their earliest years in a wing of their father's hospital, the Hôtel-Dieu, a labyrinthine public institution. Dr. Flaubert's dissection room looked onto the family's garden, and, by climbing the trellis and clinging to the vines, Gustave and his sister could see the corpses laid out, abuzz with flies, and their father standing above them with a sharpened blade. At the age of five or six, he told Sand, he had wanted to " 'send my heart' to a little girl I was in love with (I mean my actual heart). I could see it on a bed of straw, in a hamper, a hamper full of oysters." In the same period, the Flauberts employed a fetching, "simple-hearted" peasant nursemaid called Julie. Fetching, simple-hearted peasant nursemaids seem to occupy an inordinately prominent place in French literature and biography. Julie (not her real name, she said) liked to overexcite her pet, "Monsieur Gustave," with amorous kisses and fairy tales of the grimmer, more fabulous variety. She also told him—dubiously, considering her station—that she had once spent an entire year reading in bed. "All our lives we still smell of our nurse's milk," Flaubert wrote. In his case, however, the smell of childhood was of a sunlit garden, *cuisine bourgeoise*, and a warm, lactating breast mixed with blood and rotting flesh.

By the time of the *Madame Bovary* trial, Flaubert, at thirty-five, was prematurely decrepit. He would always tower above his contemporaries—he was over six feet tall—but he had lost the striking Apollonian beauty of his youth to the Nubian desert sun; to a sedentary life; to his venereal souvenirs from the dives of Esneh; to an excessive fondness for his pipe; and to the periodic attacks of epilepsy that, with syphilis, probably killed him. He had become a nearly bald and paunchy giant with a heavy, saturnine countenance chronically plagued, as was his body, by eczema and boils—the sort of man, he once joked, whom "whores wince at when it comes to the shagging."

Not every woman winced, however. It is true that Flaubert was celibate by choice for long periods; that he never consummated his greatest love (for Mme. Schlésinger); and that masturbation—the vice of the self-employed—was his most reliable source of release. But Flaubert also dallied with housemaids, actresses, artists' models, society hostesses, and the English governess of his niece, Caroline. The story of his longest, most flamboyant affair has probably enthralled more readers than any of his obscurer fictions, and, while this irony might or might not have amused him, it certainly would have confirmed his opinion of the book-buying public.

Wall describes the mistress in question, who was eleven years Flaubert's senior, in the style of the *Dictionary of Received Ideas*. Louise Colet: "Socialist-feminist writer . . . victim of much misogynist ridicule, notoriously vain and spiteful. An impossible person." She and Flaubert were thus ideally suited to drive each other crazy, and they did. At the beginning, his frustrated ardor responded ecstatically to her vitality. "You would breathe love into a dead man," he told her. He paid her the compliment, which she resented, of using her the way he used his most intimate male friends, as a sounding board for his work in progress and his literary enthusiasms. ("So what the devil do you want me to talk to you about if not Shakespeare?") But she was more interested in flowery raptures and perhaps a baby. Quite soon, Gustave was correcting her "illusions" about him—"You deserved better"—and then he took to shouting, as if at someone stone deaf, that for him love could never be "the main dish of existence."

A pious utopian (bleeding hearts are a leitmotif of Flaubert biography), Louise objected, Wall writes, to "Flaubert's 'aristocratic ideas' about women," and she complained that his mockery had killed her love. Confident about her looks ("My bust . . . and arms are extremely beautiful . . . My nose is charming . . . my legs are perfect") and their effect on men, she had always been generous with her favors. But she cherished the touching hope of marrying well—indeed, of marrying Flaubert—and she didn't like being treated "as a woman of the lowest order." The passionate sincerity with which, at first, he defended himself against her accusations and demands gave way to frigidly ironic politeness and, as time passed, to exasperated brutality: "If you could have been content with gallantry spiced up with a little sentiment and a little poetry, perhaps you would not have met with this fall which has caused you so much suffering." Even then, she was impossible to shake off.

The egomania of Louise Colet, unlike the egomania of Gustave Flaubert, was so unpolluted by self-consciousness that it achieves a certain comic grandeur. She lived in Paris on the margins of the demimonde, dependent on a series of celebrity protectors (Alfred de Musset, Alfred de Vigny, and Victor Cousin, among others), and valiantly eked out a debt-ridden living, like Mlle. Vatnaz in *The Sentimental Education*, by contributing to bluestocking journals, writing about fashion, and composing mawkish verse that she proudly sent to her paramour, who—ever incorruptible—felt morally obliged to savage it: "Do not imagine you can exorcise what oppresses you in life by giving vent to it in art." For nearly a decade, on and off, Louise and Gustave met every few months for what he was pleased to call a "big fuck," usually at a cheap hotel near the railway station in Mantes, a town conveniently situated halfway between their two abodes. ("O bed! If you could speak," Louise exclaims in one of her poems, a twelve-part opus.) These erratic trysts were hardly enough to gratify a woman of her socio-literary aspirations. While she obsessed about meeting Flaubert's mother, pined for his devotion, griped about his ingratitude, schemed to arouse his jealousy, bristled at his insistence on coitus interruptus, and sent him a lock of Chateaubriand's hair, he toyed with her feelings in immortal epistolary prose laced with quite a bit of infantile whining. "You have hurt yourself on the secrets of my heart," he chided her. And he compared himself to an angry leper turning against the misguided do-gooder who stops to dress his sores.

Flaubert was acquitted of the charges against him in the case of Emma Bovary. In certain quarters—having been cast as the Ted Hughes of the nineteenth century—he has never been acquitted of the charges against him in the case of Louise Colet. In one respect, perhaps, justice was served divinely: wherever posterity entertains the great man, his ex-girlfriend is invited. But "with [her] passing," Wall writes, "some portion of Flaubert's inner life disappears from view . . . A new, unexpected, public figure now enters the scene . . . a man of the salon and the boulevard, master of intrigue, expert in 'the art of shaking hands,' an author indeed."

Even before *Madame Bovary* was finished, Flaubert had warned his friends that he was feeling "a need for immense epics." He yearned for a vacation from the austerity of his style and the claustrophobia of his subject matter, and now he was free to take one. In 1858, he spent six weeks touring the ruins of Carthage and enjoying the taverns of Tunis (and perhaps its male brothels—his letters refer to them in passing). When he returned, he began to distill his impressions of the trip and his avid reading of ancient history into *Salammbô*, the kind of febrile costume drama his friends had once urged him to feed to the fire. Fastidiously documented tales of half-dressed pagan practitioners of human sacrifice sold well, and this redolent "stew" of barbaric horrors, perversities, and sacred rites was the most popular of Flaubert's novels among his contemporaries. It became a "cult book" to the decadents, then an opera, and inspired a school of kitschy salon art, most of it featuring some version of a dusky princess in deshabille posed ecstatically with a snake. When the manuscript of *Salammbô* was nearly completed, Flaubert invited a small party of friends, including the prissy Goncourt brothers, to a private reading—or, rather, a declamation, for he liked to bray his work at the top of his lungs—that lasted for ten hours. "To mark the occasion," Wall writes, "a special Oriental dinner was to be served. The menu included 'human flesh, brain of bourgeois and tigress clitorises sautéed in rhinoceros butter.' "

Corruption and hypocrisy, the former as lavish as the latter was rank, were the hallmarks of the Second Empire, and the same regime that had prosecuted the obscure degenerate responsible for *Madame Bovary* now feted the best-selling *érudit* who had conceived *Salammbô*. The emperor's witty cousin Princess Mathilde, whose nickname was Notre Dame des Arts, asked him to her Wednesday receptions, and their friendship generated a correspondence that was ardent though high-minded on both sides. The courier who delivered her dinner invitations, in a uniform "bristling with medals," Wall notes, "always made a great impression on Flaubert's Parisian concierge."

At the princess's mansion on the rue de Courcelles, Flaubert was introduced to the empress Eugénie, who asked his permission to copy one of Salammbô's costumes for a ball gown. He also met the czar of the Russians ("a slob," he told George Sand) and many other literary and imperial luminaries. "Elegantly dressed and copiously perfumed," Wall writes, and "joking that he looked like Almanzor, the worst of de Sade's old aristos," Flaubert eventually penetrated even the royal country house at Compiègne. As he paid his respects to the emperor, he must have recalled—with what bemusement?— that remote banquet of impudence at the Tuileries in 1848. Later, he would use his influence as a courtier to dispense patronage, fixing lawsuits and securing commissions for his friends. And in August of 1866, he received—ostensibly for *Salammbô* but surely also for deploying his powers to make bears dance—the Legion of Honor. I agree with Wall that "the last word" on the paradox of what Flaubert called his "prolonged moral cohabitation with the bourgeois" should be his: "Legion of Honor, Medal of the: To be sneered at, even though you rather covet one."

In the fourteen years left of his life—he died in 1880—Flaubert consorted with the friends he deserved: Turgenev, Zola, Maupassant, and Sand. But Louis Bouilhet died in 1869, a few months before *The Sentimental Education* was published, and Flaubert mourned the loss not only of a man he had loved for over twenty years but of "my midwife" and "my compass." Afflicted by syphilis, and perhaps even more so by the remedies prescribed for it, his health declined. France declared war on Prussia, and the ignoble defeat and capture of Napoleon III at Sedan was followed by a murderous civil uprising. "I feel we are entering into darkness," Flaubert prophesied to Sand. "Perhaps race wars are going to begin again? Over the next hundred years we shall see several million men killing each other at a single sitting. All of the Orient against all of Europe, the old world against the new." Then he added, typically, "Why not?"

In 1875, the brothers Flaubert discovered that their nephew-in-law, Ernest Commanville—a quintessential Second Empire speculator and profiteer—had accumulated debts of one and a half million francs. In an attempt to avert the ruin of his niece, Flaubert sacrificed his inheritance. Early the next year, he learned that Louise Colet had died. That summer, Sand succumbed to stomach cancer at Nohant. "My heart is becoming a necropolis," Flaubert told Princess Mathilde. He and Sand had exchanged visits to Nohant and Croisset, and some of the most eloquently fraternal letters on the métier of literature ever written, but they had never ceased to argue about his artistic "intransigence" and her metaphysical "idealism." In one of their last sallies, she begged him—because "you *must* have a success"—to write something a large public could love. "Retain your cult for form," she said. But "don't hold true virtue to be a cliché in literature." He replied that he had begun a humane "little work" that would show her "I am not as obstinate as you think."

In writing *A Simple Heart*, his tribute to Sand—a story that makes a true virtue of love but refuses to derive any moral from it—Flaubert briefly experienced a buoyancy he had rarely known and would never recover. It was midsummer, and he was living at Croisset. In the heat of August, he swam in the Seine, parsing phrases in his head, and his sentences came back to him once he fell asleep, rolling "like the chariots of some Roman emperor, and they wake me with a start by . . . their endless rumbling." He had recently brought his old nurse Julie, now ancient and blind, to live in the country with him. She enjoyed the air, and a child led her around the garden. The week she arrived, Flaubert had also acquired a stuffed parrot—his model for Félicité, Loulou in the tale. It stood on his writing table and stared at him through a glass eye. "The sight of the thing is beginning to annoy me," Flaubert told his niece. "But I'm keeping him there, to fill my mind with the idea of parrothood."

—May 6, 2002

Where There's a Will

On February 17, 1936, *Time* ran a cover story about the Fourth Winter Olympics, which Adolf Hitler had inaugurated earlier that month in Garmisch-Partenkirchen, a German ski resort near the Austrian border. The summer games, Olympiad XI, were to open on August 1 in Berlin, and the Führer had given Leni Riefenstahl virtual carte blanche to film them. Her debut as a director, with *The Blue Light* (1932), a fairy tale set in the Dolomites, had excited his admiration. So had her dishevelled beauty: she had cast herself in the starring role of Junta, a mountain nymph and outcast doomed by her purity. Riefenstahl had subsequently proved to be an epic propagandist with *Triumph of the Will*, a celebration of the 1934 Nazi Party rally in Nuremberg, and she had gone to Garmisch in part to observe an Olympic documentary being made by Carl Junghans, in preparation for her own *Olympia*. But she was also there to bask in the sunshine of celebrity.

At thirty-three, Riefenstahl was a strikingly attractive if hectic figure, with dark hair, chiseled features, and an obsidian gaze intensified by eyes set slightly too close together. Their look of adoration in the Führer's presence, and (as her rivals saw it) his indulgence of her every whim, fueled rumors of a Valhallan romance, which heightened curiosity about her in Germany and abroad. *Time* might have devoted its cover to a Winter Olympian like Sonja Henie, the Norwegian figure-skating champion, but the building controversy over the August games, which represented a windfall of legitimacy for the

Reich, decided the editors on a more electric candidate: "Hitler's Leni Riefenstahl." The sensational portrait that they chose, a departure from the usual head shot of a statesman or grande dame, is reproduced in a first-rate new biography of Riefenstahl, by Steven Bach, *Leni: The Life and Work of Leni Riefenstahl* (Knopf), though without mention of the photographer, Martin Munkacsi.

Munkacsi (1896–1963) was a Hungarian Jew who is widely credited with inventing modern photojournalism and with reinventing fashion photography in the same dynamic mold. Like Riefenstahl, he was a consummate stylist obsessed with bodies in motion, particularly those of dancers and athletes, and in 1930, some thirty years before Reifenstahl "discovered" the comely and artistic Sudanese people she called "my Nuba," Munkacsi returned from an assignment in Africa with a picture—of three naked boys running into the water— that became iconic, particularly to his disciple Henri Cartier-Bresson. The Nazi superstar and the Jewish émigré met at least once before the race laws precipitated his departure for New York in 1934, and they had much in common, including international prestige and a penchant for self-mythologizing. But the source of rapture in Munkacsi's pictures is freedom. In Riefenstahl's, it is idol worship.

One of Riefenstahl's most cherished ambitions, ironically, was a Hollywood career like that of Munkacsi's fellow émigré Marlene Dietrich, and she clung to this fantasy tenaciously even after Kristallnacht, in November 1938, which derailed what was supposed to have been a triumphal cross-country American publicity tour with *Olympia*. Upon docking in New York and hearing the news, she refused to believe it, and dismissed the hostility that greeted her at nearly every stop as a plot fomented, she told an interviewer on her return, "by the Jewish moneymen."

After the war, Riefenstahl was vehement that not only had she "thrown no atomic bombs"; she had never "spoken an anti-Semitic word." She lamented the fate of her Jewish friends in the film industry while claiming, on the one hand, that she had been ignorant of the Reich's racial policies and, on the other, that she had protested them personally to the Führer. Bach offers considerable evidence to the contrary, as does Jürgen Trimborn, the author of *Leni Riefenstahl: A Life* (Farrar, Straus and Giroux), translated by Edna Mc-

Cown. Both cite a letter first published thirty years ago in a biography of Riefenstahl by Glenn Infield in which Riefenstahl appeals to her friend and admirer Julius Streicher, the editor of *Der Stürmer* and the most fanatic anti-Semite in a crowded field (he was hanged for his war crimes in 1946), for help with, as she puts it, the "demands made upon me by the Jew Béla Balázs." Balázs, Riefenstahl's dramaturge and co-screenwriter on *The Blue Light*, was an avant-garde film critic who had also adapted Brecht's *Threepenny Opera* as a screenplay. She expunged his name from the credits so that a *judenrein* (Jew-free) version of the film could be released, and Balázs, hearing of its success, wrote to her from exile in Moscow to ask for his deferred fee. It was an easy and no doubt gratifying minor task for Streicher to deprive him of it.

Despite Walter Winchell's memorable epithet for Riefenstahl— "pretty as a swastika"—she lacked the smolder of a putative rival like Dietrich, who, she might also have noted, could speak English. In her own country, however, Riefenstahl had become an important movie star in an indigenous Teutonic genre, the "Alpine film." Arnold Fanck, its leading proponent, scorned the decadent fictions that cosmopolites like Josef von Sternberg produced in the luxury of a big studio. He pioneered location shooting in extreme conditions and prided himself on authenticity, at least where daredevil feats of skiing and mountaineering were concerned. His actors were an elite fraternity of athletes who performed their own harrowing stunts, and Riefenstahl was the only woman among them. The six films, three silent ones and three talkies, that she made with Fanck between 1926 and 1933 were a showcase for her courage—if courage can be imputed to a nature that denies fear—in scaling glaciers without safety ropes and schussing down them. They were also the shop in which she served her apprenticeship for *The Blue Light*, a film with the unique distinction of having impressed not only Hitler but Chaplin.

Riefenstahl's acting roles, however, like her impetuous sexual adventures of the period, tend to blur. Beginning with Fanck, her fellow cast and crew members constituted a virile harem irresistible to an emancipated sultana inclined to take her pleasure where and with whom she chose (even if she later boasted of "my well-known, almost virginal sexual history"). The bruised egos that she left behind earned her an unsporting epithet, "the nation's glacial crevasse." And jealousy, perhaps, encouraged Fanck's habit of subjecting his star and muse, in repeated takes, to immersion in freezing water, near suffocation by avalanches, and the barefoot ascent of a sheer rock face. At least he respected her prowess. On the Nazi films, Bach writes, the supremely organized and imperious Riefenstahl "was competing with men she had displaced through a relationship with the Führer that invited speculation she actively encouraged," and who were "disposed to view her presence behind a camera as illegitimate no matter how she got there."

Considering that Munkacsi's *Time* portrait was taken before he left Germany, it encrypts a prescient reading of Riefenstahl's art and persona. She is posed in cross-country skis, appearing to ascend a slope dressed in nothing but a clingy bathing suit that flaunts the physique of a cartoon action heroine—all curves and muscle. This was the outfit, *Time*'s reporter wrote, that she liked to train in. Munkacsi photographed her from a low angle, so that her steely thighs and booted feet dominate the lower half of the frame, and its vertical composition draws the eye upward past the dark V of the crotch and the swell of the breasts to a determined chin. Fanck used the same aggrandizing camera angle in his signature panning shots of men on mountaintops, and Riefenstahl echoed him in her heroic iconography of the Führer. Had she been fully clothed, the picture might have made a travel poster for the pure and fit New Germany that Goebbels was promoting as Minister of Propaganda. But Riefenstahl's grandiosity is laid bare for the world to snicker at, all the more so as she doesn't seem to notice that Munkacsi has seduced her into modeling for the subtle parody of an aesthetic—her own—that he, like Susan Sontag, perceived to be "both prurient and idealizing," as Sontag wrote forty-five years later in her essay "Fascinating Fascism."

In 1936, Riefenstahl had two-thirds of her life yet to live. "I *am* the marathon," she declared, more prophetically than she knew, in the course of filming *Olympia*, and any writer who embarks on the grueling course of her biography deserves admiration simply for crossing the finish line. Trimborn, who set out long before Bach, is a university professor and film historian in Cologne. He interviewed Riefenstahl in 1997, when he was twenty-five, having already spent six years of "intensive labor" on the project, and he briefly entertained the quixotic hope of writing a definitive book with her blessing and collaboration. Unwilling to misrepresent himself as a hagiographer, he was doomed to fail, though his disappointment does not seem to have warped his fair-mindedness. But I also suspect that the seeming absence of a talent for seduction—he writes in the patient, tongue-biting monotone that one adopts sensibly with a hysteric—turned Riefenstahl off.

Trimborn's aim was to correct the murky published record and the "attitudes" of his compatriots. One has to admire the sniperlike precision with which he takes out fugitive falsehoods that have lived under cover for a century. His primary audience, however, was more familiar with, and thus perhaps less likely to miss, the kind of richly fleshed-out portraiture and social history that Bach—an experienced biographer, a former movie executive, and the author of a superior bestseller on filmmaking, *Final Cut*—is able to supply.

Helene Amalie Bertha Riefenstahl, a native of Berlin, was born in 1902. Her father, Alfred, a plumber who prospered in the sanitation business, was an autocratic paterfamilias in the classic mold. Leni, rather than her younger brother, Heinz, inherited his temperament. It gave her a lifelong aversion to bullying, though not when she was the one doing it. Alfred's wife, Bertha, a lovely seamstress much tried by her husband's tantrums, had once dreamed of an acting career and was vicariously invested in her daughter's. Bach offers fresh evidence for a rumor circulated by the intriguing Goebbels, among others, that Bertha's Polish-born mother was half Jewish. She died young, and Bertha's father married his children's nanny, whose name seems to have appeared on, and falsified, Riefenstahl's certificate of Aryan descent. The family owned a weekend cottage on the outskirts of Berlin, where young Leni swam and hiked and exercised a body that always gave her supreme delight. "I do not like civilization," she later told a journalist. "I like nature, pure and unspoiled."

No one could ever persuade Leni Riefenstahl that there was

something she couldn't do, and she made her mind up, in her late teens, to become a dancer. Her father tried everything he could to keep her off the stage, but, through an obstinacy like his own, she admits in her memoirs, she wore him down to the point that he rented a hall for her debut. Riefenstahl's dance teachers had warned her that, with a scant two years' training, she wasn't prepared to perform as a soloist, but she defied them, too. By then, she had done a little modeling, entered a beauty contest, and was shortly to pay her dues as a silent-movie starlet in a bare-breasted cameo. She had also decided to lose her virginity to a thirty-nine-year-old tennis star and police chief whom she didn't yet know, Otto Froitzheim. Riefenstahl recalled the tryst, which took place on his sofa, as "repugnant" and "traumatic" (though the affair lasted for years), and when it was over Froitzheim tossed her a twenty-dollar bill—in case she needed an abortion—which, Bach writes, was, within a few months, worth eighty-four trillion Deutsche marks.

In the meantime, Riefenstahl had found a rich admirer—a young Jewish financier, Harry Sokol—to bankroll a road show. With an arty program of her own device, she played some seventy engagements in seven months. It isn't fair to judge her talents on the basis of the stiff-necked Spanish dancing, leaden with vanity, that she does in *Tiefland*—her last feature, a melodrama based on the opera by Eugen d'Albert—because by then she was over forty and, by her own admission, too old for the part. One also can't say whether she could have achieved the international renown that she believed was just on the horizon, because a serious knee injury ended her tour. And the scrapbook of reviews that she collected did not include any of the critical passages that Trimborn supplies. Instead, as she exulted in her memoirs, "Everywhere I went I experienced the same success—which transcends words."

Without her beauty, Riefenstahl might yet have accomplished something notable, although the career she forged is inconceivable without it. She had neither scruples nor—in the absence of an intellect, an education, or social connections—much of a choice about using her looks as a calling card. Fanck and Hitler were both prepared to be smitten before she took the initiative to arrange the meetings that would change her life. Though Fanck was originally skeptical of her inexperience, Hitler's enthusiasm, at least according to Riefenstahl, was unreserved from the beginning. In May of 1932, two months after *The Blue Light* was released, he summoned her to a village on the North Sea and, in the course of a long walk on the beach, effused about her grace. He also, she claimed, made an awkward sexual advance and announced impulsively that, if he came to power, "you must make my films."

Though the pass was, almost surely, a fantasy (even in 1936, *Time*'s reporter discreetly describes the Führer as "a confirmed celibate"), the job offer wasn't, and no director in history was more lavishly subsidized or indulged by her producers than Riefenstahl was by Hitler. His first commission was for the Nazi Party rally film *Victory of Faith* (1933), a clunky practice run for *Triumph of the Will* that was conveniently made to disappear, along with the porcine co-regent on the dais with Hitler—the leader of the brownshirts, Ernst Röhm, whom Hitler had had assassinated seven months after the premiere. *Day of Freedom*, which Riefenstahl denied having directed, until 1971, when a copy surfaced, was a twenty-eight-minute afterthought to *Triumph of the Will*, intended to placate the Wehrmacht. (Footage of the resurgent German Army was conspicuously missing from both rally films, in part because they were finished before Hitler formally renounced the Treaty of Versailles.) *Olympia* is a hybrid: servile to Fascist ideals in some respects, defiant of them in others— particularly in the radiant closeups of Jesse Owens, America's black gold medallist. It was marketed as an independent production, though it was financed by a shell company and paid for entirely by the Reich. Rainer Rother, the author of an authoritative filmography published five years ago, points out that the closing sequence of Carl Junghans's documentary on the Winter Games—a slow-motion montage of ski jumpers—was shot by the same inventive cinematographer, Hans Ertl (one of Riefenstahl's former flames), who shot the slow-motion montage of divers that ends *Olympia*. But even if Riefenstahl cavalierly appropriated imagery and techniques, and profited from the priceless gift that Hitler and history had given her—of a duel between the designated champions of good and evil—her use of multiple stationary and moving cameras, and her inspired placement of them (underwater; in trenches and dirigibles; on towers and saddles; or worn by the marathon runners in their prerace trials), brought a revolutionary, if not strictly documentary, sense of immediacy to the coverage of sporting events.

In the course of a dark century, Riefenstahl seems to have suffered at least one spasm of something like doubt, and the moment was captured in a photograph. When Hitler invaded Poland, on September 1, 1939, she mustered some of her most seasoned technicians into a combat-film unit. They left for the front about a week later, reporting for duty "on Hitler's orders" to the small, predominantly Jewish town of Końskie. Waking under fire the next morning, September 12—the day the Reich's news bureau promised a solution to "the Jewish problem in Poland"—Riefenstahl was on hand to witness an improvised beginning to the exterminations. Claiming that Polish partisans had killed a German officer and four soldiers, the occupying troops herded a Jewish burial detail to the main square. When the soldiers guarding the gravediggers began to kick and club them into the pit, Riefenstahl tried to intervene, she said, but they turned on her with cries of "Get rid of the bitch." Bach writes, "An amateur photographer captured her distraught expression."

The subsequent massacre at Końskie left a toll of thirty victims. An eyewitness testified that Riefenstahl had a "sobbing fit" when she saw the Wehrmacht open fire on civilians, and she later claimed to have been "so upset" by this experience that she asked for permission to abandon her assignment and return to Berlin. In reality, however, she hitched a ride on a military plane to Danzig, where she lunched with Hitler (he expressed "shock and anger" at the story, she said) and accepted his invitation to hear the victory speech in which he blamed England for the war.

Riefenstahl never made another Nazi propaganda vehicle. She grappled for a while with a project long dear to her heart—a film version of Kleist's *Penthesilea*, starring herself in the title role of an Amazon queen. Hitler had promised to finance this epic from his privy purse, but it foundered, Bach writes, on the absence of a coherent script, Riefenstahl's inability to create one without the help of a collaborator like Balázs, and the outbreak of war. *Tiefland*—a sappy flop

that tells the story of a Spanish village oppressed by its cruel lord—
was the production she turned to. There would be little reason to recall it if the logistical challenges of filming abroad had not forced her
to re-create her Iberian sets on German soil and to find some
swarthy-looking peasant extras to lend her the rude eloquence of
their physiognomies. Handily, the Nazis had rounded up the German
Sinti and Roma and interned them in "collection camps" while they
debated how to annihilate them. Riefenstahl later denied having visited the camps, but there was no denying that ninety-one selected
prisoners, including children, worked without wages on the film and
were returned to the camps when their scenes were done. After the
war but before her de-Nazification hearings—which remarked on her
lack of "moral poise" and her Nazi "sympathies" but cleared her of
crimes—she sued the publisher of the German magazine *Revue*,
which reported the story of the *Tiefland* extras, most of whom died
at Auschwitz. With courtroom sympathies on the director's side, the
defendant was found guilty of libel. In the 1980s, however, Nina
Gladitz, a documentary filmmaker, located a few of the extras who
had made it out alive. They testified that Riefenstahl, accompanied by
a police escort, had indeed chosen them herself, and had seen the living conditions to which they were condemned.

Riefenstahl survived the debacle that her idol wreaked upon humanity to be reborn, in late middle age, as an amateur (or, according to
the professionals, pseudo) ethnographer, in the Sudan. In exchange
for beads and oil, but also apparently with a measure of good will,
the Nuba let her photograph their ceremonial dances and wrestling
matches and rituals of body painting and scarification. (When they
didn't, she used a telephoto lens.) Those beautifully composed and
reverential pictures, taken between 1962 and 1977, are Riefenstahl's
African *Olympia*. To explain the absence of imperfect specimens from
her gallery, she later told an interviewer that old, ugly, or disabled
Nuba hid themselves in shame.

   The Nuba of Kau and *Last of the Nuba*, Riefenstahl's lucrative
coffee-table books, financed a new career. At seventy, claiming to be
fifty, she was certified as a deep-sea diver, and for the next thirty years

she trained her cameras on the peaceable kingdom of marine life. She still looked rather fetching in flippers and a wetsuit in her late nineties. In the course of an expedition back to the now war-torn Sudan, in 2000, she boogeyed with the Nuba maidens for a German documentary crew, and then barely survived a helicopter crash under fire from rebel troops. The pain of her physical injuries often required morphine, but the stab wounds of her persecutors, as she regarded nearly anyone who questioned her blameless version of the past, were harder to anesthetize. Yet the controversies had an upside: they were life support for her mythos.

Riefenstahl's more conscientious compatriots might stubbornly persist in treating her as a pariah, but, as she aged, a new and mainly American audience embraced her. It was led by celebrities from the entertainment world and by critics and artists who hailed her as a great auteur. Among her boosters were the organizers of the first Feminist Film Festival, in Telluride, who, in 1974, touted Riefenstahl as a role model for women directors, impervious to the irony that she had used her singularly privileged role to glorify a cult of violence and misogyny. L. Ron Hubbard briefly collaborated on a remake of *The Blue Light*. Mick Jagger invited her to take his picture with Bianca. Andy Warhol added her to his collection of divas. Madonna, then Jodie Foster, aspired to star in her life story, but Riefenstahl judged neither to be worthy. George Lucas praised her modernity and acknowledged the indebtedness of *Star Wars* to *Triumph of the Will*, particularly, Trimborn notes, in the Caesarean victory celebration that concludes Part IV. And, in 1998, Riefenstahl was one of the guests of honor at *Time*'s seventy-fifth-anniversary banquet, along with hundreds of other newsmakers from its cover. Unshackled at last from the caption of Munkacsi's photograph, she received a standing ovation. But perhaps as it died away she heard an echo of Streicher's paean to her in 1937: "Laugh and go your way, the way of a great calling. Here you have found your heaven and in it you will be eternal."

Riefenstahl devoted the better part of her last two decades to fortifying her legend and to suing her detractors (though not only them: she tried to disinherit her only living relatives, a niece and a nephew, with a spurious will that laid claim to her brother's estate).

Marcel Ophuls declined her invitation to celebrate her career in a television documentary, so she awarded the job to an unknown German, Ray Müller. He released *The Wonderful, Horrible Life of Leni Riefenstahl* to wide acclaim in 1993, and, seven years later, agreed to film her return visit to the Nuba. Though he himself narrowly escaped from the helicopter crash, she was furious that he hadn't caught her being pulled from the burning wreckage. It wasn't easy, she wrote at eighty-five, "to leave the present behind," but she managed to write an enthrallingly disingenuous seven-hundred-page memoir, taking her epigraph from a complaint of Einstein's: "So many things have been written about me, masses of insolent lies and inventions, that I would have perished long ago, had I paid any attention." Finally, having joined Greenpeace and celebrated her thirty-fifth anniversary with Horst Kettner, her handsome sixty-year-old companion, she died in bed, at a hundred and one—living, working, loving, lying, and litigating with prodigious vitality until her heart gave out.

Narcissism is often a kind of trance that insulates its subject from feelings of worthlessness, and Riefenstahl suffered periodic breakdowns and bouts of colitis at moments of loss or crisis that fractured her glassy-eyed assurance. Her love for the Führer was the paradigm of her self-entrancement, and she never disavowed it, although she later expressed some mild distress at the atrocities perpetrated in his name. Her life after the war would have been much easier if she had, but to do so was to betray something more essential than loyalty to a dead master. It was to endanger the ruthless suspension of self-doubt that her identity had, from childhood, depended on. And in one respect it was logical for her to love Hitler: he had the insight to recognize what her love could give him—a perfect reflection of itself.

Riefenstahl's "genius" has rarely been questioned, even by critics who despise the service to which she lent it. (Bach's cool resistance to the "often slavish lenience" of her rehabilitators is an exception.) Yet one has finally to ask if a creative product counts as a work of art, much less a great one, if it excludes the overwhelming fact of human weakness. That fact is the source of soulfulness and dramatic tension in every enduring narrative that one can think of. A seductively exciting surface, such as the morbid spectacle of a mass delusion, may distract from, but cannot insure against, a slack core, and in Riefenstahl's case a handful of sequences singled out for their formal beauty and a quality that Sontag calls "vertigo before power" have achieved an influence disproportionate to their depth or originality. They are played over and over, and many people, even film buffs, seem never to have seen—or are unaware of never having seen—Riefenstahl's documentaries in their entirety. But *Olympia* (three and a half hours long) and *Triumph of the Will* (two) both have their longueurs: endless scenes of shotputting and pole-vaulting in the former, of ranting and marching in the latter. In both, Riefenstahl relies heavily for her transitions on portentous cutaways to clouds, mist, statuary, foliage, and rooftops. Her reaction shots have a tedious sameness: shining, ecstatic faces—nearly all young and Aryan, except for Hitler's. If, by definition, the trailer for a so-called masterpiece can never be greater than the film itself, then Riefenstahl's legacy fails the test.

—March 19, 2007

III

EMINENT
VICTORIANS

"Reader, I Married Him"

The Reverend Patrick Brontë died at eighty-four, blind and child-less. His five daughters and one son had all predeceased him. Charlotte, the third born, survived the longest. Brontë blamed her demise on marriage—by which he probably meant sex—asserting that she wasn't strong enough for it. Perhaps he was right: modern biographers believe that the cause of Charlotte's death was emaciation and dehydration caused by three months of unremitting, violent morning sickness.

Charlotte Brontë had been married for less than a year—to her father's attentive but prosaic curate, Arthur Bell Nicholls—when she died. She was not quite thirty-nine, and had published three novels, under the pseudonym Currer Bell. The greatness of the first one, *Jane Eyre: An Autobiography* (1847), was acknowledged by readers as diverse as Thackeray, Dickens, George Lewes, and Queen Victoria, although Currer Bell achieved notoriety in almost equal measure with glory. "His" work was widely execrated for "coarseness," and the author, whoever he or she might be, was described as "soured . . . grumbling . . . alien . . . from society, and amenable to none of its laws." Matthew Arnold later complained that Bell's last novel, *Villette* (1853), was one of the most "hideously disagreeable books" he had ever read, and that "the writer's mind contains nothing but hunger, rebellion, and rage."

These charges expressed the discomforted fascination of her contemporaries with a Brontë heroine's sense of autonomy; her typical lack of gratitude toward her betters and benefactors, particularly those who were ordained; and, in the case of Jane Eyre, her "heathen passions" and the assertion of equality with a lover whose superior rank and reprobate past had both failed to intimidate her. "Do you think, because I am poor, obscure, plain, and little, I am soulless and heartless? You think wrong!" Jane storms at Mr. Rochester in a famous passage:

> I have as much soul as you—and full as much heart! And if God had gifted me with some beauty and much wealth, I should have made it as hard for you to leave me, as it is now for me to leave you. I am not talking to you now through the medium of custom . . . it is my spirit that addresses your spirit; just as if both had passed through the grave, and we stood at God's feet, equal—as we are!

The controversy aroused by the "Jacobinism" and "moral perversity" of *Jane Eyre* naturally intensified the public's curiosity about Currer Bell, who was variously suspected of being a fallen woman, a defrocked vicar, a gentleman and a lady working together, or an infatuated governess—perhaps William Thackeray's. (Thackeray, like Mr. Rochester, had a mad wife, and Charlotte, ignorant of this misfortune and grateful for his praise, had dedicated the second edition of *Jane Eyre* to him.) Harriet Martineau was so impressed by the description of Grace Poole sewing curtain rings that she wondered if Currer Bell might not be an upholsterer. It was appropriate, however, that Charlotte Brontë's readers should be obsessed with Currer Bell's identity. Identity is her own obsession, and she has a strikingly modern—embattled and internal—notion of it. She also puts the device of mistaken identity to a modern use. All her narratives and many of her finest letters are concerned with and really driven by the solitary struggle of an orphan—a Perdita—to repossess a lost birthright: not to a kingdom or a marriage portion but to a true self.

Charlotte Brontë's own sense of entitlement to a true self is what is most definitive, most glamorous, and most problematic about her, and about her heroines. A gypsy (Rochester in disguise) scrutinizes Jane Eyre's face and tells her, "That brow professes to say—'I can live

alone . . . I need not sell my soul to buy bliss. I have an inward treasure born with me, which can keep me alive if all extraneous delights
should be withheld.' " The provincial clergyman's mousy daughter
likewise knew (or professed to know) who she herself was—even if
she also took a perverse delight in being misjudged and underestimated. And the gauntlet that she throws down so defiantly but
yearningly to her heroes, suitors, friends, critics, readers, and biographers is the challenge to recognize her.

A Danish biographer I know once described his vocation to me by
saying, "I track the process of individuation to the point at which it
fails." That excellent definition of biography suggests why some glittering, eventful lives are in fact repetitive and depressing, and why
some chaste, deprived lives, like Charlotte Brontë's, are riveting. It's
the drama of individuation that gives a biography its suspense and cuts
through the trivia of a life to its vital mystery. In that respect, Charlotte Brontë and her family make exceptionally dramatic subjects, and
it is probably why their biographies are regularly rewritten.

The first biography of Charlotte Brontë was published in 1857
and is still in print, as a Penguin Classic. It was written by Elizabeth
Gaskell, who was one of Charlotte's few friends from the world of
the Victorian literary aristocracy. Novelists generally don't make
good biographers (novel-writing seems to be a work of high-minded
betrayal and biography a work of dirty-minded fidelity), but Mrs.
Gaskell is an exception. She has, as one would expect, a gift for the
pacing of a big nineteenth-century narrative: she has a mild and wise
precision of style, which complements her subject's vehemence, and
she champions Charlotte's "pure heart" without attempting to suppress the "circumstances [that] forced her to touch pitch." Her tolerance of paradox applies as much to her own character as to
Charlotte's. The respectable Mrs. Gaskell set out to vindicate Miss
Brontë of the charge that she was "coarse," despite admitting to the
reader that there was "coarseness here and there in her works, otherwise so entirely noble." She concluded that she could proceed only
by "withholding nothing," by laying the life "bare"—in other words,
by doing Charlotte literary rather than moral justice.

While Mrs. Gaskell's biography may have seemed bare to her contemporaries (she was pressured into revising and essentially bowdlerizing a subsequent edition), the next century could take a less defensive and restricted view of Charlotte Brontë. In 1967, Winifred Gérin published *Charlotte Brontë: The Evolution of Genius* (Oxford)—the standard against which all other modern Brontë biographies are measured. Gérin is definitive on Charlotte's childhood, and illuminating on that obscure process by which the roots of an artist's life take in their ideal nourishment of myths, values, images, and taboos. She writes with Brontëan fever, but, if her valuation of Charlotte's work is somewhat infatuated, her feeling for the woman isn't infatuated at all. Hers is precisely the sort of imaginative sympathy and penetration that Charlotte craved in a lover, created for herself in Rochester and M. Paul, but otherwise never found.

Close upon Gérin's heels came Margot Peters's *Unquiet Soul* (Doubleday, 1975). This is one of those rare distillations of a life that become works of literature in their own right, although in places, where the biographer turns letters into passages of dramatic dialogue, it seems a little too proprietary and novelistic. Peters belongs to a younger and more analytic generation of Brontë scholars, informed by feminism, and inclined to find Charlotte's rage "admirable" but not inclined, as Mrs. Gaskell was, to glorify her as a martyr. She is also a greater ironist than her predecessors: as much aware of the pressures that shape her own bias as of those—the extremes of "submission and revolt," in Jane Eyre's words—working on Charlotte.

Rebecca Fraser's *The Brontës: Charlotte Brontë and Her Family* (Crown, 1988) would deserve mention even if it were not the most recent entrant in the Brontë lists, published late last year. Like its subject, its author is the scion of an Anglo-Irish family in which everyone writes. Fraser's mother, Lady Antonia Fraser, and her grandmother Lady Longford have earned their eminence tackling grand, unwieldy British lives, which resemble the kind of dilapidated mansion a tenant with their sort of credentials may lease from the National Trust—if she promises to make it livable.

Rebecca Fraser's choice and treatment of her subject fit this pattern. Her scholarship is authoritative, and her style is fluent. The weakness of her biography is Fraser's reticence, or lack of curiosity, about those chambers of the life that don't have external windows—the chambers a biographer can enter only speculatively, through her subject's fiction, and through her own fears and experience. Neither Gérin nor Peters, I think, would have described one of Charlotte's most eloquently tormented outcries as "overwrought."

Like all changelings, the Brontë children grew up motherless, and with something more and less than a father: they had a *sire*. Patrick Brontë dominated their lives without having much to do with them on a daily basis. He shared his newspapers and literary reviews, and his passions for politics and the English language. They also inherited his brilliance, his contentiousness, and his misanthropic pride.

Of all the children, Emily was probably the most like their father. She had a bent for tyranny, which she exercised over the more anxious, less egotistical Charlotte; and their Belgian professor, M. Heger, asserted that, with her "powerful reason" and her "strong, imperious will," Emily "should have been a man." That isn't certain, though: it was profoundly daunting to be the son of a man like Patrick Brontë. The sisters fared much better than their volatile, red-haired brother, Branwell, who failed as a poet, a painter, a tutor, and a railway clerk, and eventually became a laudanum addict and an alcoholic.

Fraser tells us that Branwell was "considered destined for great things by his family," and that his father "sympathised with such ambitions—he had once had them himself." Patrick's own life, like Napoleon's (Napoleon was his contemporary) and like Jane Eyre's, was, as Charlotte puts it, that of a "lusus naturae"—a sport of nature. His family, the Bruntys, were peasant ditchdiggers and road menders who lived in squalor in Northern Ireland. Patrick managed, almost as incredibly as Bonaparte, to jump the tracks of his class. He escaped to Cambridge on a scholarship, and in England he embraced Tory politics and Evangelical Methodism, taking Holy Orders in 1806. In 1812, he courted Maria Branwell, the pious, intellectual daughter of a burgher from Penzance. Her family's acceptance of the penniless, obscure Brontë as a son-in-law testifies to the strength of his character and to the allure he had as one of the Church's most promising young preachers.

Both Patrick and Maria were impatient to marry, and they proceeded to have six babies in seven years, after which the exhausted Mrs. Brontë died, at thirty-eight. Her body was interred in the village church at Haworth, near Bradford, in Yorkshire, where her husband had just assumed the duties of "perpetual curate." Four years later, her eldest daughters, Maria and Elizabeth, aged twelve and eleven, were buried there, too. Branwell, Emily, and Anne Brontë, aged thirty-one, thirty, and twenty-nine, died within nine months of one another.

Haworth is now the Vatican City of the Brontë cult, and annually receives some two hundred thousand tourists and pilgrims. It was then an isolated hamlet whose drinking water was polluted by its cemetery. The curate ministered to a rough and inbred flock of millworkers, mill owners, and farmers. His living of two hundred pounds a year included a stone parsonage next to the church, with its back to the moors and surrounded by gravestones, at the top of the precipitous main street. Brontë sent out a few marriage prospectuses after his wife's death but failed to recruit a replacement for her, and lived out his days as a dyspeptic and eccentric widower, much respected by the parish. By day he went abroad, and by night he went to bed armed against the "Luddites," discharging the pistols he had slept with out the bedroom window.

Charlotte Brontë told Mrs. Gaskell, after a stay with her in Manchester, that going home to Haworth was a return to "barbarism, loneliness, and liberty." "Beautiful, benevolent Mrs. Gaskell, with her busy happy life," as Fraser calls her, felt sorry for her friend and considered her the prisoner of her father's egotism. She never quite understood the satisfaction Charlotte took either in Haworth itself or in her thralldom there to Mr. Brontë.

Beautiful, benevolent Mrs. Gaskell was also horrified by the accounts of the Gothic childhood that she pieced together from Charlotte's confidences and fiction. The children's maternal aunt had come to live with them, "bent on doing her duty by her nieces," which was to prepare them for "a life devoid of pleasures." The Methodist religious education that she gave them was a particularly "joyless exercise, tinged by the melancholy of her own dry temperament," and it apparently didn't make the impression it was intended to. When the ten-year-old Jane Eyre is asked by the rich hypocrite who runs the Lowood school if she understands how to avoid the burning pit, she replies, "I must keep in good health, and not die."

Under the circumstances, the children were fortunate that their aunt was intimidated by the "wildness" in their eyes, and that both she and their father were self-absorbed hypochondriacs who took their meals alone. The children wouldn't otherwise been able to gorge on Byron, to roam the moors, or to fantasize communally around the kitchen fire. Later, they paired off—Charlotte and Branwell, Emily and Anne—to write and illustrate their own gory, wanton, and heroic Byronic sagas. At the age of fourteen, Charlotte cataloged twenty-two volumes of her prose and poetry, each one an obsessively revised, minutely transcribed manuscript of between sixty and a hundred pages. It was only in her early twenties, according to Gérin, that Charlotte "began to realize that the atmosphere in which she had grown up, which had generated the excitement and heat of the fantasmal world of her childhood—the 'Burning clime' as she called it—was a serious threat to even a moderate expectation of happiness in a workaday world."

For Charlotte Brontë, a changeling princess from the kingdom of Angria (the setting of her sagas) who disliked children ("I find it so hard to repel [their] rude familiarity") and was destined to be a governess, hopes of job satisfaction were never very bright. In theory, at least, a private governess lived on equal terms with her employers, but in reality she was as much a glorified domestic as is her counterpart today, the au pair. "If teaching only were requisite," Charlotte told her friend Ellen Nussey, "it would be smooth and easy; but it is the living in other people's houses—the estrangement from one's real character . . . that is painful."

Emily, who was more like a Masai than like a Victorian maiden, was an even less likely governess than Charlotte. And as they entered their late twenties the sisters decided that their best chance to earn the money that would keep them from "slavery" was to found a girls' academy at Haworth—but they first had to finish their own educations. As it was more practical to do so abroad than in England, they eventually fixed upon a boarding school in Brussels, run by a well-reputed couple named Heger.

Had the Brontës been two provincial spinsters from Albany rather than from Yorkshire, their voyage to the Continent, their earnest desire for self-improvement, their disgust at and sense of superiority to Papist manners, and their curious relations with the Hegers would have made the stuff of a James novella—though James would have treated them more lightly and luxuriously than life or Charlotte did. Her version of the experience is the subject of *Villette*, which is one of the best studies of claustrophobia and depression in our literature. It is also a paradigm for the brilliant life made entirely of drab materials. As Tony Tanner explains the feat in his introduction to the Penguin edition, Brontë's fiction "constantly moves towards those moments when 'the boredom of living is replaced by the suffering of being.' "

Charlotte was continually being mistaken for a more committed radical than she ever was. She used fiction to repay her debts and to exact credit for what was owed to her by individuals and by society, and *Villette* shows her an honest bookkeeper, but one who is unforgiving and not a little self-congratulatory in her "truthfulness." Poor, sneaky Mme. Heger is pilloried as the devious, coldhearted, prying, complacent Mme. Beck, "a most consistent character; forbearing with all the world, and tender to no part of it." She is also divorced, by Charlotte, from her devoted husband. M. Heger is cast as Mme. Beck's "cousin," Paul Emanuel, who for most of the novel is relegated to the subplot—displaced from the romantic spotlight by that paragon of manly British virtue Dr. John. But wherever, molelike, M. Paul pokes through, he announces himself (usually by a fit of temper) to be the true hero. He is the only kind of hero Brontë has any use for: a great Recognizer, a sharp-eyed St. George who perceives that the dragon is only the perversity of the princess—that they are the same creature.

> "Que vous êtes dur, monsieur!" I [Lucy Snowe] said, affecting dejection.
> "One ought to be 'dur' with you" [M. Paul replies]. "You are one of those beings who must be *kept down*. I know you! I know you! Other people in this house see you pass, and think that a colourless shadow has gone by. As for me, I scrutinized your face once, and it sufficed."

Constantin Heger was in his early thirties when Charlotte enrolled at the pensionnat. He was an astute pedagogue who quickly took a connoisseur's interest in the Brontë sisters, esteeming Charlotte's character more highly but realizing that Emily had the greater mind. According to Fraser, his contemporaries thought of him as "an incomparable, almost charismatic teacher"; according to Peters, he was a "whirlwind of energy and imperiousness"; according to Charlotte, he was "a little black ugly being" with the "lineaments of an insane tom-cat"—just her type, and she was madly attracted to him. Mme. Heger understood the nature of the attraction, if Charlotte didn't, and she eventually managed to detach Miss Brontë from her establishment by means of Charlotte's own resignation; in the face of outraged protestations by Monsieur that Charlotte was needed; and without any suspicion by anyone except Charlotte that a ruthless campaign had been played out.

There has always been conjecture about Charlotte's relationship with M. Heger, fueled by her letters and by *Villette*—and anticipated almost clairvoyantly by Madame. She rifled the trash in her husband's study for the letters that the bereft, hysterical, and abject Charlotte wrote to her "master" from Haworth, and which he never answered but tore up. Madame then sewed the pieces together, and kept them as evidence that nothing *inconvenant* had occurred.

M. Heger himself later described his former pupil's "*pauvre coeur malade*," and then amended the phrase to read, more poetically, "*pauvre coeur blessé*." If you know where to look for the evidence, however, Mrs. Gaskell's biography confirms that he did conduct a kind of affair with Charlotte. It reproduces one of the exercises that she wrote for her professor in 1842, with his corrections in the margin, and there are few more erotic moments in any Brontë novel. One can sense, between the lines of a short French composition entitled "Portrait de Pierre l'Hermite," a young woman who thought of herself as "stunted" undressing before the first man able to perceive her beauty. M. Heger's response, conscious or not, is precisely the one to excite the greatest ardor and gratitude in return. He doesn't judge her the way the shallow Dr. John—"a smile so critical, so almost callous," playing on his lips—judges the actress Vashti, which is "as a woman." Monsieur judges her as "an artist." One could say, in fact, that Heger initiated Charlotte into the secret of her craft, which is to treat meaning like desire. "When you are writing," he exhorted her, "place your argument first in cool, prosaic language; but when you have thrown the reins on the neck of your imagination, do not pull her up to reason."

"What [was] the motivation of Currer Bell's novels, if not the *expectation of love*?" Gérin asks.

Well, there was Branwell. Writing distracted all three sisters from his pathetic disintegration. When they embarked on their careers as Currer, Ellis, and Acton Bell, he was involved with a married woman whose husband had dismissed him as their son's tutor, and he was asleep all day and drunk all night. (The woman's coachman periodically brought him drinking money.) Their brother's "illness" placed them and the parsonage under moral quarantine: they could hardly plan to advertise it as a girls' school. Then there was Mr. Brontë. His health and eyesight were failing; his income was burdened by Branwell's debts; and his morale was depressed by his having to stand guard over his son at night, lest he shoot himself. Under the circumstances, the daughters had to consider that the living might soon pass to the next incumbent, and they would be out on the moors. Finally, there was the prospect of their having to accept employment as governesses.

Emily's *Wuthering Heights* (considered, Peters tells us, "revolting, coarse, loathsome, and savage") and Anne's *Agnes Grey* ("commonplace") were published in 1847 by T. C. Newby, a vanity press, which had rejected Currer Bell's first novel, *The Professor*. Charlotte persevered, and found a sympathetic reader in W. S. Williams, at the house of Smith, Elder. She sent Mr. Williams the manuscript of *Jane Eyre* as soon as it was finished. He recommended it unconditionally to the publisher, George Smith, and Mr. Smith took it home with him for the weekend, turned away callers, ordered a sandwich for lunch, sat up that night to finish it, and wrote an acceptance letter to Currer Bell the next day.

As a type of Englishman—the gentleman publisher—George Smith has survived into this century, still ensconced in a Bayswater house among his charming things. Urbane in his tastes, bourgeois in his habits, he is a little soft and plump, but from bonhomie rather than effeteness. He cultivates his authors almost maternally but is hard-nosed about their contracts, and he is famously stingy with his employees. He is often seen with interesting older women but is obviously destined to marry the right kind of girl, and his true devotion is reserved for his mother, his wine cellar, and the family firm.

Mr. Smith became very attentive to Charlotte Brontë, whose success brought him considerably more profit, socially and financially, than it brought her. But she also genuinely fascinated him. He had been flabbergasted when she appeared in his waiting room, trembling and shabby, and introduced herself as Currer Bell. Her trust in his judgment flattered him; her inexperience excited his gallantry; and, despite their age difference (he was slightly younger) and her plainness, he found the same fire in her eye that was in her prose.

For her part, Charlotte enjoyed Smith's attentions, and even though she described the relationship to her friends as that of an older sister and a younger brother, she attached a certain romantic hope to it. One has the feeling, however, that Smith was ultimately too desirable to Charlotte. He was also, perhaps—as she suggests in the character of Dr. John—too conventional in his attitude toward women to be adequate as a Recognizer. Peters remarks, "His conclusion that Charlotte would have forfeited genius for beauty seems to bear out her characterization."

Charlotte's biographers should nevertheless be grateful to Smith, if for no other reason than that he managed to pry her loose from Yorkshire and so gave them a different sort of scene—something a little more *Vanity Fair*-ish—to write about. He took her to Edinburgh, an outing that excited a certain amount of gossip, and Charlotte stayed at the house in Bayswater as often as the Smiths (he and his mother) could entice her to London. She overcame her horror of self-display sufficiently to have a few decent dresses made for these forays into society, and at first she seemed eager to taste the pleasures that were served up to her: Thackeray's lectures (where she was lionized) and her first opera; visits to the Crystal Palace, the Royal Academy, and Parliament; a glimpse of her hero, Wellington, and tea with her heroine, Harriet Martineau; and encounters with Carlyle, Millais, Lewes, George Richmond, Lady Ritchie, Richard Monckton Milnes, and the Earl of Carlisle ("Will you permit me, as a Yorkshireman, to introduce myself?").

Thrilled at first to meet Thackeray, whom she worshipped, Charlotte had expected him to be purer, and was somewhat disappointed by his venality. She also got furious at him when he introduced her to his mother as Jane Eyre. And finally, unlike Jane, who had "desired . . . more of intercourse with my kind," Charlotte—pleading a headache or extreme timidity, and aloof to the point of rudeness—began refusing to enjoy her new connections. Their richness, literal and figurative, seemed to make her sick. When her hostess, at a loss to entertain her further, asked Miss Brontë to suggest her own program, Charlotte said she wanted to visit a mental hospital and a prison. Like her more direct refusals of fine food and company, this was a coded message of disdain, a way of dramatizing her ravenousness and her deprivation, which had spoiled more than her appetite.

"Anybody may blame me who likes," Jane Eyre declares. "I shall be called discontented. I could not help it."

Winifred Gérin was right after all about Currer Bell's motive for writing: the expectation of love. Matthew Arnold wasn't wrong about the contents of her mind: hunger, rebellion, and rage. Harriet Martineau didn't speak as a prude when she called Charlotte's heroines "morbid in passion." Rebecca Fraser objects not impertinently to her "hysterical prose." And Virginia Woolf, who writes about Charlotte's "genius" with greater intimacy and more fairness than anyone else, also gives the best account of its failure:

> It is clear that anger was tampering with the integrity of Charlotte Brontë the novelist. She left her story, to which her entire devotion was due, to attend to some personal grievance. She remembered that she had been starved of her proper due of experience—she had been made to stagnate in a parsonage . . . when she wanted to wander free over the world. Her imagination swerved from indignation and we feel it swerve. But there are many more influences than anger tugging at her imagination and deflecting it . . . We constantly feel an acidity

which is the result of oppression, a buried suffering smoulder-
ing beneath her passion, a rancour which contracts those
books, splendid as they are, with a spasm of pain.

That kind of rancor is a grandiose sense of entitlement which
sometimes takes the paradoxical form of what Rebecca Fraser calls
"furious, almost aggressive stoicism," although it is really a version of
the same romantic self-indulgence that destroyed Branwell. Yet if
rancor compromised the integrity of Brontë the novelist, it finally
didn't compromise the integrity of Brontë the woman. She realized
that the damage done to Perdita—to the one who has been humbled, repressed, robbed of her identity, and cheated of nurture—isn't
magically reversible. And she chose to face that reality, neither holding out for a romantic apotheosis, as Jane Eyre did, nor succumbing
to the bitterness of Lucy Snowe. So her life turns out to be more
courageous than her fiction.

Her bravest experiment may have been her nine months of marriage to her father's curate. Nicholls was a man of "feeling and sullen-
ness," of great tenacity and little imagination; a narrow-minded cleric
who would attempt to censor Charlotte's friendships and letters, but
also a reader who could laugh at her caricature of him in *Shirley*; a
lover who accepted temporary exile rather than renounce his suit,
even though on the day of parting he leaned against her gate "sobbing as women never sob."

Jealous as much of Charlotte's glory as of her virginity and her
usefulness to him, Mr. Brontë loathed the idea of the undistin-
guished Nicholls as a son-in-law. Nicholls, however, refused to be
discouraged by any insult or rejection that father *or* daughter meted
out to him. His persistence became almost a comic spectacle: a stern,
bigoted, literal, beef-and-pudding Puseyite storming the paternal
citadel to rescue a nearsighted, reluctant middle-aged intellectual en-
cumbered by migraines, anorexia, fevers, incipient tuberculosis, and
gum disease, not to mention desperate griefs and a great name.

Brontë's biographers have all given perfectly adequate descriptions
of Mr. Nicholls's character. None of them, however, has disclosed his
identity. It is now time to reveal that her bridegroom was the unvar-
nished "Truth" that Charlotte had always championed, solidly em-

bodied. He was "*le vrai*," as Flaubert (a fellow realist) enviously called it, from a safe distance, without the nerve for its clumsy, sincere embrace. "My destiny will not be brilliant . . . but Mr. Nicholls . . . offers a most constant and tried attachment." Mr. Nicholls also offered her an opportunity she had been waiting for and sublimating all her life: to defy, punish, and forgive her father for his indifference.

Rebecca Fraser wonders, with Mrs. Gaskell, what Charlotte Brontë's "transcendent grandeur" might have been. The real question—which Fraser's own sensible book leaves us to ponder—is what Charlotte Brontë would have made, as a woman and as a novelist, of ordinary happiness. That was the subject of a conversation Charlotte had with Mrs. Gaskell one leaden September afternoon in 1853 as they walked on the wild Penistone Moor together, shouting into the wind. Charlotte maintained, as she had in *Villette*, that some beings were born to suffer, and that it was nobler to "submit faithfully" to such a fate than to pine for a sweeter one. Firm in that conviction, she told Mrs. Gaskell she was "trying to school herself against ever anticipating any pleasure."

Mrs. Gaskell always conceded and admired Charlotte's superior "vehemence of power and nature." But she was one of those enviable and rare creatures who, at peace with themselves—equally unafraid to feel and able to reason—aren't seduced by depression. *Villette* worried her, and she tried to persuade Charlotte that happiness "comes only in *drams* to anyone."

Rebecca Fraser isn't seduced, either. She lacks Mrs. Gaskell's maturity as a psychologist; and, as the narrator of *The Brontës* lights her readers' way through a house she doesn't acknowledge to be haunted, she inevitably reminds one a little of "steady, reasonable," though oblivious, Nelly Dean, the caretaker at Wuthering Heights. In other respects, though, Fraser is Gaskell's rightful heir. "Beautiful, benevolent" Rebecca Fraser! She projects an assurance of her own place in the world which makes us weep over Brontë's struggle to the death with her estrangement.

—March 20, 1989

· TWO ·

Angels and Instincts

There used to be an exit off the expressway to Boston's Logan Airport marked MYSTIC RIVER BRIDGE. I passed the sign a thousand times when I was a student, and always wondered what made the river mystic. I assumed that it had something to do with Puritan theology—a passage to the afterlife. Not at all. According to historians, the explorers who first mapped the region either corrupted the Indian word for "great tidal stream"—Missi-tuk—or, and I prefer this explanation, they gave the river its name because they never were able to locate its source. A biographer cutting tracks through the backcountry of an artist's life in pursuit of its enigmas also discovers that there are rivers without a source. A protean talent is one of them. A capacity for happiness is another. In that sense, there is something doubly "mystic" about the career of Julia Margaret Cameron. She took up photography in 1864, at the age of forty-eight, having raised eleven children—five of her own, five orphaned relations, and a ravishing Irish beggar maid whom she employed as a model and married off in fairytale fashion to a gentleman. She taught herself to use a twelve-by-ten-inch sliding box camera and the volatile chemicals necessary to develop her own pictures. In a prolific career that lasted little more than a decade—while she was caring for an invalid husband and running a household on the Isle of Wight that was, in essence, a resort hotel for the Victorian intelligentsia—Cameron pioneered the close-up, experimented with soft focus, manipulated her negatives to produce painterly effects, and confirmed the legitimacy of the photographic portrait as a work of art. Although she never earned a living from her pictures (and didn't have to), she sold them widely and promoted herself with an entrepreneurial flair for hype. Her "aspirations," she told a friend, were nothing less than "to ennoble Photography." In retrospect, her immodesty strikes one as both just and endearing. Her subjects, however, like her children, servants, critics, and dealers, were often cowed by her. On one of her many studies of Tennyson, she inscribed a boast that would make a nice epitaph: "A column of grandeur—done by my will against his will."

A common trait of great talent in whatever sphere seems to be an exceptional tolerance for, or perhaps blindness to, self-contradiction. Cameron's work embodies the paradoxes of a nature that was tyrannical and benevolent, gushing and steely, flamboyantly eccentric and devoutly Christian. Her best portraits seem to challenge the Victorian pieties that her lesser work exalts. One might almost call her a closet feminist, except that she excluded women fairly systematically from her album of geniuses (Carlyle, Darwin, Herschel, Browning, Arnold, Trollope, and Longfellow, among others) and saw little interest in the face of any female older than eighteen. There was room in her pride for only one lioness: Julia Margaret Cameron.

The virtue of the lady was the collateral that secured the artist's freedom. Cameron's shooting ratio was about ten misty-eyed Madonnas to every Sappho, Hypatia, or Beatrice Cenci, but somehow the potent erotic undercurrent in her work was never perceived as an affront to respectability, and it still isn't. Blameless, dumpy Mrs. Cameron was as promiscuous, in her way, as a rake—flitting from one to another great man or pretty girl whom she just had to have. She staged love scenes between child models and posed them nude, then gave the photographs titles like *An Angel unwinged by your desire*. Yet, as far as I know, she has not been accused, as has her friend and contemporary Lewis Carroll (with whom she shared Alice Liddell), of latent pedophilia. Cameron managed the remarkable feat of accomplishing everything that convention expected of her as a mother and a matron without sacrificing any of the originality that she demanded of herself. And if one can believe the evidence—a big if, since the study of photography, like the practice of writing lives, instills in one a healthy skepticism toward the notion of objective truth—she was that rarest of creatures: a sovereign artist content with her lot as a little woman.

Cameron is "rediscovered" periodically, even though she is probably the most widely studied of photography's old masters, and her work never sinks from the radar screen of major collectors and institutions. The Art Institute of Chicago mounted a major show, "Julia Margaret Cameron's Women," a little over four years ago. A comprehensive exhibition of more than a hundred prints opened early this month at the National Portrait Gallery in London, and moves to the J. Paul Getty Museum in Los Angeles in the fall. Two publications accompany the show: *Julia Margaret Cameron: A Critical Biography*, by Colin Ford (Getty Trust Publications, 2003), and a catalogue raisonné, *Julia Margaret Cameron: The Complete Photographs*, edited by Ford and Julian Cox (Getty Trust Publications, 2003). Ford's biography is a handsomely designed, oversize illustrated volume that is much more compelling to look at than it is to read. The text is informative on social and art history, but, in certain respects, Ford's view of Cameron here, as in his catalog essay, resembles those crisply focused Victorian studio portraits that she imperiously disdained as hackwork because they favored the details of their subjects' dress, posture, accoutrements, and class at the expense, she thought, of their soul. Ford isn't a psychologist, and he doesn't, as he writes of a Victorian memoirist, have "a way with words." But the six-hundred-page catalogue raisonné he co-edited with Cox is a sumptuously presented monument of scholarship. (It's heartening to see the Getty millions spent so well.) Cox, for his part, takes the measure of Cameron's methods and achievements with erudite finesse.

Julia Margaret Pattle was born in 1815 into a well-off Anglo-Indian family living in Calcutta, which was then the subcontinent's capital city. The Pattles moved in the upper echelons of colonial society, although the resemblance of their name to the common native patronym Patel inspired a certain amount of unkind genealogical snickering. For nearly a century, the men had worked for the East India Company or the Bengal Civil Service, which Cameron's father, James, entered at fourteen. According to a family tale as colorful as it is dubious, the dead body of James Pattle, "a notorious liar and drinker," was shipped home to England in a cask of rum. The cask exploded violently during a storm at sea, so terrifying the widow that she expired, raving mad, leaving the sailors to finish off the tasty embalming fluid. "This Pattle story," writes Hermione Lee, Virginia Woolf's biographer, who tells it with relish, "was always popping up." Woolf's mother, a muse of the Pre-Raphaelites, was the austerely beautiful Julia Stephen, née Jackson—Cameron's niece, namesake, godchild, and favorite model. Cameron's fascination with her bordered upon obsession, and Julia posed for more studies—nearly fifty, including one that the artist called "My Favorite Picture of all my works"—than anyone else whom Cameron photographed. The favorite, with the maiden's downcast eyes averted from the lens, is considerably more sentimental than the dramatic frontal views in which the subject stares back at the photographer assertively, as if to say, "I am, like you, my own woman." If a portrait is a contest, it is also a collaboration, intimate though unequal, and an overbearing artist like Cameron probably achieves the best results with a sitter who exerts some inner resistance. (It was often small children, annoyed by their silly angel wings, who did so.) The great pictures of Julia Jackson treat her face like a telescopic close-up of the moon, half flooded by light, half scoured by shadow, lending it the mystery of a celestial body seen through a long lens. The closer Cameron brings those luminous human features, the more she magnifies one's sense of their goddesslike autonomy and remoteness.

Cameron's photographs decorated the Stephens' house in Kensington and, later, the Woolfs' Bloomsbury drawing room. It was Lady Stephen who wrote the biographical sketch of her aunt for the *Dictionary of National Biography*, edited by her husband, Sir Leslie. (Among 420 entries, Cameron was one of eighteen women, and the only photographer, so honored.) The Woolfs' Hogarth Press published a selection of Cameron's portraits, *Victorian Photographs of Famous Men & Fair Women*, with a fond profile by Woolf and an essay by Roger Fry, who concluded that the pictures would "outlive most of the works of the artists who were her contemporaries."

One of those contemporaries, Thackeray, coined the expression "Pattledom" to describe the deliciously exotic family culture that bred Cameron and her six sisters. According to Woolf, they were all great beauties, except for squat, clever, emphatic Julia Margaret—a fact that shouldn't be underestimated in view of her lifelong fixation on nubile grace and the absence, amounting to a horror, of homeliness from her portraiture of women. Their mother, née Adéline de l'Étang, was a minor French aristocrat with a racy ancien-régime pedigree and a noble Indian ancestress whose dark complexion and "Pondicherry eyes" were passed down through the generations. Among themselves, the girls preferred to speak Hindustani, and even when they spoke English, they gesticulated with a distinctly foreign animation that would surely have been considered alarmingly woggish. Julia left India at the age of three and spent much of her childhood with her maternal grandmother in Paris and Versailles. One would like to know more about those early years, in part because the eroticism of Cameron's work and the glamour that a carnal, even predatory, appetite imparts to it are, I suspect, a product of them.

As the art critic Carol Mavor has observed, Cameron's pictures look as though "they have been touched all over," and, literally, they were. For her, Julian Cox writes, "the collodion and varnish were elemental skins that were susceptible to, and invited, touch. Once committed, the hair, oils, dirt, and fingertip smudges were eternally suspended in the plates' cutaneous layers. Cameron considered these blobs and 'flaws' . . . artifacts of the experience." The sexual charge one feels in otherwise chaste portraits comes, I think, from her conflicting impulses to worship and to despoil. She made her virgins, unthinkably for the period, let down their hair, and she tousled the heads of her little angels to get rid of their "nursery primness," as one of them recalled; in the same way, she roughed up her old heroes and poetic swains. Children embrace, often suggestively. In an allegorical study entitled *Spring*, a moody toddler hikes up a corner of her crumpled shift to expose the almondine sliver of her labia. Lust, Cameron told her son Hardinge, was not to be despised, for the "animal side" of human nature was "the rich soil that bears the golden fruit but if good seed is not sown in that soil it then degenerates into a dung heap does it not?" Here one can see that not even her syntax is properly English. Cameron's work thrums with a seductive accent, and there is an untidy seam in the excitable prose of her letters where some more corporeal language has been taken in. Although she spoke Victorian fluently, it wasn't her mother tongue. True daughters of Britannia like the Brontës, George Eliot—even Woolf—were raised to believe that their greatest worldly leverage, their route to influence in art, politics, or any public arena, resided in abstention. Despite misogynistic traditions, French culture, like Indian culture, has always prized woman's desire.

Julia Margaret was twelve years old and still living in France when, in 1826, Nicéphore Niépce, an inventor who had already patented a combustion engine, succeeded in arresting the image projected by a camera obscura on a pewter plate coated with bitumen varnish. The exposure took eight hours. Louis Daguerre, who painted scenic backdrops for the theater using a camera obscura, was also trying to develop a photographic process, and the two men became partners. When Niépce died suddenly, in 1833, Daguerre continued to refine the precision of his equipment and greatly reduced the exposure time by steaming the plates with fumes of mercury. On January 7, 1839, his process was introduced with the fanfare its significance deserved to the French Academy of Sciences: the age of mechanical reproduction had begun.

An English scientist named William Henry Fox Talbot had, in the meantime, invented a method for taking photographs using paper instead of a metal plate, and generating a reproducible negative—a Talbotype—rather than an irreproducible, direct positive like the daguerreotype. He now hastened to publish his experiments, and three weeks after the announcement of Daguerre's success, Michael Faraday described Fox Talbot's "light drawings" to the fellows of the Royal Institution in London. The revolutionary nature of both discoveries was immediately obvious, though they couldn't be exploited for portraiture until the exposure time was again radically reduced (Cameron's studies took between two and nine minutes, depending on the hour of the day and the brightness of the sun) and a remedy was found for a problem that became apparent when the first daguerreotypes were only a few months old—they faded to invisibility.

The third great pioneer of photographic technology, Sir John

Herschel, was an astronomer, and thus a connoisseur of light. It was he who coined the words "photography," "snapshot," and "negative," and who solved, as he put it, "Daguerre's problem." Having concocted his own photographic base, with carbonate of silver, he took a picture of his father's forty-foot telescope at Slough (Herschel *père* discovered Uranus), and froze the development of the image by washing the negative with a solvent that he had invented twenty years before—hyposulphite of soda—which became known in the trade as the preservative hypo. Something miraculous (all miracles defy death) was suddenly possible: to fix forever an ephemeral moment.

In 1839, Herschel sent an account of his discoveries and of Daguerre's and Fox Talbot's to his young friend Mrs. Cameron, who was then twenty-four and living in Calcutta. They had met three years earlier, in Cape Town, where he had built an observatory. The Cape was a popular spa for English colonials escaping the fevers of India, and Julia Margaret, still Miss Pattle, was convalescing there. So was her future husband, Charles Hay Cameron, a colonial civil servant and liberal jurist twenty years her senior. The couple married in 1838, and it's worth noting that her romance with photography recreated the scenario of her infatuation with Charles: its leading celebrants are an august patriarch and a well-born virgin.

Though twenty-five years passed before Cameron took up a camera—one of the longest exposures in history—the interval was by no means blank. Charles Hay Cameron had collaborated with Thomas Babington Macaulay on reforming the Indian Penal Code, and in 1843 he inherited Macaulay's seat on the ruling Supreme Council. A year later, when the new governor-general arrived without his wife, Mrs. Cameron became the presiding hostess at Government House. The Camerons had been buying coffee plantations in Ceylon, intending to live off the income these generated when Charles retired. He did so prematurely in 1848, apparently for reasons of health, although Ford suggests that his views on Britain's duty to provide a "proper education for all Indians" and to integrate them into the civil service hadn't endeared him to either the East India Company or the Colonial Office. The Camerons abruptly moved back to England. She was thirty-three.

Thackeray's daughter, Anne Ritchie, recalled meeting Mrs. Cameron at her house in East Sheen, south of the Thames, soon after her return from India:

> I remember a strange apparition in a flowing red velvet dress, although it was summer time . . . When we left she came with us bareheaded, with trailing draperies, part of the way to the station as her kind habit was. A friend of mine told me how on one occasion she accompanied him the same way carrying a cup of tea which she stirred as she walked along.

About this time, one of the artist celebrities whom Fry so rightly predicted Cameron would come to outshine, George Frederic Watts, painted a very different portrait of her. It is a study of a wan young woman in a white shirtwaist, with delicate features, a high forehead, dark hair simply parted, prominent cheekbones, and faraway eyes devoid of fire. In another picture—a photograph with two of her sons—she is gussied up in a taffeta gown, and plumpness has filled in her hollows. Around 1858, she posed for an unknown photographer staring fatuously at her watch, as if she had a soft-boiled egg on the stove. Ten years later, she leaned glumly against a high-backed chair, looking like a spinster with a case of indigestion after a big lunch. There is only one image of her returning the camera's gaze, and she does so warily—almost with hostility. No one ever wore down Cameron's resistance to capture a glimpse, in the woman, of the ardor that radiates from the work.

When she was middle-aged (in her early forties—she died at sixty-three), Cameron cut a figure of "courtly charm," as Tennyson's wife, Emily, put it tactfully, which is to say she was a somewhat affected, voluble, self-conscious eccentric given to hyperbole. "Mrs. Cameron alternates between the seventh heaven and the bottomless pit," a friend wrote. "She lives upon superlatives." The flowing robes that Ritchie describes ("uniting Paris art and the draperies of Raphael") anticipated the rage for "Artistic Dress" that reached its height in the 1880s. They gave her a sibylline, vaguely Eastern air, and although they hid more of the body than a corseted gown with conventional crinolines, they were considered bohemian. Cameron was extremely conscious of fashion, even though she projected a sublime disregard for it, shrouding her models from the neck down in black velvet or the folds of a shawl. It was an inspired survival strategy, because dress is the perishable flesh in a photograph, emotion its bones, and her greatest portraits have thus been preserved from the rot of quaintness.

The same cannot, on the whole, be said of the hammy tableaux vivants that she called "My Fancy Subjects"—groups of figures illustrating scenes from myth, Shakespeare, Renaissance painting, the Bible, and Tennyson's *Idylls of the King*. Critics have been nearly unanimous in finding these pictorial narratives, which might be the stills from an early silent film or an old-fashioned Vassar senior play, "ludicrous" and "amateurish," and Ford doesn't persuade me that they deserve a reevaluation. One can too easily imagine bossy Cameron fiddling ungently with the costumes and props she has rustled up from a steamer trunk and barking brusque orders at the hapless houseguests drafted to serve High Art when they would much rather be having high tea. Her husband, Charles, "with his craggy face and trailing white hair and beard, made an ideal model for the aged Merlin," writes Sylvia Wolf, who curated the 1998 show of Cameron's women, "but his tendency to laugh throughout the sessions ruined a number of negatives."

Cameron's family circle was a photogenic trout pond of pulchritude and distinction, and when she needed a May Queen, a foolish virgin, or a hirsute sage, all she had to do was fish one from her stock. The Camerons' neighbor Sir Henry Taylor, a once eminent writer now forgotten, posed for her both as himself, looking like one of Rembrandt's burghers, and as Prospero and Friar Lawrence. The Taylors introduced the Camerons to Tennyson and his wife, who became their closest friends. Cameron's glamorous sister Sara Prinsep also lived nearby, at Little Holland House in Kensington, where she presided over a salon of Pre-Raphaelite painters, poets, and aristocrats with artistic pretensions. It was here that the teenage Ellen Terry was "rescued" from her abominable family profession—acting—by the Prinseps' artist in residence, George Watts, who married her when she was sixteen and he forty-seven. She unrescued herself after a miserable year of child-bridehood to fulfill her destiny on the stage. In Cameron's startlingly modern portrait of Terry—dewy of cheek, scantily dressed in the kind of deluxe peasant blouse one can find at Saint Laurent, and toying with a strand of beads—she looks just like what she was: a melancholy Lolita.

Charles Cameron and his two elder sons left England for Ceylon in 1859 to survey their estates. Julia Margaret paid an extended visit that year to the Tennysons, who were living in the seaside village of Freshwater on the Isle of Wight, and she was so enchanted with the neighborhood's supply of rustic charm and urbane company that, "impulsive as ever," Ford writes, she bought two substantial cottages and an adjacent property that she called Dimbola, after one of her coffee plantations. The poet laureate had decamped from London in part to escape importunate fans, but he succeeded only in helping to transform the island into what Phyllis Rose, in an essay for Sylvia Wolf's catalog, impishly calls a Victorian Martha's Vineyard. Cameron took it upon herself to succor the big-name pilgrims. A contemporary Irish visitor compared the community to "a French salon . . . We had our Chateaubriand in Tennyson and . . . our Madame Récamier in [her]." Despite the fact that she was constantly occupied with entertaining her illustrious company at what she described as "feasts of intellect" (dinners at Dimbola lasted for four hours, and guests were expected to sing, play, recite poetry, or, at the very least, pontificate), she managed to feel bored. When, in 1863, her husband embarked on another long trip to the colonies, her daughter and son-in-law Julia and Charles Norman gave her a camera for Christmas with the wish that "it may amuse you Mother to try to Photograph during your solitude." And so her career began.

Colin Ford argues plausibly that Cameron's first camera had to be a gift that she was already at least partially competent to use. She set up a laboratory right after the New Year, and it took only four weeks of fumbling to make her first satisfactory print, the portrait of a nine-year-old girl named Annie Philpot. "I was in a transport of delight," she wrote in an autobiographical sketch, *Annals of My Glass House*. In the month that followed, she produced what Cox calls a "torrent of magnificent pictures"—more than three dozen, a remarkable number considering the labor that each one required. She was working with fragile twelve-by-ten-inch glass plates. First, she washed and polished them; their fastidious cleanliness was essential. Next, she treated them with a freshly mixed collodion emulsion. Its distribution had to be perfectly even. The plates were bathed in light-sensitive silver nitrate, exposed while still wet, rushed to a darkroom and developed with a solution of pyrogallic acid, then rinsed twice—with water and potassium cyanide—and sealed with a coat of varnish. To make prints from the negatives, she floated sheets of fine writing paper in a solution of egg whites, left them to dry, then soaked the albumen-coated paper in the silver nitrate. Negative and paper were exposed to daylight; then she fixed the fresh print with hypo and washed off the fixative with buckets of well water. The color of the image was adjusted with a sequence of toners, some of them toxic. Most of these operations were performed more or less blindly, in darkness. The chemicals stank; the collodion streaked and peeled; dust on the plate left white blotches; the hypo turned her prints green; the silver nitrate reddened the albumen; the lethal cyanide blackened her clothes, table linens, and skin, and rightly terrified her—it was probably responsible for the chronic breathing problems that she, like so many nineteenth-century photographers, suffered as the years passed. She wrote to Herschel frequently for technical advice and moral support in that experimental period ("Pray! Pray!" he replied. "Be more cautious!"), and she "felt [her] way literally in the dark thro' endless failures."

But Cameron, as Cox notes, worked by "embracing accidents." The short focal length and fixed aperture of her first lens produced an image that was sharp only at a small "sweet spot" at the center, and she adopted what she called "the fluke" of her first out-of-focus portraits as a hallmark of her style. Even when she mastered the physics and geometry of taking an impeccable image, she preferred suggestion to definition. Before almost anyone else, she grasped the power of photography to iconify a face, to mythologize a name, to propagate a desire—and that intuition is at the heart of her modernity.

Every canonical figure on a ten-greatest list is, however deserving, the chance beneficiary of a capricious riptide that disperses some bodies of work, smashes others or pulls them under the waves, and sweeps a handful, intact, to the shore of the next century. As Cox points out, Cameron's innovations are deeply indebted to the portraiture of David Wilkie Wynfield, a painter who, in the early 1860s, published an album of "fancy" photographic portraits: close-ups in soft focus that portrayed his friends costumed as literary or historical characters. Wynfield and Cameron corresponded, and he apparently gave her at least one lesson in the use of a camera. "To my feelings about his beautiful photography," she wrote, "I owed *all* my attempts and indeed consequently all my successes." She was perhaps even more indebted to the tutelage of her friend and model George Watts, "an artistic missionary," Cox writes, whose "classical treatment of the human form separated him from the prevailing fashion for verisimilitude so favored by the early Pre-Raphaelites." Although Watts was primarily a painter of allegorical scenes, he made his living as a celebrity portraitist, specializing, as Cameron would, in eminent Victorians. He achieved a kind of immortality by association, in part with her. And, as the Ellen Terry fiasco suggests, he was himself eminently Victorian: a man who invoked the highest of principles to justify the baser of self-delusions.

Yet Watts also sensed precisely where Cameron's weakness lay: in complacence. For someone both bold and worldly, she was remarkably provincial. There is a beauty in the low, the strange, the corrupt, and the commonplace that she never saw, and a nobility in ugliness— the face of George Eliot is a good example. Cameron jubilated equally over good pictures and bad. "You must not be satisfied," Watts exhorted her. "There is more to be done."

But I wonder if that streak of complacence in an otherwise conscientious nature doesn't explain Cameron's mysterious buoyancy. She never paid attention to her critics, even those she respected, like Ruskin, whose dismissals might have sunk her. She wasn't a woman given to regret. So, in 1875, when her husband—who had always supported her art "with enthusiastic applause" and tolerated the mess it made with "sympathy" and "indulgence"—decided, at the age of eighty-one, that he wanted to spend his last years in Ceylon, she packed in her English life at the peak of her career and they sailed off with their coffins. Charles's health improved in the tropical climate, and he died in 1880, having outlived his wife by a year. She did a few fine portraits of her Tamil farmworkers, and the only extant portrait of a fellow woman artist at work, the botanical painter Marianne North, who left a last impression of Cameron:

> The walls of the room were covered with magnificent photographs; others were tumbling about the tables, chairs, and floors with quantities of damp books, all untidy and picturesque; the lady herself with a lace veil on her head and flowing draperies . . . She also made some studies of natives while I was there, and took such a fancy to the back of one of them (which she said was absolutely superb) that she insisted on her son retaining him as her gardener, though she had no garden and he did not know even the meaning of the word.

"Portraits," Carlyle wrote, "are the candle by which we read history." Cameron, in that sense, is a votive artist. But the builders of great pantheons seldom get to rest in them. She was an exception.

—February 17, 2003

· THREE · ꙮ

A Reader's Companion

People who devote their lives to literature often have their first love affairs with the great dead writers, and through a subsequent addiction to what A. S. Byatt calls "the delectable drug of understanding," they graduate to a consuming romance with language, in comparison with which other forms of pleasure seem mundane. An excellent recent novel describing that romance was Julian Barnes's *Flaubert's Parrot* (Knopf, 1985). It was as precious an artifact for the bookish reader as the stuffed bird of its title was for Barnes's narrator, Geoffrey Braithwaite. Braithwaite is the amateur's amateur. He "hates" Flaubert's professional critics, because they give themselves such airs of omniscience yet get things so wrong, and he compares biography to a trawling net that lets slip all but a fragment of what it might have captured. "Words came easily to Flaubert but he also saw the underlying inadequacy of the Word," Braithwaite tells us. And he sets an example, if not of humility, then of the humble pose becoming to biographers, by giving to his own enamored, select, contentious reflections on the Master the form of footnotes or appendixes to a true life that can't be written.

Braithwaite also makes a wishful demand for a twenty-year injunction against novels set in Oxford or Cambridge and a ten-year ban on other university fiction—a demand that may have been aimed in part at Byatt. She is one of England's most visible literary dons: an authority on Iris Murdoch and the Romantics; an editor of George Eliot's essays and poetry; a busy television commentator; and a reviewer of books. Her leading characters, too, all seem to teach, preach, broadcast, or write, and her novels seethe with the spiritual competitiveness and the sublimated lust of university life, which is that of any cloister. There is probably no one who understands better than Byatt the heart of the "reading woman." Responsive quotation is her preferred form of foreplay. She finds a suitor's fiction pedestrian and therefore cannot love him. A man can seduce her by chastising her taste in modern writers, then lending her his copy of *La Nausée*.

Byatt's latest novel, *Possession* (Random House, 1990), which has just won the Booker Prize, belongs to that genre of ingenious books—by Nabokov, Borges, Fowles, Eco, et al.—in which a scribe or pedant solves an esoteric mystery by threading a labyrinth of clues that an omnipercipient author has laid out for him. Most of these postmodernist literary thrillers descend from *The Purloined Letter*, and *Possession* is no exception, although Byatt might have done well to observe the warning of Seneca that Poe posts as an epigraph: "*Nil sapientiae odiosius acumine nimio*," or "Nothing is more hateful to wisdom than too much cunning." *Possession* demands exegesis with the imperiousness of a masterpiece. It isn't one, but it is more heartfelt and more fun to read than *The Name of the Rose*, and its prankish verve suggests it was fun to write. The monstrous richness of detail gives you a taste of the tedium and obsessiveness of literary research. *Possession* also represents every biographer's fantasy of a next book: a novel in which one will invent the life, archives, oeuvre, and critical canon of a master whose secrets haven't yet been told.

At the core of *Possession* is an epistolary novel whose scattered fragments begin to compose an image of a clandestine love affair between two prolific poets of the last century—the great Randolph Henry Ash, who seems to be modeled on Robert Browning, and Christabel LaMotte, who bears a resemblance both to Emily Dickinson and to Christina Rossetti. This romance nests like a Russian doll within the love story—"a vulgar and a high Romance simultaneously," the narrator calls it—of two sexually bashful modern scholars, Maud Bailey and Roland Mitchell, who are stalking the Ash-LaMotte relationship through "the twists and turns of [its] syntax."

Early in the novel, the scholars discover a cache of letters—"It's

both sides. It's everything"—which has been buried for a century in
LaMotte's dolls' bed. The letters are as remarkable for Byatt's intuitive reading of her characters as for her fluency in the "excited
prolixity," the "ambages and sinuosities," and the pre-Freudian
innocence of their prose. Ash's greatness becomes convincing. He's
an iconoclast but not, by temperament, a transgressor. He is both
worldlier and more conscientious than his contemporaries, and he
sees through LaMotte's terrible feigned demureness:

> At her worst . . . she would look down and sideways . . . and
> this smile would come near a mechanical simper, for it was an
> untruth, it was a convention, it was her brief constricted ac-
> knowledgement of the world's expectations . . . Most men, he
> judged, if they had seen the harshness and fierceness and abso-
> lutism, yes, absolutism of that visage, would have stood back
> from her. She would have been destined to be loved only by
> timid weaklings, who would have secretly hoped she would
> punish or command them, or by simpletons, who supposed
> her chill look of delicate withdrawal to indicate a kind of fe-
> male purity, which all desired, in those days, at least ostensibly.
> But he had known immediately that she was for him . . . or in
> freedom might have been.

Each poet is the ideal reader of the other. Their coquetry takes
the form of disagreements on religion, spiritualism, history, and the
role of gender, and their notion of ecstasy is to be of one mind. Ash
writes:

> I speak to you as I might speak to all those who most possess
> my thoughts—to Shakespeare, to Thomas Browne, to John
> Donne, to John Keats—and find myself unpardonably lending
> you, who are alive, my voice, as I habitually lend it to those
> dead men—Which is much as to say—here is an author of
> Monologues—trying clumsily to construct a Dialogue—and
> encroaching on both halves of it.

Christabel later writes:

I say nothing of Honour, nor of Morality, though they are weighty matters—I go to the Core, which renders much disquisition on these matters superfluous. The core is my solitude, my solitude that is threatened, that you threaten, without which I am nothing.

Eventually, though, she will agree with Ash's conclusion that "we must come to grief and regret anyway—and I for one would rather regret the reality than its phantasm, knowledge than hope, the deed than the hesitation, true life and not merely sickly potentialities."

Roland Mitchell has earned a meager living researching the footnotes for an edition of Ash's complete works. While digging for marginalia in Ash's copy of Vico, the great proto-Hegelian Renaissance philosopher of science, he discovers two drafts of what seems to be a love letter from Ash to an unidentified woman. One draft is impassioned: "Since our extraordinary conversation I have thought of nothing else." The second has been diluted with propriety: "Since our pleasant and unexpected conversation I have thought of little else." Mitchell, "shocked . . . then . . . thrilled"—there has never been the whisper of an attachment in Ash's life outside his marriage—purloins the letters.

Their trail of allusions leads first to LaMotte and then to Maud Bailey, the poet's descendant and leading critic. Maud is ashamed of her beauty, Roland of his background. He remains a nonentity, while she comes to embody the cerebral excesses and solipsisms of Byatt's style. Here she is one night, undressing for bed, listening to Roland's ablutions through a thin hotel wall, and—her head full of Lacan's theory of subjectivity—reflecting on her identity: "Narcissism, the unstable self, the fractured ego, Maud thought, who am I? A matrix for a susurration of texts and codes?" And neither she nor Byatt seems dismayed at this predicament.

Maud amplifies what Roland already knows: that LaMotte was the daughter of a famous French mythographer; that she made her life with an obscure painter named Blanche Glover, who committed suicide; and that her work—"disquieting" neo-Gothic fairy tales for

children, and an epic, *The Fairy Melusina*—which was neglected in its
own day, has become part of the modern feminist and lesbian canon.

Both scholars pride themselves on an interest in immortal texts
rather than in "vanished bodies": sleeping in the poet's bed or palm-
ing his inkwell isn't their style. Byatt admires their priggishness while
indulging their "narrative greed." Where the letters end, the two
sleuths proceed on foot. They dust the poets' archives and texts for
prints of the affair, and of its aftermath. Using the poetry as their
treasure map, they tramp through Brittany, where LaMotte spent an
undocumented nine months, and through Yorkshire, where Ash
went with a scalpel and a microscope to study sea anemones and to
search for "the origins of life and the nature of generation." They
must also evade rival scholars who begin closing in on them: Mor-
timer Cropper, the fastidious and perverse American biographer
of Ash, who, with his millions, has cornered the market in Ash artifacts and manuscripts; the flamboyant Leonora Stern, a bisexual
part-Indian LaMotte specialist from Tallahassee; and James Blackad-
der, the overscrupulous Scot, who has been editing Ash's complete
works for forty years. In a scene that resembles the finale of *It's a
Mad Mad Mad Mad World* with a commentary by Julia Kristeva, several carloads of pedants from both sides of the Atlantic converge
upon a country graveyard, with raincoats and shovels, to exhume
Ash's remains.

Barnes's method was to exhibit the biographer's net with all its
holes. Byatt's is to simulate the oceanic slosh. The reader is given a
stiff final exam in critical sifting and selection. We thus have at our
disposal not only epigrams and stanzas but page after page of *Rag-
narök, Swammerdam, Ask to Embla, Mummy Possest, The Incarcer-
ated Sorceress*, and *The Garden of Proserpina*, all of which are epics or
dramatic monologues by Ash; entire chapters from LaMotte's *Tales
for Innocents*, and the proem, with Book I, of her *Melusina*; generous
extracts from the public correspondence of both lovers in addition to
the cache of secret letters; weeks from the diaries of Ash's wife, Ellen,
and LaMotte's companion, Blanche Glover; the forty-five-page journal of LaMotte's teenage cousin Sabine de Kercoz, translated from
the French; lengthy quotations from the memoir of a Victorian psychic patronized by LaMotte and despised by Ash; and substantial

segments of *The Great Ventriloquist*, Cropper's biography, and of Leonora Stern's feminist-Lacanian ravings on LaMotte.

Possession is so enormous that it can't be maneuvered into the studio apartment of a review without a great deal of grunting and swearing—and of metaphor. It's a Niagara of allusions. It's a rope of pearls grossly disparate in luster and value. It's a one-woman variety show of literary styles and types. It's a high-tech handbook of professional thought tools adapted for the consumer. It's one of those deluxe museum shops that hang real art on the walls and sell cheap bric-a-brac, costly replicas, esoteric puzzles, popular histories, the perfect watch, the pen that writes upside down, protest art, Zen calendars, and Currier & Ives place mats. You search for the artistic reason for so much pastiche, when half would have been twice as beguiling. The long poems, in particular, seem to exist in such plenitude mainly to be admired as the feat of mischief, erudition, virtuosity, and "ventriloquism," which indeed they are. But if Byatt treats other people's academic cant with a terrific glee one cannot help sharing, the pedantry on display in *Possession* sets the bar for it. She points out every implicit dialectic and expropriates every possible response, including exasperation at her "polysemous perversity." One can't decide if she is mocking herself for showing off so unrepentantly or falling prey to the anxiety and hubris of postmodern critics, who tend to deconstuct their own texts defensively rather than surrender any fertile passage to an invading analyst.

The don and the novelist have been cast as sibling rivals in Byatt's fiction, and the artist and the didact within Byatt seem to compete for possession of her work. Toward the end of the novel, Roland sheds some light on this conflict. He suddenly finds that he can write poetry, and he sees that he has been taught, and has accepted, that "language was essentially inadequate, that it could never speak what was there, that it only spoke itself." Now, though, the ways "in which it *could* be said had become more interesting than the idea that it could not."

Isak Dinesen once remarked that a hostess wants only to be thanked, and perhaps one can say that a writer wants "only" to be read—by the man or woman best suited in temperament, education, and experience to meet all the "twists and turns of his syntax" with understanding. But the ideal reader deserves a particular kind of reciprocity. Byatt wants to prove that she can write anything and everything, and nearly succeeds. Now she needs to abandon her unreadability—her insistence that we savor the minutiae, the ironies, and the heroics of her struggle with all that can't be said.

Possession is called *A Romance*, and to explain her subtitle Byatt refers us to Hawthorne's definition: a tale with greater latitude than a novel, "both as to its fashion and material," and one that attempts "to connect a bygone time with the very present that is flitting away from us." But *Possession* also wants to be a less theoretical sort of romance. It is one of Eco's humble scribes—Adso—who reminds us that *amor est magis cognitivus quam cognitio*: that we know better through love than through knowledge. What is finest in *Possession* isn't what the didact tells us about language but what the artist illuminates about those, including herself, who love the word.

—November 19, 1990

This Old House

At midday on March 6, 1970, Charles Lockwood, a senior at Princeton, and his friend Robert Mayer, a photographer, were taking pictures of a particularly fine Greek Revival doorway on West Eleventh Street in Greenwich Village for Lockwood's undergraduate thesis on the history of New York row houses (three- to five-story attached dwellings of brick or brownstone, most of them built in the nineteenth century). Their work was interrupted by an explosion at the Fifth Avenue end of the block, followed by a terrific shock wave. Quickly deciding to document whatever disaster had taken place, they ran toward the flames and debris spewing from No. 18, shot a roll of film, and brought it to *The New York Times*, which printed one of the pictures on the front page the next morning. Lockwood and Mayer learned that the blasted house (also a Greek Revival gem), which burned to the ground when the gas lines ignited, was owned by a Midwestern media mogul named James Wilkerson, whose daughter Cathlyn was a member of the Weathermen. She and her comrades were using the basement as a "bomb factory," and, through inexpertness or bad luck, they had blown themselves up. I was working in Union Square that spring, and I often walked past the site. After the rubble was cleared and before the new owner of the lot erected an anomalous modern house on it—with diagonally canted bay windows that obscurely commemorated the explosion—the gaping hole between Nos. 16 and 20 depressed me. It was as if a healthy

tooth had been extracted violently from a familiar smile, transforming it into the grimace of a memento mori.

In 1972, Lockwood's much expanded thesis was published as a
book, *Bricks and Brownstone: The New York Row House, 1783–1929*,
illustrated by Mayer's photographs, and it became a bible for buffs,
architects, and preservationists. It has just been reissued by Rizzoli
(2003), with sixty-six new color plates by Madeleine Isom, a section
suggesting walking tours of the best row-house blocks in Brooklyn
and Manhattan, and an introduction by Paul Goldberger. Though
Lockwood describes the explosion on West Eleventh Street as an isolated adventure, the story he tells is that of the demographic explosions and economic shock waves that have transformed New York
City. The row house is an artifact of the same periods, culture, and
upheavals that shaped the novel. They originate together in the late
eighteenth century and, a hundred years afterward, jointly arrive at a
golden age. The serene frontage of a venerable street in Murray Hill
or Park Slope—the consensus expressed by its aesthetic unity about
what constitutes moral virtue—is an image for the predicament of a
stifled James hero or a warped Wharton heroine struggling against
prudery and beholdenness to break the social mold. From Lockwood's work, a contemporary novelist might construct a narrative
about the enduring intrigue, romance, poison, and nuance of class
privilege—the rise and fall of the house of Wilkerson. It would consider the way that successive American generations ruthlessly dese-
crate the past so that their rootless heirs will have something to
idealize.

In one of Louis Auchincloss's many fictions that treat or at least
graze the same theme, a patrician hero suffers a reversal of fortune
and moves his family from Park Avenue to much humbler quarters: a
small brownstone on an unfashionable street in the East Eighties—
making do there, as I recall, with a skeleton staff of a cook and a
maid, and adjusting to the disgrace of being déclassé. Their stoicism
in having to crowd themselves into four floors amused me when I
read the story, for I was, at the time, subletting a studio that had
once been the third-best bedroom of a grand house on East Tenth

Street—a residence of the sort that Auchincloss characters are born in or inherit and take for granted until fate serves them an eviction notice. Though I once briefly owned a Tribeca loft (before the neighborhood was developed), I had, like everyone normal, spent my entire New York life in a shoe box. There was a sordid hovel on East First Street that was torched during the immolation-murder of a Hells Angel; a railroad flat on a gang-infested block in the West Eighties; a garret in Little Italy where I shared a toilet in the hall with the drag queen next door; a derelict though charming former push-cart stable; and an illegal crash pad in a brick firetrap above an Irish bar on Water Street, where I cohabited with a jazz trombonist and his roommate, a baby-faced heroin addict. Below us lived two elderly Collyer-like brothers who never saw the light of day and who, for fifty years, had been collecting manhole covers, pornography, cigar boxes, orthopedic prostheses, and the carcasses of old radios. If there were, in 1970, any other residents of the Financial District, they were moles, like the brothers, and we never saw them. My mother, who never saw me, thought I was studying Milton while rooming with a widowed piano teacher on Riverside Drive.

I eventually outgrew my youthful contempt for "bourgeois," which is to say habitable, apartments, though never for those in modern buildings. Like Charles Lockwood, but without his sense of purpose, I roamed the brownstone blocks of lower Manhattan and Brooklyn Heights, often at dusk, just as the lights came on and before the shades were drawn, peeping into the parlor windows of old houses inhabited by rich bohemians, and lusting for a saffron-yellow library with floor-to-ceiling bookshelves and a sliding ladder; a gilt pier glass with chipped gesso above an Eastlake mantel; French doors opening to a little balcony or a cobbled patio; a lumpy recamier with a broken leg propped up by an unabridged dictionary; slanting pine floors; a high ceiling with a plaster rosette; a spitting fire; and a piano in the corner under which slept a shaggy dog. I was gratified to read in *Bricks and Brownstone* that James Fenimore Cooper was an errant voyeur of my ilk. "There is," he writes in *Notions of the Americans* (1828), "a species of second-rate, genteel houses, that abound in New York, into which I have looked when passing with the utmost pleasure. They have, as usual, a story that is half sunk in the earth . . .

and two floors above. The tenants of these are chiefly merchants, or professional men, in moderate circumstances, who pay rents of from $300 to $500 a year. You know that no American who is at all comfortable in life will share his dwelling with another." The relish with which he describes the tasteful opulence of these mediocre houses' mahogany appointments suggests that he did more ogling from the sidewalk than passing by. Fashions in and prices of New York real estate are, as one knows, eminently labile, but the habit of yearning for a poetic old house is so ingrained in some of us—me in particular— that I sometimes forget I have one.

My own reversals of fortune are too predictable to relate, but my son and I now live in a narrow Yorkville brownstone with a deep garden dominated by a majestic elm which has miraculously weathered the epidemics that have decimated its species. Our house has also weathered the epidemics—of decay, development, and conversion— that have decimated its species, and about which Lockwood writes with artless passion and consummate authority. It is part of a row built in the early 1870s for middle-class families, possibly those of the foremen or managers at the Ruppert Brewery, which opened in 1867 and was, for a century, a major employer of the neighborhood's German and Hungarian immigrants. In 2003, one needs real nerve to call any single-family house in Manhattan second-rate genteel, though mine was originally not even that. It is fifteen feet wide (most town houses are from three to ten feet wider), with two rooms to a floor and a basement that was once the coal cellar. One block to the east, a "better" class of native New Yorker lived in more lavish dwellings with "English basements" and Anglo-Italianate façades. My son, however, doesn't care about such nice, and in any case antiquated, social distinctions: he complains that we have too much room (and perhaps we did until a friend gave him a drum set), and wishes that, "like everybody else," we lived in an ordinary two-bedroom apartment. To console him for the embarrassments of privilege, I make him do chores, and one is to lock up at night. In the dead of winter, when the dogs are howling in the backyards and the wind is high, he sometimes guiltily professes a desire for a doorman. We bought the house—and it's why we could—at a moment when most New Yorkers were, like my son, wary of a shadowy garden, a front door that opened from the street into their kitchen, and bed-room windows accessible by a painter's ladder. Insecurity, however, is a luxury on which I never economize.

Having studied Lockwood's text with relative assiduity, I set out one morning shod in cross-trainers to give my reading comprehension a pop quiz. I wasn't sanguine about my powers of discernment, as I've failed similar exercises in the Central Park Ramble, where I practice bird-watching for dummies and am scarcely able to distinguish a rook from a duck. There are fewer principal styles of New York row-house architecture than avian species, though there are still plenty: redbrick Federal (the earliest and the sparest of ornament); Greek Revival (fluted columns with Doric or Ionic capitals are the give-away); Gothic Revival (creepy); Italianate (the classic brownstone with protruding stoop); Second Empire (mansard roof); Neo-Grec ("squared-off forms and incised detail"); Queen Anne (asymmetrical and gloomy, with recessed porches); Romanesque (rounded arches and Byzantine leafwork); Renaissance (pale limestone or yellow brick with fancy pilasters); Colonial Revival (fanlight windows); and my fa-vorite multiple-choice option—"Eclectic." A few "countrified" wooden frame houses still exist, as does the odd brick dwelling with a crenellated Dutch gable. I was quickly able to identify a steel-and-concrete private house with walls of translucent glass as an homage to modernism, but I found it difficult to tell one nineteenth-century style from another—partly, of course, because so few row houses are still virginal. My own, for example, which should, in principle, have been budget Italianate, was deflowered in the 1930s by a fashionable architect who performed a "neoclassical" makeover inside and out—stripping the façade of its stoop, cornice, and lintels, and the interiors of their black-walnut woodwork and florid detail. Thus have innu-merable overwrought maidens been relieved of heavy petticoats and transformed into women of the world.

I know that one should resist the impulse to anthropomorphize, but town houses have a presence and a civility missing from more monolithic forms of residential real estate, particularly high-rise apartment buildings. Those "human" qualities are obviously a function of scale, age, and the imprint of hand labor, though perhaps not merely. The mien of old houses—their solidarity and defiance as survivors—makes them seem animate. There are graffiti-scarred terraces in Hell's Kitchen that remind me of painted girls in shabby finery (most hopelessly degraded, a few improbably intact) lined up in a cheap dance hall. There are uniform brown ranks in Fort Greene as solemn about their virile dignity as a phalanx of cadets in their class picture. One of the functions of a high-rise is to deflect curiosity and contamination, and it returns one's gaze with the stony inscrutability of a thing. I've always felt that there was something inherently soulful about row houses, and, with Lockwood's help, I can now say what: a house may guard the mystery of its inner life, but its face invites us to imagine that it has one.

—December 1, 2003

IV

NOBLESSE

DE ROBE

Scenes from a Marriage

I once had a chance to buy a couture suit by Chanel that was made sometime in the 1950s, her comeback years. She had closed her *maison de couture*, on the rue Cambon, when war was declared in 1939, and reopened it in 1954, when she returned to France, at seventy-one, from self-imposed exile in Switzerland. The stories of her attempts to wrest control of Chanel Parfums from her partners, the Wertheimer family, by exploiting the Nazi race laws, and of her startling offer to Hitler's secret-police chief to broker a negotiated peace with her old friend Winston Churchill—a farcical operation code-named Modellhut (fashion hat) by Chanel's S.S. handlers—have always somewhat dampened her charm for me. But the suit was a classic tweed in opalescent pink, with flecks of mauvish blue and a selvage trim, a slightly flared skirt that grazed the knee, and a boxy jacket with her signature cropped sleeves and narrow armholes. The dealer who was selling it, a Frenchwoman, sized me up—literally—before she let me try it on. She had been keeping it under wraps in her back room like a rare piece of erotica, waiting for the right customer.

Except for the thrilling virtuosity with which it is made, there is very little sex appeal to a mid-century Chanel suit. It is a conventional and even dowdy uniform if one wears it without some wink of impiety. But it keeps faith with an enlightened notion that refuses to die, no matter how hard its adversaries—the Versaces of the world—try to kill it, and one which we owe almost entirely to Chanel: that a woman is entitled to dress with the same dignity, comfort, and self-possession as a man.

Chanel died in 1971, at the age of eighty-seven, with no heirs except a trusted manservant. She left her estate to a foundation in Liechtenstein, and, according to Axel Madsen, the author of a thorough biography, *A Woman of Her Own* (Henry Holt, 1990), its value was estimated at $30 million. By then, the Wertheimer family, secretive patricians who amassed a fortune in cosmetics, owned the House of Chanel. For a few years, they did nothing with it except to continue to market the perfumes, and to pay rent on a small boutique on the rue Cambon that sold accessories. Eventually, they hired a new designer, who has since vanished from the scene, and introduced a line of ready-to-wear. In 1983, the president, Kitty D'Alessio, lured Karl Lagerfeld away from Chloé and made him the creative director. His mandate was to raise the profile of the brand and to rejuvenate—which in the aggressive fashion climate of the early eighties meant to sex up and trick out—the Chanel style, and he did so with a bravura or a brashness, depending on one's point of view, that seemed to some critics and clients a betrayal of the Chanel patrimony. But as Lagerfeld began to define a creative identity that was both separate from Chanel and consonant with his interpretive role as her steward, he reliably produced superior collections.

A new show of couture, ready-to-wear, jewelry, accessories, and toiletries by Chanel and Lagerfeld, which opened at the Metropolitan Museum, pays homage to Chanel's purism. It is curated by Harold Koda and his associate, Andrew Bolton, of the Met's Costume Institute. They have mounted a number of exhibitions in the claustrophobic basement where couture is usually displayed, which nevertheless captured the poetry of fashion. This production involved bigger interests and egos. It received "extravagant support" from its sponsor, Chanel, Inc., Koda told me, though he declined to quantify it; "additional support" from Condé Nast; and advice from Lagerfeld, a man of imperious opinions that he has never been shy about expressing. (A Chanel show planned five years ago by Koda's predecessor, the late Richard Martin, was canceled by mutual agreement when the Met bridled at Lagerfeld's demands.) But this time, Koda said at a press conference on the day of the annual Costume Institute Ball, speaking in the Great Hall of the museum, "there couldn't have been a show without Karl's interventions." The catalog *Chanel* (Metropolitan Museum, 2005), is a luxuriously pristine example of the printer's art, thanks in part to Lagerfeld, who hand-tinted the cover and the digitally processed photographs.

The installation, elevated to the Met's main floor, was designed, on Lagerfeld's recommendation, by Olivier Saillard, a program director at the Musée de la Mode et du Textile, in Paris. Its cool, almost clinical rigor celebrates Chanel's allegiance to the aesthetics of modernism. Nineteen modular "vitrines"—white cubes open on one side—are aligned in a grid against the black walls of a windowless gallery, giving visitors the illusion of strolling through the shopping streets of a bungalow colony on the dark side of the moon. Within each module, two, three, or six mannequins, faintly rouged and coiffed in white feathers, display sixty-three ensembles from eight decades. The earliest is an evening gown by Chanel, circa 1917–20, of black silk tulle with a fringe of paillettes; the latest an evening dress by Lagerfeld from spring/summer 2005, of black silk lace and chiffon. The ensembles are grouped by color, mood, shape, material, and affinity (little black dresses; Gypsy exuberance; "orientalist-moderne" lamé; romantic lace; permutations of the suit) rather than by period, as they would be in a retrospective, a genre for which Chanel seems like an obvious candidate. But Lagerfeld is quoted in the show as "detesting" retrospectives, and the curators believe that couture deserves to be looked at without extraneous or sensational distractions. "We don't do the biography thing," Koda told me. "That's my bias. Chanel wouldn't be remembered if it wasn't for the work."

The deceptive simplicity of Chanel's work makes her an elusive subject. Her couture is easy to find beautiful, but its artistry, Koda noted, is "hard to read," which might have been a good reason to provide some context for it—a social history, one of several filmed interviews, or a portrait of Chanel at work. A visceral sense of the woman has been sacrificed to aesthetics, the way personal objects are banished from a modernist decor (though Chanel's decors were rich and eclectic). Koda hoped that by using Lagerfeld's work as a "foil" he could start "a dialogue" and supply some of the missing tension. But the conceit of then-and-now Chanel suits side by side in a white

box isn't a recipe for lively conversation. Perhaps the foils to juxta-
pose with Chanel were her contemporaries in fashion. She wasn't a
fount of invention, like Schiaparelli; a technical innovator, like For-
tuny or Vionnet; or an impresario, like Poiret, although she did design memorable costumes for Cocteau, Diaghilev, and Jean Renoir.
Her own rules of the game, distilled over the decades, were a core of
beliefs that were as much about womanhood and its paradoxes as
about clothing.

"Balzac has invented everything," Colette wrote, and he might have
invented Chanel, had she not done it with such panache herself.
Gabrielle Chanel was born in 1883, in Saumur, a city of the Loire Valley, where her parents, who already had a mildly retarded daughter
and were not yet married, had settled briefly. Her father, Albert, was
an itinerant peddler descended from peasants and tavern keepers, and
her mother, Jeanne, was a seamstress with a fragile constitution that
was further strained by a vagabond's life, a faithless husband of incorrigible charm, and the birth of six children. She died at thirty-two,
when Gabrielle was eleven, and Albert sent his sons to live with relatives and his daughters to a high-walled convent orphanage (he never
came back to retrieve them) where the nuns taught them to sew. Six
years later, Gabrielle was given the choice of taking the veil or leaving.
Her maternal grandmother arranged for another convent to take her
in—a boarding school in Moulins, a garrison town where the elite
10th Light Horse Cavalry happened to be stationed—and in 1903,
when she was twenty, her teachers found her a respectable situation.
She went to work for a draper and his wife who liked to employ the
nuns' charity cases—humble maidens, they imagined, handy with a
needle. Many years later, Chanel described herself at that age as a restless misfit "with a hot little body." She told her friend Paul Morand,
"Arrogance is in everything I do. It is in my gestures, the harshness of
my voice, in the glow of my gaze, in my sinewy, tormented face."
    There were no respectable situations for a girl like Chanel in a
garrison town. She freelanced at a local cabaret as a *poseuse*—one of
the pretty extras who filled in between the artistes' numbers with a
few songs, then passed a hat. Though she couldn't carry a tune, the

soldiers found her adorable, and they called her Coco, the name of a pet in one of her coy ditties. On weekends, she moonlighted at a tailor's shop patronized by the officers, and it was there that she met Étienne Balsan, her first protector. He was the black sheep of a rich family, a famous polo player and horse breeder who owned a château near Compiégne, where Chanel learned to ride, and acquired a number of other skills that the nuns had neglected. For a while, she overlapped with Balsan's outgoing mistress, Émilienne d'Alençon, the great Belle Époque demimondaine and one of Coco's early promoters.

Though Chanel never referred to her convent years, and in her novelistic memoirs translated the word "nuns" into "aunts" and the orphanage into a farmhouse of dour spinsters, she also never outgrew what Edmonde Charles-Roux, one of her best biographers, calls "a yearning for austerity." However gratefully Chanel might have recalled the gallants who initiated her into the idle and racy life of an apprentice courtesan, it came with its own set of humiliations. Perhaps as a result, the little grisette passed among playboy friends refused ever to fetishize another woman—and that was the moral principle (one of the few) on which Chanel founded her career.

Modernism was in part a response to the artifice and dandyism of the fin de siècle, which may have suggested another of Chanel's working axioms: the simplest solution has the greatest authority. She made her debut in fashion as a milliner who, in an era of exorbitant plumage, stripped the trimming from her hats, and went on from there. In Charles-Roux's recently reissued *Chanel and her World* (Vendome, 2005), a life in pictures adapted from her biography, there is a photograph of Coco at thirty (she always looked a decade younger than she was), posing on the rocky beach at Deauville, hatless and windblown, in front of a weathered cabana. One hand is deep in the pocket of a chunky fisherman's chemise with a middy collar and rolled cuffs, and she has thrust a flower into the belt. The picture was taken in the summer of 1913, when Chanel opened her first *maison de couture* on a fashionable street next to the Deauville casino. It was financed by the English polo player, writer, and industrialist for whom she had left Balsan, Arthur (Boy) Capel, her great love. And it was here that Chanel staged her coup: the introduction of supple cardigan suits, devoid of embellishment, that skimmed an uncorseted body. They were made from jersey tricot—a cheap fabric used for the men's underwear and work clothes that her father had peddled. The ladies of Deauville woke up one morning to discover a shocking deficit of chic between their own clothes and *la mode* Chanel. It was the difference between a regime of frivolity and one of nonchalance.

The First World War made Chanel's name—rich Parisians escaping at short notice to Deauville flocked to her shop to replenish their wardrobes. (Among her many gifts, one of the greatest was a genius for timing.) She, in turn, gave a clientele who were suddenly emancipated by adversity, and by the departure of their men, clothes they could walk, drive, and work in. By the early twenties, those women and their daughters were game for sports, cigarettes, enterprise, speed, divorce, short skirts, bobbed hair (Chanel had cropped her own luxuriant tresses in 1917), and the exquisitely unpretentious "little black dress"—"a Ford signed Chanel," as *Vogue* captioned one of them. Paul Poiret, her leading rival, dismissed her sumptuary reforms as *la misére de luxe*, and in one respect he was right. To wear them smartly, you needed the adolescent body of the undernourished waif she had been.

Chanel was always her own best model, and she was proud to say that she never designed a dress that she wouldn't have worn. Her style was a synthesis of feminine softness and masculine ease, the gossamer and the tweedy. If she appropriated certain virile entitlements the way she borrowed her lovers' sweaters and overcoats—and elements from the uniforms of their grooms, gamekeepers, and crewmen—there was no militance to her chic. Her original distinction was to have rescued the "New Woman" of the Belle Époque not only from her frumpy bloomers and didactically mannish tailleurs but from her status as an object of ridicule to the "Old Men" of either sex who feared her modernity. Chanel's respect for the appearance of propriety was the adaptive trait of the orphan and shopgirl. Like Joan of Arc, another daughter of the people who acquired a large following of aristocrats, Chanel did so by outclassing them in the lists of purity.

Chanel's tastes were virtually infallible except in romance and politics. She had many passions but few loves, and it amused her to keep younger men, one of whom was Grand Duke Dmitri Pavlovitch, the czar's nephew and an alleged assassin of Rasputin. She also hired his sister, the Grand Duchess Marie, to direct the embroidery workshop that produced her sumptuous Russian tunics and tabards of the twenties. Dmitri repaid her generosity with an introduction to Ernest Beaux, a chemist and perfumer who, in 1920, concocted the formula for Chanel No. 5. Though Chanel conceded the distribution rights to the Wertheimers and litigated with them for the next forty years, the royalties made her one of the richest women in France. She moved into a mansion near the Élysée Palace and spent her fortune with abandon on a Rolls-Royce; Coromandel screens; cascades of diamonds and pearls that she mixed rakishly with her ropes of "amusing trinkets"; and a villa at Roquebrune, in Provence, where she cohabited with the grandest of her consorts, the duke of Westminster, and entertained the Churchills. Chanel and the duke tried very hard to conceive a child—he had no heirs—and when they didn't (she was by then forty-two), he married someone else. She consoled herself gamely with a defiant boast: "There have been several Duchesses of Westminster, but only one Chanel."

Despite her wealth, Chanel was a notoriously stingy employer, and she saw no reason that her underpaid fitting models, having spent the day immobile on their feet, shouldn't find it natural—as they were beautiful girls—to spend the night in a supine position earning overtime. But she was generous to her embarrassingly rustic brothers (in part to keep them out of sight), and she quietly paid the expenses of penniless artists, poets, godchildren, and friends. The last of Chanel's known gentlemen gigolos was Hans Gunther von Dincklage, alias Spatz, the suave German officer who shared her suite at the Ritz during the Occupation. When she was arrested after the liberation of Paris by the Comité d'Épuration, and questioned about this unfortunate alliance, she supposedly retorted to her interrogator, "Really, monsieur, a woman of my age cannot be expected to look at his passport if she has a chance of a lover."

Chanel was released after three hours, and there were, amazingly, no further repercussions. Madsen, who had access to files of the British Foreign Office that were "inadvertently declassified" in 1972, explains why. Churchill's old friend possessed secret information that might have embarrassed him: from 1940 until the end of the war, he had violated his own country's trade embargo with Germany to pay for the upkeep of the French properties owned by the Duke of Windsor. This information was apparently not shared with the Resistance, and neither was the file on Operation Modellhut. Though Chanel was never persona non grata in France, she prudently moved to a resort town near Lausanne, where Spatz joined her, and she later paid "a large sum," Madsen says, to suppress any mention of her name or her activities in the memoirs of Hitler's former police chief.

Lagerfeld was a sixteen-year-old star fashion student in 1954, the year that Chanel went back into business with a critically disastrous first collection of silk and jersey suits and lace evening gowns that recalled her couture of the thirties, and which the French and British press soundly panned as mumsy and passé. Lagerfeld later told Madsen that he thought Chanel "got it right," and the Americans agreed with him. She was relaunched on this side of the Atlantic by the enthusiasm of editors, buyers, and fashion civilians for ageless, undemanding clothes that restored the comfort women had surrendered to Dior's New Look, and offered relief from the tiresome comedy of the hemline wars that dominated postwar fashion. The youthquake of the sixties never shook Chanel's convictions ("I hate the old little girls," she said of matrons in miniskirts), and she wasn't troubled by the disdain of futurists like Courrèges, who called her "an old Rolls, still in working order, but inert." Her pronouncements grew more oracular, and they acquired an acidity she took no pains to dilute. Jackie Kennedy had "horrible taste," and was responsible for "spreading it all over America." (Madsen notes that Chanel had evidently forgotten about the pink suit.) Saint Laurent, on the other hand, was a young man with "excellent taste," she said. "The more he copies me, the more taste he displays."

Chanel always shrugged at the knockoff artists and pirates who rushed copies into mass production, and she wasn't as vulnerable to them as other designers. Her strength was never novelty, and reproductions couldn't possibly compete with the work of her couture atelier. "She considered imitation homage," her assistant said (to which one might add, she paid herself that homage all the time). When the Chambre Syndicale de la Couture tightened the rules governing press access to the collections, Chanel resigned. "Come to my place and steal all the ideas you can," she told the media. "Fashion isn't made to be canned." As Rhonda Garelick writes in a thoughtful catalog essay, "shopgirls riding city buses" in head-to-toe faux Chanel "delighted the narcissist" in her "and perhaps the secret populist as well."

Whatever Chanel would have made of the Met show, it is just the sort of meal she preferred—a lean banquet, beautifully plated, that leaves you hungry. But the "narcissist" might have wondered why on earth her seven decades of "iconic" work needed Lagerfeld's as a foil, and the "populist" might have resented the show's solecism. Chanel spoke and speaks to a host of other artists and designers across the spectrum, with whom an open forum would have been more stimulating than a hermetic "dialogue." Koda assured me that Lagerfeld did not have or expect veto power, but the curators made no secret of their anxiety to please him. And here one touches upon the inherent problem with the "extravagant" corporate sponsorship of museum fashion shows—the trap of gratitude. The unseemly promotional hyperbole of the message from Chanel's chief operating officer which introduces the catalog serves as a reminder that the sponsor's interest, however philanthropically packaged, is brand awareness, and publicity is the forge that heats the double "C." A museum's obligation is to retain its cool-headed autonomy.

Lagerfeld in his own right is a virtuoso, and more versatile than Chanel in certain respects. Some of the loveliest couture in the show—the ivory cocktail suit of spun-sugar bouclé, with a dissolving hem; the romantically tiered evening dress of black tulle, with a trompe l'oeil cummerbund of silver threadwork and rhinestones—is, in fact, his handiwork. But Chanel asked one unsparing question of every stitch she made, of every flourish or tuck on a dress: Is it essential? And if one asks the question about Lagerfeld's place in this show at the Met, which should have been Chanel's show, not a Chanel show, the answer is no.

—May 23, 2005

Mother of Invention

Elsa Schiaparelli's signature color was a violent magenta that she admired, she said, because it was "life-giving, like all the light and the birds and the fish in the world put together, a color of China and Peru but not of the West." She called it "Shocking." In French lingerie shops, it is still referred to as *le shocking*, and Yves Saint Laurent describes it in his foreword to Palmer White's knowledgeable 1986 biography (*Elsa Schiaparelli: Empress of Paris Fashion*, Rizzoli) as a pink with "the nerve of red . . . an aggressive, brawling, warrior pink." Saint Laurent characterizes the woman herself—whom he dressed, revered, and borrowed from extensively—in even more harrowing terms of endearment. "Her particular charm?" he writes: "Her brutality, her arrogance, her self-possession, disdain, storms of anger, odd whims, her Gorgon's mask." She was a majestic thunderhead whose bolts crackled unpredictably. The electric theme recurs in the title of Schiaparelli's autobiography, *Shocking Life*, published in 1954, and in the name of her most famous perfume, also Shocking, first marketed in 1937. But what is most shocking about Schiaparelli in 2003 is her obscurity.

History tends to remember those who have one big idea—monotheism, penicillin, the little black dress—rather than a host of good ones. Coco Chanel and Elsa Schiaparelli launched their fashion houses in the first decades of the last century like two rockets with equal payloads of ambition. Chanel settled into the lower and brighter—more visible—orbit, which the gravity of convention has begun to erode. Schiaparelli exerts her influence like a distant celestial body on women and designers who may see hot pink when they free-associate her name, but who otherwise have no precise image of her work. Beautiful, low-born Chanel, the daughter of a peddler and the mistress of a duke (Schiaparelli, splitting the difference, referred to her as "that dreary little bourgeoise"), was, of necessity, a great student both of class and of men, and she became a master of the irreproachable, distilling a notion of lithe simplicity that was radical for its time into an enduringly desirable modern uniform. Homely, aristocratic Schiaparelli—"that Italian artist who makes clothes," as Chanel called her—was abandoned by her only mate and never cohabited with another. But the possession of an impeccable social pedigree combined with a passionate allegiance to the avant-garde inured her to reproach—or perhaps whetted her appetite for it. She was a poet of couture rather than a prose stylist like Chanel. She designed clothes for an emboldened and unbeholden New Woman. And she probably did more to enrich the language of twentieth-century dress than any of her peers.

A mammoth retrospective of Schiaparelli's couture at the Philadelphia Museum of Art charts the topography of a legendary and protean, though submerged, career: fashion's Atlantis. (The show is amplified by the curator Dilys E. Blum's excellent companion volume, *Shocking!: The Art and Fashion of Elsa Schiaparelli*, Yale, 2003.) Excluding, for the moment, Schiaparelli's collaboration with the Dada movement and the surrealists, in which art and fashion were equal partners in a fertile if kinky celebrity marriage, the roster of her innovations includes items now so commonplace and indispensable that it is easy to forget how much prescience they represent.

There is nothing in the graphic knitwear from Schiaparelli's first collections (1927–29)—a sailor's middy with a trompe l'oeil bow; a sleeveless tank with a motif of tropical fish; daringly cut one- and two-piece woolen bathing suits with stylized nautical emblems (including a seaman's tattoo)—that would date them if they suddenly appeared in a show by some edgy young Italian like Antonio Marras. Helmut Lang's flapper dress of last year, composed entirely of zippers, seemed cheeky and fresh, but Schiaparelli rakishly scarred her evening gowns with plastic "lightning closures" in 1935. Diane von

Furstenberg is often given credit for the wraparound dress with which she launched her career in the early seventies. But Schiaparelli showed its prototype in 1930—the same year she introduced mix-and-match separates and engineered a backless swimsuit (to promote a tan without strap marks) whose built-in bra received a U.S. patent. Months later, she provoked the outrage of the British press by appearing in London, on a buying trip for tweeds, in a pair of svelte culottes cropped at the calf, and by dressing the tennis champion Lili de Alvarez in a short divided skirt of white silk that, like the culottes, brazenly proclaimed that women—even ladies—have two thighs with a space between them. Followers of fashion also owe Schiaparelli the wedgie, the jumpsuit, the overall, paper clothes, transparent raincoats, folding eyeglasses, fun furs, the scarf dress, colored hosiery, athletic wear, the shirtwaist jacket, ethnic-themed collections (one of Saint Laurent's many debts to his Gorgon), and the ready-to-wear boutique. Designers are apparently still mining her archives: a suit from Schiaparelli's 1933 winter collection, in a bias-cut navy-and-white tweed jersey, with a wrapped jacket belted slightly above the natural waistline, looks uncannily like recent Prada.

It must be said of lists like the above that there are rarely any pure "firsts" in fashion, and Schiaparelli was herself indebted to predecessors, most notably Paul Poiret. It must also be said that not every Schiaparelli was a masterpiece. In a photograph by Huene published in *Vogue* in November 1933, the dumpy, middle-aged couturier appears to be modeling a bedspread and matching pillow sham, though Blum informs us that her outfit is a taffeta dinner suit and cape in a quilted fabric called "Armada." But the authority of Schiaparelli's talent and her character was such that she could subvert convention, redefine beauty, and impose an aggressive silhouette, a goofy print (white rabbits riding bicycles), or a funky synthetic (she made garments of "Rhodophane," latex, "Jersela," oilskin, "angel hair," and "tree bark" rayon, as well as of straw, horsehair, mattress ticking, and sackcloth) on a timorous public. "Twenty percent of women have inferiority complexes and seventy have illusions," she declared with the impunity of a Pygmalion in her oracular "Twelve Commandments." Though one cannot accurately say that she single-handedly corralled women into pants, the lean swank of the trousers that she proposed in the mid-thirties went far to sanction their acceptance by the herd leaders of chic. One also can't say that she invented shoulder pads, because couturiers before her—and, of course, men's tailors—had employed them correctively. But Schiaparelli was the architect of the power suit, and of what contemporary fashion journalists called "hard chic," and she styled the racy swagger of the stars who embodied it: Dietrich, Garbo, Katharine Hepburn, and Tallulah Bankhead—all faithful clients. She squared the lines of the jacket, tapered them like an inverted trapezoid, and bulked up the shoulders to minimize the natural pear shape of the average woman, who was exhorted, in another commandment, to train her body to the modernist geometry of her clothes rather than fit her clothes to the baroque curves of her body. Joan Crawford brought her Schiaparellis back to Hollywood and threw them like a gauntlet at Adrian, who made their linebacker shoulders and lavish embellishment his own trademarks, and those of nearly every sinewy, flat-hipped, chain-smoking, man-eating, social-climbing, scarlet-clawed screen temptress of the thirties. Schiaparelli called this new look "the Wooden Soldier silhouette." Her nutcracker princesses—still cracking nuts—have morphed into the skeletal centurions who stride the modern runway.

Schiaparelli was an unlikely couturier, and not merely because she never learned to sew. She was born in Rome in 1890, in an apartment in the Palazzo Corsini, near St. Peter's, into a conservative family of aristocrats and intellectuals. Her father was the head of the Lincei Library and a translator of Arabic literature. Her Neapolitan mother was descended from the dukes of Tuscany. Both parents were pious, as was Schiaparelli's older sister, Beatrice, who devoted her life to refurbishing churches and illustrating a children's Bible. It seems unfair that Beatrice inherited the smoldering maternal beauty that her naughty, rebellious sibling would certainly have used to commit erotic arson. Elsa was short and wan, with the severe features of a Spanish duenna, though her smile could irradiate the stony contours of her face like the stormy light of an El Greco landscape. Nerve generates its own radiance, and in retouched portraits by great photogra-

phers Schiaparelli is almost lovely and always intriguing. As a young
woman with a pixie haircut and trim ankles, she was mistaken for
Anna Pavlova, who was dancing in Havana when Elsa visited Cuba as
the traveling companion of a beautiful and richly kept though tone-
deaf Polish opera singer who was booed off the stage. A distinguished paternal uncle, Giovanni Schiaparelli, the astronomer who
discovered the canals of Mars, tried to console his brilliant niece for
the cluster of birthmarks on her right cheek by noting their resemblance to the Big Dipper—a mark of good fortune, he said—and she
eventually decided to believe him. Her mature work asserts that there
is nothing so lowly or absurd—lobsters, pork chops, insects, dancing
cows, garden vegetables, even flayed skin—that it cannot be transformed into an object of provocative beauty, and she fashioned her
lucky stars/ugly moles into an oversize diamond brooch. Strong
women, Schiaparelli once remarked, intimidate men, so they are
rarely happy in love, but she also understood that strong men secretly
relish a frisson of intimidation. Her ideal client was a pugnacious jolie
laide like Maria Casarès, who played the role of Death in Cocteau's
Orphée, and whom she costumed as the vengeful society woman in
Bresson's Les Dames du Bois de Boulogne: a she-devil like herself.

Sacred monsters often begin life as enfants terribles, and little
Elsa, like the grande dame Saint Laurent describes, "didn't wish to
please. She wanted to dominate." She once jumped out a window to
prove that she could fly, and "planted" flower seeds in her nose and
ears, hoping to make beauty bloom. She also kissed a boy, then told
her confessor, whose outrage seems to have permanently discouraged
all subsequent candor—with anyone—on intimate subjects. Her parents discovered that their wayward daughter had written and published an ecstatically received volume of philosophical love poetry
entitled Arethusa when they read the reviews. (They refused to read
the book.) Two years later, at twenty-three, and by now dangerously
bored, Elsa was dispatched to live with family friends who ran a progressive home for orphans in the wholesome English countryside.
On a day off in London, she wandered into a lecture on theosophy
given in French by a charismatic and impossibly handsome half-Swiss,
half-Breton nobleman, Count Wilhelm Wendt de Kerlor. He and
Elsa became engaged twenty-four hours later and married before her

parents could intervene. In 1916, the impetuous young couple emigrated to New York, where Kerlor's soulful, orotund drivel and chiseled profile earned him a rapt feminine following. According to White, Elsa was "greatly impressed" by the city's "stark, vertical lines"; its gridiron streets; its corsetless, enfranchised women; the ubiquity of household appliances and violent movies (particularly those with car chases); and by American social mobility, all of which influenced her sense of style. Unfortunately, her sexually mobile husband abandoned her for an affair with Isadora Duncan, and she was left pregnant and practically penniless to fend for herself. (Here I must confess to feeling base gratitude, on Schiaparelli's behalf, to Dilys Blum, for noting in her chronology that Duncan caught her scarf in the axle of a car and was strangled to death a month after the succès fou of Schiaparelli's bow-knit sweater.) When her baby arrived—Maria Luisa, nicknamed Gogo, the mother-to-be of the actress Marisa Berenson and the late photographer Berry Berenson Perkins—Schiaparelli parked her with a nurse in Connecticut "for her health" and moved to Patchin Place, in Greenwich Village, where she picked up a series of odd jobs and a circle of artistic friends. Man Ray and Marcel Duchamp introduced her to the nascent Dada movement; Edward Steichen educated her about modern architecture and photography; and the musician Gabrielle Picabia—the wife of the Dadaist painter Francis—gave her a disastrously uncongenial first job in fashion, as a sort of Avon lady, helping to sell, out of a hotel room, a collection of French couture designed by the sister of Paul Poiret.

The rustic air of normalcy wasn't at all beneficial to Gogo's health: she contracted polio. In 1922, Schiaparelli returned to Paris as a thirty-two-year-old divorcée with a toddler in desperate need of expensive care. Elsa's father had died, and her mother provided a small allowance that would have been more generous had the prodigal moved back to Rome. New York, however, had given her a taste of freedom. "Poverty forced me to work," Schiaparelli told an interviewer, "and Paris gave me a liking for it." Necessity may explain a knack for invention but not a genius for it. Schiaparelli had no schooling or background in her exclusive and arcane métier, and very little hands-on experience with making clothes. Yet her ascent, as noted by nearly every contemporary observer—including Janet Flanner, the Paris correspondent for *The New Yorker*, who profiled the couturier in 1932—was "cometlike." In 1923, she was improvising amateurish though fetching garments for her girlfriends and shepherding rich Americans around the couture showrooms. In 1925, she was hired to design dresses for a small house funded by a Mrs. Hartley that closed in 1926. A year later, her first collection was being lionized by *Vogue* and snapped up by New York department stores. In 1934, *Time* put her on its cover. Her addresses kept pace with her fortunes, and in 1935 she settled her salons and workshops into a ninety-eight-room mansion on the place Vendôme. Jean-Michel Frank designed the interiors and Alberto Giacometti the ashtrays. From her front windows, Schiaparelli could contemplate the effigy of another short, saturnine upstart who conquered Paris: Napoleon.

Schiaparelli did her greatest work in the latter half of the 1930s, her period of collaboration with Dalí and Cocteau on dresses and accessories that blurred the boundaries between art and fashion. In his autobiography, Dalí describes Schiaparelli's salon as the true, beating heart of surrealist Paris: "Here new morphological phenomena occurred; here the essence of things was to become transubstantiated." The futurists had celebrated the power of machines and science to transform human nature; the surrealists explored the possibilities of metamorphosis while disavowing any faith in its benignity. The beauty of Schiaparelli's surrealist couture is both troubling and hilarious—surrealism is a tragicomic genre—and it anticipates the experiments of fantasts like Alexander McQueen and of mad scientists of couture like Margiela or the young New York collective As Four, whose hybrid creations seem to reflect mimetically on the manipulation of nature by genetic research and transplant surgery.

Cocteau supplied the line drawings that Schiaparelli transformed into embroideries on two memorable pieces in her 1937 collection, and she designed the costumes for the heroine of his play *Les Monstres sacrés*. A painting by Magritte suggested her shaggy ankle booties of black monkey fur. Her vagina-shaped fedora, photographed by Man Ray, was used to illustrate a theoretical text by Tristan Tzara. With Dalí, she conceived her famous cocktail hats shaped like pork chops and high-heeled shoes. Dalí's painting for the June 15, 1936, cover of the surrealist magazine *Minotaure*, edited by André Breton, was the inspiration for several of her dresses. It shows a woman with a bull's head; an open bureau drawer where her breasts should be; a lobster emerging from a cavity in her stomach; and legs—one of them sutured, à la Frankenstein—hollowed out with compartments for an absinthe glass and a bottle. Schiaparelli subsequently designed a suit with "bureau-drawer" pockets; a "skeleton dress" with a padded rib cage; and the notoriously phallic "lobster" frock, embellished with sprigs of parsley, that Wallis Simpson chose for her trousseau (along with seventeen other Schiaparellis). Dalí had wanted Schiaparelli to smear the skirt with mayonnaise, but she demurred. Cecil Beaton persuaded the future Duchess of Windsor to model the creation in a gauzy engagement photograph intended to soften her image, though it is difficult to see how the lady's reputation as a predator could have been improved by association with an avant-garde *revoltée* (Schiaparelli); the fetishist who painted *Necrophiliac Springtime* (Dalí); and a bottom-feeding crustacean. The last and most shocking, at least in retrospect, of Schiaparelli's duets with Dalí was the "tear" dress of 1938. The silk of a simple sheath with a swallowtail train seems to have been tortured by a hunting knife, as if it were the skin of a furry animal flayed to expose the bloody flesh beneath. Appliqués on the matching veil reproduce the trompe l'oeil incisions in three dimensions. Hitler invaded Poland a year later.

Chanel spent the war shacked up with a Nazi officer at the Ritz, on the place Vendôme, from whose windows she could have looked down upon her rival's salon. Schiaparelli fled to New York, where, in 1942, she helped Marcel Duchamp organize "First Papers of Surrealism," an exhibition that raised funds for a consortium of French relief charities. She settled in Princeton, promoted her perfumes, lectured on fashion to adoring crowds, and volunteered as a nurse's aide at Bellevue. The Roosevelts entertained her at the White House. Though various manufacturers offered to bankroll a collection, she refused to design clothes in exile, out of loyalty to, and solidarity with, the couturiers and artisans of Occupied Paris. When the war ended, she reclaimed her seventeenth-century mansion on the rue de Berri, which had been commandeered by the Germans. White relates that she found a desk drawer filled with the visiting cards of French celebrities who had been received there, "and she never invited one of them again." She cranked up her business, doubled the salary of everyone on her staff, and staged a comeback with bustled gowns, wasp-waisted suits, and sportswear influenced by British Army uniforms. Her postwar collections were critically well received, and her licensing agreements with America continued to provide a handsome source of income, but the economics of couture had changed, and, while searching for her bearings in a much altered landscape, she began, for the first time—fatally—to look back.

On February 3, 1954, two days before Chanel emerged from retirement to reopen her atelier on the rue Cambon, Schiaparelli presented what would prove to be her farewell show. She filed for bankruptcy ten months later. Her work was out of tune with the tastes of a conservative postwar public unwilling to think too hard, and weary of irony and aggression. Chanel became a household word, and Schiaparelli a name that the world forgot how to pronounce. It's skYAP-a-relli. The "ch" is hard: like her chic.

—October 27, 2003

THREE

The Absolutist

In March 1956, CBS aired an episode of the *I Love Lucy* show—
"Lucy Gets a Paris Gown"—in which the Ricardo and Mertz families
explore the City of Light. Lucy and Ethel are determined to see a
fashion show, so they persuade Ricky to wangle four invitations from
the exclusive couturier Jacques Marcel. Fred, however, alerts his
buddy to the horrifying price of a Marcel creation: five hundred
bucks. After the show, the husbands deliver their critique: the dresses
look like potato sacks. Undeterred, Lucy goes on a hunger strike until Ricky agrees to buy her a Marcel. When he discovers that she's
been cheating, with Ethel's connivance, the husbands plot their revenge. They commission a local tailor to run up two shapeless frocks,
made from burlap potato sacks, which they pass off as Marcel's top-
secret looks for the next season, completing the ensembles with two
chapeaux: a wine bucket and a feed bag. The foursome then repair to
a café—America's first public fashion victims dressed in their barn-
yard finery—where Marcel, an oily-looking character in a beret, happens to be sitting at the next table with two house mannequins. Lucy
wants to thank him, at which point the miscreants confess their
prank. Marcel, in the meantime, seems to have had a sudden inspiration, and rushes off. Back at the café a few hours later, the couples
again find Marcel with his mannequins, who are now wearing his latest handiwork: couture potato sacks.

There was, of course, no Jacques Marcel, but the news from Paris
in 1956 was of a radical new silhouette: the sack, a waistless wool

shift that skimmed the body and squared its curves. Its creator was the Spanish couturier Cristóbal Balenciaga, and nothing so crude as burlap—not even an uncovered seam—ever touched his clients' skin. (The closest he came to using sackcloth was in a bolero of embroidered natural straw described by its owner, Pauline de Rothschild, as "the color of Inca gold.") Arbiters of fashion generally agree that Balenciaga, the son of a Basque fisherman and a seamstress, was the greatest couturier of the last century. Dior considered him the primus inter pares, and Chanel conceded that Balenciaga alone could construct a perfect garment from start to finish with his own hands, whereas everyone else was merely "a designer."

It is hard to imagine the aloof Spaniard warming to Lucy and Ethel, much less to a bandleader perturbed by a five-hundred-dollar dress. Among the grandees who stoically paid up were de Rothschild's husband, the baron Philippe; the banker Paul Mellon, whose wife, Bunny, ordered her gowns by the score; the Spanish sherry king Rafael de Osborne, whose effervescent queen, the former Claudia Heard, an oil heiress from Texas, rented a suite at the Paris Ritz for her couture; the Duke of Windsor; Loel Guinness, whose incomparably chic Gloria was "a little afraid," she wrote, "of not being good enough" for the clothes; Prince Rainier; Gianni Agnelli; Francisco Franco; Prince Radziwill; and "the utilities king of America," Harrison Williams, whose bride, Mona (later Countess Bismarck), won the title of "best-dressed woman in the world" the first time it was awarded, in 1933, and even had her gardening shorts tailored by the Master. The only big-time balker I can think of was John F. Kennedy, who was outraged by the first lady's couture bills (his father settled most of them). But the regal opera cape of ivory silk ziberline that Jackie wore, with a Franco-Kabuki hairdo, to dine in Paris with de Gaulle was a tribute to Balenciaga by his intimate and protégé, Hubert de Givenchy.

The exorbitant labor and materials invested in a couture dress (one of Claudia de Osborne's favorites had a bustle of ermine tails) have always been reflected in its price, but Balenciaga was the most expensive house in Paris, and its directrice, Mlle. Renée, once put off a faithful client who had asked if she might bring a friend to the lugubrious salon on the avenue George V by noting coldly that "curious" strangers were unwelcome. Curious strangers, however, will have ample opportunity, this year and next, to see what happened in the inner sanctum. The first of four ambitious Balenciaga exhibitions, curated by Givenchy, opened last March in Paris, at the Mona Bismarck Foundation. The second and grandest of the shows, also in Paris, a retrospective curated by Pamela Golbin of the Musée de la Mode et du Textile, with Nicolas Ghesquière, the current designer of Balenciaga ready-to-wear, opens on July 6. The third, curated by Myra Walker, the director of the Texas Fashion Collection, at the University of North Texas, in Denton, will occupy a suite of galleries normally dedicated to visiting collections of Spanish art at the Meadows Museum, in Dallas, next February. And the fourth, scheduled for September of 2007, will celebrate the completion of a new multimillion-dollar museum and headquarters for the Balenciaga Foundation in the couturier's birthplace, Guetaria—a fishing village on the Bay of Biscay between San Sebastián and Bilbao.

Balenciaga's work was treasured by its owners and, on the whole, lovingly preserved. He designed some three hundred originals a year, from which a staff that numbered, at its height, five hundred tailors, seamstresses, fitters, pattern cutters, milliners, and specialists in embellishment filled thousands of private orders. At any stage, Balenciaga might decide to tear apart the muslin pattern or the finished garment, even when it was wrapped for delivery. Many clients recalled his obsession with sleeves, and he was capable of spending a sleepless twenty-four hours to redo one. Chitchat or smoking in the studio was forbidden (although the silence was periodically fractured by the Master's rages at an imperfectly set shoulder). Sumptuous fabric was a house signature, and the great couture textile firms often collaborated with Balenciaga on innovative silks or woolens with a firm body that lent itself to sculptural treatment. He told Givenchy, "The cloth is like a living skin: it must never be ravaged or insulted."

Balenciaga commuted frequently between France and Spain, where his sister and relatives supervised his two busy satellite houses (their label, Eisa, was an abbreviation of his mother's patronymic, Eizaguirre). Courrèges and Ungaro both served a provincial apprenticeship at Eisa before returning to the avenue George V, and they perfected their craft by helping to translate the Paris models for a slightly staider and more frugal clientele. (According to Balenciaga's grandnephew Agustín, Doña Carmen, General Franco's wife, had the "annoying" habit of showing up with her own discount fabric.) There is enough extant couture to give each curator the luxury of drawing upon different archives. Pamela Golbin told me that she and Ghesquière will leave the Spanish work and its history to the foundation, and Myra Walker said that she will focus on the bequests of Osborne and of Bert de Winter, a glamorous divorcée who became the star millinery buyer at Neiman Marcus, and whose discreet romance with a married mogul financed her own couture shopping.

Balenciaga opened his Paris couture house in August 1937, at the age of forty-two, and closed it in 1968, in the midst of the May uprisings. The fall of the Spanish monarchy, in 1931, and the ensuing Civil War were unpropitious for anyone in a carriage trade, so Balenciaga, whose business in Spain had collapsed, followed his clients abroad. Having failed to find work in England (he revered British tailoring), Balenciaga formed a partnership with two fellow émigrés: a Basque financier, Nicolás Bizcarrondo; and a debonair Frenchman of Russian extraction, Vladzio Zawrorowski d'Attainville, who was, Walker told me, "Cristóbal's great love." They put up a hundred thousand francs, which financed—barely—a debut that was greeted with ecstasy by the French press. "Let us dream a little," a radio journalist told his listeners the next year, "before an enchanting collection as heady as a Spanish wine . . . that is all instinct and sensuality." He went on to describe "a procession of ravishing and inspired" dresses for a fairy queen, an infanta, or a Pompadour, "which pass from violent colors to exquisitely sweet pastels," while "a liturgical black and white are treated with genius in evening gowns for the cruel consorts of a doge." This delirious effusion set the tone for many, if not most, future reviews, and it was amplified by lucrative praise from England

and America for the "dramatic simplicity" of Balenciaga's daywear, which, *Harper's Bazaar* noted, "abides by the great rule that elimination is the secret of chic."

Balenciaga himself abided by the rule that the refusal of compromise is the secret of couture. When other couturiers capitulated, in the fifties, to the inevitable democratization of their business and began to produce prêt-à-porter, he stubbornly rejected the terms—and windfalls—of surrender. Whatever his politics, he had the prudence, while doing business during the Occupation, never to discuss them (although, according to his most reliable biographer, Lesley Miller, an English art historian, he did scoff at Hitler's suggestion that the haute couture should be relocated to Berlin, saying, "He might as well take all the bulls there and try to train matadors"). His career was that of a royalist, and the sometimes puzzling extremes of his style—austerity and pomp, extravagance and reserve, humility and intolerance—prove to be the paradoxes of his devout Spanish Catholicism.

Piety and chic may not obviously be compatible, but penitents and perfectionists tend to have a lot in common. Balenciaga's confessor described him as a "haunted" soul, and he was a man obsessed with his own flaws, as well as with those of women, who aspired to transcend them by creating an infallibly beautiful body of work. That struggle left him eternally dissatisfied, according to his friend Bettina Ballard—"at times, hungry and empty, at other times, filled with a great sense of injustice." When Dior reaped the glory for reviving the French luxury business with his *corolle* silhouette of 1947 (later repackaged, more commercially, as the New Look), Balenciaga—who, before and throughout the war, had shown similarly shapely suits and dresses with an hourglass waist and a voluminous skirt—felt the slight keenly. "You have to understand that M. Balenciaga's couture was not only a style of dress but a code of conduct," Givenchy explained to me last March, at the opening of his show. "He took the old-fashioned view that a woman should confide herself to a single couturier. When the New Look began turning heads, and some clients deserted him, he was profoundly grieved by their fickleness,

and that of the press. Afterward, he became a more introverted figure, refusing to make public appearances or to supervise the fittings
of all but a chosen few." Devastated by the sudden death of d'Attainville the following year, Balenciaga was dissuaded from retiring
only by an appeal from Dior himself.

Balenciaga was never willing to do the kind of self-promotion that
Dior did, which he considered demeaning. Nor would he pander to
headline writers with seasonal novelties and catchy names to describe
them. But Balenciaga's mandarin reticence asserted his supremacy,
and the double shocks of 1947 and 1948 ultimately galvanized his
talent and revealed him as a formidable competitor with an insolent
streak of pride. When he defied the Chambre Syndicale de la Couture
to show his collections—with Givenchy—a month later than his
peers, buyers and journalists obediently trudged back to Paris. The
renegades got exclusive coverage in every style column or magazine.

The sack made headlines in 1956 in part because to the average
man it seemed so militantly unsexy. (Fellini, however, was intrigued.
According to his biographer Hollis Alpert, he spoke of the sack as a
"fantastic and extraordinary" new style that "set light to my imagination.") But Balenciaga's counterrevolution had begun the previous
year, when he showed his first streamlined tunic dress—a monkish
tabard with three-quarter sleeves worn over a straight underskirt.
Throughout the fifties, his designs became purer of line, airier of volume, and more geometric. The historian and curator Richard Martin
described the chemise and the trapezoidal "baby doll" dress as
"cages" for the body—though they freed it from elaborate corseting
and offered an imperfect figure a kind of protective custody. His
gourd-shaped wraps of the same period were cocoons in which a
woman could imagine herself—or in which a man could dream of
finding—a butterfly. The tunic, however, as Myra Walker writes in
the catalog of the Dallas show, *Balenciaga and His Legacy* (Yale,
2007), "was a genie that could not be put back into the bottle." In
abolishing the waist and stripping his daywear of its surface detail,
Balenciaga gave his apprentice Courrèges (who left the house in
1961) a template for the space-age look of 1965, which gave the
mods a template for the miniskirt. The least subversive of couturiers
thus became, despite himself, a sire of the youthquake. "People used

to keep telling me that fashion came from the streets," Diana Vreeland told Eugenia Sheppard in 1973, "but I had always seen it at Balenciaga first."

The modernity of late Balenciaga isn't of the street, however, even if he was one of the first to show high boots with harlequin tights under a shorter skirt, and cheeky sportswear in transparent plastic and faux fur. Of the two clear—and conflicting—sets of instruction that he left to posterity, one is addressed to a dying imperium, and the other to an improbable utopia. The former legacy, perhaps, reflects the nostalgia for grandeur of a fisherman's son steeped in his national folklore and art history, who costumed his clients in the draperies of a Zurbarán Madonna, matador boleros encrusted with jet embroidery, and fantastical bubbles of beribboned lace that seem to have come from a Murano glassblower. The latter legacy contains the runic musings of an ascetic who progressively whittles away at the inessential. He adapted the vestments of his parish church—the cope, the chasuble, and the casula—for the wardrobe of a worldly woman, and he experimented with feats of minimal tailoring, like the one-seam coat and the no-seam dress: an asymmetric jersey wrap shaped by two darts and fastened at the shoulder like a toga. By the end of his career, Balenciaga seemed less interested in clothing a body than in treating it as an armature for thrilling and sometimes weird abstractions that the camera loved. (The history of modern fashion as we think we know it is actually the history of fashion photography.) In this work, Balenciaga married couture to modernism.

Any piece of couture by Balenciaga is a collector's item, but that doesn't make it a masterpiece. The early work is sometimes difficult to distinguish from that of his contemporaries. The famous opulence of his beading and embroidery evokes vanished Xanadus, yet it also recalls state dinners at the Reagan White House. The workhorse of Balenciaga's stable was a boxy, semifitted suit with a standaway collar and a cropped sleeve. He showed it most often in a fuzzy mohair or a tweed bouclé and sometimes in a mannish windowpane check. And no matter how deftly Balenciaga "adjusted" the waist, or handled the bulk of a stiff fabric, the suit looks dowdy today. There were dozens of versions in the archives in Guetaria, Denton, and Paris, and they elicited in me—as they might, I suspect, in anyone old enough to have burned her bra—a faintly morbid shudder at a world of claustrophobic gentility that an army of daughters set upon, around 1970, in a frenzy of sartorial matricide. The sexpots went elsewhere: to Saint Laurent, whose little black dresses and severe tailleurs owed almost everything to Balenciaga but which turned the attractive trick of perverting his bourgeois sense of propriety—the *Belle de Jour* effect.

Mostly because the work of Irving Penn, Richard Avedon, Louise Dahl-Wolfe, Bert Stern, Tom Kublin, and, later, Hiro was primarily in black and white, it is startling to realize that Balenciaga, like the ancient Greeks—but also like the doyennes who winter in Palm Beach—had no qualms about showy, if not garish, color: cerise and lime; puce and royal blue; the purples and yellows of a pansy bed. Woman-as-flower is a recurring motif, though it is most poetic when least literal, as in his "cabbage cape" of 1967, a sensuous whorl of silk ruffles that tops a columnar sheath in which the body becomes a stalk for his sublimely abstract corolla. The other extreme is a parachute-silk evening pajama of 1966 smothered with three-dimensional floral appliqués: dainty camouflage for a she-yeti. And at the Bismarck show I marveled at an evening coat that was somehow as unsettling as a fetish. Its bell-shaped inner shell of absinthe-green tulle was completely feathered with curly, translucent ostrich plumes, each no thicker than a false eyelash and individually sewn on at a random angle, so that its wearer's slightest movement caused the surface to tremble. Before she lit a cigarette and took a drink, the slavishly admired Countess Bismarck, who owned the coat, must have seemed like some hybrid divinity—half human, half bird.

Each of Balenciaga's legacies had its cohort of disciples, and the courtly knights of the old order are Givenchy, Ungaro (who told me last March that the Master taught him everything he knows about a "woman's mystery" and "moral rigor"), and Oscar de la Renta, who learned the romance of the ruffle by heart, in his youth, and is still reciting it. "I don't like to speak of fashion now," Givenchy admitted with good nature, "so I have my blinders on." We were sitting alone in Mona Bismarck's conservatory (the Bismarck Foundation is housed in her former mansion, on the Seine), and Givenchy, who is seventy-nine, pulled his gilt chair closer to mine. "I was seventeen when I came, timid and quaking with respect, to the avenue George V with my portfolio. Mlle. Renée sent me away—M. Balenciaga wouldn't see me, she said. But we met at a cocktail party in New York about seven years later. My passion for the vocation moved him, and I think he saw in me someone he could share his own with. 'No cheating': that was his cardinal rule."

The guests for the opening reception began arriving, and Givenchy politely left me to stand on the receiving line and kiss their hands. Many were petite, exquisitely groomed old ladies in couture suits who had their granddaughters in tow—the kind of *jeunes filles comme il faut* that one rarely sees on the streets of Paris anymore, and you had to wonder in what convent they had all been stowed. The girls were most interested, as I was, in a gallery of bridal gowns—the only pieces on display that had not belonged to Mona Bismarck, despite her five trips to the altar—and a small gaggle of them, sisters and cousins, perhaps, with the same corn-silk hair, stood for a long while before a display mannequin in a corner that was facing the wall. The arms were bare, and the head and shoulders were opaquely veiled in a cowl of ivory gazar. The back of the gown, which was all one could see, fell in an unbroken parabolic sweep of full-bodied silk that tapered into a train. It had one seam, like the axis of an elm leaf. Yet despite its weight and stiffness—and its nunlike solemnity—the dress was a Brancusi. This is the prophetic Balenciaga, the one who taught the schismatics of fashion—like Courrèges, Paco Rabanne, Geoffrey Beene, and, after them, an avant-garde of Japanese and Belgians—how to cut free.

Balenciaga was born in Guetaria in 1895. A century ago, the harsh monotony of village life would have been relieved by the beauty of a spectacular landscape and the tumult of the sea. Today, an ugly baffle of condominiums is going up above the beachfront, and a cluster of low-cost modern housing strung with banners supporting the Basque separatist movement occupies the high ground south of the corniche. But the old town still consists of four narrow medieval streets, a slanted Gothic church of worn ocher stone, a marina, a small square with a large statue of the explorer Juan Sebastián Elcano, and a cemetery on the windswept hill, where Balenciaga is buried, along with his parents and siblings.

Balenciaga's father supplemented his modest living as a fisherman by acting as the village mayor. He died young, and his widow took in sewing to help support their three children. Cristóbal, the youngest, may have graduated from the local grammar school, but, according to Aberri Olaskoaga Berazadi, of the Balenciaga Foundation, he received no further formal education. He was destined for a sailor's life, or perhaps the seminary—his uncle was a priest. Though little is known about his formative years, Cristóbal seems to have helped his mother with the relatively menial needlework that she did for the women of a noble family, the Marqueses de Casa Torres, who summered above the village in the Aldamar palace, a fussy nineteenth-century mansion—vaguely alpine, vaguely rococo—with wooden balconies and a façade of raspberry-pink stucco. It currently houses the offices and archives of the foundation, and behind it is a vast excavation site where a new museum wing—a long horizontal tube of articulated-glass sections—will be erected.

The legend of Balenciaga's rise seems more cinematic than likely when one has walked Guetaria's unevenly cobbled streets, whose ancient tenements are swagged with drying laundry, and which smell of fish grilling on outdoor braziers even today. Cristóbal was thirteen when he followed his mother's patron, Doña Blanca, as, presumably, she made her way to Mass, for where else could she have been going on a summer day, alone in the village, in a couture suit? He begged her to let him copy it, and she is said to have agreed. Whatever the truth, Marie-Andrée Jouve, Balenciaga's former house archivist, notes simply in the chronology of *Balenciaga* (Assouline, 2004), a brief, illustrated memoir recently reissued, that the Marquesa "encouraged" his career. Some fifty years later he made the gift of a wedding dress—a majestically prim confection of satin and mink—to her granddaughter Fabiola de Mora y Aragón, when she married the king of Belgium.

Balenciaga spent his teens as an apprentice to society tailors in Madrid and San Sebastián—the summer residence of the Spanish court—and he became the consummate court dressmaker. It was a point of honor, for such a man, to flatter the conventions of an exalted clientele. His business was built on the premise that a lady changed her clothes three times a day, disdained the familiarity of inferiors, flaunted her diamonds but never her indiscretions, and traveled with several steamer trunks and a maid. (The jet plane, Givenchy pointed out, dealt one of the death blows to couture.) That lady, like Balenciaga himself, was apt to be hostile to the mood of disaffection that became glamorous when a new generation embraced the louche, the epicene, and the plebeian. Even though the theater of the barricades of May 1968 attracted its share of chic walk-ons in Saint Laurent, it is hard to imagine any of Balenciaga's house stalwarts as a rock or flower thrower. And, whether or not the festive insurrection that helped topple de Gaulle influenced Balenciaga's decision to retire, it would end his era. "I have given enough," he later told Givenchy. "There is no one left for me to dress."

San Sebastián was a sophisticated spa and casino town, built on the lines of Biarritz. The local Basques were prosperous, and the summer population, from both sides of the border, rich. The city was famous for its seaside promenade, its luxury shopping, and, in particular, the men's haberdasheries that made it a center of what Lesley Miller calls "Spanish Brummellism." According to Jouve, young Cristóbal, in 1913, is "employed at the shop 'Louvre,' and rapidly rises to the top." In 1919, at the age of twenty-four, he opened his first fashion house, and then two more, and began traveling to Paris for the couture shows. He had somehow borrowed or earned enough capital to buy originals at Chanel, Vionnet, and Schiaparelli, and he assiduously studied their construction. The female couturiers were his greatest mentors, but by then he probably knew that he loved men. He was the kind of romantic-looking youth, dark and slim, with a repressed,

Proustian intensity, who would have been attractive to the Brum-
mells. Golbin believes that he met d'Attainville in the twenties, and it
seems plausible that this artistic polyglot, who later designed the
witty house millinery, became Balenciaga's Pygmalion, refining his
persona and finishing its seams. Their relationship was never clandestine, and they lived together on the rue de Boétie. But once Franco
had come to power, and his wife and daughter began dressing at Balenciaga, the two lovers would have had to be circumspect.

Flamboyance, in any case, was alien to the nature of a laconic and
touchy man who was a cipher to outsiders, and who preferred to say
nothing about himself rather than to strike a false pose. After 1948,
he shunned the press, which he despised (he banished from his shows
journalists deficient in reverence); refused to give interviews until he
retired, and then gave only one; and worked in silence in an all-white
room. "Don't waste yourself in society," he told the textile magnate
Gustav Zumsteg, and between collections he retreated from Paris to
one of his houses in France or Spain, where he is said to have enjoyed
knitting, collecting fashion plates and bric-a-brac, and shopping for
antiques, which piled up in storage. Another guilty pleasure, according to Ungaro, was a penchant for fresh eels with garlic.

Balenciaga's inner circle included Givenchy; Aimé and Marguerite
Maeght, who built one of Europe's great contemporary-art collections; Bettina Ballard; and Carmel Snow, the editor of *Harper's
Bazaar*, with whom Balenciaga later had a falling-out. But, for the
most part, his close friends were Basque. Sonsoles Díez de Rivera
met Balenciaga as a schoolgirl in the 1940s (he designed her First
Communion dress). She is a lively patrician, still striking in late middle age, and her manners belie one of Balenciaga's rare, flippant remarks: that you can tell a distinguished woman by her disagreeable
air. We met at the Bismarck show, and Díez de Rivera spoke in passing about her mother, the Marquesa de Llanzol, a beauty whose
swanlike aplomb recalls that of Babe Paley and who is often described
as Balenciaga's Spanish muse. He dressed her and her daughters for
twenty-five years, and, in the catalog for a show of the family couture, Díez de Rivera recalled Balenciaga as a "bighearted, affection-
ate" friend with "a joy for life" and a "sense of humor." To support
this surprising claim, she described her mother's first encounter with

Balenciaga, around 1942, at the Eisa atelier in Madrid. The Marquesa was pregnant, and, as the dress she was having made would no longer fit her after she gave birth, she asked for a discount. The house refused, so she confronted the Master in a corridor of the salon. Díez de Rivera wrote, "Balenciaga looked at her over his glasses, and asked, 'Why should I have to give you a discount on a dress just because you are expecting? I'm not the one to blame.' "

Balenciaga made few concessions, either to private clients or to the better department stores that paid a premium for his originals with the strictly controlled right to make copies at different price points. But he was generous to other couturiers, dressing the great Vionnet after her retirement, supporting the work of Givenchy, and lending Courrèges the money to open his own house, then refusing repayment when Courrèges was successful. The two offenses that Balenciaga never pardoned were careless workmanship—a form of disrespect to the cloth—and personal disloyalty. Chanel lost his friendship and esteem forever with a spiteful remark to a reporter about his decrepitude. He wept with chagrin when he heard it, Givenchy told me, and sent back all her gifts. "But M. Balenciaga," he continued, "made a point of going to Coco's funeral, saying to me"—apparently without irony—"one must know how to forget."

There is perhaps nothing the fashion world does better than forget. Balenciaga died in 1972, and his name is best known to the youth of today as the label in a sought-after handbag with punkish hardware—studs, buckles, and a zipper festooned with leather streamers. There have been a series of slight variations on the basic design, and a medium-sized version of the ever-popular motorcycle bag, in pink or silver, retails for around $1,200, about half the price of a suit by the Master in the 1950s. The prototype was designed by Nicolas Ghesquière in 2000. "My generation doesn't have any sense of the collective patrimony that Balenciaga represents," he told me in New York last March, "and initially, I suppose, neither did I."

Ghesquière is a slightly built man of thirty-five—wary but not withholding—with arctic-blue eyes that are set off by a stubble of dark beard. He has something of the young Balenciaga's sultry air of hypersensitivity, and he, too, speaks about himself without affectation. He was born near Lille, an industrial city in the north of France, and grew up in the Loire valley, not far from Chanel's birthplace, in Saumur. His father taught physical education and hoped that his son would do the same. At eighteen, however, Ghesquière left home for Paris, aspiring to a career in fashion, and he was hired as an assistant at Jean-Paul Gaultier. After two years, he quit to support himself designing knitwear. In 1995, he was offered a job by the owners of Balenciaga, Groupe Jacques Bogart, which had bought the company from a German firm that bought it from Balenciaga's heirs. Though Balenciaga officially disdained ready-to-wear, Golbin believes that he was "fascinated" by its possibilities and constraints. In 1968, he told the Marquesa de Llanzol that he regretted not being younger, for he might have produced "amusing but tasteful" ready-mades for "the era we live in." He had licensed his name for a line of hosiery; the house had marketed several profitable scents for men and women; and in 1968 he accepted a commission from Air France to design the uniforms for its flight attendants. (I traveled to Paris for the first time in 1969, on an Air France charter, of which I remember nothing but the hostesses' chic. The new uniform consisted of a short, svelte skirt in navy blue serge, with in-seam pockets, hemmed slightly above the knee; a trim jacket in the same fabric; and a white blouse and gloves. Only the silly hat, shaped like a baba mold, marked these ensembles as corporate livery.) It was Balenciaga's sole foray into mass production, but the practical challenge of dressing a legion of Mariannes—the public face of Gallic womanhood—was apparently irresistible.

Several forgettable creators had tried to make a viable luxury brand of Balenciaga before Ghesquière, who found himself consigned to turning out golf outfits and funeral clothes for the Japanese franchises. In 1997, the managers fired their chief designer, Josephus Thimister, and failed to lure their leading candidate, Helmut Lang, to replace him; in desperation, they asked Ghesquière to produce a collection. After doing so, he was also fired, but was called back and promoted when the sales figures came in. The moody swagger of his clothes—gaunt leather blousons and stovepipe pants—suggested the costumes for a biker *Hamlet* set in a bleak metropolis like Lille, a century from now. Their success assured Ghesquière's continued employment when Balenciaga was sold to the Gucci Group, in 2001. He says, "I got the job because I had my own vision, and because of my youth. It was intimidating enough just to be at the house. I hesitated to explore Balenciaga's archives until a few years ago, when I realized I could just go downstairs for an hour at a time, without feeling pressured, to see what caught my eye."

Ghesquière has, at times, clashed with Gucci executives, including Tom Ford and Domenico De Sole. He had a reputation for being difficult, and he, in turn, felt hobbled by a lack of confidence and financial support. Nor, as Cathy Horyn wrote in *The New York Times* last year, did it help his status "as fashion's new messiah when he was caught copying, line for line, a patchwork vest by the late Kaisik Wong, a California designer of the 70s." In 2003, Ghesquière was about to resign—though more in frustration than disgrace—when Ford and De Sole left Gucci abruptly after failed contract negotiations.

Whatever embarrassment he may have felt about the Wong episode, Ghesquière realized that he could begin citing Balenciaga without sacrificing his bohemian integrity. In 2004, he introduced Edition, a costly line with couture detailing based on archival designs, and last February his ready-to-wear show, a dauphin's canny homage to a king, was the sensation of Fashion Week. Tickets were perhaps even harder to come by than invitations to Balenciaga's excruciating two-hour *défilés* (conducted in total silence, though smoking was allowed). Ghesquière started promptly on a rainy morning, without extraneous theatrics, and out came a procession of eerily familiar tweed suits with standaway collars and bubble skirts; boxy, molded jackets with raglan sleeves and bejeweled gum-ball buttons; austerely cut sheaths in gorgeously stodgy materials like quilted silver lamé. But Ghesquière had given these elderly ghosts an elixir of youth that made them more desirable—at least to look at—than the originals. The comparison was a bit unfair, because Balenciaga created his classics for a body of average height with a bulge here and there, and his house mannequins were hired for their cool dignity rather than for their sex appeal. Ghesquière's runway models were nubile Giacomettis, and, to exaggerate their legs, he sent them out in seven-inch platform boots. But the clothes were not just cleverly updated vintage. By shrinking, squeezing, cropping, stretching, or inflating their proportions, Ghesquière endowed them with an exotic buoyance—like that of anime—and he reminded his audience that modernity in dress reflects the sense of dislocation which defines modern life.

A sense of dislocation often hones the instincts of a gifted gay youth from the provinces, like Ghesquière, or like Saint Laurent forty years ago. They are able to recognize a closeted seductress—a Buñuel heroine, like Belle de Jour—and help to realize her potential for transgression. That, perhaps, is how they both saw, and saw through to, Balenciaga's latent eroticism. Yet the secret life embodied in Balenciaga's couture—his own—cannot be discovered in a fashion show, a photograph, or a retrospective. You have to examine his seams from the inside out. If no ready-to-wear can approximate them, it isn't because a machine can't make perfect stitches. A machine doesn't suffer from the terror of failure and exposure inherent in virtuosity. Fashion plays upon the same fear when it attempts to persuade gullible women that a dress can make them as unassailably lovely as the inhumanly perfect teenager who models it. But Balenciaga, who refused to cheat, took the true measure of a woman's sins, and forgave them.

—July 3, 2006

FOUR

Hidden Women

The Café des Beaux-Arts is a Parisian *bar-tabac* on the corner of the rue Bonaparte and the place de l'Institut, half a block from the Faculty of Fine Arts. It has been a bohemian hangout for decades, if not centuries, and it has changed very little since Richard Avedon used its awning and a stack of its rattan chairs as the backdrop for his rapturous photograph of Suzy Parker in a white chiffon gown by Mme Grès. "Note how much you see of the bosom," Carmel Snow, the editor in chief of *Harper's Bazaar*, wrote on the back of the engraver's print, which was air-mailed to Alexey Brodovitch, her art director, in August of 1956, so that it could be processed for the fall couture issue.

Fashion is no longer, or only rarely, photographed in the Latin Quarter. The currency of the picturesque has shifted to the anomic modern, and editors prefer locations like Fresno or Levittown. But for a decade after the Second World War, Avedon was doing something daring by wetting the ancient cobblestones, strafing them with klieg lights, staging tableaux vivants at a pool hall, a circus, a casino, or in a kitschy boîte, like the Scheherazade. "Most of the pictures had a historical subtext," he says, "and I spent weeks before a sitting documenting it with research and snapshots. Maybe the Maquis had used the basement of a bar, or the Jacobins had raised a guillotine in a courtyard where I assembled a troupe of acrobats, scattered a bale of hay, and posed a model in a New Look suit." In 1948, he contrived to photograph Chanel against a crudely plastered wall under a painted slogan that asked POURQUOI HITLER? But even if the photographs weren't explicitly political—and they weren't (*Bazaar* refused to run the Chanel picture)—there was a subversive shimmer to them. It comes, in part, from the birdlike poignance of the models, captives of their finery, their stoicism masquerading as insouciance. And it comes, too, from the high contrast between somber rigor and hectic frivolity; the earthy and the ethereal; the aristocratic and the plebian. It's hard to remember, in an age of blatant and ceaseless dissonance, that such incongruities in a fashion magazine were once—joltingly—new.

The decor and clientele of the Beaux-Arts still gratify a tourist's preconceptions about the Left Bank—more so than the Flore or the Deux Magots, which are crowded with other tourists. The last time I had breakfast there, I chose a corner table, ordered *un express bien serré*, unfolded *Libération*, and listened to the two students next to me discussing their philosophy exam. As everyone is a provincial on his first day in—or back in—Paris, I'm not ashamed to admit that the scent of their tobacco, rising in lazy plumes backlit by the sun, was as intoxicating as the bittersweet sediment in my cup, the view of the Seine through half-curtained windows, the heated sibilance of their babble about Lacan, the scowl of the bartender, and the interested glances of a lone drinker enjoying his first *petit rouge* of the day. He was a lean man of about my age (a generation older than the students), scruffy in a rakish and impeccably calculated way, Parisian to the core. His motorcycle helmet sat like a paperweight skull on a ravaged leather attaché case which could have belonged to a novelist or a professor, but just as easily to a courier. Prudence triumphed over the temptation to act upon my luxuriant (and banal) reverie about him, though not entirely. I found myself, as in a trance, rising from the banquette, buying a pack of Gauloises from the obese cashier and—after a decade of abstinence—starting to smoke again.

Smoking, like joining a revolution, is one of the Parisian beaux arts, as is cruising a stranger. In this light, consider Avedon's remark about the sexual intimacy of a portrait and its beholder: "The moment you stop to look you've been picked up." I was also interested to read that his "first erotic experience"—he was ten—was watching a girl smoke. She was an invalid who lived in his building on East Eighty-sixth Street, and she spent her days confined to bed, like the young Proust, with a bad case of asthma, for which her doctors had prescribed, fantastically, some sort of medicinal cigarette. In the late afternoons, he would sit beside her as she inhaled "the smoke slowly into her lungs, holding her cigarette sideways, like someone floating down the Nile." The American boy couldn't know that this languid beauty on her imaginary barge, drugged and doomed, is a ubiquitous figure in French fiction from the Romantic period through the fin de siècle to the novels of Françoise Sagan, which are contemporary with the photographs in this volume (*Made in France*, Fraenkel Gallery, 2002). He already knew, however, that "women are a foreign country." He also knew, like every other precocious young aesthete raised among philistines and hungry for distinction in both senses of the word—glory and separation—that Paris is the capital of that foreign country: the place one flees to (or fled to) for an advanced degree in Sentimental Education.

In the course of transferring his archives from a warehouse in Long Island City to the Center for Creative Photography at the University of Arizona at Tuscon, Avedon found twenty-seven engraver's prints in a carton where, he says, "I'd forgotten them." The pictures were taken between 1955 and 1959, and in the earliest ones, he points out, "I had really just come to grips with the eight-by-ten format. For the first decade of my career, I couldn't handle its distortions, or perhaps didn't want to. Brodovitch was always cropping in to eliminate the nineteenth-century frame of the skylit studio. The eight-by-ten is what Nadar, Brady, and Atget used—a direct descendant of the camera obscura—and the only things that have changed since its invention are the speed of the film and the sharpness of the lens. It has a very shallow depth of field, which means you can throw the background out of focus, reducing the sum of detail and creating an ambiguous narrative relation between the knowable (what's sharp) and the unknowable (what's blurred), which is what René Clair does, with gauze, in a film like *Le Million*. But tracking is impossible with an eight-by-ten, and there's no spontaneity. After years of photo-graphing with a Rolliflex, which gives you too much information and feels too easy—as if the camera is taking the picture—I wanted that discipline. You set up your photograph, then stand to the side of the tripod directorially, gauging the discrepency between the image in the viewfinder and the scene as your eye perceives it. There's some-thing poetic in that disconnect—like the experience of a child who sticks a pencil into a glass of water and notices that the point ends somewhere else." That humbling demonstration of refraction—of reality's recalcitrance to art, the point always ending somewhere else—was, he concludes, "important for my work."

The young Avedon's luxuriant reveries of Paris refract, playfully, certain conventions of the films of Ernst Lubitsch, which inform the mad-for-France Hollywood movies of the 1950s, which mirror the reveries of Richard Avedon. *An American in Paris* (1951), *Sabrina* (1954), *Funny Face* (1957), and *Gigi* (1958) all are set, at least par-tially, in that operetta City of Light to which the Café des Beaux-Arts belongs. One might add to the list of period Francophile romances Grace Kelly's wedding to Rainier III of Monaco (1956), whose back-drop wasn't Parisian, but which, as both a love story and a fashion show made in France, had many of the movies' trappings, and whose heroine fits their mold: a ravishing ingenue, high-spirited and ambi-tious for experience, who captures the heart of a jaded prince, receiv-ing, in the process, both a glamorous makeover and an old-world education in erotic wisdom and feminine cunning.

The left and right banks of this madcap Paree, its high and low life, its monde and demimonde, its dissipated pleasure-seekers and folkloric, bohemian working class of showgirls, midinettes, and bar-stool philosophers occupy separate, nearly hermetic universes—both imaginary. The dichotomy is a venerable literary and boulevard con-ceit, as old as Balzac, and Avedon plays with and off the contrast—the erotic thrill of miscegenation—the way the filmmakers do, though without resorting to burlesque. They go for the kaleidoscope of postcard sights. He wields his camera like a jeweler's loupe, prying a costly gem from a vulgar setting and remounting it austerely. He had just begun reading Colette, and his vignettes have an affinity with hers—"The Hidden Woman," in particular—a short story *Bazaar* had published in 1955, in which a rich bourgeoise trapped in a numb marriage goes alone, disguised, to the Opera Ball. She thinks her husband is out of town, but he has trailed her secretly, expecting to surprise her with a lover. She throws herself into the orgy of masked revelers, and as he watches from the shadows she yields to the embraces of a naked wrestler and a Dutch girl, and to the lips of a nubile boy. Instead of rushing forward to separate them, her husband disappears into the crowd, having discovered a more demoralizing secret than simple infidelity: her "monstrous pleasure" in the freedom conferred by a mask. Avedon's pictures capture the same festive melancholy and the same mysterious solitude of a beautiful woman at a quintessentially Parisian moment: deciding capriciously, and with no faith in true love, whether she'll resist or surrender to temptation.

Funny Face is also the story of a costume party, an *inconnue*, and an awakening, though of course in a much frothier vein. Avedon's early adventures in the fashion business were, loosely, its inspiration, and the hero, named Dick Avery, is a photographer played by Fred Astaire. While they are both elegantly kinetic ectomorphs, Astaire was a dapper gent in his mid-fifties, sere at the edges when he made the film, and Avedon a meltingly handsome dark colt in his early twenties when he arrived in postwar Paris to cover the couture for *Bazaar*, and—as the practical Mrs. Snow put it—to help revive the French luxury business by whetting the vast, lucrative American appetite for its wares. While *Funny Face* is the artifact of a remote, lost civilization, three of its purest pleasures haven't dated: Hepburn's face, Givenchy's couture, and Astaire's dancing—all pertinent, the dancing in particular, to Avedon's work in this volume. Astaire's *ballon* (his impossible buoyancy), the classical discipline he applied to a popular genre, and the virtuosity that makes a strenuous, artificial, endlessly rehearsed feat seem joyful and spontaneous are the attributes of these pictures, and they, too, suggest that there is probably no chagrin for which the grace of perfection can't console us.

All but three of the photographs were published in *Bazaar*. A majority have been reprinted in previous collections of Avedon's work, included in his shows, or both, though never precisely in this form: unretouched (or barely retouched) originals marked with a grease pencil for Brodovitch; the gowns titled and described by Snow; the images numbered, dated, and rubber-stamped with a notice of copyright, and signed by the artist in his acrobatic scrawl. "A picture in a magazine," he says, "is a view without a window. Here you have the window—the context of production. It's pure chance that these prints escaped the garbage pail. So many from the same period, even from the same sittings, were lost or stolen." As there is almost no chance in his work, the random nature of the prints' survival and the accident of their discovery make an apposite foil for the laborious collaboration that created them.

Avedon's models—Suzy Parker, Dorian Leigh, Barbara Mullen, Dovima, China Machado, Carmen, Audrey Hepburn—were his contemporaries. ("Notice that they all have noses. The heroic age of the nose has since ended.") Like him, they were handsomely paid and well-known. But unlike the society women who posed for an earlier generation of genteel European photographers, they were thoroughbred only in their silhouettes. The elegant creatures were workhorses, and their sense of complicity was that of performers who sweat behind the footlights and are separated by a breach of caste and an experience of professional discipline from the spectators in the hall—but also by a breach of glamour from the dowdy fans at the stage door. When Avedon first began working for *Bazaar*, he met his colleague the Russian baron George Hoyningen-Huene in the elevator of the Hearst building. Huene, a fitness enthusiast, used to ride his bicycle to work from his estate on Long Island and leave it with the attendant. "Are you the new photographer?" he asked the twenty-two-year-old. Avedon replied that he was. "Too bad," said Huene. "Too late." "What he meant," Avedon explains, perhaps construing the remark in its kindest light, "is that fashion had become a business, and that the days of court portraitists like himself, Baron de Meyer, and Cecil Beaton, who belonged to the same *gratin*

as their subjects—aristocrats modeling their own clothes—were finished." They were hardly finished: there have been several successive
generations of titled beauties eager to pose for fashion magazines in
or out of their own clothes, and Avedon himself has made some of
the most alluring images of them. But there is often nothing more
tonic for the resolve of a fiercely competitive young artist than the
dismissive snobbery of an old master. One would like to have the
Avedon portrait of the towering Huene in the mahogany coffin of
that elevator cab, bicycle clips on the trousers of a bespoke suit, the
overhead light harshly contouring the bald crown, the voluptuous
tie, the planes of an incongruously boyish countenance, its shaken assurance masked by a thin smile.

Avedon and his womanly girls had started working together in
their late teens or early twenties, after the war, and had, over the
course of a decade, become a family of troupers—a small repertory
company of which he was director, ballet master, and impresario.
"Our rapport was built from sitting to sitting and from season to season," Avedon says of his artistes, "and I would never have dreamed
of using a picture they didn't like." Each of them seems to have possessed a different expressive speciality. Carmen provokes, smolders,
and withholds—her forte is reluctance. Parker projects what Avedon
describes as "a radiant, unearned ecstasy." Dovima is a brushstroke,
in human form, of inspired calligraphy. Machado subverts the clichés
of Asian compliance and feminine passivity. Her beauty is fragile but
her aura steely—even defiant. "In 1959, when I first photographed
China, she wasn't considered 'white' enough for *Bazaar*," Avedon
recalls dryly. "I had to threaten that I'd leave for *Vogue* if they didn't
use her pictures. They placated me by using a couple of them and
played up the diplomatic background she'd run away from. There
was actually no mention that she had lived with a bullfighter—the
great Dominguin—or that after leaving him she had earned her living
as a nightclub singer on the Riviera. It was a compromise on both
sides. Three years later, China was hired to succeed Diana Vreeland
as *Bazaar*'s fashion editor. Times were changing."

Eleven of these photographs, including Avedon's study in grisaille
of Machado veiled in black lace, inscrutable as a maja, were shot
against a stark felt background in the *Bazaar* studio on the rue Jean

Goujon, directly behind the House of Dior. "From the balcony," he says, "I could wave to the seamstresses." His resident assistant was the French technician and printmaker André Gremola, who "seemed ancient" to the young photographer—"he was probably fifty"—and whose fairy-tale name, which suited his legend, suggests one of those thralls with magic powers who, in the sagas, do the gods' dirty work. "There was hardly enough room to unpack the dresses," Avedon recalls. "In a tiny kitchen on the mezzanine, a maid cooked French lunches, and the darkroom smelled of the garlic sausage on Gremola's breath. He never slept and was always wearing a soiled lab coat. Every night, he'd string clotheslines from wall to wall and hang up the negatives to dry, making his prints the next morning, one at a time, in his simple trays. He used Portriga paper, which has a special warmth to it. Gremola was the perfect artisan. These silver-bromide prints are his handiwork, and you'll never see their like again."

One day, Avedon and Gremola climbed up to the roof, and together they ripped off the layers of tar paper and plaster that had, under the regimes of his predecessors—Baron de Meyer, Huene, and Louise Dahl-Wolfe—covered the skylight. "It wasn't a self-conscious attempt to be modern. I was interested in the challenge of shooting with no props, no artificial light, no background, little help—just a dress, a model, and her pensive beauty in isolation. This is precisely how and where photography begins: in Paris, in this daylight studio—a miniature version of the gritty, romantic places that Nadar had worked in, and Daguerre before him. I wanted to use that frame and history for pictures that were new." One of the first post-demolition pictures, which appears on the cover of *Made in France*, is of Suzy Parker in a gray faille "dinner dress" by Dior, with a deep décolleté and a fringed stole spread out like the wings of a coasting hawk. At first glance, the stole appears to be a piece of felt that Parker has ripped from its staples on the wall behind her—an impudent, even heretical gesture that relates the makeshift bohemian setting to the fastidious chic of the gown, the cheap, pressed cloth to the swanky, woven silk. Avedon says that the effect was unintentional, but it suggests the spirit of iconoclasm that animates his Parisian project, and the shock of its vitality.

That shock (indeed, any shock) is difficult to appreciate in the present fashion climate: it needs some relief. Avedon wasn't the first to shoot clothes lyrically, or on location using movie lights, or to liberate models from their static poses and their petrified expressions, and he has always acknowledged his debts to predecessors. The first and most influential was Martin Munkácsi, the 1930s master of "action realism," who, Avedon wrote in 1962, "brought a taste for happiness and honesty and love of women to what was, before him, a joyless, loveless, and lying art." Then there was Brodovitch himself, whose mystical blurred-motion images of the Ballets Russes, published in 1945, revolutionized performance photography. But Avedon's performance photography—a good description of it—is more psychologically astute than his forerunners' about that elaborately choreographed performance called femininity. "Any extreme gift is alienating," he says, "beauty no less than genius. It's a sport of nature. I've spent my life with these aberrant creatures—exceptional beauties. My sister was one of them, and all my models have been memories of Louise. Her looks were the only thing our mother talked about. 'With skin like that, you don't have to open your mouth, Louise,' and she never did." Louise Avedon withdrew from her family and the world and ended her short life in a mental hospital. But great photography gives a voice to the mute, even to the inanimate, and sometimes a dress can speak. One of the most eloquent pieces of clothing in Avedon's oeuvre is a voluminous plaid overcoat that was obviously not made in France, that indeed might have come from the immigrant family's bankrupt department store—Avedon's Fifth Avenue. His dark sister is wearing it in Central Park on a sunny autumn day of 1940, and it seems to shield her protectively, even from her brother's tender gaze, like some dumb, familiar spirit. "Cocteau understood what's moving about fashion," Avedon says. "That it dies young."

While the women in his early work certainly aren't liberated, they aren't puppets or victims either: they're escapees. It is both chilling and illuminating to revisit the world they've escaped from as it is reflected in the issues of *Bazaar* where these images first appeared. In January of 1959, the editors published, in gazette form, a roundup

of events, celebrities, inventions, and obsessions that had shaped the
preceding decade. They included Stop & Go pills (downers and up-
pers); the Korean War; the belted chemise; quality paperbacks; the
McCarthy hearings; the "Capri look"; filter cigarettes; the Salk vaccine; strontium 90; *Rashomon*; Dynel hair; "thinking machines";
Brigitte Bardot; the Dead Sea Scrolls; private planes; the conquest of
Everest; the coronation of Elizabeth II; and Dior's greatcoat. The
editors also noted the advent of "ads with humor," which, however,
are conspicuously absent from their own pages. Here, despite
Brodovitch's modernist art direction and the tony fiction (Gordimer,
Auden, Chekhov, Borges, Welty, McCullers, and de Beauvoir were
some of the contributors), one encounters the shades of Avedon's
tragic sister and asthmatic neighbor grown up, tranked up, and living
in a claustrophobic suburban harem where they have nothing to do
but "sleep away the inches" on a vibrating lounge chair (the Relax-a-
Cisor), or to interrogate their mirrors for "heartbreaking truths." "If
you smoke a lot, shouldn't it be Kent?" On a more hopeful note:
"The husband you get may be your own!" (This is the promise of a
corset named, rather vindictively under the circumstances, the Merry
Widow.) And then "there's this to be said for the age we live in—the
man in the white suit has come out of his laboratory and entered our
lives," bringing the miracle of an "estrogenic" cream. The man in the
white coat was only a step behind.

I was particularly arrested by an unsigned opinion piece—a little
dose of saltpeter—in the issue of July 1956. It is subtitled "A Threat
to American Beauty." The writer (who seems to have a bone to pick
with Avedon) complains about what she calls "the fashion for Bottled
Lightning." This expression, she explains, was coined by William
James to describe the undignified tendancy of Americans to grimace
with a "too desperate eagerness and anxiety," or a "too intense re-
sponsiveness and good will . . . It is not by chance that fashion photographers . . . usually snap their shutters when the models' faces are
intensely animated. Amazement, ecstasy, alarm, joy, wonder, glee—
and a $29.50 dress . . . But after the teens, don't men get a little
weary of high-key women?" And she exhorts her readers to follow
the "serene" example of their "Oriental" sisters. They should "learn
to sit, so that even waiting at an airfield can be restful." One begins

to appreciate the proto-feminism mixed with old-fashioned gallantry and barely contained panic in Avedon's message: run for the plane.

Fashion is by definition unstable, but the fashion photograph has one enduring imperative that hasn't changed since the early 1930s, when, thanks to the advance of mass-printing technology, photographs largely replaced illustrations of the latest modes in the women's press. The imperative is to depict a supremely desirable garment worn by an archetypically desirable individual—until fairly recently, always female. At this point (so vulnerable both to corruption and to interpretation), it is up to the artist to balance the conflicting demands of his talent for autonomy and his career for reemployment, as well as to accommodate his own illusions and disillusions about class and sex. Fashion photography is an indisputably promotional genre, but if one takes the view of John Berger and Claude Lévi-Strauss, so is much of traditional portraiture and still life since the Renaissance— and perhaps since the first commissioned likeness of a well-heeled sitter was rendered on a wall, a tomb, a piece of linen, or a clay jar. "If you buy a painting you also buy the look of the thing it represents," Berger writes. According to Lévi-Strauss, "It is this avid and ambitious desire to take possession of the object for the benefit of the owner or even of the spectator which seems to . . . constitute one of the outstandingly original features of the art of Western civilization." Berger's distinction between a piece of "hackwork," however technically adept, and a "masterpiece" is useful in considering what makes a great fashion photograph. "The average [oil painting] was produced more or less cynically . . . It is the result of the market making more insistent demands than the art."

Not all of Avedon's fashion photography meets Berger's somewhat doctrinaire criteria for what constitutes a masterpiece, as Avedon himself would readily agree. "It meant something to me for the first twenty years of my career," he says. "But just when I got the art of it down, the feeling wasn't in it, there was too much narcissisim and disenchantment. I kept at it, but it became a craft—a means of support for my studio, my family, and my art, which turned to portraiture. This book documents the last time the sensibility of my fashion work wasn't commercially driven." Yet the rift isn't so absolute. A deeply felt, artistically insistent consciousness of fashion—of the relation between an envelope and its contents—is never incidental to an Avedon portrait. The dress and grooming of his subjects are essential features not only of a photograph's graphic composition but of the tension between exposure and concealment, resistance and submission, manipulation and authenticity, the social and the primal selves. Cover any of Avedon's faces, and the garbed body takes up the burden of emotion—even when that garb is nothing but a black lacework of live bees on the immobile torso of a youth, albino pale. And perhaps once one has been, like Avedon, a high priest of fashion's most sacred rites, one may, as in the Catholic Church, repudiate one's vows, but one can never formally be released from them. The obligation to describe and inform has also trained him to encrypt in clothes, as if they were genes, a compact code of self-expression— that of an organism's vital intelligence. Even in some of his harshest and most troubling studies of character, the photographer's gaze conveys a prestige one can't help but experience as glamour: a state that Berger defines as "the happiness of being envied," but which, in Avedon's best work, is also something rarer—more fearful and precious—the happiness of being seen.

—June 2001

FIVE

Man of the Cloth

In 1968, Giorgio Armani had recently been promoted from his first job as an adult, styling department-store windows, and was designing menswear for Nino Cerruti. I was a young American living on a shoestring in Rome. A wellborn woman whom I knew slightly invited me to a Halloween party at her villa outside the city. The Halloween of fright masks and trick-or-treat is not an Italian tradition, but she had spent some time in New York and wanted to celebrate with a costume ball. "It won't be stuffy," she assured me. "No bella figura. I've ordered everyone to wear something silly and fantastic!"

My homemade costume, of which I was immodestly proud, was a sheath of lime-green polyester chenille, ruched to resemble the casing of a caterpillar—a plump one. Two muslin wings, stiffened with picture wire, emerged at the shoulder blades, one artfully half crumpled, as if it had been bruised in the birth struggle. A pair of quivering antennae were attached to a headband of matching plush. Luckily, I got lost on the labyrinthine ring of roads around Rome, and by the time I arrived at the villa, the party was well under way. It was a warm autumn night, and the French doors were open to formal gardens. From a distance, I could see that all the female guests, and my hostess, were in evening dress, and all the men in tuxedos.

I needed Armani that night, although he had not yet gone into the business of providing the illusion of breeding and confidence to women who are not born to it. Perhaps because he was a provincial

boy—the son of a trucking-company manager from the unstylish industrial city of Piacenza—he has always been particularly sensitive to
the risk of courting ridicule in overly ambitious or exotic clothing
and bright colors. Armani is the champion of the insecure, the newly
hatched, the self-doubting and ingenuous, and that has been his
charm for the ingenues of Hollywood, male and female, of all ages.
The French have never cottoned to Armani for the same reason,
though in part, too, because he is a foreign upstart who challenged
their preeminence in ready-to-wear. They tend to look with disdain
on any Prometheus who presumes to steal the fire of sacred chic for
mass diffusion.

Leaving the Guggenheim Museum under the influence of the new
Armani retrospective, I was struck by the resemblance of Frank Lloyd
Wright's modernist ziggurat to one of Edith Sitwell's ambitious, exotic turbans. A girl of Sitwell's generation learned at an early age that
she could aspire to express herself through fashion in one of two
roles: the priestess or the object of worship. With a prominent nose
and a great deal to say, she was probably destined to be a priestess.
This dilemma was current as late as my own youth, and it was Armani
who helped abolish it.

Wright himself was a man of fashion, a canny dresser who, like Armani, understood how to make his clothes project aesthetic flair
without sacrificing professional sobriety—a sort of cross between J. P.
Morgan and Ezra Pound. On my piano, I have a photograph taken in
1938 of Wright with an uncle of mine who was his business partner
in a big, doomed real-estate venture. The architect and the entrepreneur are both wearing confidence-inspiring bespoke suits: Wright's a
single-breasted navy pinstripe dandified by an Edwardian tie and a
gold loupe on an opera-length chain, my uncle's a double-breasted
British tweed with a matching waistcoat that surely exuded a clubby
scent of malt whiskey and tobacco. These are the kinds of suits that,
with a dart or two, Dietrich and Garbo modeled with such transgressive glamour around the same time, and the images of those northern
sirens commandeering a mogul's battle garb made their impression on

the young Armani, always a big fan of movies and broad-shouldered enterprising women.

Most of the hussies who affected trousers before the late 1960s were only flirting with transvestism. They wanted the convenience and modernity of men's clothes, and with them a just portion of social virility (not the same as sexual virility). Armani's sartorial innovations have less to do with "androgyny"—a ubiquitous word in *Giorgio Armani* (Guggenheim Museum Publications, 2000), the four-hundred-page, six-and-a-half-pound catalog to the exhibition— than they do with camouflage. He did not "deconstruct" gender. He deconstructed a jacket, ripping out the lining or interlining, adjusting the placement of the buttons, and changing the proportions of the collar, lapel, and shoulders.

In 1975, Armani showed a woman's version of the same garment—radical but not militant—that he had designed for men a season earlier. Its slouchy drape skimmed the body in a sensual way, without flaunting or constraining it. The cut, slightly oversize, like the pajamas of a Pierrot, flattered the heavy and gave the thin a waifish charm. As a working uniform, it was neutral and dignified enough to pass muster with both feminists and bosses. The look, in fact, functioned "semiotically"—another favorite catalog word—like a good pair of sunglasses. You could read into it what you wanted to: power, nonchalance, sexual cool, entitlement, but also a hidden vulnerability—the priestess and the object of worship in one. An Armani suit steeled the nerve of women without masculinizing them, just as it disarmed men erotically without unmanning them. Whether this really helped create more equality between the sexes or just equalized their narcissism, I'm not sure.

It can't be a coincidence that Armani's low-risk, evasive chic— evasive about class, age, aggression, and desire—conquered the headlines at a moment of high-risk sexual behavior and violent political struggle, or that it dominated the luxury market, at least in America, throughout a decade of rapacious economic speculation. In an essay in the catalog, the Italian journalist Natalia Aspesi reminds us that Milan in the 1970s was an "epicenter" of protest and terrorism. Remembering "the rotten eggs . . . hurled at their dazzling ensembles at the historic opening of La Scala in 1968," the rich had disguised themselves on the street in "irreproachable garments." Armani, she notes, "remained detached from the enraged city," working on his first collections, which would redefine the irreproachable.

A week before the Guggenheim retrospective opened, I visited the Armani flagship store on Madison Avenue. The racks looked a bit picked over, perhaps because the choicest merchandise is often set aside for the most faithful customers. Many of the shoppers were foreign, and no one was under fifty. A South American was vetting the classically cut dark suits and feathery chiffon blouses with a younger woman who was either her daughter or her personal shopper. There was a mother of the bride with her best friend, and a business executive on her cell phone, pulling together a travel wardrobe while she booked her flight. They were all attractive women of substance, but fashion civilians. The elite commandos have not worn Armani for some time. Fashion on the front lines is by nature subversive, and Armani prefers, as he once put it, "to be a reassuring figure." His customers need that reassurance—to receive it and to project it. The last time I was in a courtroom, both the prosecutor, a woman, and the defendant, a Dominican drug lord, wore Armani suits, or decent copies.

Armani's reach is still wide, and his profits are commensurate. The company is Italy's leading fashion house in sales. And there is also something proud, perhaps even noble, in his refusal to deviate from principles he once articulated to the Italian style oracle Anna Piaggi: "First of all, I must preserve my own image . . . an image which has, in turn, created a certain kind of woman. Consequently I must never allow avant-garde or retro tendencies to work their way into my own personal backdrop."

But avant-garde and retro describe everything that is in fashion. And Armani's retrospective at the Guggenheim, timed to celebrate his twenty-fifth anniversary in the business, has received more editorial coverage this autumn—almost all of it loving—than his collections. That, surely, was its main point.

Critics of the Guggenheim have long complained that the curved walls and open well of Wright's rotunda make an uncongenial exhibition space for art, particularly painting, and some have even suggested that the architect intended his dynamic container to forever upstage its contents. The architecture does invite you to keep moving, while a picture requires that you stand still. That sinuous unfurling of planes and bays, however, proves to be nearly ideal for a high-end retail showroom, perhaps because to shop is to navigate an alimentary canal of desire.

There are four hundred appetizing and deluxe pieces of Armani's work in the show, served up against a background of taupe walls, ivory screens, and alcoves finished like the surface of a crackled riverbed. The floor of a room full of black-and-gold dresses glows like a light box; a crescent of stylized beach is spiked with fiber-optic reeds. The museum's spiral terraces have been scrimmed by Robert Wilson, who designed the installation, in a continuous bandage of taut, theatrical gauze that follows the curvature of the ramps. The clothes are cleverly mounted on headless, nearly invisible armatures spotlit by A. J. Weissbard, and invested, like those partygoers I once glimpsed through the windows of the Roman villa, with hauteur.

I had always thought that Armani's gift was for a kind of sensuous abstraction—that, say, of an urban landscape. This show suggests that I was mistaken. The pensive daywear in his signature monochrome palette looks a little thyroid-deficient next to a collection of evening clothes that display a dazzling range, not only of inventiveness with pattern and texture but of emotion. There are tunics encrusted with pearls and embroidery whose surface richness is tempered by their simplicity of line; a strapless, fluted column of black-and-white bugle beads that pays homage to a rug dealer's fly curtain; a gray silk tea gown cut from a Gauguin print bleached of its color and tattooed with steel beads; a gossamer shift of chamomile tulle and spun gold appliquéd with jeweled spiders; floral chiffon dinner suits plastered with sequins that brave (and defy) vulgarity; and—best of breed—the frock of a Fragonard shepherdess, stripped of all embellishment, and rendered in sooty velvet.

I usually work the Guggenheim the way I do Takashimaya, taking the elevator to the top floor and walking down. At the Armani show, I started at the bottom, but when I got to the top I decided to take another look, and on the trip back the installation seemed to give off a faint whiff of embalming fluid. All the wrapping and muffling—the floors have been carpeted, too—creates a disembodied effect, which is heightened by the dreamy ashram music of Michael Galasso, but even more so by the absence of any useful program notes or critical focus.

This so-called retrospective invites you to worship Armani's virtuosity in a vacuum. The exhibits have been grouped by color and theme, without regard for chronology or, in fact, content. There is almost nothing from the 1970s—Armani's formative years—and very little from the eighties. A handy number of ensembles are still for sale, and, indeed, a vast chamber on the top floor is devoted to the wishfully youthful, tepid pastels for spring 2000.

The curators' choices in general seem precious and repetitive. There are none of the uniforms Armani has designed, over the years, for ordinary people like taxi drivers, policemen, soccer players, flight attendants, and military personnel, which might have helped offset the impression—however expensively cultivated by Armani himself—that his raison d'être is to dominate the Academy Awards. His Oscar-wear gets—as it deserves—its own shrine, papered with blurry star close-ups and raked by a spotlight. On the far wall, one can watch a silent video collage of scenes from the films for which Armani has designed the costumes. They are often films in which the costumes have more affect than the actors. The most engaging is a clip from *American Gigolo* in which a nubile Richard Gere, naked to the waist and grooving to inaudible rock music, packs his overnight case with Armani shirts and ties.

Only a fool or a mystic seeks the moral high ground on a commercial floodplain. A museum can be "both a theme park and a cultural institution," the director of the Guggenheim, Thomas Krens, told reporters after the press preview. So be it. (I've also accepted that I'll probably never spend a night with Arnold Schwarzenegger, but at least I got to stand next to his empty tuxedo.) Unfortunately, the show's catalog fulfills neither the expectations one has of a theme-park brochure—which usually provides a map of the rides—nor those of a scholarly publication that purports to document an exhibition.

With the exception of the endnotes, it is devoted almost entirely to puffery. Some is delirious, like that of the curator Germano Celant, who describes Armani's work as "a dynamic, nonstatic notion that went so far as to allow clothing to exist as an open-ended, formless condition covering the closed form of the body." Other contributions, like John Travolta's, are all too painfully intelligible: "When I first met Giorgio Armani in 1979, he made me the best-dressed American there was. Today, he's made everybody around the world the best-dressed person they can be, and we all love him for it. Thank you, Giorgio."

There is a lot more of this goofy drivel, otherwise known as advertising copy, not only from other celebrity recipients of free clothes but from well-known figures once on the designer's payroll, like Lee Radziwill, his "muse" and public-relations consultant, and from prime-time product ambassadors, like Pat Riley, who modeled Armani suits to so many high-rolling sports fans at Madison Square Garden. A great artist—and surely one is a great artist if the Guggenheim gives one a retrospective?—deserves more artfulness.

Perhaps some of the airheaded doting is a case of the museum world succumbing to the fashion world's delusion about its artistic purity. Everyone's collection—from Valentino's to that of the East Village designers Imitation of Christ—is art for art's sake. Never mind that "trauma and insanity" were popular runway themes this season, or that Alexander McQueen showed his work in a padded cell. Designers don't even have "shops" anymore, since no one's in trade. You now visit ascetically curated "spaces," and the most prestigious of them have been conceived by an architect who is also responsible for some great modernist public building, like Rem Koolhaus (Prada's) or Richard Gluckman (Helmut Lang's).

But hagiography is almost invariably a symptom of beholdenness. In January of 1999, Thomas Krens proposed the retrospective to Armani, who accepted. A few months later, Krens contacted Armani again, suggesting that he become a "global sponsor" of future, unspecified Guggenheim projects. Armani subscribed to his appeal with a contribution in the neighborhood of $15 million. When bugged by ten journalists in a row about "promotional considerations" and the appearance of impropriety created by the conjunction of the large gift and the major show, Krens responded with barely suppressed impatience. "Life is promotion," he said.

The famously reticent designer, who didn't attend the dinner party after the gala preview for six hundred of his most photogenic friends, wasn't giving interviews. But in an old issue of his in-house style magazine, *Emporio Armani*, I found a nice epigraph. "I hate to see my clothes exhibited as a symbol of discretion tainted by a veil of hypocrisy," he said. Whatever that means.

—November 6, 2000

Noblesse de Robe

I never bought a piece of clothing by Bill Blass, although I inherited one of his down coats from my mother. It was a shapeless bed sack of reversible two-tone gray cotton, ash on one side, slate on the other, and there is nothing better for walking the dog on a frigid morning. Blass was a great dog lover. Indeed, the only slobbering he could tolerate—he had a horror of effusions—was that of his adored retrievers. I'm fairly sure, however, that Blass himself didn't design that coat—at least I hope not. It was among the merchandise that he licensed for production and ennobled with his signature, not always with impeccable discrimination—jeans, luggage, chocolates, linens, eyewear, a backgammon set, and perhaps best known of all, a Lincoln Continental. He consulted with the maker about color schemes, even though he candidly admitted that he'd never tested the product personally. He couldn't drive.

The man behind the label, a patrician by affinity, was an autodidact of considerable culture and disarming humility. I have heard admiration for his character expressed by a surprising cross section of New Yorkers—surprising because the disillusionment with the rich that followed the Reagan decade, during which Blass was a frequent guest at the White House, and the more recent falls from grace of so many posh felons haven't tarnished him. "There was nothing ersatz about the Blass style," said a friend of mine, a downtown architect who voted for Ralph Nader in the last presidential election. "In that respect, it reminds me of Cesar Pelli's World Financial Center. Nei-

ther Pelli nor Blass is a visionary, and in both cases the work celebrates money and power, but somehow you don't hate it. I think it's
because they represent a republican rather than an imperial image of
capitalism. It's not the Wall Street of junk bonds and boiler rooms.
And it's not the fashion Disneyland of Ralph Lauren. Blass looked
like the president of an old family bank—someone you would trust
with your life savings."

The Blass family didn't have a bank, or even much of an account
at one. To understand desire, one has to be, or remember having
been, hungry, and perhaps that is why the history of fashion has
mostly been written from the outside in—not by scions of the ruling
class but by provincials shaking off the dreariness of their milieu.
Charles Worth started out as a shop assistant. Chanel, who grew up
in an orphanage, was the bastard daughter of a peddler. Paul Poiret
was a draper's son. The father of Adrian (a Mr. Greenburg) made
hats for the matrons of Naugatuck, Connecticut. Mainbocher, né
Main Bocher (his names rhyme with "plain" and "rocker," not
"élan" and "cachet"), worked briefly as a wholesale florist in Chicago.
And then there is Bill Blass. Those two clubby monosyllables are as
crisply percussive as the slapping of a jib in the breeze off Hobe
Sound. Yet "Blassy," as he was known to his school friends, grew up
in a middle-class house with a singularly hideous brick porch next
door to a costume-rental company in Fort Wayne, Indiana. A favorite
treat was a white-bread sandwich of cold, leftover mashed potatoes
with mayonnaise from a jar. His vowels were flat, and he wasn't much
of a sport. As a teenager, he owned a pair of dubiously tasteful pearl-
gray shoes. His classmates at South Side High School nevertheless
voted him "the best dressed and least likely to succeed." His greatest
ambition was "to get out." The movies of the 1930s taught him
about penthouse life and the quainter locutions of the gentry. He
fanned the flames of his escape fantasies with his mother's back issues
of *Vogue*. Ethyl Blass was a dressmaker and the widow of a traveling
hardware salesman. The mother who sews seems to be a folk arche-
type, particularly in stories of rags to riches. (Wallis Simpson had one.
So did Eva Perón.) Her selfless needlework provides her child's—her
changeling's—first noble disguise.

Halston and Norell also both happen to be Hoosiers. But then most interesting Americans were originally someone else, and we can make too much of the fact that so many of our seminally debonair men of the world—Scott Fitzgerald, Fred Astaire, and Cole Porter, to name the big three—hailed from midsize Midwestern cities of the Rotarian persuasion. The geniuses (like Astaire), the aesthetes (like Blass), the bohemians (like Fitzgerald), those brimming with effervescence (like Porter) can't stand the stasis and the conformity—they have to emigrate. "There is nothing like the dull, unattractive childhood to give a bedazzled boy the *right* push," Blass observes in his memoir, *Bare Blass* (HarperCollins, 2002). In 1999, the year he sold his company for a reported $50 million and retired from fashion, he decided to break a self-imposed lifetime taboo against airing his private affairs, and he began reminiscing to his collaborator, Cathy Horyn, a fashion critic for *The New York Times*, in the autumn of 2000, a few months after he had been diagnosed with throat cancer. "Of course, the beauty of my upbringing was in its plainness," he writes. "As a consequence of having little money ourselves and no social standing above my mother's widowed respectability—and even here we might have stood to gain some ground if my father had died instantly and unambiguously in a highway crash rather than by a self-inflicted gunshot wound in our front parlor—I learned . . . how to occupy myself." Blass was five, and he dates from that time both a "budding genius for avoiding anything unpleasant or ugly" and a lifelong preoccupation, the strain of which was always stoically dissembled, with "keeping up appearances." He recalls making one of his first sketches about a year later, of a butler serving drinks on a Manhattan terrace. One wonders what role in that scene he imagined for himself: the dapper host or the suave friend of the house? It presumably wasn't the retainer.

Blass died on June 12, 2002, ten days shy of eighty, done in by a lifetime of "joyous smoking." He was a man who savored his hard-earned pleasures without apology or regret, but without sanctimony or pretension, and that is how he tells his tale. His prose has the gruff chic, the virile aplomb, and the elusiveness of his persona—qualities the French call *retenu*, though one would never mistake Blass for anything but a Wasp of the bite-your-tongue, count-your-blessings, take-your-licks, elbows-off-the-table old school. What he has the nerve to call "the fag elements of fashion" were alien to him. The "presentable young man" on the make who grew so seamlessly into his impostures that he was described by nearly every one of his friends as the "perfect gentleman"—perhaps because he possessed the flair and refinement of a snob without actually being one—knew that pathos, like complacency, is fundamentally vulgar and unamusing. He gets all the heartbreaking stuff about his arid Depression childhood out of the way wryly in his first two chapters. His grandfather's suicide is an aside, and his mother's silence on the subject of these two painful paternal secrets a tolerable chagrin. He alludes only briefly to the death, in a training accident on Parris Island in 1942, of Ed Guild, his "first real friend" (and, one suspects, his great unrequited love), and declines to dwell upon the unctuous local "Humberts" of Fort Wayne who, posing as benefactors and playing on the longing of a fatherless boy for a man he could talk to and admire, preyed on him from the age of eight. "I can't claim," Blass writes, "that these experiences put me for or against homosexuality (nor would I bother to)." Insouciance can be an expression of dignity—it can even be heroic—and *Bare Blass* reminds one that the suppressed grief and shame seeping from the hairline crack in a highly veneered character is often more affecting than a confessional Niagara.

The memoirist deflects any pity his confidences might inspire by noting that "everybody had troubles" during the Depression. He also notes that, throughout a life that was hardly celibate or reclusive, but which he never chose to share with a partner of either sex (he neither concealed nor flaunted his preference for men, though he enjoyed a series of *amitiés amoureuses* with women), he made a specialty of the unceremonious exit from the "emotional entanglement." Blass was famous for his bonhomie as a dinner companion, and for his ribald garrulity on every topic but himself, yet in his own grandly austere Sutton Place apartment and the eighteenth-century stone house in Litchfield County that was practically Cistercian, he eschewed comfortable furniture because it might encourage a visitor to settle in. Having "cooled" it, as he calls dying, he forbade his friends to hold a funeral or a memorial service. One has the feeling that perhaps he didn't stick around for his book party or for the opening of a retrospective of his career at the Indiana University Art Museum—accompanied by a glossy *Festschrift* (*Bill Blass: An American Designer*, Abrams, 2002)—because he dreaded the fawning.

Blass was single-minded about being in fashion, in both senses, from a young age. At fifteen, he was selling sketches of evening gowns to a New York manufacturer. While still in high school, he won second prize in a design competition sponsored by the *Chicago Tribune*, and as soon as he had graduated, in 1940, he moved to New York, where he got a job as a sketch artist with the Seventh Avenue manufacturer David Crystal. A salary of $35 a week paid for a room in an Upper West Side apartment and tuition for night classes in design. After Pearl Harbor, he enlisted in the army and was recruited for the 603rd Camouflage Battalion, a company, he writes, of "creative types," mostly artists, admen, or recent art-school graduates. (Ellsworth Kelly and the Hollywood set designer George Diestel were among them.) The unit shipped out shortly after D-day, arriving on Omaha Beach in July of 1944, and took part in the last big offensives of the war, though not as combat troops—as decoys. Their highly classified missions, carried out at night in the mud of rural France, behind the front lines, were intended to keep the Germans guessing about the movements of Allied armor or infantry, and they involved deploying a column of inflatable rubber tanks and simulating traffic and battle noise, "so, when Von Ramcke looked the next morning through the haze and battle smoke with his field glasses, he thought he was seeing Patton's forces." Before each operation, the 603rd had to change the insignia on its vehicles and uniforms; Blass's valor consisted, appropriately, of painting, sewing, impersonation, and "dreaming up marvelous new uses for chicken feathers." His best friend kept a field diary recording their secret maneuvers, but Blass's notebooks were filled with "miniature drawings of ladies' hats, shoes, gloves, and dresses," and with doodles of the mirrored "B"s that became his logo. In all his photographs, he points out, he's "smiling idiotically."

The army made "a mama's boy" into a man, and it was apparently the only place that he felt free to risk loving: not an individual but an ideal of fraternity.

After his discharge, Blass reapplied for his old job, but Crystal rejected him on the ground that he was "too ambitious." He worked briefly for Anne Klein, who put out the word that he had beautiful manners but no talent and fired him. He then settled into what he describes as a period of peonage as an assistant at the dress firm of Anna Miller, which was later absorbed into the larger house of her brother, Maurice Rentner, where Blass spent a decade designing adroitly detailed Diorish suits and drapey chiffons that were flattering to a mature clientele. Only when Rentner died, in 1960, did his grudging partners put Blass's name on their label. He then began to turn out "some of the best work of my career—snappy minidresses and fur-trimmed coats," and to experiment with his signature incongruities: flannels and sequins; ruffles and tweed; gingham and lace; a mink peacoat; a taffeta ball skirt worn with a long cashmere cardigan; or a corduroy topper tossed with nonchalance over beaded trousers. But he was still seething about his accumulated humiliations fifty years later. Designers, he reminds us, were "considered trade" and expected to "keep their heads down," and they were sometimes even asked to use the service elevator. He once compared the stigma of his profession to that of being an actor in sixteenth-century France: it "denied one the right of Christian burial." One particularly insufferable "garmento" had summoned Blass to his apartment for a job interview, then kept him waiting in the butler's pantry while he entertained his friends at a cocktail party.

Blass is widely credited with being the architect of the "bridge" that links fashion to society. It is now such an essential feature of the cityscape that one forgets how remote from each other, and how parochial, those two island cultures were. "I think that I'm partially responsible for bringing a respectability of a new kind to this business," he said. Cathy Horyn's assessment of Blass's importance is less measured: "It should be obvious to almost anybody that no designer has more profoundly influenced American life," she wrote in a profile. "More than Ralph Lauren, more than Calvin Klein . . . he changed the status of designers." Fashion being fashion, ergo perverse, the minute designers got some respect, a younger generation without gratitude for the sacrifices that were made on its behalf wasted no time in becoming as louche as possible. But, in part because Blass's work is so devoid of proletarian or subversive tendencies and in part because his guerrilla camouflage was a bespoke tuxedo, it is hard to think of him as a catalyst for social change, much less as a liberator of untouchables, the Gandhi of Seventh Avenue.

In the early fifties, Blass was still a lowly "cloakie" by day, but by night—armed with his urbanity, his chiseled profile, a hollow leg, wicked repartee, a faux Jockey Club accent, and the potent charm that resides in an upstart's infallible instinct for the insecurities of the powerful—he embarked on a career in café society as a ubiquitous extra man. "It was an era of great chanteuses—and clean hair and long, long necks," he writes. The action was at the Stork Club, El Morocco, and the Blue Angel, where he cravenly told the swank strangers he got drunk with ("occasionally very drunk") that he was "in advertising." He also kept the glamorous "gals" on the leopard-skin banquettes "under surveillance," though not, of course, sexually: he was interested in what they had on. The mothers of debutantes were reassured by his table manners, and the grandes dames by his courtier's tact as a "listener." He eventually made some impressive conquests: Mrs. Gilbert (Kitty) Miller, who, according to C. Z. Guest, "was a hell of a snob"; Missy Bancroft, a young socialite who did some modeling; movie stars like Kim Stanley, Claudette Colbert, Gary Cooper, and Cary Grant; and the droll, fastidious Baron Nicolas de Gunzburg, an editor at *Vogue* who was the first to ferret Blass and his talent for "jazzy realism" from the back room at Anna Miller and, as Blass puts it, to "shove" Diana Vreeland "in my general direction."

By the end of the decade, Blass was doing ingratiating and handsome but derivative clothes influenced by Norell, Mainbocher, Saint Laurent, and, even more so, by a small coterie of muses—American beauties with big allowances and blue blood who had "the confidence to mix things up" and who embodied the "lean, agile, racy" style that he aspired to. They were women like Chessy Rayner, then a junior editor at *The Ladies' Home Journal*, who patronized Mme. Grès but also shopped for men's chinos at the Army Navy Store and wore them with a dressy jacket; or like Gloria Vanderbilt, who casually threw a sable coat over a pair of gray flannel trousers; or like Mrs. Guest, who wore her country-house uniform of twinset and tweed skirt to lunch at the Ritz in Paris. None of these women were, like their contemporary Jacqueline Kennedy, exclusively besotted with what Blass endearingly calls French "snottiness." "And so it came to me," he wrote in *The New Yorker* five years ago, "that there could be a way of designing for women that was, in the best sense, *American*."

What was most American about Blass was his success as a businessman and his frank relish for its perks: a penthouse with a river view, a staff (valet, driver, and chef), a Savile Row wardrobe. The entrepreneur was more adventurous, by far, than the designer—an intrepid pioneer of self-promotion. While still indentured to the Rentner partners, he began, despite their misgivings, to market his own "Blass-famous" glamour, in an advertising campaign conceived by Jane Trahey. It was unique for its time, and it featured Vreelandish lists of his likes and dislikes about women. (He liked one who could "cuss in five languages" and disliked one who did the crossword puzzle in ink.) He had himself photographed under the Brooklyn Bridge with two machine-gun-toting hit women wearing fedoras, kitten heels, and tasteful "little nothing" dresses: "Next time you want something knockout that won't be knocked off . . . invest in Bill Blass." He appealed to the vast, lucrative market of the unsvelte with the image of a model in a voluminous caftan eating a mound of spaghetti above the tagline: "The Blass Diet: Feel Free." In 1967, he was the first American designer of upscale women's wear to introduce a high-fashion line for men (although the swagger of the plaids suggested the kind of men who did armed business out of limos under the Brooklyn Bridge). Once Blass became his own master, in 1970, he followed the example set by Pierre Cardin and began to amass a fortune from licensing agreements. "The couture," he told John Duka in 1980, with his typical distaste for hypocrisy, "is . . . the come-on. It's not the moneymaker, it's the bait. If I didn't have my clothes, I couldn't have my licensees, and if I didn't have those, I couldn't live the way I do." The clothes might be the bait, but their hook was the Blass charisma, and his presence at trunk shows spiked sales dramatically. He never had any priestly qualms about peddling his wares in provincial department stores or hotel ballrooms, where, squinting through the smoke from a Carlton, he flirted gamely with the "old broads" from Houston or Grosse Pointe, bossing them around as they emerged from the fitting room, cheeks flushed and checkbooks in hand.

Plenty of rich scoundrels make it through the needle's eye into fashion heaven: all it seems to take is an acquaintance with Karl Lagerfeld's diet doctor. It's the man who lives by appearances yet isn't deceived by them who's the rarity. Blass never mystified himself or posed as an artist: fashion was a "craft," and it was "pretentious to be in awe of it." He certainly did nothing to hurt his reputation for human decency by giving $10 million to the New York Public Library, or raising important sums for AIDS research, or, without publicity, supporting the careers of younger designers.

The Blass fashion legacy is less obvious, at least to me, someone who does crossword puzzles in ink. Blass used to bristle when his work was called "wearable" by critics or by fans, though he eventually accepted the term as a badge of honor—a decoration for gallantry to women. He respected the intelligence of his customers, particularly those who didn't live in New York, wear black, and weigh nothing, and he treated them as constituents rather than as subjects of a monarch. But what, in principle, is most refreshingly democratic—not only about Blass but about American style, in general, and about much of American fashion journalism—is often, in practice, what is most pedestrian: it's too remedial.

The best of Blass (and it isn't the Reagan-era ruffled poufs or lamé dinner suits) is difficult to date, though is that because the clothes are ageless or because contemporary fashion is so anarchic that every period and impulse seems modern? He uses a perceptive phrase to describe the 1960s: "cruelly demographic." The demographics of fashion are cruel to every generation as it ages. Blass liked to think that his work spoke to a free spirit, a woman with her own identity, not a "clotheshorse." But looking through the photographs in *Bare Blass* of his friends and clients, I don't see any models for the kind of glamorous old witch I would like to become. Beneath the surface dazzle, there is something extinguished about the Blass Ladies—a flame smothered by convention. When style burns true, it's cooler and more cryptic. You can't place it or decode it at a glance. And, for all his generosity, Blass couldn't bestow it, though he had it himself to a sovereign degree. It's the chameleon's trick of plainly being not what you seem.

—September 9, 2002

SEVEN

The Misfit

Does it really matter what one wears? I sometimes think my life might have been different if I had chosen the other wedding dress. I was getting married for the second time, and until the overcast morning of the ceremony I dithered between a bland ecru frock appropriate to my age and station, which I wore that once and never again, and a spooky neo-Gothic masterpiece with a swagged bustle and unraveling seams in inky crêpe de laine, which I still possess: hope and experience.

The black dress—and other strange clothes in which I feel most like myself—was designed by Rei Kawakubo. In 1981, when she brought her first collection to Paris, Kawakubo was nearly forty and preeminent in Japan but largely unknown in the West. Mugler and Versace were the harbingers of a new moment: of a giddy, truculent materialism embodied, in different guises, by Margaret Thatcher, Madonna, Princess Di, Alexis Carrington, and Jane Fonda, and by legions of newly minted executives who wore block-and-tackle power suits to the office and spandex stirrup pants to the gym. These women were tough and glitzy and on the make without apologies, and so was fashion. Then, the following year, a collection that Kawakubo called "Destroy" hit the runway. It was modeled by a cadre of disheveled vestals in livid war paint who stomped down the catwalk to the beating of a drum, wearing the bleak and ragged uniforms of a new order. Few if any spectators were left blasé, and some went home dumbstruck with rapture, while others lobbed back at the invader what they perceived as a blast of barbarity, tagging the look "Hiroshima's revenge." Kawakubo has never quite lived down (she has at times played up) that show of audacity, whose fallout is still being absorbed by fashion's young, yet which was much more Parisian than it seemed—a piece of shock theater in the venerable tradition of *Ubu Roi* and *The Rite of Spring.*

Kawakubo works under the label Comme des Garçons ("like some boys"), though she has never wanted to be like anyone. There are few women who have exerted more influence on the history of modern fashion, and the most obvious, Chanel, is in some respects her perfect foil: the racy courtesan who invented a uniform of irreproachable chic and the gnomic shaman whose anarchic chic is a reproach to uniformity. They both started from an egalitarian premise: that a woman should derive from her clothes the ease and confidence that a man does. But Chanel formulated a few simple and lucrative principles, from which she never wavered, that changed the way women wanted to dress, while Kawakubo, who reinvents the wheel— or tries to—every season, changed the way one thinks about what dress is.

Early Comme, as devotees winsomely call it, gave comfort to the wearer and discomfort to the beholder, particularly if he was an Average Joe with a fondness for spandex stirrup pants. Kawakubo's silhouette had nothing to do with packaging a woman's body for seduction. Nearly any biped with sufficient aplomb, one thought, might have modeled the clothes, though especially, perhaps, a self-possessed kangaroo, whose narrow shoulders and well-planted large feet are a Comme des Garçons signature. The palette was monochrome, with a little ash mixed into the soot, and one hears it said that Kawakubo "invented" black—it was one of the "objective achievements" cited by the Harvard School of Design when it gave her an Excellence in Design Award in 2000. What she objectively achieved was the revival of black's cachet as the color of refusal.

The French Old Guard, needless to say, reviled Comme des Garçons, but the line immediately became popular among women of the downtown persuasion. In Kawakubo's voluminous clothes, one felt provocative yet mysterious and protected. They weren't sized, and they weren't conceived on a svelte fitting model, then inflated to a sixteen. Their cut had the rigor, if not the logic, of modernist architecture, but loose flaps, queer trains, and other sometimes perplexing extrusions encouraged a client of the house to improvise her own style of wearing them. Shop assistants showed one the ropes—literally. A friend of mine who included Kawakubo in a course on critical theory suggested that these "multiple open endings" were a tactic for liberating female dress from an "omniscient male narrator."

Conventional fashion, and particularly its advertising, is a narrative genre—historical romance at one end of the spectrum and science fiction at the other, with chick lit in between—and Kawakubo doesn't have a story line, insisting, not always plausibly, that she works in a vacuum of influence and a tradition of her own creation. "I never intended to start a revolution," she told me last winter. "I only came to Paris with the intention of showing what I thought was strong and beautiful. It just so happened that my notion was different from everybody else's." Yet so many entitlements were challenged by the black regime of Comme des Garçons that it is hard not to see its commandant as a Red. The hegemony of the thin was one target, and the class system that governed fabrication was another. Kawakubo ennobled poor materials and humbled rich ones, which were sent off to be reeducated in the same work camp with elasticated synthetics and bonded polyester. She crumpled her silks like paper and baked them in the sun; boiled her woolens so that they looked nappy; faded and scrubbed her cottons; bled her dyes; and picked at her threadwork. One of the most mocked pieces from 1982 was a sublimely sorry-looking sweater cratered with holes that she called (one assumes with irony, though one can't be sure) "Comme des Garçons lace."

Kawakubo's most radical challenge to the canons of Western tailoring lay in her cutting. Couturiers before her had experimented with asymmetry in the one-shouldered gown or the diagonal lapel, though they were still working from a balanced pattern with a central axis—the spine. She warped her garments like the sheet of rubber that my high-school physics teacher used to illustrate the curvature of space, and she skewed their seams or closures so that the sides no longer matched. Just because a torso has two arms, she didn't see any reason that a jacket couldn't have none or three, of uneven length—

amputated and reattached elsewhere on its body. Among the many mutants that she has engineered are a pair of trousers spliced to a skirt; the upper half of a morning coat with a tail of sleazy pink nylon edged in black lace; and her notorious "Dress Meets Body, Body Meets Dress" collection of 1997—"Quasimodo" to its detractors— which proposed a series of fetching, body-hugging pieces in stretch gingham that were deformed in unsettling places (the back, belly, and shoulders) with bulbous tumors of down. The historian and cu- rator Valerie Steele sees "a kind of violence—even a brutalism—to Rei's work that made most fashion of the time look innocuous and bourgeois, and from that moment an avant-garde split from the mainstream and hurtled off in its own direction." Steele was, she adds, "an instant convert."

Yet if Kawakubo consents to call her style "rebellious" and "ag- gressive," it is also intensely feminine in a bittersweet way. Her clothes suggest a kinship with a long line of fictional holy terrors: Pippi Longstocking, Cathy Earnshaw, Claudine—motherless tomboys who refused to master drawing-room manners and who, when forced into a dress, hiked up their petticoats and climbed a tree. Crushed frills are a leitmotif at Comme des Garçons, as are fraying ruffles; droopy ruffs; distressed pom-poms; drab roses of wilted tulle, eyelet, crinoline, and broderie anglaise; and the round collars and polka dots that Kawakubo wore as a fauvish girl. In March of 2005, she showed a fall/winter collection whose theme was "The Broken Bride," which was almost universally admired. (I doubt that she was entirely happy with the reviews—when everyone understands her, she seems to get depressed.) The models wore whiteface and antique veils anchored by floral crowns. The ensembles, despite their sovereign refinement, had an eerily familiar air of desperate, last-minute indecision. They were trimmed with passementerie that might have been salvaged from a Victorian steamer trunk in which the finery of an old- fashioned maidenhood had been abandoned along with its illusions. The show, in its melancholy romance, captured the tension between vigor and fragility that dominates most modern women's lives, in- cluding Kawakubo's.   .

Tokyo was enjoying an unseasonable warm spell when I arrived at the beginning of February, and the famous allées of cherry trees in the Aoyama cemetery had been lured into bud. In the labyrinth of paths that fret this verdant tract of incalculably expensive real estate, which is sacred to Buddhists, Shintoists, Christians, and fashion photographers, I kept running into an old man and his two whippets, all three in Hermès coats. The dogs upset the great flocks of crows—*karasu*—that nest in the foliage or perch insolently on the tombs and whose bitter cawing fractures the peace. A *karasu* was said to be the messenger of the sun goddess, Amaterasu, Japan's mythical progenitress, from whom the imperial family claimed descent. Through the millennia, this brazen and potent female deity hasn't been much of a model to her countrywomen, particularly once they marry. Of the numerous characters for "wife," the most common, *okusan*, means "a figure of the inner realm."

Japanese girls still tend to sow their wild fashion oats before they settle down with a mate and disappear, if not into the shadows, into a Chanel suit. But Kawakubo started out making clothes in the seventies, she said, for a woman "who is not swayed by what her husband thinks." (She was then deep into her black period, and her devotees were known in Tokyo as "the crows.") Two decades later, and shortly after her own wedding, to Adrian Joffe—a South African–born student of Asian culture ten years her junior, who is the president of Comme des Garçons International—she told an interviewer from *Elle* that "one's lifestyle should not be affected by the formality of marriage."

Kawakubo owns an apartment near the cemetery, in one of the modern towers on its perimeter, not far from her headquarters and her company's three stores in the smart Aoyama shopping district. The apartment's precise location is a secret (very few friends and none of the longtime employees whom I met had ever crossed its threshold), and she lives alone there with her twenty-year-old cat, the last of five. Joffe, who is based in Paris, sees her, he says, at least once a month, and between collections they take a week to travel—generally choosing somewhere off the fashion radar screen, like Yemen or Romania. He is a slight, intense man who speaks five languages, including fluent Japanese, and he acts as his wife's interpreter. Small talk—indeed, any talk—is not Kawakubo's forte. She doesn't take invisibility to theological extremes, like Martin Margiela, fashion's Pynchon, who is, with some of his fellow alumni of the Antwerp School (Ann Demeulemeester, Walter van Beirendonck, Olivier Theyskens, and Raf Simons), one of her acolytes, though she rarely poses for a photograph or gives an interview anymore, and, several years ago, she stopped taking a bow after her shows. From the beginning of her career, she has insisted that the only way to know her is "through my clothes." Her employees, including Joffe, treat her with a gingerly deference that seems to be a mixture of awe for her talent and forbearance with her moods.

Kawakubo is now sixty-two. She is the sole owner of a company with a dozen boutiques and some two hundred franchises on four continents, which manufactures twelve lines of clothing and grosses about $150 million annually. But despite her wealth, her only apparent major indulgence is a vintage car, a monster Mitsubishi from the 1970s, which attracts the kind of stares in Tokyo that her clothes attract in Houston. The recreations common to designers of her prestige, such as collecting villas or art and socializing with celebrities, don't appeal to her, and the atmosphere of her office "is more monastic than commercial," as the journalist Deyan Sudjic puts it in *Rei Kawakubo and Comme des Garçons* (Rizzoli, 1990), a monograph on her career. But she recently learned to swim, and on her way to work she sometimes takes a detour through the Aoyama cemetery to feed the stray cats.

Before I met Kawakubo in Paris, Joffe and I spent a day in Berlin at a Comme des Garçons "guerrilla store," which then occupied the former bookshop of the Brecht Museum, on a seedy block in the eastern sector of the city. It is part of an experiment in alternative retailing (inconspicuous consumption) which the company launched in 2004. There are now seven such outposts, most in northern Europe, in cities like Helsinki and Ljubljana. Each of the stores is an ephemeral installation that opens without fanfare and closes after a year. Their decorating budgets are less than the price of some handbags at Gucci and Prada, and original fixtures, including raw cinder block and peeling wallpaper, are left as they are found. Brecht might have approved the poetic clothes and the proletarian mise-en-scène, if not the insurrectionary conceit. "But the word 'guerrilla' as Rei understands it isn't political," Joffe says. "It refers to a small group of like-minded spirits at odds with the majority. She's fascinated by the Amish, for example, and the Orthodox Jews."

Part of Joffe's role is to help make his wife intelligible whether or not she is present, and an unease sometimes creeps into his tone: the anxiety of a parent who resents the injustice yet accepts the inevitability of having to subject an antisocial prodigy to a school interview. "Are you scared of her?" I asked him bluntly over a Wiener schnitzel at the Café Einstein. "No," he said, "but she can be dictatorial, and I'm sometimes scared of the way she might treat people." Kawakubo treated me with a courtly if reticent politesse, and our conversations weren't unlike a tea ceremony: exquisitely strained. She is a tiny woman with taut cheekbones, a graying pageboy, and an aura of severity. When we were introduced in her showroom last January, she was wearing a pair of trousers most easily described as a hybrid of a dhoti and a jodhpur, with a trim cardigan and a corsage of safety pins. Though she cultivates a reputation for being both timid and intimidating, some of her friends—among them Carla Sozzani, the Milanese retailer and gallerist, and Azzedine Alaïa, the couturier—assured me that, in private, Kawakubo can be a charming pal, congenial and even "hysterically funny." (I duly asked her what she laughs at, and she answered deadpan, "People falling down.") She patiently entertained the speculations with which I tried to prime her, and allowed that some of them "might be true." "But I'm very grateful that you haven't asked me about my 'creative process,' " she said as I was leaving one afternoon. "I couldn't explain it to you. And, even if I could, why would I want to? Are there people who really wish to explain themselves?"

Kawakubo was born in Tokyo in 1942. She was the oldest of her parents' three children and their only daughter. (One of her brothers works as a director in the commercial department of Comme des Garçons, and the staff refers to him as Mister, to differentiate the two siblings in conversation, because there can be only one Kawakubo-san.) Their father was an administrator at Keio University, a prestigious institution founded by the great Meiji educator and reformer Fukuzawa Yukichi, a champion of Western culture and, according to Kawakubo, of women's rights. She admires Yukichi as an "enlightened man," but she has never belonged to a movement, followed a religion, subscribed to an ideology, or worshipped a hero, "because for me belief means that you have to depend on somebody."

Sudjic relates a few anodyne details about Kawakubo's girlhood (that she bunched her socks down as a revolt against the conformity of her school uniform, for example). Her home was "comfortable," he writes, and her family "a close one," and she told me that her mother made all the clothes. The trauma of war and the privations that Japan suffered in its aftermath didn't, she thought, have an appreciable effect on her. Yet however ordinary she felt her upbringing to be ("You think I'm not normal because you're looking at the clothes," she said to me somewhat plaintively when we met in Tokyo. "But I am. Can't rational people create mad work?"), her biography neglects to mention that she grew up with divorced parents. Her mother was trained as an English teacher—Kawakubo understands and speaks the language better than she lets on—and when the children were of a certain age she wanted to work. Her husband disapproved, and for almost all Japanese wives of that class and era, his word would have been law. Kawakubo's mother left him, however, and got a job in a high school. "She was unlike other mothers," Kawakubo says. "I always felt like an outsider." But she also had a model of defiance and autonomy.

In 1960, Kawakubo enrolled in her father's university and took a degree in "the history of aesthetics," a major that included the study of Asian and Western art. In 1964, the year she graduated, Japan hosted the Olympics. "The postwar period of poverty, humiliation, and, until 1952, Allied occupation was finally over, and the boom years of the economic miracle had begun," Ian Buruma writes in *Inventing Japan*. Kawakubo's generation discovered—and in varying degrees embraced—the counterculture of the sixties. At twenty-two, with a nod toward her mother's act of lèse-majesté, she left home "without telling my parents where I was going or what I was doing," and moved into a shared apartment in Harajuku, which was Tokyo's East Village and is still a mildly louche neighborhood of clubs and boutiques where pierced teens (most of them home by dinnertime) hang out wearing outré street fashions and trying to look ghetto. Kawakubo was never a druggie or a rebel, she says, "though in my head I liked the bohemian lifestyle." On the other hand, she went to college with "a lot of rich people—that's who goes to elite institutions, and they are generally conservative." She found the solidity of their lives appealing, and she considers herself to have a dual character: the right half "likes tradition and history," the left "wants to break the rules." Nearly every statement Kawakubo makes about herself is hedged or negated by a contradiction, and she resists being defined even by her own words. The desire to be unique and the sense of isolation that the feeling generates are a predicament common to artistic people. What makes Kawakubo's clothes so attractive to them is precisely her genius for wrapping up the paradoxes of being a misfit and a cipher in something to wear that is magically misfitting.

Tokyo in the sixties was not yet the world's capital of luxury consumerism. Many women still made their own clothes or patronized a local tailor, and the best-known Japanese couturier, Hanae Mori, worked in a decorous Parisian mode. Kawakubo wasn't thinking of a fashion career: her only vocation was for a life of self-sufficiency. She found a job "at the bottom of the ladder" in the advertising department of Asahi Kasei, a textile manufacturer. Her boss was sympathetic to her ambitions. He accepted her unusual refusal to wear the standard uniform of an office girl, and he allowed her some modest creative freedom in helping to scout props and costumes for photo shoots. After three years, one of her older colleagues, Atsuko Kozasu, who later became an influential fashion journalist and an early booster of Comme des Garçons, encouraged Kawakubo to go freelance as a stylist. When she couldn't find clothes suitable for her assignments, she began to design them, and she often says that she's grateful to have skipped fashion school or an apprenticeship because, in the end, even if she can't sew or cut a pattern, she had no preconceptions to unlearn, and no master to outgrow.

By 1969, Kawakubo's work as a stylist had become a sideline that helped finance the production of the youthful sportswear that she sold through trendsetting shops like Belle Boudoir, in the Ginza, whose communal fitting room—"just like a London boutique"— impressed her. She rented office space in a graphic-arts studio and hired a few assistants. Tsubomi Tanaka, who is Comme des Garçons' chief of production, has been with her almost from the beginning. Tanaka was then a country girl who had left home to work in a Hara-juku shop and, she says, "do my own thing," and she first noticed Kawakubo on the street. "Even in those days, she had an aura," Tanaka says, "and I asked a friend if she knew her name, because I wanted to meet her."

Sudjic writes, "Kawakubo's experiences as a stylist had taught her the importance of creating a coherent identity"—a philosophy of de-sign that is followed as strictly in the company's Christmas cards as it is in the flagship stores. But the styling of that signature is a collabo-rative effort that demands an almost cultish attunement among the participants, and it is one of the paradoxes of Comme des Garçons that a designer obsessed with singularity and an entrepreneur allergic to beholdenness have spun such an elaborate web of dependence. In the workplace, Kawakubo's laconic detachment—the refusal to ex-plain herself—forces her employees, particularly the pattern cutters, to look inward, rather than to her, for a revelation of the all-important "something new." Tanaka says, "The work is very hard, and I have to delve deep into my own understanding because her words are so few. But there's always some give to the tautness. And I'm still moved by the collections. That's why I've been here for so long."

Comme des Garçons' chief patterner, Yoneko Kikuchi, a thirty-year veteran of the firm, describes the arduous, if not mildly perverse, esoteric groping in the dark through which a collection comes into focus. It begins with a vision, or perhaps just an intuition, about a key garment that Kawakubo hints at with a sort of koan. She gives the patterners a set of clues that might take the form of a scribble, a crumpled piece of paper, or an enigmatic phrase such as "inside-out pillowcase," which they translate, as best they can, into a muslin—the three-dimensional blueprint of a garment. Their first drafts are in-evitably too concrete. "She always asks us to break down the literal-ness," Kikuchi says. The quest proceeds behind closed doors, like a

papal election, and successive meditations on the koan produce more
or less adequate results. The staff calls the process by a deceptively
playful English word, "catchball," though as the deadline for a collection approaches, and Kawakubo is still dissatisfied, the "anguish
and anger" mount in the cutting room. "We all want to please her,"
Kikuchi explains, "and it's sometimes hard for patterners who have
come from other companies, because they just want you to tell them
how wide the collar is supposed to be. But you can't teach people to
let go, and some end up leaving." ("They make it sound more interesting than it is," Kawakubo says dryly. "The ideas aren't as abstract
as they used to be.")

The business flourished, and was incorporated in 1973. By 1980,
Comme des Garçons had a hundred and fifty franchised shops across
Japan, eighty employees, and annual revenues of $30 million. Fans of
the house had none of the designer's scruples about hero worship:
they went on camping weekends together organized by the fran-
chisees, and there was talk of a Comme des Garçons restaurant where
the faithful could meet. The clothes they loved were inspired by the
loose and rustic garb of Japanese fishermen and peasants. When I
asked Kawakubo what those early designs looked like (she hasn't kept
many pictures in her archives), she answered after a long, perhaps
embarrassed, pause, "Denim apron skirt. Very popular. I made different versions of it." Their chicest detail may have been the Comme
des Garçons label, typeset in a font created by Kawakubo, with a star
for the cedilla, which hasn't changed. It isn't obvious how she made
her evolutionary leap, but it occurred in the early eighties, when she
abandoned representational fashion and introduced the notion of
clothing as wearable abstraction.

Most people naturally assume that Comme des Garçons is not just
a logo but a slogan, and when Kawakubo was still giving interviews
she compared her work with menswear, in its ideals of comfort and
discretion, although she has denied that there was any message to the
three words: she had just liked their French lilt. They mean what they
mean, however, and there are few women who personify the ideals of
seventies feminism with greater fidelity. The phrase comes, with a
slight tweak, from the refrain of a pop song, by Françoise Hardy, in
which a wistful teenage girl enviously watches happy couples walking

"hand in hand" and wonders if the day will come when—"*comme les garçons et les filles de mon âge*"—she will find someone to love her. One may have such yearnings at any age, and Kawakubo was into her thirties when she met the love of her youth, Yohji Yamamoto. There was something pharaonic about their glamour as a couple, that of two regal and feline siblings with a priestly aura, and they shared the regency of a new generation in Japanese design. Both are alumni of Keio University (Yamamoto was two years behind her) and children of enterprising single mothers—his a widow who owned a dress shop. Yet, as the eloquent idiosyncrasy of their work suggests, a match between equals is rarely a balanced pattern whose cuts and edges align.

Like Kawakubo, Yamamoto is an anomaly in the fashion world on a number of counts, his proclivities among them. He married young and fathered two children. A different union produced a third child six years ago. For some years in between, he and Kawakubo were "travelling companions," as Kiyokazu Washida coyly puts it in an essay he contributed to Yamamoto's book, *Talking to Myself* (Steidl Publishing, 2002), a sumptuous pictorial chronicle of the designer's career. Malcolm McLaren remembers Kawakubo and Yamamoto as a petite, stylish couple of "excellent customers" (he didn't yet know they were designers) who, in the seventies, turned up at Sex, the mother of all guerrilla shops, an outpost of seditionary music and fashion that he and his partner, Vivienne Westwood, had opened at World's End in London. (Decades later, Westwood told Kawakubo that she considered her a "punk at heart.") They made their Paris debuts the same year, and were invariably linked, or lumped, together as part of an emerging Tokyo school that was challenging the conventions of Western couture, and of which Issey Miyake was the doyen. Kawakubo bridled at the group portraits. "I'm not very happy to be classified as another Japanese designer," she told *Women's Wear Daily* in 1983. "There is no one characteristic that all Japanese designers have."

Yamamoto was unavailable for an interview, but his friend and associate Irène Silvagni, a former fashion journalist, speaks of "the enormous competition between Rei and Yohji that she, I think, needed and thrived on." As far as Silvagni knows, they never collaborated, but "they both wanted to break the rules, and Yohji likes to say that 'perfection is the devil,' which I think is true for Rei. Japanese temples were always left unfinished for that reason." It is her perception that "they admire each other deeply, but there's a lot of baggage between them." She referred me to the baggage depot at the end of *Talking to Myself*, in which Yamamoto sets down some fragmentary aperçus on a variety of existential subjects, including alcohol, gambling, insomnia, and women. "I'm always assuming that if she's my girlfriend she won't create a scandal," he writes of a nameless consort. "I'm sure of this even if it's unfounded."

The relationship ended in the early nineties. When a childless single woman nearing fifty suddenly starts to do her best work, she often has a broken heart. Joffe had joined Comme des Garçons in 1987, and on July 4, 1992, he and Kawakubo were married at the city hall in Paris. The bride wore a black skirt and a plain white shirt. That winter, she showed a hauntingly lovely collection that is still a favorite. It was composed of ethereal chiffon layers yoked to cone-shaped knitted turtlenecks which masked the face from the nose down, worn over flowing shifts with sorcerer's sleeves. Their color was nightshade, and their inspiration the myth of Lilith—a female demon of Jewish folklore, whom God created of "filth and sediment" when Adam, like the girl in the Hardy song, complained that he was the only creature on the planet without a mate. In Robert Graves's version, Adam and his first wife "never found peace together," because she rebelled at "the recumbent posture he demanded." When he "tried to compel her obedience by force, Lilith, in a rage . . . rose into the air and left him." So much for girlfriends who don't create scandals.

Lilith's heretical divorce was a juncture for Kawakubo, too. She was tiring of black (but she tires of anything once it catches on, and being avant-garde, she said recently, has become a cliché). She began to play with the opulent fabrics she had once disdained: damask, brocade, and velvet; with brilliant, sometimes lurid colors; and even with the staples of drag and bimbohood—sheer lingerie (worn with winkle pickers) and campy bustiers (layered over bulky topcoats). For commercial reasons, she says, she started sizing the clothes and narrowing the gap between dress and body. She edited the guest lists for her shows to a sympathetic coterie of editors and buyers, in part, as Amy Spindler wrote in *The New York Times*, because "multiplying the attendance figures . . . only serves to increase the number of people who don't get it." But Spindler also noted that Kawakubo "typically throws a bone to those who still believe clothes are for wearing outside fashion focus groups without being gawked at." Her easier-to-wear subsidiary lines, particularly Robe de Chambre (now called Comme des Garçons Comme des Garçons)—a microcosm of her own wardrobe—streamline the runway concepts to reach a broader public. "I'm not an artist, I'm a businesswoman," Kawakubo says. "Well, maybe an artist/businesswoman."

Despite the relative accessibility of "The Broken Bride," Kawakubo denies vehemently that she has mellowed ("I am still as aggressive as I've always been"), and every few years she reasserts her militance by exploding another bomb on the Paris stage. In 1995, the presentation of her menswear collection, which included a series of baggy striped pajamas reminiscent to some critics of the prison uniforms at Auschwitz, happened to coincide with the fiftieth anniversary of the camp's liberation. Kawakubo apologized for any offense she might, unintentionally, have given, and Jewish organizations who reviewed the videos were satisfied that no sacrilege had been committed. But she was perfectly conscious of the storm she conjured two seasons later with "Dress Meets Body." (Her own staff loved the sexy and salable silhouette, but there were worries about its bulges, and Kawakubo ultimately decided to make the troubling wads removable, though she wore them herself, and adapted them as costumes for a dance by Merce Cunningham. On perfect bodies in motion, they transcend their morbidity.) The collection was inspired, Joffe says, "by Rei's anger at seeing a Gap window filled with banal black clothes." Kawakubo concedes, with an ambiguous grimace that might just be a grin, "I may have been especially angry at the time, but I'm more or less always angry anyway."

Early one morning in Paris, the cobblestones of the place Vendôme were varnished by a drizzle, and a row of limousines idled in front of the Ritz, waiting for clients in town for the menswear shows. The couture had just finished, and, in the terribly chic restaurants where fashion people eat their tiny portions of mediocre food, they were complaining that the couture *was* finished. Only eight designers had bothered to mount a show, and there was a sense that a once festive, feudal tournament of virtuosity had become a Renaissance fair with demonstrations of spinning and horseshoeing in period costume. But no one had informed Armani, a couture debutant. In *Le Figaro*, he discoursed with a quaint gravity on *les tendances de la mode* and affirmed his belief in "simplified lines that are easy to understand," because "true success means pleasing everyone"—a succinct résumé of everything in fashion that Kawakubo doesn't stand for, in both senses.

Across the square, in a narrow courtyard adjacent to the showroom of Comme des Garçons, the company's Paris staff, joined by a contingent from the Aoyama headquarters, who were groggy with jet lag, assembled for the morning salutation—a monastic ritual of solidarity performed daily in Tokyo. They formed a circle, shivering a little, and waited in silence for Kawakubo. Her protégé Junya Watanabe, who has a wrestler's physique and a cherub's face, squeezed in near Mister, who looked, in his business suit, a little like the hired mourner at a rocker's funeral. Joffe was surprised at his wife's delay ("She's a stickler for punctuality"), but she arrived at her habitual gait—the anxious scuttle of a sparrow with a broken wing—and took her place.

Kawakubo was sporting her favorite accessory: a dour expression. A collection, she says, is never not "an exercise in suffering," and she "starts from zero every time," destitute of confidence. It is ironic to her, she said at our last meeting in Tokyo, that a career she undertook "with one objective: to be free as a woman" has become a Spartan life of self-imposed servitude. But sympathy and compliments both annoy her, perhaps because they rub salt into the incurable and necessary wound of her discontent. The only consolation she can imagine "is an hour to spend with animals."

When she wants to, however, Kawakubo smiles through her clothes. That morning, she had chosen a black sweater strategically appliquéd with two white circles and a triangle that one could read as either a face or two breasts and a pubis, and which was meant as an homage to Rudi Gernreich's bikini and its muse, Peggy Moffitt. On her way to the rehearsal of her menswear défilé, Kawakubo threw on one of her cheeky biker jackets from spring 2005: a crudely sutured leather blouson bred to an unbroken-in catcher's mitt, then taught some charm by a vintage couture bolero with a standaway collar. "Balenciaga on steroids," as an assistant put it.

Cristóbal Balenciaga, who died in 1972, was a chivalric holdout from a courtlier age whose passing he lamented. If anyone "invented" black, he did. The ecclesiastic lines of his sculptural couture liberated women from the tyranny of the wasp-waisted New Look, and later from the ruthlessness of the miniskirt. His clients were the kind of *grandes bourgeoises* at whom Parisian spectacles of shock theater have always been aimed, but Balenciaga himself might have recognized Kawakubo as a kindred spirit. They are both idealists whose work devoutly affirms that it matters what one wears—something pure in its distinction—and in that sense they have a common ancestor. He was an aging and spindly Spanish samurai who, like Kawakubo in her faintly obscene trompe l'oeil bikini, was never afraid to cut an absurd yet heroic figure in a cynical world: the ridiculous made sublime.

—July 4, 2005

The Kimono Painter

Traditional cultures that set a high premium on conformity often prescribe their members' attire. Ethnic and regional costumes have largely disappeared from urban life in the West, with one exception—an example of folk garb that defines modernity. The American blue jean, like a mutant seed, has supplanted native varieties wherever it is sown. Japan, however, is rare, if not unique, among industrialized countries in having retained its national dress, the kimono, into the twenty-first century.

Women (or men) in kimonos may no longer be a common sight, but they don't turn heads—at least not those of their compatriots. Last summer, at rush hour in the Tokyo subway, there seemed to be about one passenger taking dainty steps in a kimono to every three hundred in Western street wear. Above the symphonic rumble of a moving crowd, the entrance of a kimono produced to my ear a soulful trill—like that of an archaic flute. When a wimpled nun passes you on the sidewalks of Rome, she strikes the same high, fleeting grace note.

The kimono is a long, ample robe shaped like a capital "T," which is wrapped closely around the body and fastened with a cloth sash. It was introduced to Japan in ancient times, along with so many other arts and refinements, from China. A twelfth-century illustrated edition of Lady Murasaki's eleventh-century novel *The Tale of Genji* depicts the elaborate court dress of the Heian period (794–1185), when the nobility of Nara and Kyoto swathed themselves in as many as a dozen kimonos, each successive layer exposing an edge of the one beneath, along with a wearer's faults of taste in mixing and matching, which were punished, as they are everywhere, with lashes of ridicule.

Kimonos have loose sleeves of varying length, and are classified according to the width of their opening at the wrist. A simple white *kosode* (which means "small sleeve") was the Heian undergarment. Its practicality relative to the *osode* ("big sleeve"), with its even more flaccid dewlaps under the arms, gradually prevailed. Courtesans, who have always been arbiters of style in Japan, preferred the svelter silhouette of the *kosode*, and commoners adopted it as outerwear. Since the Edo period (1600–1868), the proportions of the kimono have scarcely varied. It is cut from a bolt of fabric thirteen yards long by fifteen inches wide, using the full width of the cloth. Every garment is basically identical, consisting of a flat collar and eight panels, two each for the back and front, and four for the sleeves.

Fashion may be ephemeral, but solving the conundrum of how to stand out while fitting in seems to be one of its eternal functions. Though conspicuously lavish kimonos flouted the frugal ethos of both Buddhist and samurai culture, the desire to own them couldn't be suppressed—not even by the strict sumptuary laws of the Tokugawa shogunate. These measures were intended to curb the inflationary spending (and the social pretensions) of a rising merchant class by forbidding its members to wear embroidered silk or cloth woven with gold thread. In that respect, the fourth shogun made a grave miscalculation when, in 1652, he "liberated" three thousand concubines who were taxing his purse. The ladies went home to their fathers—wealthy traders, for the most part—and their kinswomen, seeing their finery, competed to outdo it.

Kimonos with a painted surface cleverly circumvented the sumptuary laws, and artisans learned to produce noble-looking embellishment with common materials. By the late seventeenth century, *yuzen-zome*, a technique of resist dyeing, was a flourishing cottage industry, centered in Kyoto. *Yuzen* imparts an indelible design—waterproof and washable—with the minutely intricate detail of a weave or a print, to the kimono fabric while preserving its suppleness.

The art is still alive in its birthplace, more than three hundred years later, even though hand labor has become the exorbitant luxury that golden embroidery used to be, and the costliest kimonos are now worn only on ceremonial occasions.

Kunihiko Moriguchi is one of Japan's preeminent kimono painters. At sixty-four, he has practiced *yuzen* for almost forty years. Last summer, when I visited his workshop in Kyoto, and renewed a long-interrupted friendship, he surprised me by saying that the likeliest client for one of his unique creations (which cost between $40,000 and $80,000) isn't a geisha or a rich man's wife but a self-made woman, often a business executive in her forties, who buys it for a family wedding or a corporate social event. Each robe requires at least six to eight weeks of meticulous workmanship, and Moriguchi's three-man studio can finish about two a month. "If I didn't feel so responsible to my apprentices, I'd probably be much lazier," he said. "But no one becomes a *yuzen* painter just, or primarily, for the livelihood. It is a way of life."

Moriguchi and I first met in Paris, about twenty years ago. I used to stay there at the apartment of an old friend, a literary hostess and retired curator, in Montparnasse. On a winter evening in 1986, I was sitting alone in her salon, watching the news. The key turned in the front door, and I assumed that it was my friend, home early from a weekend in the country, but a stranger entered. He seemed as startled by my presence as I was by his, though, with a disarming smile and a slight bow, he simply said, "*Bonsoir.*"

This second houseguest introduced himself familiarly as Kuni, presuming correctly that I would recognize his nickname. He was a diminutive Japanese man with a handsome face, a boyish aura, and a thatch of dark hair. Had it not begun turning gray, one would never have guessed that he was well past forty. He spoke excellent French, and was smartly tailored, yet his ease of manner was bohemian. I knew of him as an artist, and a protégé of our hostess, who had played the same role in his youth that she had in mine. So I found another wineglass, and linens for the spare room, and Moriguchi and I quickly established our adoptive fraternity.

The Japanese did not make a hierarchical distinction between the fine and applied arts until the nineteenth century, and in the world of animation they are remerging. Moriguchi's career blurs the borders, too. He is a well-esteemed "pure artist" (he uses the term ironically, because no one knows better than a purist that there is no such thing) who was in Europe that winter for one-man shows of his abstract works on paper at a Left Bank gallery and a Swiss museum. He also has a distinguished résumé as a curator, and he helped to design the Japanese wing at the Metropolitan Museum. (Thanks in part to his advice, the galleries feel more like a temple pavilion and less like a showcase for imported treasures.) But his renown in Japan, and among connoisseurs of Asian textiles in the West, is as a *yuzen* master and spokesman.

Miyazaki Yuzen (1681–1763), who gave the genre its name, was an artist-monk whose painted fans attracted a passionate following in Gion-machi, Kyoto's geisha district. Yuzen's motifs were traditional, and he depicted flowers and landscapes with surpassing elegance, but he added fresh and, to the contemporary eye, radically new elements: vignettes with human figures; famous monuments (which were popular as souvenirs); and literary allusions—in particular, to *The Tale of Genji*. According to Ken Kirihata, a textile historian, the style first caught on among the "big spenders" who patronized the city's pleasure quarters and the women who entertained them. (*The Life of an Amorous Man*, a quaintly comic novel about libertine intrigue, by Yuzen's contemporary Ihara Saikaku, devotes considerable attention to the subject of *yuzen* as an aphrodisiac.) But fashion often behaves like an epidemic, and *yuzen*'s appeal could not be contained. The mistress and her serving maid were equally beguiled.

Eventually, the industrious monk branched out into clothing, and as the demand for his textiles grew he perfected his resist techniques. Artists like Moriguchi have continued to refine them. "The shape of the kimono has ceased to evolve, and tradition dictates the process," Moriguchi says. "My aim is to preserve its dignity for posterity. But the simplicity of the construction is precisely what favors the complexity of design. And tradition also dictates, paradoxically, that the expression of *yuzen* has to keep changing. I want to make sure it remains a living art."

About 10 percent of Moriguchi's kimonos are designed for Western collectors and museums or for competitive annual exhibitions of traditional crafts sponsored by the Ministry of Culture. The fiftieth of these group displays took place last week in Tokyo, where Moriguchi mounted a simultaneous solo show of his latest robes. At this stage of his career, he says, he is more interested in the kimono as a work of art than as a wearable object, but one of his most startling innovations was a softened cummerbund—more of a "self-belt" than an obi—that he treated as an integral element of the textile design rather than as a contrasting accessory. It remains to be seen whether his private clients will warm to the experiment. They typically own at least four of his pieces, and one patron has a wardrobe of twenty.

A kimono destined for such a woman begins with her visit to Moriguchi's workroom. Her age, size, and station will influence the direction he takes, and she may look through his sketchbooks and suggest a palette, but the commission is otherwise an act of trust on her side. On his, it is part architecture, part couture, and an act that keeps faith with the romantic spirit of *yuzen*—what Moriguchi's wife, Keiko, calls "a man's homage to an ideal woman."

The original charm of the monk's fans was what Kirihata calls their modernity, and Moriguchi's sophisticated work has a strong mathematical component. In one kimono, and without help from a computer, he set out, in the footsteps of Dürer and Escher, to disprove a geometric theory of tessellation which holds that a flat surface can't be completely covered by pentagons. (He succeeded, with a little fudging.) Op art was an early influence, and his boldly graphic kinetic patterns were considered revolutionary when he introduced them thirty years ago. Many of his designs have been inspired by the principles of Buddhist landscape architecture. They are abstract distillations of sand, snow, moonbeams, a riverbed, a flowering cliff, or a harrowed field. "Dawn" is a vertical arrangement of white trapezoids on a turquoise ground. "Darkness" has the somber beauty of a raked gravel garden. But his latest kimonos, like their sashes, take liberties with a certain notion of decorum. They are enlivened with freewheeling circles, triangular sawteeth, or asymmetrical zigzags in grayed pastels. A pattern of silvery filaments against a pointillist sky seems to celebrate Japan's famous suspension bridges.

One does not casually embrace a traditional Japanese vocation. It is almost a religious calling, and the path to grace in kimono painting, as in many devotions, is through surrender. Students of traditional crafts submit to long apprenticeships, some lasting a lifetime. Moriguchi was old for a *yuzen* beginner—twenty-six—when he entered the studio of a legendary sensei, his father, Kako.

The senior Moriguchi is considered one of the greatest *yuzen* masters of the past century. He is now ninety-five, and he worked until two years ago. The empress Nagako, Hirohito's consort, was an appreciative client, and hanging in the family dining room is a color photograph of her wearing a Moriguchi kimono—pale blue, with a bamboo motif—to receive the queen of England on a state visit. Kako was relatively young—fifty-eight—when he was elevated to the rank of *ningen kokuho*, an honorific meaning "holder of an intangible cultural property." This makes him one of Japan's hundred and seventeen Living National Treasures. The designation was established at the end of the American occupation, in 1950, in part to prevent Japan's traditional handicrafts (woodwork, cloisonné, swordmaking, art-paper production, doll-making, lacquerware, metalwork, ceramics, and textiles) from succumbing to oblivion in a rapidly modernizing society. "Tangible cultural properties" (landmarks and monuments) and performance arts (Noh and Kabuki) are similarly protected.

The eldest son in a family of artisans is traditionally the heir apparent, although Kako's firstborn, Masafumi, chose to become an architect. Kunihiko helped in the studio as a schoolboy, and studied Japanese painting and art history, but he wasn't yet prepared to assume the mantle. In August of 1963, with a degree from the Kyoto City University of Arts, he sailed for Europe. Competing against two hundred other applicants, he had won a two-year French government scholarship to the École des Arts Décoratifs, in Paris.

Traveling abroad with him were several hundred treasures from five centuries of Japanese art destined for an exhibition at the Petit Palais, including a portrait attributed to Takanobu of the first shogun, Minamoto—a mysteriously expressive study that is, in its way, Japan's *Mona Lisa*. Neither the twenty-two-year-old kimono-painter's son nor the eight-hundred-year-old warlord had ever left his native country. Japanese museum officials, impressed by Moriguchi's French and his knowledge of the works on loan, asked him to interpret for them during the voyage, and they later invited him to help install the show. Sometime in late September, as he was choosing wallpaper for the galleries and directing the carpenters, a lordly figure, dressed in the trousers of a Camargue cowboy, made an entrance. Moriguchi had no idea that this "insanely chic" personage was the curator of the exhibition and a great painter in his own right—Balthus. They began to argue in a courtly though heated fashion about the proper way to hang some eighteenth-century Zen drawings—hell sketches and hungry-ghost sketches, among others—with Moriguchi defending his traditional approach and Balthus explaining that "orthodox principles" were of less interest to him than the "fantasy" of the monks who made them. Charmed both by the upstart's ignorance of his fame and by his deep, if still unworldly, refinement, Balthus invited Moriguchi to lunch, and then to a weekend at the château of a former mistress, and they embarked on a lifelong friendship.

While Balthus was touring Kyoto's temples choosing art for the exhibition, he had fallen in love with his interpreter, Setsuko Ideta, a young student who became his second wife. On a visit to her parents in 1964, the couple called upon Kako, and Balthus later told Kunihiko that he was staggered by the painterliness of his father's work, and had stayed until the early morning discussing their common artistic ground. Kunihiko, in the meantime, spent a summer in southern Europe singing for his supper in Greek tavernas. His two school years passed quickly, and after graduation he received a tempting job offer from a graphic-arts studio. Balthus urged him to reconsider it. He had recently been posted to Rome, to direct the French Academy, and he was restoring the Villa Medici, the grand Renaissance palazzo where the academy is housed. He invited Moriguchi to be his guest for six months while he sorted out his fate. There was one stipulation: that Moriguchi cease painting for that interval. "I was just supposed to live—and to reflect," he told me. "But I knew Balthus wanted me to succeed my father, believing that any career I might have as a graphic artist in the West would be mediocre in comparison."

At Christmas, Balthus took Setsuko to Switzerland. Moriguchi was on his own at the villa, and, once he had made his choice, it seemed easier not having to say goodbye.

Kako Moriguchi's studio is now his son's, an attic loft of about seven hundred square feet whose low ceiling is latticed with bamboo drying racks. The air is close—the dust from an open window would be fatal to wet silk—and a heady mixture of odors (fixatives, solvents, tobacco smoke) stings one's nostrils. In an alcove at one end is a small library of art books and a computer station. An array of brushes hangs on the wall behind a drawing table, close to the wooden floor. Moriguchi's two apprentices (his father employed a much larger staff) kneel or sit cross-legged on mats, working with trancelike concentration in pools of lamplight.

Moriguchi still sounds and looks like the boyish stranger I met twenty years ago, and he is so relaxed in French, his third language (he learned English at a Protestant elementary school), that the magisterial persona he projects in the studio came as a surprise. When he introduced his apprentices, explaining my visit and inviting them to speak frankly, they looked perplexed, if not horrified, and an awkward silence ensued. The junior man, Takashi Ashida, is thirty-two. He has the finely modeled, ascetic beauty of a Heian bodhisattva. (Moriguchi says that he counts on Ashida's serenity to rescue him from his "creative panics.") Ashida's long fingers move at a dreamy pace, and that is how he speaks. "I do not think I am very patient," he said. "With time, though, I have learned. It has taken eleven years." The senior man, Kazume Abiko, is an opera buff, and was listening to *Don Carlo*. Abiko has been working for the Moriguchis since he entered Kako's service some forty years ago, at the age of fifteen. He asked Kunihiko to keep him on because, he said, "one must live *yuzen*, and I could only do so where there is love." He had also long since admitted to himself that "any kimono of my own would only be an epigone of my master's. It is not my place to discuss creation." Moriguchi told me later, though, that Abiko can be vehement if he doesn't like a design, and that the otherworldly Ashida, who has a wife, two children, and a degree in textile design, is quite ambitious, and will undoubtedly open his own studio when his training is complete.

Some *yuzen* painters use ramie or cotton, but Moriguchi prefers white crêpe spun by Brazilian or Chinese silkworms, and woven in Japan. Once the garment has been made up, and the design modeled to scale, he sketches it freehand onto the fabric, with a fine brush dipped in soluble ink derived from a tiny blue wildflower, the *aobana*. When the ink is dry, the kimono is unstitched, and its panels are pinned tautly to ribbed bamboo stretchers. At this stage, it is ready for a first coat of resist. There are many genres of resist decoration, and children practice a simple one when they stencil their names onto lunch boxes. Whatever the resist—starch, paper, wax, or wood—it protects each discrete area of detail from taking color, or losing its definition, as the adjacent area is treated. *Yuzen* painters use rice paste, which is squeezed, like icing, through a brown mulberry-paper cone that has been waterproofed with persimmon tannin. The diameter of its nozzle controls the relative thickness of the resist, which is sometimes no wider than a hairbreadth. Then the underside of the silk is sprayed with water to dissolve the *aobana* ink, and to increase the absorbency of the rice paste, and it is primed for the dye. Moriguchi prepares the colors from scratch—indigo, cochineal, shell powder, onionskin—steeping plants or insects and grinding minerals. He delegates many chores to the apprentices, but never the painting, because a brushstroke, like a fingerprint, is unique to its hand.

Abiko's forte is a resist technique of the Edo period—*makinori*—which was originally inspired by the sand garden at the Silver Temple. It had been lost until the elder Moriguchi noticed an Edo *kosode* at the Tokyo National Museum which had a patch of mottling that intrigued him. It took him some fifteen years of trial-and-error experimentation to reproduce it, and it became his hallmark. *Makinori* are tiny grains of pulverized zinc that resemble poppy seeds. They are mixed with rice paste and sprinkled on the wet silk, individually or in pinches, then coated with wood wax to prevent cracking, and fixed with soy juice, before a graduated wash of color is applied. Then the *makinori* are tweezed off and rinsed away, leaving a delicate speckled pattern that is whiter or grayer (a mist or a flurry) depending on the density of the resist. "With Kako-san, the grains are a background for the figurative motifs," Abiko said. "In the work of Kunihiko-san, the nuances of *makinori* are themselves a motif. The effect is more severe, and the labor of applying and removing them intensely demanding. There is no room for error."

A *yuzen* master's reputation, however, depends not only on his consummate virtuosity as a technician but on his ability to imagine how a two-dimensional composition will translate into a three-dimensional object—"kimono" literally means "the thing worn"—and how a specific woman's body and gestures will bring it to life. At that moment, the robe acquires what Moriguchi calls its "fourth dimension": it becomes a moving picture. (His elegiac work "Darkness" plays an emblematic role in a recent film shown on Japanese television in which the father of the heroine, a geisha, is a *yuzen* master.)

The workshop occupies the top story of the family house, which seems more venerable than its actual age, about a century. It is a rambling wooden dwelling with an interior garden, in the old quarter of the city. Kunihiko and his siblings grew up here among their father's disciples, who shared their meals and living space, and on the morning after his marriage to Keiko Terada, in 1975, she joined them. "Our communal household wasn't simply a practical arrangement," he told me, as Keiko served us tea and sweets in their tatami room. "It was about the transmission of a culture, and it required a lot of sacrifice from my wife and sons. When I proposed to Keiko, whom I met through a friend—a former sumo wrestler—I asked if she could accept it. She said yes, perhaps without reflecting what it meant. We married four months later. She had incredible courage."

Keiko is a pale, radiantly pretty woman in her mid-fifties. Her composure is a foil for her husband's intensity. ("If I am successful in the world, it is because of her profound tact," Moriguchi says.) She is the daughter of a Tokyo dentist, and when she met Kunihiko she was working as her father's hygienist. "I wasn't prepared for the world of *yuzen*," she told me, "even though my parents were of the old school." Her mother had neglected to give her a domestic education, on the principle that a future mother-in-law should have that prerogative. On Keiko's wedding day (she wore two kimonos painted by Kako, including a white robe with a crane motif that is one of his masterpieces, and a black-and-white robe with a rainbow of stripes by her journeyman fiancé, which he labored on for six months), she embarked upon a feudal vassalage of her own.

Keiko's tact was never more essential to the household than in 1999, when Kako had a stroke that left him partially paralyzed, and he had to relearn to use his right hand. His lucidity also suffered. Moriguchi says that his father's mental decline was "particularly hard for me to accept. He had been my spiritual companion for sixty years. We set an example of a father and son working together with mutual respect. I carried on his work, but he always left me free to differentiate myself."

Until last year, when Moriguchi was finally persuaded by his friend and patron Madame Takako Shimazu, the former princess Suga—Hirohito's youngest daughter, who knows something about dynastic obligations—to ignore "shaming lectures" from busybodies and move his parents into a private nursing home, Keiko, their full-time caretaker, had never, in thirty years, had a real vacation. "I owed her a honeymoon," Moriguchi told me sheepishly. "I bought first-class tickets and took her to Paris."

Many of Japan's most prominent artisans are the scions of dynasties going back ten or even fifteen generations. The Moriguchis are an exception. Kako, born in 1909, was the first member of his clan to practice *yuzen*. The family's forebears, Kunihiko says, were village chiefs who, for at least half a millennium, had owned land in the Shiga Prefecture, east of Kyoto, where the waters of Lake Biwa nourish the mussels that produce Biwa pearls and irrigate some of Japan's most fertile fields. They collected the taxes—which, like the wages of the samurai, were usually paid in rice. But with the opening of

Japan to Western influences, in the Meiji era, and the introduction of a money economy, the Moriguchis "suffered a loss of caste," Kunihiko said. Their fortunes were definitively battered by a famine in 1913–14, and Kako was forced to leave school at thirteen and find employment.

According to the family folklore, Moriguchi children tended to be either "sickly" or "exceptional." Kako showed his hardiness in both senses: resistance to disease and an unconquerable self-assurance. The future Living Treasure received the lowest marks in his art class for submitting heretical pictures. Asked to draw a locomotive, he sketched a black triangle flanked by two swaths of yellow and green. "The train left already," he said. "The green is spring wheat, and the yellow is rapeseed, on either side of the track." Kako's freehand painting on kimono silk—exuberant plum blossoms, chrysanthemums, and birds in flight—would assert the same defiance of academicism. It reflects nature like a dream, rather than like a mirror.

One of Kako's uncles was a pharmacist in Kyoto, and he took his nephew on as an apprentice. The work was menial and included washing the windows and hanging flyers for soap, aspirin, or toothpaste, which were supplied by manufacturers. But the paper was of high quality, and Kako used its blank side in lieu of a sketch pad. Sometimes he had the temerity, Moriguchi said, to turn the drawings around with the ad facing in. The uncle made no objection to the use of his shopfront as an impromptu gallery, and his nephew's work attracted the interest of an elderly gentleman who came by every morning.

As in a fairy tale of a penniless changeling recognized by a passing burgher, the old man introduced Kako, by then fifteen, to the *yuzen* painter Kason Nakagawa, who became his master. Moriguchi showed me Nakagawa's picture in an old album: a scowling figure in a fedora too small for his head. Despite appearances, he was "an open-minded man" who gave Kako leave to study art in the evenings with Hosho Hikita, a painter and a sage. The master's liberality had its limits, however, because after five years of service, in 1929, when Kako asked Nakagawa for his freedom, the request was denied. He stayed on for another nine years, and was paid well enough (as are Moriguchi's apprentices) to buy a house and, through a matchmaker, arrange his marriage. Masafumi was born in 1937, and Kunihiko in 1941, ten months before Pearl Harbor.

Immediately after the war, Kako supported his family (a daughter, Etsuko, was born in 1946) by painting cherry trees and American eagles on souvenir handkerchiefs and silk bomber jackets, which were popular with the occupation troops. By the fifties, though, the expanding economy had begun to reproduce some of the conditions that favored the heyday of *yuzen* three hundred years earlier: loosened social constraints and a rising middle class avid for luxury goods. "We started to get huge commissions," Moriguchi says. "The merchants and industrialists who made their fortunes supplying war matériel for Korea were good clients. Two years in advance of a wedding, they would order kimonos for all the women in the bridal party. The studio worked from morning to night, and there was another virtue to the nouveaux riches: they always wanted something new. My father was doing some of his most original work."

In 1955, one of Kako's kimonos, speckled with *makinori*, won the grand prize at the first exhibition of "intangible national treasures" organized by the government. The empress saw the show, and three years later Princess Suga paid an official visit to the Moriguchi studio. The imperial Mercedes blocked traffic in the narrow street, and all of the neighbors turned out to see their monarchs' teenage daughter, who was attended by a sour-looking duenna and several equerries. "I didn't know much about *yuzen*, and I was curious to see the process," Madame Shimazu told me in Tokyo, in the restaurant of a grand hotel. She is still a beauty at sixty-six, slim and wiry, with cropped hair brushed off her high forehead, though she wears an incongruous braided rattail at the nape. It is perhaps symbolic of a flair for rebellion, since she was the first member of the imperial family to defy protocol and take a paid job—working as a design consultant. She had come from a business meeting, and was dressed simply in a summer pantsuit. "I could never get used to wearing kimonos in daily life," she said. "They are too valuable, for one thing, and uncomfortable. My actions and walk change when I wear them, and, like most people, I prefer Western clothes." When an important occasion calls for Japanese dress, she often calls Kunihiko for advice, "but I don't always take it," she added with a laugh. "I wear things the way they suit me." She has no memory of meeting Moriguchi at his father's house. They were introduced formally at the French embassy in the late sixties, and have been close friends since. "Kunihiko has something rare," she said, "a sense of balance, and I suspect it derives from his relationship with his father." In a portrait of Madame Shimazu by Hamada Taiji, whose style is reminiscent of David Hockney's, she poses in profile, with her elegant hands folded in her lap. In homage to Moriguchi—or perhaps just because it suits her—she is wearing one of his kimonos.

While I was in Kyoto, Moriguchi started work on a new commission that was causing him trouble—"Maybe," he suggested with a grin, "because the lady has such long arms"—though beneath his sunny demeanor, which was also a form of politesse, he was finding it hard to concentrate. His older son, Motoharu, had called from Paris, in something of a quandary about his future; his younger son, Hiromitsu, who lives at home, was in an anxious mood and causing both parents concern. "I've probably indulged them," Moriguchi said to me one afternoon. The French ambassador had just left after a studio visit, and Keiko was reverently refolding the kimonos. "I'm still supporting them while they find themselves. Keiko and I grew up in a different world, and I wanted to be a modern father."

Motoharu and Hiromitsu are bachelors of twenty-nine and twenty-six. According to his father, Motoharu's hobbies are rock music and photography. Hiromitsu is a surfer. But each has entertained the prospect of taking up the family profession. Motoharu left home after high school and lived abroad—mostly in the Hamptons—for eight years. He studied graphic design, and for a while he tried to program his father's work on a computer—which proved to be impossible. Hiromitsu helps in the studio, preparing the *makinori*, but not as an apprentice. "He tried it for two years, though he didn't have the patience for it," Moriguchi said. "He made one or two interesting things, with a lot of help, and won a prize for his art. But everyone was hoping for a third-generation Moriguchi, and the pressure was too great. He could never be sure, he said, that his talent, and not his name, had impressed the judges." Keiko still hopes, however, that at least one of her sons will follow his father. "*Yuzen* is in their DNA," she says.

My last day in Kyoto was a Sunday. The Moriguchis invited me to lunch at Sorin-ji, a Zen temple on the outskirts of the city. It was surrounded by a blighted landscape of strip malls and auto-body shops. "Kyoto is a funny place," Moriguchi said. "The birthplace of *yuzen*—but also of Nintendo." After our meal, we drove up into the northern hills, to Ohara, an idyllic village that is thronged with tourists in foliage season. The nursing home where Kako and Chie Moriguchi live is tucked away at the foot of a mountain, next to a stream, surrounded by deep woods. It is a cheerful modern building with the atmosphere of a spa hotel. When we arrived, about fifty of the residents had gathered for tea in the lobby. Their social director was playing a grand piano, and they were singing what sounded like Stephen Foster songs.

Kako was in his room at the end of a hall. When a nurse announced that his children had come to visit, he found his glasses, bowed to me from his wheelchair, and for a brief moment he embraced all of us with an incandescent smile. Then I went off with Keiko to find her mother-in-law, and to deliver some laundry. Moriguchi stayed with his father for a long time.

On the drive home, he seemed pensive, and concentrated on the winding road. After a while, almost as if he were thinking aloud, he began speaking about *yuzen*. It needed an infusion of new ideas, and a closer rapport to modern fashion. "I admire the Japanese avant-garde," he said. "They understand what Balthus meant by 'fantasy.' And we have to answer the challenge of modernity: What is a kimono, or what will it become, if it ceases to be a thing worn?"

We said goodbye at my hotel, and I thanked him for the honor of meeting Kako. "How strange it still is," he replied, "to leave my parents up there and drive home without them. Yet I think my father would be happy to know that I feel freer as an artist than I've ever been."

—October 17, 2005

Penn à la Carte

Happy pictures are all alike. Every perfectionist is unhappy in his own way, and his art reminds us that life is a losing battle. Fashion, on the other hand, is the domain of promise, where youth and beauty are perpetually solvent. The conventional purpose of fashion photography is to excite envy (the wellspring of desire) while promoting the illusion that there is almost nothing one can't have. In that sense, the fashion world is an alien habitat for an artist, and the most gifted guest workers who make a living there often attempt to flee its balminess to a more congenially cold climate, an anti-Eden where the perfect couple bicker and decay.

The photography of Irving Penn is one of the twentieth century's most important bodies of work. Penn makes a distinction between his art and the pictures of clothing or accessories, which he dismisses as "commodities," but even though the fashion photographs exist to celebrate the salable, there is always something eating at them, implacably. A disembodied tongue; a splayed peach; a grotesquely slathered maw; an insect; a spoonful of caviar glistening obscenely— all are ready to consume or to be consumed. The nude women in the black-and-white pictures that Penn was discouraged, for decades, from exhibiting (for no better reason, it appears, than that the women were headless and fat) seem to be melting under his lights like ambitious confections whose contours have only half jelled, or are half decomposed. The will, like the flesh, must sag, they suggest.

Penn was a failed painter when he embarked on his career in fashion, as an assistant art director at *Vogue*, sixty-one years ago. He took up a camera because the staff photographers couldn't execute a picture that he had designed for the October 1943 cover. Alexander Liberman, the senior art director, told him to give it a try. Penn produced a somewhat busy, Braque-ish still life that evoked the front-hall table of a horsey matron, and he has experimented with the genre more subversively ever since. The fastidious clutter disappeared and was replaced by the detritus of louche nights on the town, memento mori, and—in some of his most famous images—cigar butts and sodden gutter swill. Employed to purvey opulence and joie de vivre (which Penn did and does better than almost anyone else living), the modern artist out of his element and homesick for discomfiture makes an aesthetic of it. In the great pictures of Penn's wife, Lisa Fonssagrives, modeling the couture of the late 1940s and early 1950s, he was the first to strip the fashion photograph of a context and props. For the portraits that he took for *Vogue* in the same period (of nearly everyone grand and notable at mid-century), he backed his elegant subjects into a shabby corner—the acute angle formed by battered wooden panels. He photographed native warriors in masks and feathers against a drab dropcloth, as if they were Fonssagrives or Giacometti. Beauty, Penn implies, makes him claustrophobic, but he has never been able to escape it.

He is now eighty-seven, and a widower. Most of his intimates refer to him in conversation not by his first name or his last, but—with quaint formality—as "Mr. Penn." Their reverence is so well earned both by the distinction of the work and by the courtliness of the man that the honorific doesn't seem servile or pretentious. If one were to translate "Mr. Penn" into French, it wouldn't be *monsieur*—it would have to be *maître*. The master has just published a new collection of photographs, *A Notebook at Random* (Bulfinch, 2004), a laconic volume with no introductory essay and very little explanatory text. Two offhand sentences by the author serve as its epigraph:

The reader might find himself traveling along a path through many countries, through years of time, distant cultures, in the presence of lovely women and brilliant men. His path would make small detours among inanimate objects, foods, drawings, paintings, amusements, and seductions.

Though the title advertises a deliberate nonchalance, it is difficult, at first, to grasp Penn's motive or criteria for selecting, from such a vast and rich oeuvre, these particular images, or how he decided upon their sequence. Some of this material will surely still be admired in two hundred years, and some, however charming, is ephemera. In addition to the famous and not-so-famous photographs, there are fragments of pictures used in testing platinum prints, preliminary sketches, an example of Liberman's cropmarks, watercolors, and a worksheet from a photo lab. Voguish frivolity consorts with existential anguish, abstraction with carnality, and, as always in Penn's work, appetite with disgust. I wondered, though, if—as he meandered through his archives and laid the prints out on the worktable in the whiteness of a studio familiarly known as "the hospital"—he wasn't thinking of Walter Benjamin.

Benjamin, like Penn, was smitten by Paris and French culture as a young man, and a central figure in his work is that quintessential Parisian, the flaneur. This idle stroller is adrift in the city, his passive senses exquisitely attuned. His greatest luxury is to have no purpose. Like the photographer and his subjects, he is a solitary figure. Even when the mud men of New Guinea, the sublime and enigmatic Mrs. Penn, the stunted children of Cuzco, and the wary old Colette return his gaze, it isolates them completely. Their mutual contemplation is that of the ambler staring—with the impartial gall of an infant or a predator—at passing strangers, one of whom may be himself, fractured in a shopwindow. There is probably no more impersonal, yet no more concentrated, distillation of intimacy.

Like Penn, Benjamin preferred phenomena to ideas and curiosities to treasures, the tinier and weirder the better (he greatly admired two grains of wheat inscribed with a Hebrew prayer), and the aim of his ramble, he wrote, was "to capture a portrait of history in the most insignificant representations of reality, its scraps, as it were." In photographic terms, that ideal might be an album as random and capricious as this one: a survey of the material world conducted, over a lifetime, with such metaphysical fidelity that it transcends the need for explanation.

—September 27, 2004

Swann Song

Of all the garments I have loved and lost, there is one whose perfection gave me such happiness that I've spent decades hoping it will surface in some thrift shop, and when I'm in Paris I never fail to check at the Père Lachaise of couture, Didier Ludot's grimly glamorous little resale boutique in the Palais Royal. This first deluxe, not to say decent, piece of clothing that I ever owned was a sable-brown Cossack-style maxiskirt by Yves Saint Laurent that zipped up both sides like a sleeping bag. It was made of thick alpaca blanket wool, lined in black silk, and ingeniously constructed without darts so that, despite its weight, it had no bulk at the hips or waist. I bought it in 1969 at the Rive Gauche boutique on Bond Street, in London, which had been inaugurated with great fanfare that year by Princess Margaret and was managed very profitably by a former fashion journalist named Lady Rendlesham. Saint Laurent has always had a penchant for aristocratic sales help.

While he didn't invent designer ready-to-wear—Pierre Cardin did—Saint Laurent was the first couturier to make a cult of it, associating the cachet of an exalted label with a line of factory-made clothing and accessories of high quality and audacious chic (he designed them himself, at least for a while) that were marketed globally to a hip baby-boom clientele. "The Rive Gauche notion of luxury had less to do with money than with attitude," Laurence Benaïm writes in her authoritative biography of Saint Laurent, which was published in France in 1993. Benaïm also notes that in 1966, when the Rive

Gauche line was launched, the ready-to-wear prices were about a tenth of the couture. But a tenth of the unthinkable was still hard for me to imagine. Except for my youth, and an inclination toward idolatry, I was hardly the target Rive Gauche customer, and I have never, unfortunately, had a Saint Laurent body—leggy and broad-shouldered, with the flat hips, shortish waist, and high, shapely haunches and bosom of the African and Caribbean models he was among the first to employ. At the time, though, I was grateful for the mercy of a long skirt: ruthless minis were the rule. I was also thrilled to have something so certifiably Parisian in a closet filled with the picturesque ethnic frippery that is back in style this year, but which stank of the embroidered sheepskin coat from Afghanistan that I'd bought in an open-air stall next to Gandalf's Garden off the King's Road. Badly cured hippie fur, patchouli, diesel exhaust, mildew, hashish rolled with stale tobacco, maté, and paraffin heating oil are the scents that summon up my remembrance of the late sixties.

I was then writing wine-dark Plathian poetry in a bedsit with imitation William Morris wallpaper facing a garage south of the river, and paying my rent by tutoring a Hollywood mogul's eleven-year-old son in Berkeley Square. When my pupil's English lesson was finished, the butler served us tea, a repast at which we were supposed to speak French. Since teatime was off the meter, I felt entitled to wrap up whatever solid refreshments we hadn't consumed to take home, and I confess that, in addition to scones and sandwiches, I sometimes also pocketed a handful of raw brown sugar lumps, and on the way to the tube station, which, like Rive Gauche, was on Bond Street, I would eat them furtively, like stolen candy. One Friday, I noticed a discreet "final reductions" sign in the shopwindow, which emboldened me to cross its intimidatingly smart threshold for the first time. The carpet, as I recall, was the color of a blood orange, and there were little mauve chairs, and futuristic lighting, and a black-and-white portrait of Himself in the style of *Blowup*. Not much was left on the sale rack, but the marvelously refined skirt with its cavalry swagger and feline nap had been marked down to fifteen pounds—one of its zippers was "as seen." I had a week's pay in my pocket: fifteen pounds. Many of my romances would begin, like this one, as a chance encounter sparked by an obscure hunger, a neat coincidence, and a fatal attraction for the defective. That is how I joined the ranks of *celles qui s'adonnent à Yves Saint Laurent* (in the words of the 1977 ad for his perfume Opium—a publicity campaign that was widely protested as pro-drug and anti-Asian): one of those women addicted to Yves Saint Laurent.

On January 7 of this year, reading from a prepared speech in a gravelly whisper, Saint Laurent, who is sixty-five, announced his retirement. The spring 2002 haute-couture show would be his last, taking the form of a retrospective. His forty-four years in fashion had, he said, been haunted by aesthetic phantoms. "I have grappled with anguish and I have been through sheer hell . . . I have known those fair-weather friends we call tranquilizers and drugs. I have known the prison of depression and the confinement of a hospital. But one day I was able to come through all of that, dazzled yet sober. It was Marcel Proust who taught me that 'the magnificent and pitiful family of the hypersensitive are the salt of the earth.' "

French television provided live coverage of this rare and emotional press conference, which generated nearly as much nasty backbiting as it did fulsome piety. The fashion press scrambled to compose its tributes. The funereal windows of Didier Ludot were promptly dressed with vintage Saint Laurent, and so, with a brighter, mod flair, were the windows of the Galeries Lafayette, the vast department store that occupies two square blocks behind the Opéra Garnier. Grasset reissued Benaïm's biography, and bookstores on both banks also gave prominence to a six-pound coffee-table tome of film stills (*Yves Saint Laurent: 5, avenue Marceau*, Abrams, 2002) from a documentary made by David Teboul, who spent three months with his crew in Saint Laurent's atelier. Teboul's made-for-television hagiography, Warholian in *longueur* but without the consolation of sex, brutality, or weirdness, was to be screened at the Centre Pompidou on January 22, immediately following the Saint Laurent couture show, and, later in the week, on television. It should have been called *Merci, Monseiur*, the refrain of its dialogue. The ash grows longer on the master's cigarette as he labors over his sketch pad. His French bulldog, Moujik, dismembers a stuffed toy. His muse, model, and collaborator Loulou de la Falaise, the director of YSL accessories, unfurls a bolt of matronly flowered chiffon and drapes it on a stoic model. (La Falaise has always been the quintessential Rive Gauche *haute bohémienne*, and her 1977 wedding to Thadée Klossowski, the younger son of Balthus—a party hosted by Saint Laurent at the Châlet des Îles in the Bois de Boulogne—was, notes Benaïm, the first great social stir-fry of "punks and baronesses.") A plump seamstress with a bad haircut irons the canvas lapel of what will become an exquisitely banal suit jacket. Every feeble nod or hoarse croak from the subject is received like a pontifical blessing by a tired-looking staff of aging parishioners who, except for la Falaise—a woman who flaunts her well-worn beauty with mermaid nonchalance and whose expression of ironical detachment belies her vigilant subservience—are touchingly unglamorous. But Teboul's homage is perhaps more revealing than it was meant to be. It leaves the impression that 5, avenue Marceau is less a couture atelier than a mad king's private theater where the actors conspire, elaborately, to humor his fantasies.

The backbiting in the press was encouraged, in part, by Pierre Bergé—Saint Laurent's formidably astute business partner and ex-lover, who has, for four decades, sheltered the master from the unpleasant realities of accounts payable. Saint Laurent has always maintained that he has no precise idea how rich he is; he just knows there's enough money to permit him to decorate beautiful houses and collect precious things. In 1994, when Bergé was being investigated for insider trading (he was cleared the next year), the judge accepted Saint Laurent's convincing protestations of fiscal imbecility. In 1993, Bergé had sold the YSL ready-to-wear business to the pharmaceutical and cosmetics giant Sanofi, which, in a complicated deal with the luxury mogul François Pinault, resold it two years ago for a billion dollars to the Gucci Group. Domenico De Sole, Gucci's chief executive, confided the design of the Rive Gauche line to the dashing American Tom Ford. After a tepid start, Ford has, with lots of grommeting, whipstitching, ruching, animal prints, peasant ruffles, and skintight leather, begun to make it profitably decadent again (though not too kinky for the American market). Since the turn of the millennium, most of the "Saint Laurents" featured in the glossies or worn by celebrities to awards ceremonies have been the pretender's handiwork. This has understandably rankled the royalists. After the press conference, Bergé announced with a flash of Nixonian bitterness that the game of haute couture was finished because the player with the marbles was packing them up and going home.

The crowd outside the Centre Pompidou, in the place Beaubourg, on the night of January 22 was behaving as if there were a Prada warehouse sale inside rather than the retrospective of a great designer's lifework. Two thousand of the elect held tickets, five hundred of them for standing room, which everyone knew meant three hours on one's feet. The flood surge of bodies when the doors finally opened was terrifying, and it's a miracle that none of Saint Laurent's original couture clients—a beautifully wrought, hand-painted set of tiny porcelain old-lady dolls—got trampled to death. The publicists themselves had been so mobbed by importunate style faxers begging for a seat that they'd stopped answering the phones. I had been told there would be absolutely no admission without an invitation corresponding to the name and gender on one's passport, but it was impossible to disengage a limb from the crush, much less a document.

More than one guest who made it past the barricades was secretly gratified by the rumor, later confirmed, that Gwyneth Paltrow—a fixture, with bodyguards and camera-ready pancake makeup, at every prior couture event—had, among other upstart celebrities, been turned away. It was a show of loyalty on both sides: creator's and audience's. Jeanne Moreau, Lauren Bacall, Bianca Jagger, Paloma Picasso, Nan Kempner, Diane von Furstenberg, Betty Catroux, and, of course, Catherine Deneuve, muse and spokeswoman for the house—who first became addicted to Saint Laurent when he dressed her for *Belle de Jour*—shared a front row with three French first ladies, an Arab princess, and the designer's mother. Jean-Paul Gaultier's platinum buzz cut and Sonia Rykiel's electrostatic carotene pageboy glowed in the dark. Hubert de Givenchy was conspicuous for his height and distinction. Vivienne Westwood, in clashing plaids and matching red hair, teetered off on platform stilettos to find a ladies' room. Many of the spectators were wearing a treasured piece of YSL, though I assume that none of them except me, ever the bargain hunter, had bought her early-seventies décolleté tuxedo jacket—structured shoulders, tapered waist, jet buttons—at the Council Thrift Shop on East Eighty-fourth Street. Outside in the cobbled square, under a light drizzle, a battalion of well-armed riot policemen with rakish berets nervously scanned a huge throng of fashion fundamentalists, some weeping, who watched the simulcast on giant screens.

After a predictably interminable delay, the epic défilé began unfurling to a soundtrack of the Beatles, African drums, Callas, Mozart, jazz, and the Stones. A hundred and seven "girls" modeled three hundred archival designs, beginning with a breezy peacoat and wide-legged white trousers from 1962. The stream of vintage creations was punctuated, erratically, by some forty outfits for spring 2002, including a suite of draped chiffon gowns in opaline colors (ravishing, though their novelty was imperceptible). The finale was a cortege of sixty tuxedos impossible to date but representing every conceivable variation: cropped, skirted, slim, padded, flared, strict, high-waisted, pleated, racy, flat-hipped, classic. The majority of the models had been culled from this season's crop of inhumanly lovely teenagers, although Naomi Campbell and Claudia Schiffer, magnificently sullen and goofy, respectively, who rarely work the catwalk anymore, consented to appear. But they were all outclassed by the womanly splendor of their elders: Mounia, Katouscha, and Jerry Hall.

Most couture shows last about twenty minutes. This one roiled on for more than an hour, in waves of staggering beauty, fauvish color, and perverse extravagance—a jacket costing half a million francs, for example, perfectly replicating van Gogh's *Irises* in seven hundred hours' worth of hand-beading by Lesage. There were sumptuously embellished tributes to other painters: Picasso, Matisse, Braque, Dalí, and Warhol; to poets and writers, among them Aragon and Cocteau; and to exotic native populations—Russian moujiks, Forbidden City courtesans, Castilian matadors, and African queens. There was plenty of cerebral whimsy to offset the noirish sex play: feather minis suitable for a showgirl's wedding to a peer; a minuscule suede tunic from the sixties worn with high-heeled waders; swanky cocktail dresses that exposed a nipple; a transparent black baby-doll disco nightie trimmed with fur; quite a bit of immaculately white-collared *Belle de Jour* respectability begging to be corrupted; a strong dose of double-breasted androgyny; and a backless evening gown cut to the cleft of the buttocks, then scored with lace. But while Saint Laurent can sometimes be pedantically outré, he's never trashy. And he displayed such encyclopedic formal invention and technical virtuosity that the occasional bomb—like a series of umbrella-shaped flowered tea frocks in what looked like shower-curtain fabric, or a shapeless wool shift worn with a dowager's turban—were like a sorbet between courses rather than a disappointment.

The event itself had the gestalt of those imperial funerals that the French Republic orchestrates with elegiac pomp and poignance for its national heroes (and, much more rarely, heroines), whether they have contributed to the glory of the *patrie* with a pen or a sword—or, as in this case, a No. 2 pencil. And it was impossible to be unmoved by the pure-heartedness of Saint Laurent's love of women; or by his appearance of leonine decrepitude; or by the tragic grimace—the expression of a man walking the plank and still riven to his core by the conflicting imperatives of resistance and surrender—with which he took his final steps down the runway. The dauphin of couture had become its King Lear.

Yves Mathieu-Saint-Laurent (he dropped the Mathieu when he opened his own couture house) was born on August 1, 1936, in Oran, Algeria. His prosperous middle-class parents, Lucienne and Charles, who owned a house in town and a villa at the beach, prided themselves on employing French, rather than Arab, servants. Yves's father was an insurance executive who also managed a chain of movie theaters. His mother was a pretty and stylish provincial coquette with great legs, who, Saint Laurent says enigmatically, "is still a child." In pictures from the family albums she also looks rather terrifyingly sunny, at least from the point of view of a fragile and depressive homosexual son who identified so passionately with Proust that he sometimes traveled under the pseudonym M. Swann and of whom Bergé has said, "He was born with a nervous breakdown." But she encouraged his precocious talents, even to the point of letting him cut up her clothes to make rag dolls, and when he was fourteen or fifteen and had begun to design ensembles influenced by Dior and Balenciaga for her and his two younger sisters, she paid a local dressmaker to run them up.

One of the most eloquent photographs of the neurasthenic aesthete as a young man is an all-boy class portrait that seems to date from his last year at the Lycée Lamoricière, in Oran, and for which he has removed his glasses. Whether or not his fellow students are as cocky and virile as they look, it is painfully obvious that the wraith in the back row, out of focus, twenty pounds thinner than the pompadoured, *pied-noir* Romeos on either side, is an alien object of locker-room contempt, and perhaps of abuse. Even Proust managed to survive his military service, but when Mathieu-Saint-Laurent, Yves, was drafted into the army in 1960, at the height of the Algerian war, and sentenced once again to the torture of a barracks full of straight boys, it shattered him so badly that he was confined in the isolation ward of a military hospital, where the doctors tranquilized him into a stupor. A common enough story: so many of those dreamy, provincial child outcasts who become the somebodies of art and literature are first driven to mobilize their powers by an urgent necessity to be somebody else.

Saint Laurent arrived in Paris for the first time in December of 1953, with his chic mother, having won third prize in the dress category of a design competition sponsored by the International Wool Secretariat. (The next year he came in first. Karl Lagerfeld took top honors in the coat category.) Through his parents' connections, he met Michel de Brunhoff, who was the editor of French *Vogue* and an intimate friend of Dior. De Brunhoff encouraged the promising teenager to study at the school run by the Chambre Syndicale de la Couture, which he did briefly. Two years later, the editor was impressed, indeed "flabbergasted," by the prowess and sophistication of a fashion portfolio that Yves, now eighteen, had brought back to Paris from his villegiatura in Oran. It included some sketches of an A-line dress—a shape that Dior was working on but hadn't yet shown except to de Brunhoff, who now persuasively recommended his protégé to the man who, in 1947, had created the voluminously skirted, wasp-waisted New Look that revived the morale of the fashion world and, with it, the postwar French economy. Saint Laurent's first coup as an assistant at the House of Dior was a graphically arresting black evening gown with long sleeves, a décolleté nicked like a rifle sight, and an episcopal-looking sash of white taffeta. Carmel Snow featured this dress in the 1955 fall fashion issue of *Harper's Bazaar*, photographed by Avedon on a model who was herself as elegant as a calligrapher's brushstroke. Her name was Dovima. He posed her at the Cirque d'Hiver, with two elephants.

A year later, Dior, who was only fifty-two, died of a heart attack at the Italian spa where he had gone for his annual weight loss and liver cure, defying the advice of his astrologer, who'd warned him that the trip boded ill. Marcel Boussac, the textile magnate who owned the couture house, briefly considered shutting it down before deciding to give Dior's "preferred assistant" a shot. Saint Laurent's first collection, the "Trapeze," presented in January of 1958, was greeted with delirious acclaim on both sides of the Atlantic. I have always believed, heretically, that the "Trapeze"—while flattering to the trapezoidal bodies of women in advanced stages of pregnancy—was just a couture version of the muumuu. But both the originals and the Ohrbach's copies sold briskly and made their obscure twenty-one-year-old creator a *Life* cover boy.

Saint Laurent's youth, his mother told Benaïm, "ceased abruptly in 1958," when the embalming fluid of celebrity started flowing in his veins. "In achieving his oldest dreams," the biographer continues, "he closed the door on his life. Yves becomes a purveyor of illusions." The flimsiest but most seductive and persistent of those illusions, which the women's-wear industry now treats as a sacred truth, is that the essence of being in fashion is to live dangerously. Poor, addled Talitha Getty, one of Yves's millionaire junkie friends from Marrakesh and an early muse—who once posed on her roof in the medina wearing a Rive Gauchiste caftan and a ring on every finger and died at thirty-one of a heroin overdose, orphaning her toddler son—has been cited by a number of young designers as their inspiration for fall 2002. Saint Laurent's own epic bingeing and self-imposed quarantine from reality begin here. "I had to request an audience in order to see him," a friend recalls.

Before Saint Laurent was drafted into the army and cracked up, there were six collections for the Dior label—not all of them, Benaïm notes, gratifying to the expectations of his backers and fans. The comfy but erotically challenged "sack dress" inspired innumerable cartoons. The hobble skirt was unpopular with couture clients, who had to disrobe in order to use a toilet. A series of jewel- and lace-encrusted evening gowns that paid homage to Goya's infantas were so ornate that critics complained about the Dior *femme relique*—the woman mummified by her opulence. But there was also a biker's jacket, the *blouson noir*; an early "car coat"; and a regal wedding gown for the new empress of Iran, Farah Diba. "Saint Laurent designs for women who lead double lives," Catherine Deneuve once said astutely, and these tentative experiments express the contradictory impulses that he would continue so masterfully to explore. He drew upon the vocabulary of proletarian work clothes and menswear, radically simplifying a woman's wardrobe and purging it of its fussy, bourgeois gestures. He replaced the tailored blouse under a suit jacket with a "see-through" chiffon halter, a T-shirt, or nothing. He gave women sporty pockets for their Miltowns and cigarettes. But he also perceived that tribal fetish worship, the past and its splendors, the Orient and its mysteries, the art world and its sacrileges, the underground, the flea market, the souk, the steppes, and the gay demimonde were all ripe for creative plunder. Saint Laurent was the designer who, in 1971, with his widely execrated but enduringly influential "Libération" collection (the title refers not to the liberation of women but to the Liberation of France in 1944), invented "retro" in the form of, among other beguilingly updated throwbacks, an absinthe-green fox chubby. Proust taught him well: art, elegance, snobbery, nostalgia, and vice distilled with supreme purity make an eau-de-vie that goes straight to the head.

The army doctors had told Saint Laurent that he would be subject to "relapses" of his malaise. Discharged to the care of his lover, he "honeymooned" with Bergé in the Canary Islands. Meanwhile, Marcel Boussac, unhappy with his dauphin's performance, had installed Marc Bohan on Dior's throne. Bergé sued for breach of contract and won a settlement. An American investor named J. Mack Robinson (who was pointed out to me at the retrospective, proudly sitting in the second row) committed $700,000 to the founding of Yves Saint Laurent Couture, and in December of 1961 the partners opened their house on the rue Spontini. Chanel was, at the same moment, back in business on the rue Cambon. The jewelry designer Robert Goossens once compared the old queen of fashion to its Young Turk by noting that Chanel embodied Bergé and Saint Laurent in one.

In a television interview broadcast in 1968, Chanel anointed Saint Laurent as her spiritual heir (though there is some question as to whether they ever actually met), and in his farewell press conference he paid homage to the predecessor "who taught me so much, and who, as we all know, liberated women. It was this that enabled me, years later . . . to liberate fashion." But the notion that any revolution can be concluded or claimed as a definitive victory is itself a relic of the past. What Chanel liberated was the natural line of the body, which entailed, as most liberations do, a new form of tyranny—the oppressive maintenance of a svelte, toned silhouette. Hers is the virile glamour of renunciation. She freed women to dress with the sobriety and nonchalance of English gentlemen, though she stopped short of putting them into trousers. That was Saint Laurent's claim to immortality. He showed his first tailored pants in 1962, and went on to commandeer other staples of a gentleman's and an officer's wardrobe: the business suit, the jumpsuit, the peacoat, the short, the trench coat, the motorcycle jacket, the safari jacket, and, most famously, the tuxedo. Yet, for all his often proclaimed debt to the "street," he was more romantic than Chanel was about the rich—she who slept her way out of poverty. And as a gay man, or perhaps simply as a man, he was more sentimental than she was about femininity. Indeed, no one has been so religiously gallant toward women or resistant to the temptation of modern fashion to make clothes as difficult, ironic, contemptuous, or ugly as modern art. Saint Laurent takes it upon himself to anticipate every potential humiliation in the bulge of a seam, the pucker of a pleat, the mockery of a bow. His cutting and drapery are a lover's discourse with the female body.

Bergé has been calling Saint Laurent "the last couturier" for years, at least since the time of his retrospective at the Metropolitan Museum in 1983. Even then the vitality of his great work—his legacy—was behind him. The only news that he delivered this January was at the press conference. But the pathos of his eclipse is proportional to the radiance of his imagination and the supreme good fortune of his timing. He came of age as an artist at the moment everything changed. With all the talent in the world, it isn't possible to be a Saint Laurent today—any more than it's possible to be an Elvis—even if one is Saint Laurent.

On the morning after the Beaubourg show, *Le Monde* published a brief interview that the designer, who was declining interviews, gave to Laurence Benaïm. "What motivated the announcement of your retirement?" she asked him. "We are living in a world of disorder and decadence," he replied. "The struggle for elegance and beauty has been causing me much sadness . . . I have been feeling marginal and alone." There was something so ingenuous about this remark, as if the speaker had just awakened from a coma to perceive the disarray of Western civilization, that I thought of Proust's last scenes, in which the Narrator returns to Paris after his long wartime convalesence in a nursing home and discovers that the world of the salons is a grotesque and degraded parody of all that he remembers. But then he is introduced to a young girl, Gilberte's daughter—Swann's grandchild—a tall beauty of sixteen, "rich in hopes," "a masterpiece . . . formed from those very years which I myself had lost." And this encounter permits him to understand that "the cruel law of art is that people die . . . after exhausting every form of suffering, so that over our heads may grow the grass not of oblivion but of eternal life [upon which] gaily and without a thought for those who are sleeping beneath them, future generations may come to enjoy their *déjeuner sur l'herbe.*" I can't think of a more hopeful insight to reconcile one with the "magnificent and pitiful" family picnic that is the fashion world. But Saint Laurent couldn't know about, and therefore take heart from, Marcel's moment of existential truth because, he told Benaïm, he's never finished reading *In Search of Lost Time.* Perhaps now he will.

—March 18, 2002

V

NOTES FOR A
TIME CAPSULE

ONE

Combat Fatigue

I was not a better person the morning after New York Fashion Week. I wouldn't have been surprised to find some strange augury of alien metamorphosis on my body: a third nipple, a patch of scales, a bar-code tattoo. From the grandstands during six days of runway shows, I had, I calculated, reviewed some two thousand ensembles. They might just as well have been light infantry or an armored-tank division. The clothes were a blur of ruched silk jersey and harness leather, of fuchsia sheepskin and vintage lace. I could barely remember what I'd worn myself.

This amnesia was less troubling to me—I knew I could refresh my memory of the collections on the Internet and of my own *toilettes* from the dry cleaner's receipt—than the shock to my dulled receptors, moral and aesthetic, when I picked up *The New York Times Magazine* and realized that I had mistaken the cover photo of a heroic African nurse in the Ebola ward of a hospital in Uganda for one of Miguel Adrover's models.

A few seasons ago, Adrover, an immigrant from Majorca, was working out of a Lower East Side basement. On the basis of two collections, which included garments cut from the late Quentin Crisp's dirty mattress and an old Burberry raincoat, as well as some sportswear of provocative sobriety, he found a backer and became a phenom. Suspecting, perhaps, that those perverse gourmets who delight in dining on fashion's young would be whetting their knives for him, he chose to show his line for fall 2001 at the old Essex Street meat-and-produce market.

It was a lupine night of bone-chilling wind. Although many spectators were turned away by the police, I was swept inside by the first wave of arrivals. The interior of the market had been tented artfully in ravaged canvas, and I recognized the waxy ambient perfume not as incense, though some was burning, but as kerosene from a space heater. Since there was only one obvious means of egress, and four hundred bodies pressed against it, this was disheartening.

Visibility was so low in the yellow tungsten gloom that the clothes got to command more attention than the celebrities, if there were any, in the front row, wherever that was. Adrover's theme was "Meeteast"—the message on the coffee-stained cocktail napkin that had served as his invitation—signifying, one inferred, East Village, meet Middle East. The designer and his business partner had spent six months soaking up inspiration in Egypt (a heartfelt thank-you to his friends in Luxor was included with the program notes) and also, apparently, a little time at Talbots.

"Osama bin Laden as fashion icon," drawled a retailer on the refectory bench behind me when the show finally started, though this wasn't quite fair. A trancelike parade of traditional Arab, colonial, and missionary garments that blurred gender distinctions was punctuated by a raincoat patterned with Stars of David made from masking tape. A Vuitton satchel balanced on a model's wrapped head overflowed with fresh lettuce. Clones in the full Talbots—blouse, blazer, and A-line skirt—teetered blindly down the runway in black head shrouds, like the cloth over a parrot's cage that stifles its squawking. Sumptuous robes of great dignity, which is to say no sex appeal, were cut from coarse, grease-stained duck or recycled sackcloth, as if to remind us that a billion Third World women have no change of clothes: that one all-purpose garment serves for fieldwork, housework, worship, and celebration.

Yet it wasn't all anthropology. There was real modernity in a series of supple cable knits, including a floor-length skirt that swirled like the petticoat of a dervish, and in whip-smart military jackets layered over voluminous tunics and *shalwar-kameez*-style leggings—evoking the way immigrants from hot Muslim countries dress for a northern winter, or a woman dragged from a fire on a cold night throws her rescuer's parka over her nightgown. And if the victims of the fire at the Triangle Shirtwaist Factory were never far from my mind on that particular cold night, it is also true that Adrover has something eloquent to say about a common plight, perhaps even in the fashion world: that of strong, hardworking women with stressed, imperfect bodies who need a sheath for their fragility.

The fragility of strong women: I can imagine Colette chortling at the concept, and not kindly. For her, the male was always the weaker and nobler creature, while the voracious female monopolizes the will to survive. It would have been fun to take her—as a writer of African descent who, though she despised identity politics, was an avid connoisseur of bad boys, hot mamas, sensational trials, virile plumage, rippling muscles, puerile exhibitionism, demimondes, and "love's barbarism"—to the Sean John show. Sean John is the eponymous line of menswear designed by Sean (Puffy) Combs, the hip-hop and fashion mogul whose trial for weapons possession and attempted bribery of a witness had been under way for two weeks.

On the morning of the show, I had driven my son, who was turning twelve, and some friends to play paintball on Staten Island. The paintball fields, which resemble a militia training camp, lie in a wooded hollow next to a state prison. It's a landscape of razor wire and garbage dunes, overgrown with marsh grass and scoured by gulls. A dozen or so excited young warriors, mostly from the outer boroughs, were already gearing up for mock combat when we arrived—the target demographic for Puffy's line of thermals, cargo pants, and bleached denims.

After signing releases with a certain guilty trepidation, I tethered my bewildered standard poodle to the rank of Portosans behind the picnic tent. Then the boys and I were issued our rented weapons, ammo belts, CO_2 cannisters, and camouflage jumpsuits. Had I known how voguish these would look later in the week at the Pierrot show—a kooky tribute by a fey Frenchman, Pierre Carrilero, to macho American backwoods folklore, which also featured a life-size rubber bear, *Blair Witch* sound effects, a naked blond Native American in a dream catcher, and a fetching knitwear *hommage* to Waco and the NRA—I might have bought one.

We moved along to a staging area for the safety briefing. Our referee was wearing mirrored Revos, olive drabs—a ubiquitous fall color—an orange safety vest, and a chunky version of the combat boots shown by Calvin Klein on bare-legged models in desirable shearling minidresses and cropped peacoats. "Keep your mask lowered at all times," he told us, "and if you shoot anyone at point-blank range, you—and your crew—are out." It was good advice for the days to come.

The fashion professionals, of whom I am not one, were nearly unanimous in proclaiming that many accomplished and salable clothes but few trends of significance emerged from the collections. New York does not have its Nicolas Ghesquière, its Rei Kawakubo, or its Alaïa. Some of the most notable shows were those of foreigners who have settled in the city, like Narciso Rodriguez, a Cuban American from New Jersey, or of natives who have left it, like Marc Jacobs, who lives in Paris. Jacobs showed his grasp of French coquetry in tidy little *Belle de Jour* dresses with pleats or ruffles and sheer bodices with trompe l'oeil collars that were just slightly disheveled—as if their owner had rushed off in haste after a *cinq à sept* to meet her husband for dinner. But I also couldn't help feeling that Jacobs's sojourn in France has made him a trifle too sexually optimistic on behalf of an American client. Ask Helmut Lang's woman: after thirty-five, there's no point in flirting like that here. Lang, a cerebral Austrian with a sooty palette, perfectly understands the seduction of withholding. His sibylline garments pose the question "What's your fantasy?" and then refuse to answer it.

Like Adrover, but much more abstractly, Lang was playing with the notion of a life lived 24/7 in one three-tiered outfit: a severe jacket over a longer, filmy chiffon wrapper and slim trousers, worn with the hottest footwear on the runways—a pointy black suede bondage boot with a spatlike cutout instep. The woman who leaves for her office or gallery dressed like this in the morning has no idea when, if, or with whom she is coming home, or of what surprises the day will bring, but she has covered all the bases of *leben und arbeiten*.

It was remarkable, though, how many designers—even the aloof Lang, who was also into thongs and drapery—had succumbed to the influence of the costumes from *Gladiator*, a story, when you think about it, that could serve as a parable for the modeling business. Every few seasons, a fresh batch of impossibly gorgeous human specimens, the more exotic the better, are recruited in the provinces and shipped to the glittering, corrupt imperial capital for a brief reign of glory. The new hopes are buffed, exercised, oiled, coiffed, painted, garbed, and hyped by their wranglers to arouse the most primitive lusts of a populace with a short attention span and a fickle appetite for sensation. They quickly adopt a defiant stare and swaggering gait. The plebes treat them familiarly—both as fodder and as idols. The patricians decide their fate.

If there was no fire to the collections, there was still a smoldering atmosphere of decline and fall, as if the Zip Codes of Manhattan were small, embattled postcolonial encampments, each ruled by a style lord or a clan and competing for legitimacy. Obscure design collectives issued manifestos. Military silhouettes, colors—even hardware—were everywhere one looked. So was a barbarian glamour that the irrepressible Simon Doonan dubbed "*haute sauvagerie.*" Anna Sui showed convict stripes. In a Chelsea auto-body shop, under fluorescent lights, Sonja Rubin and Kip Chapelle served bottled beer from a trash can, while photographers huddled beneath the carcass of a taxi from which no one, surely, had emerged alive. The interesting clothes looked dreamy and bruised, as if they had been salvaged from the wreck.

The loft space overlooking the Hudson River rented by Daryl K. was flooded with pulsating red bordello light and orgasmic music. Her runway was long enough for the sort of aircraft that drops off the arms, drugs, and contraband Prada bowling bags which help finance a coup. The models all looked a little like camp followers—adorably half dressed in the soldiers' clothes, which they flaunted like booty. One of them wore a white shirt with the FBI's sketch of the Unabomber printed on the back. (The point of reference seemed to be his hood.)

There were tom-toms at Donna Karan, and I found her theme a

little too percussive as well: the "modern urban warrior." Karan's legions wore "slashed nubuck," "ravaged layers of metallic chiffon," and a "savage shearling body bag," accessorized with "tusk body pins" by Robert Lee Morris; i.e., belts. None of this Sturm was at heart any more subversive than the wryer, less ambitious, more assured collection that Diane von Furstenberg showed at home in her converted West Village carriage house. Like their creator—newly married—the tart pleated skirts in tweed, with chiffon insets, and the molten silk jerseys seemed to purr with an air of mature feline contentment.

The charm of Karan's clothes is inert, at least to me, until they react with a woman's body, and then one understands the loyalty they inspire. Off the runway, in motion, stressed by the bumps of modern life, they have much more of an undercarriage than the tinny blather that promotes them. Unfortunately, Karan placed copies of her spring ad catalog, entitled *Woman to Woman*, on the bleachers at her show. The catalog was shot on location in Vietnam, with Jeremy Irons and Milla Jovovich playing sexual tourists. In one image, Jovovich models a rumpled white linen jacket whose cut alludes to those good old days when the country was still Indochine. In the same frame, slightly out of focus, a peasant woman with a heavy basket, wearing the jacket's prototype, stares at Jovovich with an unfeigned expression of pain and incomprehension from the shadows of her paper coolie hat. Outside on Sixth Avenue, labor activists picketing the show were distributing leaflets that alleged "slavelike conditions" for women workers in "Karan sweatshops." The motto of their campaign was "Ain't I a Woman?"

There were many small triumphs of virtuosity during Fashion Week: Behnaz Sarafpour's bolero of black satin roses; the wrap coats at Geoffrey Beene; Douglas Hobbs's molded leather camisole; a flapper's dance dress of leather and chiffon strips from Badgley Mischka; and pretty much the whole Bruce collection. But the shows that generated the greatest buzz—"controversy" would be too strong a word—laid claim, with varying degrees of hubris, naïveté, or conviction, to an old-fashioned, even Marxist moral high ground, celebrating the "authenticity" of traditional and tribal cultures; of street and club kids; of flower power; of erotic militants and champions of the proletariat. The Old Guard, in the meantime, and particularly the courtly Latin Americans, Oscar and Carolina, seemed intent on dressing the partygoers in "Exterminating Angel," while Ralph Lauren and Michael Kors—Kors to a soundtrack of hoofbeats—concentrated on racy britches and cashmere horse blankets for the Four Polo Players of the Apocalypse. Despite the resurgence of the miniskirt, it was not exactly 1968—no *imagination au pouvoir*. But the divides of age, class, and ethnicity seemed to be deepening.

Tara Subkoff and Matt Damhave, two enfants terribles who call their company Imitation of Christ (after a song by the Psychedelic Furs), made sniping at the marketplace from the heights of purity into a predinner recreation. With the help of Chloë Sevigny, their "creative director," they turn out a tiny collection of irreverently tweaked vintage rags—clothes, in other words, that they may have created but didn't make, and that are sold through outlets like Barneys and Louis Boston with price tags of four figures.

The invitation to their show, at the Beekman Theatre, solicited contributions to Free the Children and Sweatshop Watch, two humanitarian labor groups that their profits apparently help to underwrite. My own shop rules obliged me to refuse the collection plate, and when I was offered a brown paper goody bag by one of the ushers, I was leery of that, too—having read, in their "Communiqué Number III," that "ignorance is not bliss for those who bleed in the name of future bargains." Suppose the bag contained a severed finger? Luckily, there was just free nail polish.

The "event" that followed was a silent video-vérité, in extreme closeup, of the peevish audience arriving for the show, which segued rather charmingly into the emergence of Chloë Sevigny and the models from a stretch SUV. They vamped the clothes—some ravishing, even sublime, and others hideous beyond description—and then we all settled down to an amateur film of staggering pretentiousness indebted to Godard (is there any other kind?), which took aim not only at the despicable fashion bourgeoisie in the theater but at the abuses of multinational capitalism and the decadence of Western civilization.

Communiqué Number IV, Jesus to Matt and Tara: Welcome to heaven, kids. Now that you've made it through the needle's eye, learn how to sew.

Puffy Combs, a man who hedges his bets, tried to dominate the battlefield from both positions, high and low. "I wanted to be the best-dressed motherfucker on the block," he told his audience in a recorded voice-over that explained his motives for going into the fashion business. That sounded like a reasonable ambition until he sent his models down the catwalk wrapped in, or dragging, the skins of more slaughtered creatures than Teddy Roosevelt ever shipped back from Kenya to the American Museum of Natural History, and with slogans painted on the boys' bare chests: "Black Power" on a white torso; "Revolution" on a black one. A simultaneous projection spliced clips from civil-rights riots, nuclear explosions, and a sex-education documentary with shots of Che Guevara, Eldridge Cleaver, Jimmy Carter (poster boy for the cardigan), the Reverend King's galvanic oratory, and Jennifer Lopez's latest music video, "Love Don't Cost a Thing."

The coincidence of so much thuggish splendor and anarchic posturing with so much private security left me a little cowed, like the lapdog in the arms of Kimora Lee. But it also defined, in retrospect, the mood of the whole week: its surly festiveness, its tawdry sparkle, its flashes of inspired improvisation, its claustrophobia, and perhaps also its message: "Escape from New York."

—March 19, 2001

TWO

The White Ball

I once heard of an East African farmer who, in the 1920s, traded his vast flax plantation for a much smaller plot devoted to damask roses. He liked the notion of being able to transport an entire harvest to Paris in a suitcase, attar being worth more, per gram, than cocaine. I like that notion myself. Every writer's ambition is to distill the truth irreducibly from a thorny subject, and it is one reason I am such a fan of natural pearls. There is probably no product on earth that more radically dramatizes the discrepancy between the size of a treasure and its value.

The most comprehensive exhibit ever devoted to pearls, and to the paradoxes of their natural and social history, has just opened at the American Museum of Natural History. While the scholarly apparatus of the show is all one would expect—evolutionary trees, analyses of manganese pollution, artifacts from the button industry, a scale model of a pearl fishery, and an interactive display of a pearl's crystalline structure magnified fifty thousand times—its glamour comes as a surprise. Malacology, the study of mollusks, isn't a discipline noted for its sex appeal, and, despite the recent fashion comeback of mangy fur, the museum hasn't become a hangout for the Bryant Park crowd. Yet the baubles on display are as hard-core fabulous as anything for sale at Fred Leighton—jeweler to the stars—and mollusks turn out to be more creative than a lot of designers, and perhaps just as snappy when provoked: they'll sever a finger without thinking twice.

One learns, with considerable admiration, that nearly any member of the phylum—and there are more than a hundred thousand species living in salt water and fresh, tropical and temperate climes—can, in theory, produce a pearl, its shell efficiently forecasting the gem's color. The pearl from a queen conch ranges from a pale blush to a deep fuchsia, and can grow to the size of a goodly bird's egg. The black-lipped pearl oyster from the South Pacific secretes a desirably large, iridescent sphere that has a metallic luster ranging from gunmetal gray to onyx, with tinges of blue, violet, rose, or green. Baler shells from the South China Sea yield a "melo" pearl the size and color of a cavaillon melon ball. Sedentary bivalves (mollusk couch potatoes) like the clam, the oyster, and the mussel are the most reliable producers, but even a relatively antsy gastropod like the garden snail can, on occasion, deliver its non-nacreous little bundle. Abalone pearls are often cusp-shaped and nearly always baroque—an adjective that was used to describe irregular pearls before it was, in the late Renaissance, applied to art or architecture straining neurotically at its classical fetters. Jewelers have been inspired to set the suggestive, sometimes freakish bulges of baroque pearls as figurines: a swan, a snake, a dolphin, a bug, a Bacchus, an overfed baby in a cradle of gold filigree. A selection of their handiwork is on display, but none of it is as curious as the Chinese freshwater-mussel shells blistered with pearlized figures of Buddha and Chairman Mao, or the life-size model of the largest pearl ever found—a brainlike fourteen-pound excrescence from a Philippine giant clam that is known as the Pearl of Allah. These are but a few of the show's strange and luminous charms. It is hard to think of another subject, particularly these days, that could find some common ground between Muhammad and Chanel.

Pearls have been a fixture of the fashion scene even longer than Karl Lagerfeld has—about five hundred million years—and have been prized since antiquity by nearly every culture in the world. To theologians of the major monotheisms, they represented spiritual perfection. The ancients supposed them to be frozen tears of the gods. Early naturalists believed that oysters were impregnated by raindrops, or the dew, or were shocked by bolts of lightning at sea. Later it was thought that they were seeded by grains of sand. Pearls are, in fact, formed in the living slime, through the struggle of an aragonite-secreting organism to protect its flesh against an irritant that is most often nothing more romantic than a parasitic worm, although sometimes a shrimp or even a small fish will find itself lacquered chicly to the shell wall. But there is something about a pearl, as there is about a French schoolgirl, that stimulates intense erotic reverie without its/her innocence ever being sullied. As the portraits of parvenu heiresses here suggest, pearls—unlike colored stones or even diamonds—are quite miraculously proof against vulgarity, even when flaunted wholesale by vulgarians.

The earliest mother-of-pearl artifacts date from the Neolithic Age in the Middle East. The Hopewell Indians of the Ohio River Valley (200 BC–AD 500) harvested freshwater-mussel pearls by the quart and burned them in their funeral rituals. The Romans were mad for pearls—Caligula literally so. He lavished them not only upon his shoes but upon his horse. According to Suetonius, a general named Vitellius financed a campaign with a single pearl from his mother's earring. If no gem has been as alluring as the pearl to poets, folklorists, and moralists, or to novelists of manners like Colette, Scott Fitzgerald, and Edith Wharton, it is probably because there are few symbols that so intimately link the entitlements of the highborn to the privations of the lowly. Steinbeck's *The Pearl* was on the summer reading list of my twelve-year-old son, Will. "This novel is depressing," he wrote. "The moral is that when something really, really expensive is involved, evil triumphs over good." But on rare occasions, a pearl story involves a just, or just enough, reward. In the early sixteenth century, one of the many slaves forced to work in the oyster beds off the coast of Panama was able to buy his freedom when he surfaced with a pear-shaped white pearl weighing ten grams, which has since become known as La Peregrina. Having once belonged to Bloody Mary, it now nestles upon the considerably cushier bosom of Elizabeth Taylor, who has lent it to the show. Perhaps the pearl achieves its ultimate perfection as a metaphor for life's inequities.

The best grade of pearl is found in the waters of the Persian Gulf, but until the exploitation of mollusks and humans depleted supplies, some of the finest gems came from the New World. When Columbus set sail for the Indies with a high-end shopping list from Ferdinand

and Isabella—the original *"les musts"*—pearls were at the top of it. On his third voyage west, he discovered the oyster beds off the islands of Cubagua and Margarita, initiating a pearl rush that, according to the show's companion volume, *Pearls: A Natural History* (Abrams, 2001), flooded the coffers of the Old World "with such an abundance of riches that it helped usher in the flowering of Renaissance Europe." The curators estimate that in three decades 120 million pearls were harvested from American waters. Queen Elizabeth I acquired most of hers from English pirates preying on the Spanish treasure fleet. The abandon with which she used them to encrust her gowns and headgear had a delayed, plebeian counterpart in a late-nineteenth-century craze started by a Cockney street sweeper named Henry Croft, who artfully plastered a three-piece suit and a top hat with thousands of pearl buttons, and inspired a fashion cult—still in existence—known as the Pearlies. Their fantastical costumes, a form of folk-art couture, unite the two greatest strengths of British style: eccentric working-class cheek and punctilious tailoring. The Pearlies prefigure contemporary designers like Malcolm McLaren, Vivienne Westwood, and Alexander McQueen—and even that great anglophile, Chanel. There is only one photograph of Mademoiselle in the show, festooned with pearls, of course—some real, some faux. It suggests her debt to all the Renaissance queens, Mogul rajahs, Belle Époque courtesans, and Jazz Age flappers with whom she shares a gallery. But it also suggests why Chanel is the designer who defined style for the new century. With supreme irony and simplicity, she appropriated two quintessential emblems of power. One was the modern capitalist's sober, deceptively democratic-looking business suit. The other—a superfluity of pearls—distilled what was most gorgeous and hieratic about the ancien régime.

Every important natural pearl was the nucleus of a narrative that accreted new layers, just like a pearl, as the gem changed hands. The advent of the cultured product destroyed both the economy and the mystique of the pearl trade. Modern perliculture was pioneered in the early 1900s by a Japanese entrepreneur, Kokichi Mikimoto, whose scientists perfected a technology for nucleating the pearl oyster on a commercial scale (though Linnaeus had experimented with culturing pearls successfully in the eighteenth century, and the fruits of his lab work, two tiny golden globes still attached by T-shaped metal posts to a fragment of shell, are on loan from the Linnaean Society of London). A cultured pearl is just as "real" as a natural pearl, though it has been stimulated and standardized by human intervention. One of the more unforgettable installations at the show is a video on the nucleation process, in which a technician working with a very sharp scalpel implants a nacre bead from a Mississippi-bred freshwater mussel and a frilly slice of mantle tissue into the fleshy, pulsating gonad of a marine oyster. You probably shouldn't watch if you're contemplating a breast enlargement.

One is supposed to restring good pearls at least every other year, and I recently took my own pearls in for a checkup. I own two strands, the finer of which is a choker of very small natural pearls that dates from the 1890s and probably belonged to a debutante. I usually wear it with a man's white cotton undershirt—Blanche DuBois and Stanley Kowalski in the same outfit. "Most women today would rather own a strand of ten-millimeter Akoyas than the much smaller natural pearls that they could buy for the same price," observed Edith Weber, the dealer in antique and estate jewelry who sold me the necklace and who supervises its repair. "The natural pearl has, alas, become a curiosity. It represents a vanished way of life and an aesthetic ideal, a noble folly, since only an X-ray can tell the difference between the cultured and the natural." An X-ray or a lover. As Paul Claudel noted in the speech he gave at Pierre Cartier's induction into the Légion d'Honneur, the value of a pearl has one true measure: the desire it inspires.

—October 29, 2001

THREE

Altered States

Fish were once so plentiful in the Thames that they became a diet staple of the poor. According to London folklore, there was a clause in the employment contracts of apprentices stipulating that they couldn't be forced to eat salmon more than three times a week. Beauty is the diet staple of those who design and promote high fashion, and they, too, sometimes object to the sameness of their fare. So they rebel, usually unspectacularly, by hiring a model with a tiny gap between her front teeth, a broad mouth, freckles, an infinitesimally crooked nose, or some other marginal irregularity that would pass undetected in the civilian population. Then they congratulate themselves on their temerity. But a few express their grievances in a more artistically subversive way. "Beauty has a cardinal importance, for ugliness cannot be spoiled, and to despoil is the essence of eroticism," Georges Bataille asserted. It is at times the essence of fashion.

Moderately sophisticated people no longer judge art according to the criterion of beauty, and it's hard to shock them, short of spattering dung on a picture of the Virgin Mary. Not so in fashion, where much lip service but little money is paid to radical originality. The bread-and-butter work of nearly all first-rank designers, even those who consider themselves avant-garde, is a form of society portraiture. They are in the business of marketing the tailored equivalent of a painting that one can hang over a sofa. Purists—such as Martin Margiela, the J. D. Salinger of couture, who refuses to be photographed; Jil Sander, purer since she sold her name to Prada and became unemployed; Rei Kawakubo, of Comme des Garçons, who, in 1997, showed a collection of padded dresses with unsightly lumps like those of old ladies or the dreadfully ill; and Walter van Beirendonck, the edgy Belgian who likes the slogan "Mutilate"—still have to sell enough relatively prosaic garments—trousers with legs, for example—to finance their poetry. But the close of the century was a period of heightened revolt that saw the younger big names in fashion, with increasing insolence, questioning the canons of beauty (the employment contracts) of their profession, and investing their virtuosity in what the fashion critics, whose diet staple is designer self-promotion and who get sick of that, too, have sometimes disparaged as "runway stunts." The stunts tended, and were intended, to be trashy, amusing, cruel, ugly, obscene, macabre, inspired, "transgressive," or all of the above simultaneously.

Many of the showpieces could be considered "clothing" only nominally, since they were cut from nearly anything but cloth. John Galliano used a broken collapsible umbrella as the cowl for a raincoat. Thierry Mugler dressed one of his dominatrixes in a suit of chrome armor with peekaboo plastic cutouts. Issey Miyake's samurai *kamishimo* (photographed for the cover of *Artforum*) was constructed of lacquered bamboo. Hussein Chalayan, who sometimes treats clothing as furniture, showed a polished wooden body brace fastened, so it seemed, with coffin hinges. Alexander McQueen, the most pugnacious and talented of the stuntmen, fashioned a bustier with a floral excrescence out of sterling silver and a bolero from sandalwood fans. He also designed a pair of shapely wooden prosthetics for a Paralympic athlete named Aimee Mullins who sometimes models for him and who is a bilateral amputee. The prosthetics represent the feet in high-heeled shoes; the calves are ornately carved with a Dionysiac relief of vines, grapes, and leaves that seem to suggest the possibility of magical regeneration. They are part of an ensemble that includes two other garments. One is a brown leather corset molded like a medieval cuirass and scarred by thick, diagonal Frankenstein sutures. The other is a short bias-cut skirt of tiered and frothy Valenciennes lace. McQueen was accused of "exploiting" Mullins for publicity, and perhaps he was, but he repaid her. She's the muse of a haunting reverie: the tribute of a warped artist to the heroism of a damaged maiden.

These experiments and others in a similar vein form the core of an ambitious show at the Costume Institute of the Metropolitan Museum of Art that examines fashion's eternal and probably terminal ambivalence to nature. It is called—with understatement, I think— "Extreme Beauty," and there is so much opulence of texture and imagination, so much bravura and craftsmanship, seething in a small space that it's hard to digest. One can't blame the admirable curator, Harold Koda, for one's claustrophobia. It's the fault of the trustees. Every time I visit the institute, I'm indignant that armor should enjoy a palatial gallery on the main floor, while couture is relegated to an orphan's closet under the stairs.

To reach the basement where clothes are displayed, one meanders through the Egyptian wing, past the reconstructed crypt, the kids giggling at mummies, the statues of very rich and thin royal couples nude under their gossamer loincloths, and of mutant deities who are the harbingers of what lies below. "Extreme Beauty" is laid out like a gorgeous corpse on an embalming table. Each of five sections is devoted to the fetishizing of a specific erogenous zone: Neck and Shoulders, Chest, Waist, Hips, and Feet. The organizing principle, never strictly enforced (Buttocks and Crotch have crept in with Hips), is theme and variation rather than chronology. The heterogeneity of the clothes is as extreme as their distinction. Antique and tribal garments mingle with contemporary couture, vulgarity consorts with grandeur, anarchists with prudes, envy of purity coexists with contempt and reverence for it. The clothes embody such disparate notions of femininity and conflicting impulses to exaggerate, suppress, inflate, conceal, deform, exalt, or transfigure the body part in question that you begin to suspect that the warp of fashion is an occult memory of our past incarnations, and its woof a still-hazy intuition of our future ones. There doesn't seem to be much evolutionary logic to the process until one imagines each new fad, innovation, or shift in erotic focus as the rumor of a Darwinian advantage that swiftly makes the rounds of a credulous population. A cure for mortality and ugliness has at last been found! And it's a farthingale. A hobble skirt. Bell-bottoms. A penis gourd. Four-inch stilettos.

The fashionable body as it's represented in "Extreme Beauty" has talons like a bird of prey, pterodactyl wings, mammalian fur, a beetle's finely articulated carapace, a gorilla's shoulders, a pigeon's breast, a camel's humps, stork legs, amphibian scales, and a space alien's mutability. A display of bustle forms from the 1880s made of cane, wire, and batting looks curiously like a production line of unfinished tails, and a protuberantly bustled dress of the same period imparts to its mannequin the faintly comic dignity of a waterfowl. McQueen's black lace-and-feather evening gown is a triumph of bespoke taxidermy whose phallic boa morphs from a snake's body into a swan's beaked head. Freud would have liked it, and it reminded me that he collected Egyptian talismans of sex and death, and kept them in his consulting room for inspiration. The objects here are talismans of our species' strangeness, too, and if the installation resembles a Salon des Refusés for all the outfits the academy rejected as too far out, it also resembles the curiosity cabinet of a refined and perverse fin de siècle aesthete—a collector incurably infatuated with artifice who could have said, as Christian Dior did in a cryptic confession posted near the entrance to the show, "My dream is to save women from nature."

Geneticists may be close to patenting a hybrid body, but fashion has been working on the project for millennia, and its experiments with the human form have always been carried out on living subjects, not all of them volunteers. Much of the Waist section is a mausoleum of corsets. Some are purely decorative, like the beaded girdles of Dinka warriors and their couture copies by Galliano. Others are hard-working, like the nineteenth-century Sadean fantasy wrought in trellised steel. Miyake's bustier, fashioned out of wire, looks just like a Slinky. A dainty "body" in chartreuse silk comes from the personal wardrobe of Mr. Pearl, a corsetière who works with Christian Lacroix and who is himself what used to be known as a "tight-lacer." The smallest corset has the circumference of a man's neck. Few garments have been so politically controversial—the delight of rakes, cartoonists, and pornographers; the bane of dress reformers, Victorian gynecologists, and feminists—or so semiotically versatile. The corset was a neat package of sexual allure and moral rectitude tied up with pink ribbons. Women were "liberated" from its "tyranny" more than once, only to relapse, and the Empire shift in the Chest section, a figure-revealing wisp of sheer muslin as unforgiving as it is exquisite, suggests why.

The most diabolical experiment in fashion history was also the longest-lived. Chinese foot binding lasted for nearly a millennium, and it wasn't restricted to the leisure classes: many peasants subjected their daughters to the practice. There is a pair of well-worn leather work boots in the show—the size of a toddler's booties—equipped with metal cleats for an icy winter of hard labor. The intervention was performed in early childhood, when the four small toes were broken, folded under, and bandaged tightly to the heel. The dressings had to be changed frequently, and pus drained from the gangrenous wounds that often resulted. A woman with bound feet was disabled, though not utterly. Her shoes were elevated and angled to relieve pressure on the mutilated sole, so that she could eventually take small, relatively painless steps supported by a cane or a retainer. By the time she was old enough to marry, her ornamental stump had acquired the shape of a tiny, atrophied lingam, or, as the Chinese preferred to describe it, a golden lotus. There is a pair of fuchsia silk bridal slippers in the show. They measure three inches.

In a work entitled *A Short History of Decay*, the Romanian philosopher E. M. Cioran defines frivolity as "the most effective antidote to the disease of being what one is"—a useful insight for the student of fashion. Who, since the Fall, has ever been perfectly content with her body? Critics of sartorial misogyny and feminine vanity sometimes make too much of the mortifications women endure without first asking women why they submit to them and what they feel like. I, for example, am old enough to have worn, at a nubile age, a long-line panty girdle, which, for those who have never seen one, is a piece of "figure control" lingerie cut like a pair of biker's shorts, but of an inflexible lycra, with a nasty reptilian snap. A panty girdle replaced the garter belt and immobilized—indeed, anesthetized—one's lower torso (just as the hair spray of the same era flash-froze one's beehive), so that nothing could stir or be stirred. By the end of a school day, the pressure of the elastic had embedded the garters into the flesh of the thigh, leaving an imprint like that of a small crustacean fossilized by a mud slide. Yet the stricture was strangely comforting—perhaps as swaddling is to a restless infant. I've always felt that some of the most appealing garments are those in which a woman can seclude herself.

Comfort in Western dress, as Valerie Steele observes in *The Corset: A Cultural History* (Yale, 2001), is a relatively modern and liberal concept, dating from the early nineteenth century. High style derives from aristocratic, which is to say military, ideals of pride, stoicism, hardness, swagger, and snobbery—of trial by ordeal and tournament chic. Koda explains in his notes to the catalog of the show (*Extreme Beauty: The Body Transformed*, Yale, 2001) that the exhibition originated in a discussion of fashion's "competitive nature" and obsessive "one-upmanship." A scholar of couture with a courtly, esoteric bent and an academic prose style, he himself has chosen to snub popular culture almost entirely. There are none of the comic books and animations that have been, and continue to be, influential sources of extreme fashion; no costumes from science-fiction films or situation comedies (the inspired *I Love Lucy* Paris-dress episode springs to mind); no trace of punk, rap, Goth, disco, or death metal; no sporting or (explicit) sex gear; no drag-queen finery. There is, however, a vitrine of wishfully proportioned armorial codpieces in finely etched tempered steel that relates the posturings of Iron Man to the blond ambitions of Material Girl in her ruched-velvet rocket bras by Gaultier.

The extremes of fashion aspire to be as malevolent as nature's, or as benign. The piece that Koda chose for the cover of the catalog is an ethereally beautiful, Brobdingnagian ruff of tarnished polyester organza by Junya Watanabe, six feet wide, that reminds the curator, he said to me, of "a used air-conditioner filter." It alludes, more obviously, to the ruffs and collars of Shakespeare's time, lacy platters for great heads soon to be severed—a fashion that transcended sex, as Shakespeare did. In the only image we have of him, he's wearing one. But it also conjures a giant milkweed flower to wish on and blow away.

—December 17, 2001

FOUR

String Theory

In my youth, I had a weakness for the esoteric. You could seduce me by reciting the poetry of any language I didn't speak. I was charmed by the gambler who introduced me to the *Daily Racing Form* and held rapt by the physicist who tried to explain string theory. His lesson didn't enlighten me about the hidden workings of a ten-dimensional "shadow universe" where enigmatic particles, some of them hypothetical, like Wino and Zino, have the names of space creatures from a children's book. But it did enhance my sense that there existed, as researchers in the field believe, a unifying "theory of everything." Fashion journalism tends to erode such a conviction.

An esoteric work that I still prize, especially for travel, is Roberto Calasso's *Literature and the Gods.* The paperback is light, but the extreme density of the erudition makes it a kind of portable free weight that provides a strenuous mental workout before knocking one mercifully unconscious at the end of a mindless day. I packed it, along with too many shoes, for the spring/summer 2003 ready-to-wear shows in Paris early in October, and it proved strangely useful in my quest for clues to the meaning of the starry, gaseous, ever-expanding cosmos of the collections, and for the equally mysterious reasons I find myself employed in writing about them. I especially took heart from a surprising literary fact that Calasso mentions in passing. In the late 1870s, that most incorruptible of poets, Stéphane Mallarmé, single-handedly wrote, edited, and published "every word of a frivolous magazine called *La Dernière Mode*," a journal that, later in his august career, "could still, he claimed, when pulled out and dusted off, make him 'dream for hours.' " This "society and family gazette," I discovered from Gordon Millan's biography of Mallarmé, "provided an illustration of one of the latest dresses, a fashion article signed 'Marguerite de Ponty' " (who was Mallarmé), news "from the salons and the beaches" reported by Ix (also Mallarmé), and a section called "Le Carnet d'Or"—the Golden Notebook—devoted to "cooking and other practical hints." Unfortunately, neither Calasso nor Millan supplies an example of the cryptic poet's improbable output as a critic of women's wear and as the Symbolists' Martha Stewart, or describes the reveries that the diversion inspired. But, with a little effort, one can imagine that Mallarmé discerned an affinity between his own mode of writing—in which the haunting repetitive phrase supplanted the concrete elucidation—and "the latest fashion." His life's work demonstrates that it is possible to fabricate an experience of revelation from which the material presence of truth has evaporated like a volatile spirit, leaving an essence only the senses can grasp. And that's just what great clothes do.

Had one plotted the trajectory of the shows on a street map of Paris, with straight pins and string, like a nineteenth-century military campaign, one would unwittingly have tatted the kind of hideous yet touching macramé doily a first-grader brings home for Mother's Day. There were a hundred and fifty défilés and presentations shoehorned into ten days, at hourly intervals from about nine in the morning until ten at night. Rarely were two sequentially in the same venue. One staggered around a city in the grip of labor disputes and gridlock, briefly alighting at the Trocadéro, the Musée Bourdelle, the École des Beaux-Arts, the Carrousel du Louvre, the Centre Pompidou, the Stock Exchange, a tent in the place de Varsovie, a sports stadium, the Carreau du Temple, a nightclub in Pigalle (the gritty old Élysée Montmartre), a theater in the Marais, and various boutiques, lofts, suites, cinemas, consulates, and firetraps in arty double-digit arrondissements.

At some locales, there was free coffee or champagne and, occasionally, a tray of sweets, but one had no time for meals. That was probably just as well. Neoprene, the fabric of wet suits, which has an unfortunate tendency to mimic sausage casing on the wrong body, was ubiquitous. At Balenciaga, Ghesquière used it in Hawaiian prints and abstractly seamed collages of color for glamorous surfer dresses cut to the thigh. Marc Jacobs at Vuitton and Giambattista Valli at Ungaro both revived the polka-dot bikini. Flirty tennis skirts at Chanel (worn with stilettos) were microscopic. Hussein Chalayan showed urban rompers with organic cutouts that were all peek and no boo. The entire season's worth of vintage-looking chiffon slip dresses at Stella McCartney might have been packed, so gossamer did they seem, into one of those oversize Kelly bags that make the perfect assignation kit, as the French acknowledge with their charming name for such an accessory: a *baise-en-ville*.

With markets crashing and buyers anxious about matters even more serious than their clothing allowances, designers seemed to be making a collective show of gallantry, as if to say, Beauty first into the lifeboats. It wasn't quite as stirring as the singing of the "Marseillaise" in *Casablanca*, but hard times and bad news inspired some of the best work in years: flattering, inventive drapery; heat and vibrance to fight depression; and a flourish of creativity with fabric. Helmut Lang set an example by making a lighthearted collection of heavy-handed materials. A cocktail dress with a 1920s silhouette was composed entirely of silver zippers sewn in vertical strips, so that the flat black cotton edge provided the garment's body and the metal teeth its embellishment. For the daring, there was a schoolgirl's kilt, twelve inches long, of pleated sheet rubber. Thin black streamers of the same latex fluttered, like satin ribbons, from closely cut dark jackets with sleeves of *ombré* chiffon. (They might be useful for gauging which way the wind blows.) Alber Elbaz's lovely tabard dresses for Lanvin seemed strapless, but the front and back were seamed with invisible netting. Naoki Takizawa's collection for Issey Miyake was ethereal, too. He showed it among the Romanesque bas-reliefs in a reconstructed abbey at the Palais de Chaillot (where the worn stone foreheads of the saints bore an eerie similarity to those petrified by Botox in the front row). His work, according to the program, was inspired by stardust, calligraphy, waterfalls, birds in flight, and classical drapery, and it consisted of robes for a naiad sugared with translucent sequins, a bridal gown of trembling black chiffon petals, and softly pleated tunics with the purity of chitons, but done in vibrant overlays of sheer color, their volume defined by tendrils of smocking.

There is nothing new in fashion about fantasies of escape to the past, the future, or fairyland, but since September 11 of last year, a number of designers have expressed a formal interest in survivalism. At Comme des Garçons, Rei Kawakubo spun the uncut selvage of her garments into thickly plaited ropes and bulbous cables suitable for lowering oneself from the window of a prison or an ivory tower, then festooned them like leis over outsized khaki flak jackets trimmed with roses. The palette of bitter olive and shocking pink that she showed in a cramped, harshly lit studio had a Brechtian flavor. So did the scarified collection that Jun Takahashi at Under Cover helpfully entitled "Scab." This courteous young Japanese designer was making his debut in Paris. Supple cutting gave long Edwardian skirts of denim or duck a voluptuous grace. There was charm but no novelty to his layering of a miniskirt slashed to shreds over a pair of clamdiggers—it followed the current trend in Williamsburg and Tribeca for wearing ladylike dresses or vintage lingerie over jeans. The gesture that thrilled his audience was taking a box cutter to the garments before repairing their wounds with lovingly hand-stitched patches and a fretwork of red sutures. He left all the threads dangling.

Paris has become, like New York, a city of immigrants living in their own villages within the greater metropolis. But the world of fashion more closely resembles ancient Rome at the time of its fall, when barbarians within the gates outnumbered citizens. The vast majority of the so-called French shows featured the work of foreigners, many of them obscure, at least to the consumer: Risto Bimbiloski, Venera Arapu, Dice Kayek, Fátima Lopes, Miwha Hong, Christian Wijnants, Lie Sang Bong, Maria Grachvogel, and Karim Tassi, to mention a few. With the exception of the big cheeses who stand alone—Gaultier, Lacroix—and of Balenciaga, where Ghesquière has leveled out (at a high altitude) after a vertical takeoff, most of the venerable houses are under non-French direction. Galliano is at Dior, Tom Ford at YSL Rive Gauche, Julien Macdonald at Givenchy, Martin Margiela at Hermès, Marc Jacobs at Vuitton, Alber Elbaz at Lanvin, Michael Kors at Celine, Lizzy Disney at Jacques Fath, Phoebe

Philo at Chloé—and, of course, Lagerfeld at Chanel. The French Republic of Bohemia has become a Belgian colony (though Gigli still trolls the Casbah dreamily, like an expatriate milord). Aristocratic decadence and Romantic iconoclasm are the fiefdoms of two working-class Englishmen—Galliano and McQueen—while the avant-garde consists mostly of Japanese irregulars.

In a hall at the Musée Bourdelle filled with grandiose heroic sculptures that prefigure the 1930s, Junya Watanabe presented a show that seemed to mock the Fascist aesthetic of that period, and to insist on the nobility of trying, at least, to achieve serenity in a violent world. His collection paid homage to the pastoral painters of the eighteenth century—Fragonard and Watteau—whose great subject was the stolen private moment. To an operatic soundtrack, Watanabe presented a series of buoyant pastel shepherdess frocks in sprigged cotton toile and reembroidered eyelet, but their blitheness had restraints attached—the straps, buckles, and ruched whipcording of a parachute or a straitjacket. (Perhaps the contemporary equivalent of the eighteenth-century lady's maid, always on call to grapple with one's laces, is a psychiatric nurse.) In lieu of panniers and bustles, the dresses were constructed with exaggerated built-in saddlebags and fanny packs, and sleeves wired like kites. The models floated through the hall straining at reality's moorings.

Darwinian theory teaches us that we must adapt or perish. So do Martin Margiela and Yohji Yamamoto. They have both adapted to a harsh climate for purists, Yamamoto by signing a lucrative contract to design sportswear (his new Y-3 line) for Adidas, and Margiela by producing a collection for Hermès so fastidiously bourgeois that it seems almost tongue-in-cheek. But the ingenious collections that both designers showed under their own labels might have been inspired by Lavoisier's famous aphorism: "Nothing is lost, nothing is created, everything is transformed." These playful mutants reminded me of the robots my son collected as a little boy—humanoid figures with articulated plastic limbs that morphed into spacecraft. The proportions, even the identity, of the garments were as unstable as the world is. The inverted hem of a Margiela dress became a stole. A top slipped off the shoulders to zipper, like a peplum, over the hips. Sweaters with the trick backs of a magician's coffin hung from the neck like deluxe lobster bibs. He fashioned a fetching bustier entirely out of white athletic shoelaces, stitched horizontally, with the ends left dangling to tie across the bosom. In Yamamoto's cheaper line (Y's), floppy sleeves turned into obis, and a voluminous greatcoat of sludge-colored poplin could, with a snap, be trimmed or let out like a mainsail.

Anyone who is leery of sailing off into potentially troubled waters can, this spring, take an exotic virtual vacation in her own walk-in closet, although it may not be cheaper than chartering a yacht. Viktor & Rolf's giddy collection of carnival wear was generally rated the best entertainment of the week. Their show featured the infectious tunes of a Rio samba school and dancing models in clown makeup and wigs, and it was such a funfest that editors were wriggling in the aisles and gushing over the exuberantly ruffled dresses and the big ball skirts of globular silk roses stacked like pyramids of profiteroles, even though the racks at the showroom of the Dutch duo, who are much beloved by museum curators, displayed prim little pleated or tucked shifts in black silk, slightly frayed; a white satin blouse with a Pierrot ruff; and a cocktail dress of sooty nylon lace on a flesh-colored ground—tweaked versions of the Chanel classics familiar from some of Mademoiselle's most famous portraits.

Galliano, never a showman to be upstaged, condensed the festivities of a weeklong tribal wedding in an obscure province somewhere between Outer Mongolia and Kerala into a fifteen-minute display of sartorial fireworks that showered the audience with colored powder while unfurling a gorgeous panoply of gauzy saris, chiffon and tulle skirts spangled with sequins, leggings of stretch paisley lamé, and lurid prints of grimacing Hindu divinities. His models wore face paint and tinsel, and they were laden, like the bride at such a celebration, with the contents of her extended family's linen closet. Some of the poor creatures even seemed to be wearing the family yurt. It was, as intended, too much to take in, so I dropped by the showroom on the top floor of the Institut du Monde Arabe, a glass-walled aerie with a panoramic terrace just east of Notre Dame, where the transparency of the space and the grandeur of the view made a nice foil for the riot of the clothes. But lo, what pieces were being modeled for buyers? A knee-length skirt of taupe silk cut on the bias (Galliano's speciality), a chunky white cable-knit sweater, and a pair of cargo pants.

Perhaps we all secretly yearn for fate to blow our lives off their prosaic courses to some spectacularly alien Shangri-la where our senses will be employed as nature intended them to be: gathering intelligence in the service of our unfettered predatory appetites. That, at least, was the reverie of Alexander McQueen. His production opened with a giant-screen video projection of a girl (Ophelia? Miranda? Viola? the mute heroine of *The Piano*?) who appeared to be drowning. Her translucent rags and loose hair swirled around her limp body like the tentacles of a medusa. Then the models entered with their mascara streaming. Ensembles like a camisole encrusted with mother-of-pearl buttons worn with a lacy skirt of brine-colored suede might have washed up at the jungle's edge from a sunken galleon. In one sequence, the royal maidens thus swept away seemed to have borrowed the raiment of their lost twin brothers: braid-trimmed corsair jackets and rakish britches draped like dhotis, or a gentleman pirate's ruffed chemise. For the finale, they were brides of nature. Their billowing chiffon gowns had shredded skirts of a parrot-feather print or flounces like an accretion of fan coral. I suspect that one could maroon McQueen on an atoll and he would manage to turn the palm fronds and the scales of dead fish into something fabulous for his new boutique on West Fourteenth Street. Yet these were clothes one could wear—or at least that one might feel emboldened to dream of wearing—by a designer who believes that a stylish life is only worth living dangerously.

For the first time in memory, I left Paris with the same number of shoes I had brought with me. I was headed for London, which I knew would be chilly, but, inspired by Galliano, I decided I could get away with wearing everything in my suitcase at the same time: a short silk dress with a knotted hem over a long frayed slip over knitted trousers, and, on top of it all, a mohair poncho. Normally, this would have looked blimpish. Thanks to my fashion-week minibar diet of cocktail nuts three times a day, I was nearly a waif.

Three days earlier, the popular mayor of Paris, Bertrand Delanoë, the first Socialist to govern the capital since the Paris Commune, had been stabbed in the stomach by a mentally disturbed homophobe (the mayor is gay) who attacked him during a nocturnal art festival billed as Nuit Blanche—the sleepless night. Nearly half a million Parisians crowded the Métro (which, unfortunately, shut down at the usual hour) and roamed the streets in a festive mood (hungrily, too, as restaurants also shut down at the usual hour). When his assailant struck, toward three in the morning, the mayor was mingling with the public at an event in the Hôtel de Ville (City Hall). "Let the party go on," he commanded bravely.

That might have been the motto of Gianni Versace, the subject of a retrospective that just opened at the Victoria and Albert Museum in London. It is now five years since Versace was murdered, at the age of fifty, on the front steps of his villa in Miami's South Beach, by a serial killer who targeted gay men. Versace lived and died as he worked—sensationally, and surrounded by a crowd of revelers, indeed of orgiasts. Yet Mallarmé's languid friends the decadents wouldn't have considered Versace one of their own, in part because he bristled with so much energy and libido. He was decadent like an imperial Roman, a big-game shooting spree, a grande bouffe—or like Las Vegas. "I don't like good taste," he liked to say, pugnaciously. But it is too facile merely to accuse Versace of bad taste. The Victoria and Albert show suggests that he was a vulgarian by temperament; by virtue of appetite and perversity; and because it paid royally and was huge fun—not because he lacked the aesthetic subtlety or sense of history necessary for refinement.

The retrospective contains a hundred and thirty ensembles, including gowns worn by all those bold-faced friends of the house: the bad-girl blondes, the models he made super, the tragic princess—surely you know them. There is a mildly witty dress designed in collaboration with Roy Lichtenstein for the first Florence Biennale; examples of Versace's didactically outré but still masterly leatherwork, of his menswear for a special clientele, and of his sometimes regal couture (a queen, by definition, is a dominatrix). In the wake of the Guggenheim's much criticized pocketing of a multimillion-dollar donation from Giorgio Armani around the time of his retrospective in New York two years ago, the Victoria and Albert has made it clear that this show was funded exclusively from its own coffers. There is, however, a gift shop stocked with Versace trinkets and scarves; Christmas is coming, and throngs are expected.

One has to wonder about the point of being scrupulously unbeholden when the result is a spectacle more lavish in its servility than almost any that Versace—a master of self-promotion who often managed to arrange for photographs from his ad campaigns to be used on the covers of fashion magazines—ever staged on his own behalf. In her catalog notes, the show's curator, Claire Wilcox, describes a series of supremely cheeky biker jackets and bustiers heavily encrusted with sequined images of the Virgin Mary, and some flagrant metal-mesh and leather minidresses adorned with jeweled Byzantine crosses, as "a joyful celebration of ecclesiastic art . . . without sacrilegious intent." Versace, she adds, "was interested in the impact of the cross when used as a purely decorative motif in a secular context." But as the designer himself knew perfectly well—as every Italian has known since the advent of Christendom—the impact of the cross or the Madonna when used as a purely decorative motif in a secular context (in the case of these clothes, a sexual context) has no interest whatsoever except as a profanation. Nearly everything Versace did was joyously sacrilegious in intent, and he would probably be greatly aggrieved to have his credentials as a rogue thus impugned.

Versace was a brilliant tailor, colorist, and innovator with fabric. His metal-mesh dresses, for example, were made of Oroton, a brass-and-aluminum alloy that he developed with a German manufacturer and used as a signature in most of his collections. Its "intrinsic qualities," Chiara Buss writes in a catalog essay, are "symbols of the invincible woman." They are also rather pointedly the attributes of a reptile: slinkiness, hardness, and "impenetrability." Oroton molds itself almost magnetically to the body, and, despite the fact that it is cold against the skin, excessively heavy, and easily snagged, Versace loved its erotic flash. Wilcox suggests that it turns the woman who wears it into a "Joan of Arc."

Nowhere are Versace's talents more appreciable than in the section of the exhibition devoted to his costumes for the opera and ballet, many done in collaboration with Maurice Béjart. (They are bizarrely lit, however, with flashing lights that illuminate each mannequin for a second, like the stripper in a peep show, before plunging it back into the dark.) What distinguishes these deliriously beautiful garments, so far as one can see them, from Versace's commercial fashion design, including the couture, and from the "showstoppers" he designed for celebrities, isn't their technical complexity (a Versace hallmark) but the range of emotion that they express: innocence, majesty, wantonness, yearning, humor, caprice, mourning—mobility of body and spirit. Challenged by a character or a work of art with real depth to which he could respond, Versace did—and with all the virtuosity at his command. Given a movie star to dress or a bank of cameras to feed, he produced something "iconic"—a word that now simply means hyper-photogenic. He possessed an unusually rich and even deeply cultivated design vocabulary, but he used it to make the same point over and over. What is missing from the exhibition is what was missing from the man. A true artist is a well. Versace was a mirror, and he needed something to reflect that wasn't himself.

The French word for vocation—*métier*—also means "loom," and Mallarmé referred to himself as a "sacred spider" spinning threads from his mind and weaving them into "marvelous laces." He wrote about the "fretting of the veil"—the veil of convention—that took place in the temple of art at the end of the nineteenth century. Calasso relates these images to a god in the Upanishads who spun his cloak of selfhood from the "primordial matter." But every time a spider reconstructs her broken web, it is a little more imperfect, and thus less divine, a little more frayed, asymmetrical, stylized—and that warped look of desperation is what makes it creepy—but also defiantly individual and morbidly fascinating. The fretted veil is a paradigm for the way innocence becomes entangled in self-consciousness, classicism lapses into the baroque, weary cultures resist their inevitable degeneration—and for modern fashion.

—November 4, 2002

FIVE

Déshabillé Chic

Patrons of couture generally fall into two categories: wives (or ex-wives) and their husbands' other women. There is a show for each at the Museum of the Fashion Institute of Technology and, rather like marriage and adultery, they offer a choice between the prix fixe and the tasting menu. The basement galleries are devoted to a retrospective of Arnold Scaasi's five decades in fashion. Scaasi is a sort of American Hartnell. Some of his clients ride in motorcades wearing matching coat-and-dress ensembles in floral brocade. Since they do a lot of waving and smiling on behalf of their spouses, they require clothes that are splashy yet irreproachable. Scaasi also specializes in gala party dresses that awaken one's childish gourmandise like the dessert buffet at a big Jewish wedding. Several such dresses in the show are of tulle, in riotous Easter-egg pastels, with frothy appliqués that look like a swarm of butterflies or the air bubbles in a milk shake. There is no hauteur in Scaasi's rather Southern (Houstonian or Washingtonian) notion of glamour, which in a way is endearing. And not all the work is fussy: his lines are often boldly graphic. But something in the tone, perhaps a slightly forced, therapeutic cheerfulness, reminds me of Dr. Ruth Westheimer's superannuated giggle and her insistence that old married couples can still—indeed, should feel obliged to—have wholesome fun in bed.

The French believe that one should seek unwholesome fun in any bed but one's own, and seduction is the theme of "Femme Fatale: Fashion and Visual Culture in Fin-de-Siècle Paris," a small, dreamy installation on the Fashion Institute of Technology's main floor. It is curated by Valerie Steele, whose literate notes on the wall and at the base of each ensemble and accessory deserve praise for eschewing the artspeak that afflicts so many costume exhibitions. Steele concentrates on informative social history. As I squinted at the clothes (the low wattage of the lighting is, I assume, necessary to protect antique fabric), I recalled a line from the ballad "Sir Patrick Spens": "I saw the new moon late yestreen / Wi' the auld moon in her arm." At the penultimate fin de siècle, svelte, quicksilver modern woman was the new moon, but she was still burdened with her heavy-bodied, old goddess myths.

The thirty ensembles on display include a severely tailored yet sumptuous black riding costume by Denova, circa 1895—a skirt over invisible trousers with a closely buttoned pigeon-breasted jacket. One understands why the French called huntresses thus attired *amazones*: their sex appeal was intimidating whether or not they wore high-heeled boots and wielded a leather crop. At the other erotic extreme, a suite of tea gowns exudes the sensual languor of a courtesan waiting for her protector. One can imagine Odette receiving Swann in a confection by Mme. Denoix that is the color of watered absinthe, trimmed with fur, and open down the front to reveal a pink silk lining shimmering with glass beads that suggests, scandalously, the nudity beneath it. As a note points out, the tea gown (*robe d'intérieur*) was a form of glorified *déshabillé* that was worn only at home to receive one's intimates, "usually without a corset, thus combining comfort with a somewhat risqué charm."

Every age has different standards of the risqué, and at the end of the nineteenth century the costume a woman might respectably wear to a ball would constitute an actionable "outrage to public morality" on the street. A thrilling example of such a style in the show is an off-the-shoulder gown of labial red velvet from the House of Worth. It is something that a Wharton heroine with a yearning to be corrupted—say, Countess Olenska—might have bought on her Paris honeymoon, before she was relieved of her romantic illusions about corruption, along with her dowry, by a titled scoundrel. One also has to wonder about the sexual history of the lady whose hat is displayed in a vitrine of accessories, among them several pairs of satin slippers and boots as poignant in their fragility as bliss. Nestled in the brim of the hat are the actual dead bodies of what appear to be two lovebirds, although Steele's note describes them as parakeets.

Colette's first husband nicely summed up the fin de siècle by reminding a reluctant mistress in one of his novels that "adultery is the foundation of society, because in making marriage tolerable, it assures the perpetuation of the family." Steele evokes the contradictions of this age obsessed by both purity and debauchery without overstating them, and her potpourri of sources has a suitably musky pungence. A Belle Époque fashion writer named Octave Uzanne, who was intoxicated by froufrou, observes that "lace permits the indecision that simultaneously provokes and restrains desire." A nineteenth-century reviewer contemplating Manet's portrait of Zola's Nana remarks that "the aristocracy of vice is recognizable by its lingerie." Charles Bernheimer, a modern scholar, asserts that the appeal of the courtesan was "to dissolve the beastly immediacy of the female animal in a play of intriguing signs and changing masks."

The exorbitance of fin de siècle couture was proportional to the exorbitance of the labor that produced it, and Steele has the decency to include a snippet from the anonymous author of "The Revolutionary March of the Dressmakers":

> What does the delivery girl demand
> Of the House of Worth
> Or of Paquin?
> More money!
> Less work!

One should note that in an era famous for the sybaritic consumption so richly represented here, a seamstress doing piecework might earn as little as a franc a day: the cost of a gown by Worth or Paquin could be twenty-five times her yearly salary. One should also recall that for every courtesan who salted away enough of her allowance to buy a villa in the south of France, and to keep a great chef, a prize cat, and a pretty boy, there were thousands of wretched creatures selling themselves for a few sous on an outer boulevard, and nearly as many girls, some as young as nine or ten, ostensibly selling flowers in the late-night brasseries. Countless milliners, maids, laundresses, and shopgirls supplemented their meager wages with freelance sex work. Fin de siècle Paris had a population of nearly three million and, by a contemporary estimate, about a hundred thousand prostitutes.

One of Steele's favorite pieces in the show, she told me, is an afternoon or dinner dress by Émile Pingat of black cut velvet with a pattern of apples that she considers intriguingly "diabolical." Despite the gown's long sleeves and high neck, the decadents, she feels, would have read deviance and artifice into the allusion to "forbidden fruit." Yet nothing on display, not even the corsets and peignoirs, suggests that the women who wore these sublime creations did depraved things when they took them off, and that discretion, which gives the clothes their coquetry, also makes the premise of the show seem a little quaint. While the Parisian chic of the kept woman certainly made willing suckers of men, it was probably more "fatal" to other women. Genteel wives and maidens, even some "daughters of Puritan ancestors," were seduced by the splendors of the courtesans and yearned to acquire their mystique. By the fin de siècle, tarts and duchesses shopped at the same couturiers for similar outfits. (Many of their bills, of course, went to the same guarantor.) Proust, a human seismograph, was one of the first to register the significance of this social temblor, and Steele spotlights it astutely. By blurring the moral boundaries between castes of women, and between social celebrity and sexual notoriety, high fashion diluted the prestige of virtue. It also mirrored a much deeper instability in the culture, and contributed to the emergence of a new strain of glamour that was more resistant to class prejudice. The end product of this democratization process may, unfortunately, be Anna Nicole Smith.

Parisian chic was, as it still is, one of France's most profitable luxury exports, and the great couture houses drew, as they still do, high-rolling foreign tourists. Between April and November of 1900, the city hosted the first world's fair of a new century, and the fifty million visitors who passed through the main gate were greeted by a statuesque young woman known as La Parisienne. This kitsch Venus of painted stucco was twenty feet tall and posed atop a pillar on a sug-

gestive golden ball, her eyes turned rapturously toward the heavens
and her voluptuous, nearly naked bosom spilling from the bodice of
a gown designed by Mme. Paquin, president of the Universal Expo-
sition's fashion section. La Parisienne embodied the popular taste for
docile ripeness in feminine beauty and the general anxiety about in-
docile female desire. Was woman an angel or a temptress? "The uncertainty makes her into a sphinx," Simone de Beauvoir reflected
with irritation fifty years later, also noting that the Sphinx was a famous Paris brothel.

The fin de siècle was the heyday of the femme fatale in art, theater, and society in part because every male insecure in his virility (apparently the entire population) had his own fantasy about woman's
power to consume him. The decadents imagined a vampiric seductress wreathed in snakes: Wilde's Salome. The religious right, which
fiercely opposed the reforms of the Third Republic that had given
women limited entitlement to an education, a divorce, a passport,
and a bank account, conjured up an invading army of lesbian head-
mistresses spreading their vice among the innocents entrusted to
their care in the new public girls' schools. The bluestocking with a
hypertrophied brain and atrophied sex organs was a popular object of
nervous male ridicule. So was the New Woman, who was never to be
confused with a "real woman." She smoked and worked (or wanted
to), bobbed her hair and wore a mannish *tailleur* with a shirt and tie
(though it had to have a skirt, because wearing trousers in public was
considered transvestism and prohibited by law unless one had a dis-
pensation from the chief of police). But in her private moments she
could just as well have adopted Paul Poiret's luxuriously daring
"Harem" ensemble: a crushed silver gauze tunic, red chiffon Zouave
pantaloons, and a matching turban, suitable for sharing a hookah
with one's woman lover in a prettily decorated little *chambre turque*
while reading Dr. Mardrus's translation of the *Arabian Nights*.
Poiret, Steele notes, succeeded where the prudish dress reformers of
the nineties had failed, by making an unfettered body and a comfortable cladding for it stylish and alluring. He helped to do away with
the corset, replacing it with the brassiere, and to transform the florid
femme fatale into the Jazz Age sylph.

The New Woman, however, wasn't necessarily an androgyne, a

lesbian, an anarchist, a feminist, or any other kind of committed radical. She was often just an ambitious student or an unhappy wife who had asked herself a radically impertinent question: How can one refuse to be owned without renouncing the desire to be possessed? An answer is still to come.

—November 18, 2002

SIX

Broad Stripes, Bright Stars

Are you really interested in what men wear? Do you rifle hungrily through your Sunday paper to extract the semiannual color supplement on men's style? Does an outfit in the window of Bergdorf's men's store ever stop you in your tracks like the flashback from a dream? Does Bergdorf's men's store have windows? I don't recall. Most wondrous clothes that make men ineffably poetic figures are on the walls of the Met, or in news footage from Afghanistan. Since the nineteenth century, when the Western ruling class adopted the uniform of a dark tailored suit worn with a shirt and tie, men's fashion (not to put too fine a point on so obvious a truth) has been militantly prosaic. The rise of the merchant prince coincided with the decline of fashion as a theater in which men wore romantic costumes. It coincided, in fact, with the decline of culturally sanctioned male vanity, flamboyance, and insouciance. The courtier or the tribesman is freer than the self-made man in one respect: a modern identity is less stable, and demands more psychic effort to maintain, than a traditional role. The ceaseless effort to prove one's worth diverts ambition from more luxuriant forms of self-expression.

It is, in short, considerably more rewarding, creatively and financially, for most of the designers who showed their spring-summer 2004 menswear collections last month in Milan and Paris to work for the avid and knowing clients who best appreciate their gifts—women. Men's fashion represents a fraction of their business, and one that is, for the most part, in steep decline. A general sense of crisis may help to explain the lassitude of buyers and critics, though perhaps it was partly the side effect of a spectacular heat wave that broke records for June.

In Milan, an African sirocco stirred migraines, excited great swarms of mosquitoes, and, like a cosmic hair dryer, blew curls of torrid yellow dust through graffiti-scarred streets and drought-scorched piazzas. The sun faded the rainbow *Pace* banners that were hung to protest the war in Iraq. Housewives draped tarps or bed-sheets over their shutters, which gave the city's working-class districts the air of a bedraggled encampment. Its industrial outskirts, where a number of shows were held in hangars or sheds, became a giant kiln of cinder block and corrugated tin. The power failed; residents were warned to avoid taking elevators; and it was even a little dangerous to wear stilettos: they sank half an inch into the melting tar, impaling one's legs to the spot while one's torso pitched forward, headfirst, like a stone launched from a slingshot. In such a climate, a fur coat from the fall collection already in the window of Valentino's men's boutique on the via Montenapoleone was as tempting as a hair shirt, and an alligator jacket with a price tag of twenty thousand euros might have found a buyer had it come with a muddy river in which to wallow.

Many shows played to escape fantasies—of alpine lakes, luffing mainsails, crashing surf, island breezes, piney woods, and Riviera sun-sets—that tortured the parched souls condemned to review them un-der sweat-lodge conditions. Yet, even though the weather made news, the collections will probably be remembered as the season of the cowboy. *The New York Times* ran Cathy Horyn's report from Paris as a front-page story with a picture from Tom Ford's show for Gucci. The model wore a bone-white Stetson that matched his broad-shouldered jacket. His jeans were belted with a silver buckle, and he carried a pair of riding gloves. MACHO AMERICA STORMS EU-ROPE'S RUNWAYS, the headline read, and the story suggested that Ford—a native Texan who lives in Paris and who, last winter, publicly criticized America's bellicose intentions—was now fawning on the victors and eager to exploit the popularity of the rugged he-man in the White House.

Among the other labels that seasoned an eclectic summer salad with a dollop of ranch dressing (cowboy hats, pointy boots, snap-closed shirts with scalloped yokes) were Nicole Farhi, Calvin Klein, Roberto Cavalli, John Varvatos, Fendi, and Miu Miu (whose languid and urbane collection, in the shades of a tea table—chamomile, double cream, bone china, and brown sugar—revisited Fort Worth by way of Brideshead). I was not persuaded, however, that the look in whole or in part was intended as an apotheosis of the president: warhorse as clotheshorse. It seemed, rather, that with consumers resistant to spending their severance pay on anything but a conservative two-button suit for a job interview, and stores drastically reducing the space they allot to masculine fashion, a different hegemon was being summoned, from on high, to come in shooting. He happens to be a trim, monogamous, silver-haired, ranch-owning, Stetson-wearing, horse-riding, sports-loving, flag-waving multimillionaire of undisputed global dominance who has built his career on the dubiously legitimate yet irresistibly glamorous marriage of Old Wasp privilege and frontier swagger—but his name isn't George Bush, it's Ralph Lauren.

In retrospect, the cowboy brouhaha was like the weather: something ephemeral to deplore. The Stetsons were as integral to the clothes on display as a paper party hat is to a tuxedo on New Year's Eve. And the blunt certainty of the *Times* headline, with its faintly sensational suggestion of a new Yankee invasion (a reprisal raid by commandos from the David Barton Gym on the decadent wimps who opposed our war of liberation), also belied the rather anarchic diversity of the clothes that came down the runway. Valentino channeled the wolfish glamour of old Riviera playboys like Gunther Sachs. Ford's collection for YSL was saturated with hot, hedonistic color. Paul Smith revived op art squiggles and cabana stripes, while Dolce & Gabbana's prints were psychedelic. (They also got more of a kick from the sartorial theatrics of the soccer star David Beckham than did his former coach at Manchester United. Humble origins, a celebrity marriage, an enviable fortune, athletic prowess, and vast reserves of laddish credibility apparently entitle one to get away with wearing pink, ruffles, and barrettes.)

Perhaps it was symbolic of shrinking profits that the seventies, a decade of recession, inspired so many skinny ties and cigarillo suits—

such as those at Prada, Dior, Vuitton, and Gigli—cut to flatter the avian figure of a male waif like Adrien Brody. Trousers were shrunken, too. They grazed the anklebone, as if an unemployed futures trader too distracted by the help-wanted ads to read the care instructions on his pants had thrown them into a dryer at the Laundromat. That new length, which leaves a gap between instep and cuff, is a little shocking. The flash of an ankle used to represent the chasm between a sophisticate and a rube. It flagged the provincial American as surely as a taste for acrylic greens, golf-tournament pastels, and clashing plaids—three other trends of an anxious season in which designers, like the strapped revenue collectors they are, declared an amnesty for, and even embraced, the faux pas of the average guy.

Some menswear designers are discreetly resourceful in challenging the dronish taste of their customers. Naoki Takizawa's virile yet dreamy collection of rain gear, bowling shirts, and cargo pants for Issey Miyake seethed with the colors and creatures of the jungle floor, in the shape of cutouts and talismanic appliqués. At Jens, "normal people"—dancers and acrobats—modeled lithe, unpretentious warmup clothes in doodle prints. Neil Barrett showed a collection in washed leather, silk twill, and hemp that combined ruggedness with finesse. Atavistic references were encoded into the conceptually elegant "ecological" sportswear of Hussein Chalayan, whose collection celebrated the "divided history," as a publicist put it, of his native Cyprus. (A zippered pouch at the back of a cotton Windbreaker was designed for "stowing small game," and the loops on the shoulders of a T-shirt for "carrying a lance.") He played the laconic modernity of his sludge-colored clothes against the quaint charm of a "history" cloth that enlivened a collar or a lining. The pictures told a boy's adventure tale about Neolithic archers disporting in a palm forest at the edge of a modern city, where medieval knights jousted by a swimming pool and a galleon rode at anchor on the blue waves that lapped its shore while a plane buzzed an ancient minaret. It was an Eden without Eve, though each piece carried a label with the first name of a woman—the worker who sewed it.

A few purists, for better or worse, refuse to indulge the mass market with timid, crass, or banal clothes. Antonio Marras, a young Sardinian who has been called "the Galliano of menswear," experimented with dandyish Proustian jackets worn over pajamalike dhotis in striped jersey. Helmut Lang showed knitted tanks that looked half eaten by some exotic pest. They were scooped out in asymmetric, demilunar bites that revealed a navel or a nipple. Low-cut jeans, some in Mylar-colored leather, were gaffed with ribbons or swagged vertically with a column of pockets that resembled a Roman shade. Junya Watanabe used cotton cartridge belts as accessories to an ironic collection of Boer-style jodhpurs, khakis, safari jackets, orderlies' coats, middy blouses, and other martial gear demilitarized with sweetly flocked stripes and florals. It was easy to infer a timely protest from these gentle uniforms, though the Japanese hardly need Iraq as a pretext for indignation at tactics of shock and awe.

No one translates angst into fashion with more stylish intensity than Hedi Slimane. His beautifully cut suits are beloved by the lean and hungry of both sexes. The moody spectacle he staged at Dior featured an explosive laser show with a soundtrack of electro-Euro lounge music (which is the noise that the hip magazine *Wallpaper* might emit if it were a radio). But the lighting was so dim and the models in such a hurry—perhaps for dinner, since they looked as though they had been holed up in a bunker without food or shampoo—that I caught only a fleeting glimpse of the clothes as they disappeared behind a bank of mirrors: body-hugging leather pants crumpled at the ankle, slashed nylon camisoles, and hooded jackets worn over naked torsos entangled in sequined tentacles. Could they have been symbolic of the cables that fetter captive minds to the Matrix?

One never knows what form of radical protest against bourgeois complacence Raf Simons's interesting work will take. But this season the young Belgian focused his energy on repairing the broken circle of our cosmic awareness with the help of nature, crystals, and Hermann Hesse. His former bleakness has given way to a "different state of consciousness," according to the program. I suppose he figured, not unreasonably, that if he could enlighten the fashion crowd, no feat of conversion was beyond his powers. To that end, he lured us to a buggy grove in the botanical gardens at Vincennes, where his barefoot models, all tender as the grass, stood soulfully among the trees, dressed mostly in flaccid whites, though a stiffly padded coat, suitable for a druidic rite, was hand-embroidered with sacred symbols and sayings from *Siddhartha*: "There is no reality except that which is contained within us." Would that it were so.

An unreconstructed old sinner like me is sometimes grateful for Donatella Versace. At least she isn't renouncing any of the vices that are her virtue. She still smokes. Her skin is the color of Russian amber. It is rumored that she buys the corn-silk tresses of Swedish virgins for her hair extensions. Her steamy show, held in a tent and copiously perfumed with incense, had a Moroccan theme, and the clothes should appeal to dens of sharp-dressing thieves wherever they lie low rubbing lamps, though especially, perhaps, in Hollywood, South Beach, and New Jersey. In addition to tunic-length djellabas with plunging necklines embellished with gold embroidery, there were some charmingly cocky sharkskin suits. A talent agent (or a garbage contractor) with a sense of humor, if he exists, might pair one with the T-shirt that reads: "Ever get the feeling you've been cheated?"

Armani's show, the last event in Milan, quite sensibly, and with exemplary dignity, I thought, snubbed the New World Order, the Middle East, the Old West, the Left Coast, Eastern philosophy, and the various unpleasantries of recent history. His collection paid homage to the Naples of an operetta or a vintage postcard. While his program included a fogyish diatribe against cargo pants (why preach to the converted?), a défilé of boldly striped, fluidly cut, nostalgically patrician leisure wear pared to its essence—blue water and white heat— reasserted his virtuosity.

By the time I got to Paris, the heat had subsided. I did some laundry in my hotel room, went to a few shoe stores on the rue du Cherche-Midi, mentally converted euros to dollars and didn't buy anything, drank a coffee at the Flore, considered bumming a cigarette from a chic woman in white linen at the next table, dismissed the notion, remembered I had no opaque white underpants to wear under my own white linen suit, looked for a pair up and down the rue de Rennes, couldn't find any—there is no such thing, in Paris, as opaque white underpants, which is a reason to love Paris—went to a bookshop on the boulevard Saint-Germain, bought a novel, had another coffee at the Café des Beaux-Arts and considered bumming a cigarette from the art student at the next table who was wearing a cowboy shirt and discussing American imperialism with a girlfriend in adorable bangs and clashing plaids, angrily chided myself, ordered a ham sandwich, and read my newspapers. In one of them I found an interesting story. Recent studies of the Y chromosome suggest a bittersweet truth that most women manage to discover without a microscope: that the human male, however endearing or superior an individual specimen may be, is one of evolution's flawed experiments. The Y chromosome determines the gender of the fetus, and it must isolate itself from the exchange of traits with the X chromosome in the act of reproduction, for if it didn't, all infants would be male, and the shoe shops on the rue du Cherche-Midi out of business. Over tens of millennia, the gallant self-effacement of the Y chromosome has drastically reduced its endowment of genes—from a thousand to fewer than eighty—whereas its robust female counterpart enjoys a double helix as lavishly bejeweled, so to speak, as a queen's parure.

The most thoughtful collections explored a futuristic premise: the exchange of traits between X and Y chromosomes. An evolved couple the same size might share the ravishing white canvas duffle coat with rope toggles at Comme des Garçons, or one of the witty jackets lined with cartoon drawings by Alexander Stadler. At Costume National and Prada, tops with scooped necklines redefined décolletage for men, which has hitherto entailed an unbuttoned disco shirt baring a hairy chest festooned with chains. Prada's menswear seems of the moment precisely because its epicene sensuality is so blasé, and because it reflects the casual attitude of sophisticated young people who don't think they are cross-dressing when they wear the same clothes, and who don't consider themselves rebels or androgynes for doing so. The great Gaultier, on the other hand, introduced a line of makeup (though I doubt the men that it is intended for are shy about sidling up to the Shu Uemura counter at Barneys) and showed a collection that included a peach leather bathrobe, sheer baseball jackets in polka-dot mesh, and ankle-length wrapped dresses that resembled barbecue aprons. His models teetered down the runway in high-heeled boots. At the end of the show, he threw a powder puff at photographers. It wasn't a failure of creative nerve—if anything,

Gaultier has too much—that made the show seem anachronistic. It was the campiness of the provocation.

"I detest the ultrafeminine or the ultramasculine," Jil Sander told me in Milan. Sander was presenting her first collection (for either sex) in three years. She reconciled a few months ago with Patrizio Bertelli, the chief executive of Prada, which bought her company and then forced her to retire from it. "But I had become a bit of a robot, so the time-out was healthy," she said. There has always been a cerebral chill to Sander's precision, but that is its forte. "You just can't speak to everybody," as she puts it. A pleasant if unwilling sabbatical hasn't relaxed her discipline, though a new lightness showed in softly structured jackets; low-waisted trousers in crisp cotton; a Bohemian palette of chrome yellow and poppy red; and playful knits with trompe l'oeil stretch marks at the seam. I suspect a lot of women will be wearing them.

I'm not sure who will be wearing the long, priestly black skirts and strict jackets with corset lacing that Yohji Yamamoto sent forth at a Parisian lycée (perhaps an advanced human male whose desires resist conformity to any doctrinaire assignment of sexual roles). The distinguished older men, including the great Malian actor Sotigui Kouyaté, who modeled the skirts with the authority of grizzled sages and shamans, reminded a jaded audience that the soul of beauty is self-possession.

Last spring, I stopped by a suite at the Carlyle where the young Savile Row tailor Richard Anderson was taking orders for his bespoke clothes. He joined the firm of Huntsman as a teenage apprentice, left two years ago to open his own shop, and has spent most of his life dressing gentlemen who appreciate, and can afford, the obsessive perfection of masculine couture. A half-finished double-breasted blazer hung from a doorjamb. From a distance, it looked as though a column of tiny red ants were marching across the lapel. The ants were stitches, perfectly uniform yet mysteriously alive, as only the finest handwork can be. The fabric, he explained, is a blend of Andean guanaco, pashmina, and yearling cashmere. It felt to the hand as foie gras does to the tongue: exorbitantly rich, ineffably silky, and melting.

The bespoke tradition is an esoteric cult, and the tailors of Anderson's caliber who practice it resemble the Spanish or French curés who, for a tiny congregation of devotees, still say the Latin Mass. But two avant-garde designers—a Belgian who works in Paris and an Austrian in Milan—revere the ideal of artisanal tailoring without subscribing to the dogma of impeccability. The Belgian is Martin Margiela. He is partly a folklorist, salvaging the stories that old clothes have to tell, and partly a mad botanist who scavenges for vintage pieces, rips them apart, then splices their cuttings into a radically strange though pleasing new garment, like a vest with a fly closing made from an inverted trouser top. These unsettling hybrids have their own formal integrity—they aren't merely clever sleights of hand. In fashion as in science, mutation, rather than invention, seems to define modernity.

The Austrian, Carol Christian Poell, is an emaciated man of thirty-six with the stark features and eerie radiance of an El Greco. He studied tailoring in Vienna, where his parents are in the garment business, then learned about textile fabrication in Italy—not, he told me, to lay the technical groundwork for a commercial career in fashion but because he wanted the skills necessary to transcend one. Working entirely by hand, he and a small company of artisans make their limited collections (he can't afford to show them every year) in a loft whose size and openness are unusual for Milan—the backdrops for La Scala were once painted on its floor. The collective has lately been experimenting with new materials: crocheted rubber; a pigskin with the strength and lightness "of a good garbage bag"; and a special gaffer's tape they use instead of thread or ribbon both to seam and to embellish garments.

The invitation to Poell's show was a salmon-colored factory time card stamped with an hour—seven in the evening—and an address that puzzled my driver: "Alzaia Naviglio Grande Under Bridge Viale Cassala." The Naviglio Grande is the largest of the natural canals that flow through and beneath the industrial neighborhood where Poell has his studio, and which is the oldest part of the city. By the time we found the spot, the sun looked like a melon. A youthful crowd had assembled along the iron railing that protects the steep embankment. There was no evidence of a runway. There were no assistants in black, no security personnel talking into headsets, no publicist with a seating chart—indeed, no seating. The water, which was pale green and surprisingly clear, though flecked with wisps of straw, reflected a skyful of Tintoretto clouds. *"Dov'è la sfilata?"* people were asking—Where's the show?

Then, to universal amazement, we beheld—drifting lazily down the canal—two red boots, a white shirt, a pair of dark trousers. They were followed by a boy dressed in a thick vest of what looked like russet-colored steel wool. He lay supine and motionless, his limbs outstretched, his perfectly calm face framed by the swirling mass of his hair. There were sixteen of his fellow volunteers to come. Though the clothes were soggy and a little blurred, one read them—as the current turned the page—like the hand-colored images in some mildewed yet marvelous old book. Poell's idea was so poetic that the magical buoyancy of bodies and clothes (kept from sinking by an invisible flotation device) leaped the banks and infected the audience with a fit of joy. It didn't matter, I thought, what the collection looked like on a hanger or in a shop, because the show had performed a feat that is rare enough in theater or art and practically unheard of in fashion. It surprised a group of people with an emotion they hadn't been expecting to feel. That is how a child experiences a sensual revelation, and how it is transformed into a memory of being happy. "Everybody follows fashion," Poell told me later. "But change goes against the stream."

—July 28, 2003

Roots

My father had a secretary named Barbara who kept his books and managed his life for twenty years. I don't think he knew much about her, except that she lived in Brooklyn with a diabetic sister and had a son in the army. The son was a decorated soldier whom I never met, though he figured in the violent arguments that I had with my father, in the late sixties, about his conviction that Kissinger's "domino theory" was a necessary evil, and mine that anyone who subscribed to it was a war criminal. Barbara had always processed her hair, which she wore in a pageboy, à la Coretta Scott King—a rigid helmet as highly polished as a walnut breakfront. Then one Monday, without warning, she came to work in an Afro. My father looked up from *The New York Times* and choked on his Danish. "For God's sake," he sputtered. "What did you do to yourself? You look like a Zulu!" To which she replied, "It's 1968, Bill, and that's the idea."

I was, in those days, still setting my own spongy curls on jumbo toilet-paper rolls in a futile effort to transform mohair into corn silk, and, reading *The Autobiography of Malcolm X*, I had been humbled to learn about the more extreme mortifications practiced by black people in order "to look 'pretty,' " as Malcolm puts it, "by white standards." In the early 1940s, he arrived in Boston to seek his fortune—a naïve young man from Lansing, Michigan, whose "kinky, reddish hair was cut hick style." To help him acquire the veneer of a hipster while saving a few bucks at the barbershop, a friend named

Shorty gave Malcolm a list of the ingredients and gear that they would need to cook up some homemade "congolene," then showed him how to do it.

"A jelly-like, starchy-looking glop," writes Alex Haley, to whom Malcolm X narrated his memoir, resulted from pouring half a can of Red Devil lye over two white potatoes, peeled and sliced. Shorty whipped in a couple of raw eggs, and the lye heated up the Mason jar they were using as a receptacle. He then coated Malcolm's scalp, neck, and ears with Vaseline, and worked the mixture through his hair. "My head caught fire," Malcolm recalled. "I gritted my teeth and tried to pull the sides of the kitchen table together. The comb felt as if it was raking my skin off." Even after the congolene was rinsed out, the fiery sensation persisted, but there had been a "staggering" transformation in Malcolm's appearance. He had a "thick, smooth sheen of shining red hair . . . as straight as any white man's." This initiation to conking—a backseat deflowering of sorts—persuaded Malcolm that if black people "gave the brains in their heads just half as much attention as they do their hair, they would be a thousand times better off."

One of the small ironies of black history is that the modest sums spent by millions of people on "dekinking" their hair represented a significant chunk of capital that stayed in the community and enriched its small entrepreneurs. Even before the Civil War, the hair business provided the single most important source of a middle-class income and a respectable life of relative ease for men and women who were once, or whose parents had been, slaves, and whose likeliest avenues of employment were manual labor and domestic service. The most spectacular of their success stories—and a lightning rod for the controversies about class, race, and identity that have historically dogged the enterprise of dressing black hair—is that of Sarah Breedlove, who became Madam C. J. Walker. Breedlove, according to *On Her Own Ground*, a biography by A'Lelia Bundles (the subject's great-great-granddaughter), was born in 1867 to a couple who sharecropped in Louisiana. Until she was in her late thirties, she earned her living as a laundress and cook in St. Louis. Her life was hard, her diet poor, her hygiene as sketchy as the plumbing, and her hair had begun falling out. A thicket of legend obscures this larval stage of Walker's self-invention, but she probably sought treatment from a well-known local aesthetician—Annie Pope-Turnbo—who had a substantial interstate business selling tonics and restorers, and who later employed Breedlove as a sales agent. Walker, however, preferred to claim that the formula that cured her baldness, and which contained, she said, secret ingredients imported from Africa, had come to her—after much prayer—in a dream.

As Breedlove's hair flourished, so did she. In 1906, she married her third husband, the flashy and charming C. J. Walker, and, about the same time, launched her own line of products. Whatever their provenance, and whether or not they really grew hair (glossy relaxed shafts seem longer than woolly ones, but she also addressed her clients' underlying scalp problems by prescribing more frequent shampooing, better nutrition, and massage), they did grow money. By the time of her death in 1919, Madam Walker was one of the richest and most admired African Americans in the country: a philanthropist, a crusader against lynching, and a marketing genius of world renown who laid the groundwork for transforming the cottage industry of black hair into what it has become—a multibillion-dollar business. She was also, later critics charged, a parvenue who wallowed in a life of wretched excess that she financed by catering to her customers' sense of racial inferiority.

Most beauty products and advertising—whoever their target—cater to a sense of insecurity, and to an enduring belief in miracles from a jar. The jars now contain ever more potent promises of transformation, as the old taboos against the hubris of trying to improve on nature are, like nature herself, everywhere on the defensive. We tamper casually with our bodies, our faces, our brain chemistry, and our metabolisms. Mass marketing of this vast cosmetic and genetic revolution is altering the notion of identity, and of where and in what it resides. The more appearance means, the less it signifies. Wrinkles no longer define age. Clothes no longer define class or gender. Hair no longer defines race, or not as dialectically as it used to, with blacks anxious to look whiter at one extreme and Malcolm X's austere contempt for anything but "God-created" hair at the other. African

American barbershops and hair salons are now hotbeds of anarchic and confident self-expression.

The free spirits of the hair world convened in January at the Los Angeles Airport Radisson Hotel to attend Hump the Grinder's Hair Wars 10-Year Anniversary & California Hair Grammys. Hump the Grinder is the stage name of David Humphries, who is also sometimes called "the Don King of black hair entertainment." We first met in 2002, at Deitch Projects, a SoHo gallery, where a few of his stylists were participating in—and stealing—a show of fashion as performance art. Their espaliers of hair were as fanciful as the topiary in a baroque garden or the headgear of Mardi Gras queens. (Here one should probably note that the world of black hair is not predominantly gay. Flamboyance, as Dennis Rodman liked to demonstrate somewhat pedantically with his tonsorial antics on the basketball court, can be a measure of conspicuous virility.) Humphries is a soft-spoken forty-seven-year-old former teacher and copywriter who wears his own grizzled locks conservatively cropped, and who is probably the last contestant you would pick out of a lineup as the impresario of an entertainment that features, among other novelties, hair shrubbery, helipads, spiderwebs, tires, and lingerie.

The idea for the spectacle that Hair Wars became occurred to Humphries in the 1980s, when he was working as a DJ in his native Detroit. "I used to give a lot of gimmick parties in the clubs," he told me. "Hair was really happening, and I thought, Let's get exotic with it. Detroit hair was always famous for its edge, probably because it's a predominantly black city, and people were more comfortable trying things that only high-school kids elsewhere had the nerve for." The popularity of the early performances emboldened him to "take the concept on the road" and to promote it like a rap tour.

The show, which travels to some ten cities a year, is primarily a runway extravaganza, but it's also a trade fair and a convention of hair designers. Performing stylists, who pay for the privilege, compete for what Humphries calls "bragging rights." Each headliner creates an extravagantly coiffed and costumed vaudeville skit, with song and dance, to showcase his or her virtuosity. These often inspired but sometimes cockamamie production numbers call to mind the artier experiments at a high-school science fair—homemade volcanoes, Rube Goldberg kitchen gadgets, and miniature ecosystems—but endowed with the sex appeal of a music video. The models are, in most cases, amateurs recruited from among the stylists' friends and staff, and many are refreshingly ultra-Venusian. Their diversity of shape makes that inhuman and homogeneous regularity of beauty from which there is no relief or appeal in mainstream magazines, or at the collections, seem insipid.

While I was waiting to check in at the Radisson, I noticed a figure ahead of me in line who, among the nondescript budget travelers clutching the hands of cranky toddlers, was as fabulous as some temple idol from ancient Nineveh. The outré splendor of his garb suggested that we were registering for the same event, and I mustered the courage to introduce myself. He was Big Bad D—the sponsor of Hair Wars—a forty-two-year-old, three-hundred-pound, six-foot-four hairstylist, bodybuilder, salon owner, magazine publisher (of a new periodical entitled *Bobby Pin*), and billboard star. He is also the CEO of BBD Products—a company that manufactures expensive hair-growth enhancers. D considers his hair, as many African and Rastafarian men also do, a talisman of his power, so he never cuts it. A thick fascicle of dreadlocks sheathed in wax thread is slung rakishly over his right shoulder and spliced to an equally long but spindlier cable of beard. (The logistics of dressing and safely performing other activities of a strenuous or intimate nature with head and chin umbilically attached are, he admits, sometimes challenging.)

That afternoon, D was dressed in an ensemble worthy of Galliano: a pair of high-waisted patchwork leather samurai pants evocative in pizzazz and volume of a Montgolfier; a red T-shirt inlaid with gold and gems that was slashed to display his awesome pectorals; a belt of scarified alligator skin, with claws still attached, from which hung a pouch containing, he said, freeze-dried gator meat; a rawhide "coolie" hat adorned with stones, pods, and shells; and some $50,000 worth of diamonds, including a bracelet of hazelnut-size beads and a ring, about four inches wide, shaped like a pair of scissors. "I've stopped counting carats," he told me with the offhand shrug of a gourmand who has thrown out his bathroom scale. "I design my own jewelry and clothes, and my style is a blend of Asian and African, but it's mostly inspired by Conan"—the Barbarian. D's priestly gravity of manner belies his mad maximalism of dress, and there is something about him of the discreet coupé in an action film that suddenly revs up and speeds off, morphing into a silvery hot rod bristling with lethal accessories.

The hair business has been lucrative for D, and he owns a mansion on eleven acres in Detroit and an estate in Jamaica. "My typical customer spends about $350 a month on treatments and styling," he told me. "That's probably as much as on her car payments. We do a lot more to our hair than the average Caucasian. African American hair care is a $5 billion-a-year industry, and we outspend whites by about three to one. It used to be that the products were manufactured by black-owned companies, but almost all of them have been bought up by the big conglomerates, or undersold by them and forced out of business. Mine is an exception."

D's underdog tenacity in the business world suits him for his role as the patron of a show that, if only because of the concentrated talent and enterprise that it represents, has become an important ethnic-pride event. Most of the participants are too young to remember, or were not born yet, when "Black Is Beautiful" was a radical slogan. They take it, if not for granted, then as a self-evident truth. But the show's regal MC, LaToya Pearson (a prizewinning stylist now retired from salon work), has a long memory. Pearson is a churchgoing grandmother of sixty-two whose high cheekbones, strong chin, and blond wig give her a faint resemblance, at least from the neck up, to Cher. "I have a gift," she notes, for "extemporaneous public speaking," and her commentary mixes a little "tasteful" rap and discreet promotion with "lots of appreciation" for the performers, though she won't tolerate "lewdness or profanity." Pearson's father was a black Jew, and she learned her trade in "a multicultural setting, doing everything from the bubble, the beehive, the gypsy curl, and the Farrah Fawcett flip" to her trophy-winning "Moonlanding" coif (an electrified globe of hair pocked with the craters of a lunar landscape and skewered by a silver rocket).

Having come this far, Pearson would like to see the domain of black hair reviewed less exclusively from a "politically correct" perspective. Styling, in her view, is an art, "like portraiture," that channels emotion and celebrates individuality. "When I was young, it wasn't just nappy hair that was unacceptable," she recalls. "Color out of a bottle was for 'loose' women, and I would have caught heck from my pastor for looking as I do today. Braids on adults were even more controversial. Now, of course, they're everywhere—on people of all ages and races, and you have to believe that's progress."

In their suppleness, braids are, perhaps, an emblem of the changes that have taken place since the sixties in attitudes not only toward black hair but toward the potential for mobility in every sphere. There are almost no limits on what you can do with them or what they can mean. The braids of an old-fashioned schoolgirl were accessories of her nubile virtue, but braids are also symbols of strength (sinews are a form of plait)—even of ferocity. It is not a coincidence that military uniforms are decorated with braid, or the heads of NBA stars with cornrows. In Africa, as among Africans of the diaspora, braiding pays homage, intentionally or not, to ideals of valor and fertility, and to patterns probably as ancient as the first woven textiles and works of art. Braiding is also, as D observed, a "huge profitmaker" for the black-hair business—"about 30 percent of it"—in part because the process is so labor-intensive and, in other parts, because elaborate styles often involve costly weaves; braids stress the scalp and hair shafts, so they require a battery of conditioners; and, like jeans, they are a genderless fashion staple that never seems tired or prosaic.

Nina Ann Garner, the owner of Hair Underground, is a specialist in weaves and individual dreads (which resemble tiny chenille caterpillars), and Tsega Tesfamariam is a braider admired for her finesse and speed. On the afternoon of the show, they were at work in their hotel room on a crew of male, female, and child models. Tesfamariam is only twenty-two and has been braiding hair professionally since she was eight. She learned the art from her grandmother in their native

Eritrea. Cornrows, she explained, are tightly plaited kernels of short hair that hug the contours of the scalp. Microbraids have the fluidity of willow branches or the cascades of fine jets from a fountain. Like the more leonine or pharaonic styles (and one often sees working women on the subway or shoppers at the supermarket whose hairdos are identical to those in Sumerian bas-reliefs), they are often achieved with extensions, which is to say, help from someone else's head.

The demand for high-quality human hair has revived a trade that flourished for centuries: girls and women, now mostly in Asia, selling their crowning glories for the price of a trousseau, a vacation, dental work, school fees, or a VCR. Tesfamariam's dexterity is prodigious. She wields a rattail comb with mechanical rapidity, separating the hair into sections no thicker than a feather of eyelash. In about an hour, she had embellished the shapely crown of a swanlike maiden with an intricate fretwork of flawlessly symmetrical black starbursts.

Hair Wars is still a fringe happening—covered sporadically on local television, or on programs like *The Ricki Lake Show*—and there were no paparazzi, red carpet, or Joan Rivers in the lobby of the Radisson to hype the Grammys and greet the stars, among them the belles of Hair Erotica; Mike-Mike & Baby Boy, from Head Bangers; Giorgi-O, of Beverly Hills; the L.A. Braid Queen; Von Jour Reece; Dontae Dupree, of Hair Traffic Control; Infamous Lisa B.; the magisterial Kevin Carter, celebrated for his elegant spider women and hair flowers; and Steven Noss, who bills himself as "Tha Baddest Whyte Boy in Tha Hair Business" (he is the only white boy in Hair Wars). Noss, who hails from Pittsburgh, is the engineer of a crowd-pleasing "hairy copter" that takes off from a deck of braids. Like Lisa B., he specializes in faintly surreal "hair couture," which has nothing in common with the macabre ornaments, tatted from the tresses of a defunct loved one, that Victorians once hung in their drawing rooms. His collection of bras, miniskirts, and ruffled gowns is inspired, he says, "by Barbie and Bob Mackie." One might describe them as hair shirts for the terminally unrepentant.

The coach in Humphries prides himself on discipline and punctuality, so the show started, as scheduled, at five past six, the first acts playing to a semi-deserted ballroom. D was impassively resplendent in a crimson-and-gold kimono. A camera crew directed by the film-maker Regina Kimbell was shooting footage for a documentary enti-tled *My Nappy Roots: A Journey Through Our Hair-itage*, and after the Grammys were presented by Ms. Color-Me-Vic, a stylist from Columbus, Ohio, whose rainbow-tinted poodle cut and three-inch fingernails have been televised on *Ripley's Believe It or Not!*, I met Kimbell backstage. The hair industry, in her view, is rallying African Americans to shake off the fetters of their subservience to un-attainable ideals of Caucasian beauty. It is, she says, "the business of liberation."

When the hot buffet materialized, so did the audience. Of a thou-sand people or so, no one I noticed (except Humphries) wore a nat-ural. Both off and on the runway, there were wavy weaves; feather cuts; lightning-bolt bangs; punky spikes; ponytails; twists; dreads; knots; bristles; corkscrew curls; crimping; radical asymmetry; exotic color (hot pink and blue); an assortment of pinecone- and ziggurat-shaped finials; and heads on which neat cornrows exploded into fan-tails of frizz, like a terrace of cultivated paddies ringed by a forest of bamboo. But one of the most popular fashions was a thick, smooth sheen of shining red hair—bone straight, like Malcolm's.

—March 15, 2004

VI

THE QUEEN
HIMSELF

・ ONE ・

Éminence Rose

I spent my summer vacation reading four biographies of Mme. de Pompadour in a row. When a subject is ineffably delicious and none too wholesome, *l'appétit vient en mangeant,* and my appetite for the Marquise increased the more I read. She seems to have had the same effect on her lover, Louis XV, and on her young husband, the royally cuckolded M. d'Étioles. He fainted when he was told that he had lost her, along with his honor and his hopes for an heir. Louis's *droit du seigneur* was beyond appeal, and the adulteress was madly in love. D'Étioles retired with dignity and consoled himself like a gentleman—with a chorus girl from the opera.

Pompadour's life (1721–64) is minutely documented by gloriously literate and astute contemporary sources (the eighteenth century does not seem to have generated another kind), including her own correspondence and the journal of her lady-in-waiting, Mme. du Hausset. Her most recent biographers have had the tact to make themselves relatively inconspicuous, though each has a virtue and a weakness that color his or her version of the same events. Colin Jones, a professor of French history, is the author of *Madame de Pompadour: Images of a Mistress* (Yale, 2001), the companion volume to an exhibition of that name opening at the National Gallery in London. His forte is iconography (or what he calls his subject's "image management"), and he assesses her character from the vantage point of her role—inflated by posterity, he believes—as a tastemaker and a patron of painting, architecture, sculpture, and design who, he writes, "presided over a period which was, it has been argued, 'a moment of perfection in French art.' " But Jones's work is more than an erudite tour of the Marquise's private collections; it offers a commanding, indeed lofty, overview of her times. He admires Pompadour's magisterial self-invention, but deplores her grandiosity, womanish myopia, and bulimic shopping. The brisk authority of his style is, like his judgment, dry almost to the point of impatience, and at times he seems like the bishop at an orgy: embarrassed to be associated with so much obscene frivolity.

Evelyne Lever's *Madame de Pompadour: A Life*, translated from the French by Catherine Temerson (Farrar, Straus and Giroux, 2002), and Christine Pevitt Algrant's *Madame de Pompadour: Mistress of France* (Grove, 2002) are compact, sympathetic lives aimed at an intelligent popular readership. Lever's portrait is more revealing of the intimate life. Algrant is the subtler political historian. Both write engagingly, and neither feels obliged, as Jones does, to introduce any lugubrious references to "hegemony" or "gender politics." But they also left me with the question I have always asked myself about that other royal horse-whisperer, the Duchess of Windsor. What on earth did Pompadour know about men and sex (or was it image management?) that gave her such power to enthrall?

Working downward on the scale of objectivity and upward in literary distinction, I came, at last, to Nancy Mitford's passionately partial *Madame de Pompadour*, published in 1954. Mitford rather blithely overlooks the fact that Pompadour was monstrously vain and Louis a tragic blunderer, but she has a decided advantage as their biographer. She is herself a consummate woman of the world and, more precisely, a connoisseur of snobbery in all its nuances. It may also help to have been, as Mitford was, the long-suffering mistress of an aristocratic and unfaithful French politician. In her first few pages, which are devoted to Louis's childhood sufferings, she settled my question about Pompadour's secret.

The king was orphaned at the age of two, in 1712, when in one traumatic fortnight he lost his entire family—parents and siblings—to a violent contagion, though their deaths were hastened by the court physician, Dr. Fagon: "killer of Princes," as Mitford calls him. Louis escaped the same fate only because his governess, the redoubtable

Duchesse de Ventadour, refused to hand him over for treatment and hid him away. The Duc d'Orléans, his regent, and Cardinal Dubois, his prime minister, let *maman de Ventadour* assuage his terrors and indulge him without measure until the age of seven, when he was pried screaming from her arms, confided to his tutors, and dressed in the ceremonial hair shirt of his exaltation. He had inherited the throne two years earlier, upon the death of his great-grandfather Louis XIV. The first years of his reign were happy for France, and the people loved him, but even when they ceased to—blaming Pompadour for his gross neglect of their welfare—it was not because he had become a despot. Louis was a sovereign without a mind of his own, who, as the Comte d'Argenson put it, "adopted a jargon of feelings, a jargon of political arguments, composed of different comments that he has heard from other people, without the slightest inclusion of common sense . . . or even comprehension." It was a recipe for becoming putty in a woman's hands.

The orphan grew into a fitfully depressive man in chronic need of distraction from his torments. Pompadour alone could always lift his spirits, and she devoted her life to reenacting his first dramatic rescue. They were perpetually in flight. Much of her energy and a good portion of the kingdom's taxes were spent on the buying or building and doing up (with an architect of genius, Gabriel) what, in essence, was a relay of safe houses: sublimely refined châteaus and hermitages where the strict protocol of the palace didn't apply. At Crécy, Bellevue, and Ménars, or in the privacy of the "*petits appartements*" at Versailles, they were screened (though never opaquely) from the critical scrutiny of ten thousand eyes. Louis even liked to make their after-dinner coffee.

His ultimate hiding place, however, was Pompadour's love, an alloy of the slavish and the steely. The royal children expressed its nature perhaps better than they knew when they dubbed the favorite Mommy Whore.

If Hillary Clinton had held every cabinet position in her husband's administration and controlled every appointment, her influence might have approximated Pompadour's at the height of her power. She was instrumental in framing domestic and cultural policy; she promoted French craftsmanship and valor (the porcelain factory at Sèvres and the École Militaire were among her pet projects); the Paris police and postal chiefs were on her payroll, so she vetted all the most pertinent (and impertinent) mail. She held court enthroned at her dressing table in a boudoir hung with mythologized likenesses of her, and Princes of the Blood and grizzled warriors descended from Charlemagne stood humbly beside the ambassadors of foreign majesties as she applied her rouge and, just as profligately, dispensed her patronage. Though Louis kept some secrets from her, and occasionally ignored her advice, there was virtually no high commission, ministerial portfolio, alliance, diplomatic post, important public-works project, royal favor, invitation, or marriage contract authorized against the will of the Marquise. She sent battle plans to French generals at the front, enclosing maps that she had marked coquettishly with her beauty spots. "You will admit later," she told the Duc d'Aiguillon, who was fending off a British invasion of Brittany, "that I am insufferable in always being right." But the insufferable offense was that she wasn't. It was Pompadour who engineered the reversal of alliances in the mid-1750s that embroiled France in that wretched conflict the Seven Years' War.

Pompadour's trajectory is nearly as improbable as Napoleon's. She was born Jeanne-Antoinette Poisson into an obscure and dubiously respectable middle-class Parisian family, albeit one with grand connections. Her father, François Poisson, a widower of humble origins, was in his mid-forties when he married a dark-haired and "devilishly" lovely young woman from the same milieu. He had made his fortune in the service of the Pâris brothers, shadowy financiers who had accumulated fabulous wealth and insidiously pervasive influence through loans to the crown and contracts to provision the army. (In time of war, which was a lot of the time, their network was so indispensable that they virtually ran the country.)

Poisson traveled frequently in their employ, and he seems to have done some of their dirty work. In his absence, and particularly during a period when he lived abroad to avoid a prison sentence for speculating on wheat during a famine, Mme. Poisson is said to have amused herself disreputably. The paternity of Jeanne-Antoinette has long been debated. She bears a strong resemblance, if not in looks, in force of character, to her godfather, Jean Pâris, who was known as Pâris de Montmartel, but her biographers also point to the attentions that another august family protector, the *fermier-général* (tax collector) Charles-François Lenormand de Tournehem, lavished upon her and her mother. Pompadour's contemporaries found it difficult to believe that she could be the daughter of a vulgar nobody like Poisson. Yet the family name and its quick-to-rot, up-from-the-slime associations would be a boon to her enemies—authors of malicious ditties known as *poissonades*.

The little girl, however, had nothing but rapt devotees. This radiant child performer of almost Mozartian poise and precocity enchanted everyone who met her, beginning with the Ursuline nuns at the convent in Poissy where she boarded until she was brought home at the age of eight. Tournehem, a childless widower a decade younger than Poisson, was the uncle of poor d'Étioles. He paid for Jeanne-Antoinette's deluxe education, arranged her marriage, settled a fortune upon the balky groom (delightful as she was, Poisson's daughter was beneath him, though the warmth of felicity soon evaporated his reluctance), and sponsored the entrance of his "niece" into society. In the early 1740s, the delectable young matron was taken up by Mme. Geoffrin and Mme. de Tencin, and she became an ornament of their salons, where the Encyclopedists were practicing their marksmanship for the skirmishes of the Enlightenment. One of Mme. d'Étioles's fellow habitués, who became a lifelong friend, mentor, gadfly, eulogist, and sometime protégé, was Voltaire. Though his judgment may have been clouded by infatuation, he praised her for having "a mind full of refinement and a heart full of justice." He also couldn't get over how many books she had read.

When Jeanne-Antoinette was nine, her mother took her to the famous fortune-teller Mme. Lebon, who predicted that she would become the king's mistress. In 1730, Louis XV was not only a virtual divinity of absolute temporal power but a dazzlingly handsome Prince Charming of twenty. It is easy to imagine that a young girl might dream idly of being loved by him (it is easy to imagine that an entire kingdom of smitten maidens nurtured such a fantasy), though he had been married at fifteen to a homely Polish princess and was, briefly, like so many of the Bourbons, an uxorious husband. But

Mme. Poisson encouraged her precious Reinette (Queenie) to dream on. Having been reclaimed from the pious tutelage of the nuns, she was henceforth groomed, like her latter-day avatar, Gigi, with all the resources at the family's collective disposal—which were as mighty as their lack of scruples—to be, as Tournehem put it, "*un morceau de roi*" (a morsel fit for a king).

Among Pompadour's many gifts was a genius for ingratiation. She was one of those girls and women who are a pleasure to spoil. They have never, in their lives, ever had a better time or a more special treat than the one you are giving them. Such a talent tarnishes quickly without a conscientious effort to keep it bright. Pompadour was rarely ungrateful—she never disowned her embarrassing family—and she prized fidelity (to herself and the king) above all other virtues and rewarded it opulently. This criterion for state service tends to produce mediocrity and stagnation when applied exclusively, since the faithful are not, history suggests, always the wise.

Marie Leczinska, the queen of France, was seven years older than her husband, and in 1745, when Louis met Mme. d'Étioles, she was a frumpy old lady of forty-two and the mother of seven children—six hard-to-marry princesses and one priggish dauphin. She had done her duty and now turned her attention to prayer, games of *cavagnole*—she was an unlucky gambler—and charitable works. Louis's valets, one of whom was reported to have been the paramour of Mme. Poisson, often served as his procurers, and the king liked slumming with them in disguise. But, being a devout hierarch, he had, like his forebears, always chosen his official mistresses from the *noblesse d'épée*. He was now in the market for a new favorite, and every faction at court had its candidate. Speculation was high. No one, except perhaps she herself and her pit crew, considered Mme. d'Étioles, with her spotty pedigree, even a remote long shot. Her reputation as "the prettiest woman in Paris" had, however, been touted intriguingly in court circles, and the royal hunt sometimes passed through the Sénart forest, near her château at Étioles. There she stationed herself in the king's path, "and either she wore a light blue dress and rode in a pink phaeton," Lever tells us, "or she wore a pink dress and rode in a blue carriage." Note was taken.

Jeanne-Antoinette had no intention of becoming one of the sovereign's *passades*. Her chance at "the big niche," as she put it, came at a masked ball that was given at Versailles in honor of the marriage of the dauphin to a Spanish princess—an open house to which anyone properly dressed was invited. (Guests arriving without a sword could rent one from the footmen.) Like many celebrities, the king sometimes went to comic lengths to preserve his anonymity in a crowd. This time, his ruse was so fanciful that it inspired a number of engravings. He and his gentlemen were rigged up as a hedge of yew trees clipped like the topiaries in the garden. One of the yews went off with a lissome Diana, and later, with masks removed, His Majesty and Mme. d'Étioles were seen flirting strenuously. In the weeks to come, her carriage was constantly on the road to or from Versailles. Tournehem sent the husband on a business trip to Provence.

One should probably mention that in 1745 France was at war with Austria, the Netherlands, and England, to no great profit for the people, who were, as usual, being bled to death for the sake of a county here, a border there, part of a colony, an ancient quarrel, a stupid promise, or a pleasant sinecure for the eldest of Louis's daughters, Mme. Infante, who was bored at the Spanish court of her in-laws and begged Papa to help make her Duchess of Parma. Having picked a new mistress off the rack, Louis left her with his tailors for some adjustment, and went off, in high spirits, to the front. Mme. d'Étioles now retired to her estate to prepare for her presentation at court. Voltaire was one of the Pygmalions who helped prep her for Versailles, along with the seasoned Abbé de Bernis, who advised her always to "protect writers," which she tried to do until they proved too subversive. (Bernis served in high positions and as her counselor and close friend until 1758, when, judging his lucidity to have curdled into "defeatism," she arranged for his banishment.)

Louis's love letters, which arrived almost daily, were sealed with a cachet that bore the motto "Discretion and Fidelity." One of them contained the *lettres de noblesse* for the extinct marquisate of Pompadour. It came with an escutcheon, a château, and lands for which Pâris de Montmartel picked up the check (and certainly deducted it). The new Marquise was a quick study for any part, and over the summer she relearned how to walk and talk, this time like a great lady, and she mastered the esoteric codes that governed the life of every palace inmate, but especially the monarch. He was, Jones notes, "inordinately proud" of her transformation. Mitford, however, claims that the Marquise "hardly bothered" to change her bourgeois ways, always expressed herself with uncourtly frankness in a loud voice, laughed freely, and "gave herself no airs." Louis was charmed by some of her locutions. In any case, on the day of her presentation to a hostile court prepared to annihilate her with ridicule, she was perfection itself.

One almost has the feeling about Pompadour that some consortium of fairies decided, on a bet or whim, to create an ideal feminine specimen as their plaything, investing a human doll with their own attributes for the purpose of seeing how far that endowment would take her in the world, and what she would do with it. Like all great sirens, she sang hauntingly, and, in her tireless effort to keep Louis amused and besotted, she organized a repertory company that gave amateur theatricals of professional quality in the several private theaters she had constructed—each a jewel box. For the five years this enterprise was in operation, the favorite starred in and directed a hundred and twenty-two performances of sixty-one different operas, plays, and ballets, outclassing, it was said, some of the leading lights of the Comédie-Française. (Courtiers, Mitford writes, "became perfectly hysterical" in their efforts to get a walk-on role, or even simply a ticket.) Onstage, at least, the Marquise was working from a script. In daily life, her survival depended on the virtuosity of her improvisations.

Yet perhaps because perversity is the hallmark of gods everywhere, Pompadour's good fairies overlooked a few basics. She had a fragile constitution, suffering from chronic migraines, lung ailments, and a vaginal discharge recorded for posterity in a malicious quatrain disseminated by the evil Comte de Maurepas. She died at forty-two, probably of congestive heart failure, but also worn out by her hummingbird's existence. Oddly, too, for someone in her line of work, she often lamented that Louis found her, despite her best exertions, "cold and passive," although her frigidity didn't chill his ardor. He had made her his *maîtresse en titre* in defiance of protocol, and he would continue to promote her as he pleased. That was the adolescent aspect of their, and perhaps of every, enduring romance: it was the two of them against the world. For nearly twenty years, until her death, in the second-best bedroom at Versailles, Pompadour reigned as the virtual queen of France—and, perhaps one could say, its first meritocratically appointed civil servant. She had outscored her rivals on the written, oral, and physical parts of a grueling exam that was re-administered every day of her life.

I suspect that, like the most artful of Rasputins, Pompadour dosed Louis with just enough unconditional maternal comforting and just enough well-sweetened guilt to induce in him a permanent semi-coma of habit and dependence and to check his omnipotence and wrath. Then, when she needed him to throw the lightning bolts of his displeasure or shed the rays of his bounty for her benefit, she would supply the antidote of her adoration. She worked her will on him—greatly to her own glory, of course—but also sometimes to oblige other deserving parties, such as the *philosophes*, her "clients" at court, or his wife. The rightful queen was surprisingly tolerant of her new rival, and the royal mistress reciprocated with a touching and politic deference to Her Majesty. Early in their liaison, the favorite got the king to pay off the queen's gambling debts, redecorate her shabby apartments, and present her with a gold snuffbox (originally commissioned, however, for Mme. Poisson). She also eventually suggested that her own position would be morally enhanced (it never was) if the queen accepted her as a lady-in-waiting—an honor reserved for the most irreproachable duchesses. A ducal upgrade facilitated the affair, though Pompadour, with well-bred *pudeur*, never adopted the grander of her titles. She possessed the most endearing weakness of the arriviste, a desire to please, and when she made a show of groveling she always did so with impressive natural dignity. More endearing still, she had the tact to miscarry every bastard the two sinners conceived.

No royal mistress in the minutely calibrated hierarchy of the ancien régime could ever be the queen's equal, but this one made herself the king's master. Even as she lost her ravishing looks and Louis satisfied his lusts elsewhere, Pompadour consolidated her prestige. It was she, not the king, who was supposed to have said, using the royal and/or conjugal we, *"après nous, le déluge"* (though it is doubtful that Pompadour said any such thing—she was too congenital an optimist). But in her lifetime nothing could dethrone her: not the nymphets of the Parc-aux-Cerfs, Louis's private brothel; or the shifting palace cabals that were ceaselessly intriguing against her; or the vehement hostility of a populace that blamed her extravagance, plausibly, for its crushing taxes and starvation; or a clergy that saw her as the devil's handmaid for whose sake the Very Christian King had forsaken Communion and his family; or even the debacle of an abject military defeat in the Seven Years' War, for which she and her ill-chosen champions and silly maps were a good deal to blame. Except for Bonaparte, and perhaps Robespierre, whose tenures were briefer, and de Gaulle, who was in principle answerable to an electorate, no French commoner—and certainly no woman—ever achieved such imperial sway. But what did she achieve with it?

"The marquise had none of the great vices of ambitious women," the Abbé de Bernis wrote, "but she had all the pettiness and unreliability of women intoxicated with their looks and their self-proclaimed intelligence." Diderot's postmortem was more severe:

> So what remains of this woman who cost us so much in men and money, left us without honor and without energy, and who overthrew the whole political system of Europe? The Treaty of Versailles which will last as long as it lasts; Bouchardon's *Amour* which will be admired forever; a few stones engraved by Guay which will amaze the antiquaries of the future; a nice little picture by van Loo which people will look at sometimes, and a handful of dust.

Had she only served France as well as she loved Louis, it might yet be a Bourbon monarchy. What she left, besides a staggering inventory of choice possessions that took a team of notaries a year to appraise, is a mystery still worthy of contemplation: Did Pompadour fulfill a great destiny or betray one?

—October 7, 2002

TWO

The Candidate's Wife

The child of nature was a creature invented by the Romantics, whose cult of authenticity informed the literature of the next two hundred years. His direct descendant is the protagonist of countless modern films and novels: the prisoner of a false self revolting against the artifice of conventional narrative. On the face of it, Teresa Heinz Kerry makes an unlikely rebel. She is a sixty-five-year-old Catholic billionaire, born into the colonial society of Mozambique, whose tastes, pieties, and hobbies—cultivating roses and collecting still lifes—are those of a traditional, if not Victorian, lady. But when she calls herself "a child of Africa," one can hear an echo of Rousseau, and it reverberates in the impulsive salvos (playful, caustic, or profane) for which she has been ridiculed as "bonkers" and "a loose cannon." The natural woman refuses to suppress her élan or subordinate her character to a role. "I don't want to lose myself," she said to me recently, "because if I do, then I think my husband loses something, too."

Three years ago, when John Kerry was discussing a potential presidential race with a small circle of advisers, his wife "blessed his decision and accepted it as a partner," a member of the group recalled. "She said she knew what was involved, but, to be fair, no one does, and any thinking human being would have qualms. She certainly made it clear that she would be her own person, and we wondered if she was going to be perceived as a breath of fresh air or as a threat; if her straight speaking would motivate voters—women in particular—

or if we were going to spend the campaign watching our back, tensed for a blowup. We called it the Teresa factor."

The role of first lady is, in many respects, as archaically courtly as the title, and history suggests that a woman who plays it may be forgiven for weaknesses perceived as feminine—Betty Ford's depression, Jackie Kennedy's extravagance, Pat Nixon's fragility, Nancy Reagan's faith in astrology—but not for strengths perceived as manly. In a deeply pious country founded by Puritans, the spouse of a president is also, to some extent, the minister's wife. She commands sympathy and reverence only so long as her conduct is irreproachable or her husband's isn't. Though she is not ritually invested with the sins, evils, or ill luck of the tribe, she is nevertheless a scapegoat of sorts— a propitiatory figure saddled with the culture's burdensome ideals of wifely and maternal virtue.

Heinz Kerry has made a feminist issue of her entitlement to express herself, and if she were a man, she says, no one would denigrate her as "opinionated." She lectures knowledgeably on the inequities that confront women in the workplace and champions the excluded and discounted women of the Third World. One of the lucky charms that she wears on a necklace (another is a four-leaf clover that Kerry gave her one Valentine's Day) is a religious medal that her dying mother received from her confessor. He got it from Mother Teresa, who embodies the vocation for which Heinz Kerry would best like to be known—tireless caregiving. Her father, a Portuguese-born oncologist, had hoped that she would become a doctor, "and she kind of wanted to," a close friend, Wren Wirth, the wife of Tim Wirth, a former Democratic senator from Colorado, says, "though she wanted to get married and have children even more." At the height of the women's movement in the 1970s, she was the stay-at-home mother of three little boys for whom, she says, she washed cloth diapers. She calls herself "a spokesman for women's ability to be at the center of the family."

But Heinz Kerry intends to be the first spouse of a president employed outside the White House (Hillary Clinton gave up her legal career when her husband was elected), and though she performs her share of the expected campaign chores—reading to toddlers and laying wreaths—some of her speeches and seminars on the hustings would not be out of place at Davos. They have focused less on John Kerry's legislative achievements, human qualities, or political agenda than on her own eventful biography and the work of the Heinz Endowments, a charitable enterprise seeded by the family fortune of her first husband, H. John Heinz III, a Republican senator from Pennsylvania.

Many of the voters who come out to meet Heinz Kerry are middle-aged workingwomen, chafing at constraints they have outgrown, and they applaud her defiance in breaking the mold of first lady–like self-effacement. (Breaking molds is otherwise known as iconoclasm.) Kerry himself admires his wife's intellect and independence, he told me, and he seems to accept stoically, if not with relish, that she is "saucy." Even if he doesn't, "he wasn't blind," she says. "He knew what I would be like, what he was getting."

Nevertheless, recent approval ratings for the infallibly sunny and conventional Laura Bush, who is her husband's greatest booster, are vastly superior to Heinz Kerry's (72 percent, according to a poll taken by the Los Angeles *Times*, to 35 percent). Even many Democrats admire Mrs. Bush. Americans in large numbers, regardless of their party, tell pollsters that they don't vote for a first lady and that their opinions of Laura or Teresa won't influence their decision on Election Day, but the two wives have a significant influence on voters' perceptions of the candidates. Kerry's image is still sorely deficient in the warmth and human definition that Heinz Kerry herself possesses and might lend him. The adviser involved in Kerry's early strategy meetings told me that he is surprised by her reluctance "to trim the sails" of what he and others describe as a "self-referential" presentation that has often dwelled, at inopportune moments, on her memories of Heinz and on his legacy. "She made some stirring and lovely speeches, particularly during the primaries, when you thought, Goddamn right, Teresa!" he said. But her habit of running on private rails rather than on the main line has dissipated some steam from the campaign. "It isn't as if there have been no specific conversations with Teresa about the necessity to fill in the picture," the adviser said. "John had a few himself, but he would ask others to convey the message." Perhaps, he reflected, she tends to reject criticism imperiously "because she's used to tremendous deference. When you have so much money, and give so much away, everyone, from governors on down, courts your approval. I think she sometimes has problems with a secondary role."

On the campaign trail with Heinz Kerry, I occasionally closed my eyes and concentrated on her diction and accent. She pronounces folksy locutions with upper-class British vowels, sultry Portuguese "s"s, and pizzicato "t"s. Her repartee is quick, with a Gallic tartness. Backstage at a fund-raiser in New York, she bantered with her son Andre, who recently moved to Pittsburgh from Stockholm, in perfect French and the convincing Swedish of a Bergman spoof. The Hispanic press in South Florida was disappointed last spring that she declined to be interviewed in Spanish, which she speaks fluently, though with the occasional Italian verb. She explained that it would take three weeks to get her vocabulary up to speed for a serious policy discussion, but that she would be happy to oblige the reporters with a little "chitchat."

Despite her linguistic prowess and her worldliness, Heinz Kerry has, at times, a deaf ear for the nuances of slang, code, condescension, and vulgarity in English—for the emotion of the language. "There are these bizarre moments that make you shudder," the Kerry adviser said. "Like calling herself African American to black audiences." She dismissed voters skeptical of her husband's health-care proposals as "idiots," and, in a television interview with a Pittsburgh anchorwoman, employed the word "scumbags" to describe some of her detractors. I doubt that she knows the literal meaning of "scumbag," but perhaps, after forty years in America, nearly thirty of them as a political wife, observing how the flaws and contradictions of a personality as complex as hers are melted down for ammunition by the other side, she should have learned it. Close friends attribute her lapses of discretion to "naïveté." Heinz Kerry says that they are a form of resistance to enforced conformity. "I don't like to be told, for told's sake," how to behave, she says, "because I lived in a dictatorship for too long."

During Heinz Kerry's childhood, Mozambique—a colony of Portugal for some four hundred years—was ruled by the Fascist government of António Salazar. She hasn't been back to Mozambique since April of 1974, when she was thirty-five and married to John Heinz. It has changed too drastically, she says, and she is afraid the experience would be distressing. On that visit, she took her three sons to see their grandparents. Christopher, the baby, was a year old, and his brothers, Andre and John, were four and seven. The family was scheduled to return to the United States on April 25, but the borders were closed and the airport shut down. That day, Salazar's heir, Marcelo Caetano, had been ousted in a bloodless military coup. Its leaders were a cadre of young army officers, many of whom had fought in their country's African wars and returned home—like some of their American contemporaries in Vietnam—radicalized by the destruction they had helped wreak. They pledged free elections, the restoration of civil liberties, and an end to colonialism.

When the news from Lisbon reached Lourenço Marques, the capital of Mozambique, stunned and ecstatic people took to the streets. Teresa Heinz and her father attended the first open meeting of FRELIMO (Frente da Libertação de Moçambique), which had been waging a guerrilla war of liberation for more than ten years, and they joined the vast throng of celebrants marching through the "cement town." (The expression, which refers to the European enclaves in Mozambique's urban centers, alludes to their solidity rather than to their ugliness. Most Africans lived in wretched shanties on the outskirts, which were known as "cane towns.") The parade took her up and down familiar, still-well-kept avenues lined with jacaranda trees dripping pale blossoms, past the Museum of Natural History, next door to which her grandmother had lived, and past the colonial villa on the cliffs overlooking the Indian Ocean where she and her siblings grew up.

In the early months of Kerry's campaign, Heinz Kerry rarely gave a speech or an interview that wasn't redolent with nostalgia for the sensations of her childhood (the steamy vibrance of New Orleans reminded her of home, she said, as did the palm trees and tile roofs of Florida and the earthiness of Pittsburgh), and she continues to invoke what she sees as Africa's lessons about nature, race, freedom, dependence, and survival. When she urges Americans to exercise their right to vote, she likes to observe that her father was seventy-one when he cast his ballot in a free election for the first time.

Heinz Kerry's father moved back to Portugal with his wife after the Socialist regime of Samora Machel came to power in Mozambique, in 1975, and the country became independent. Machel nationalized private property. "My father wanted to die there," she told me with bitterness. "He didn't come to make money to take back to Portugal. He had nothing in Portugal." But, as crime rose and the economy crumbled, white nationalists who had supported FRELIMO felt, she said, increasingly embattled and marginalized. "The Portuguese colonials were not bad people compared to the crooks who took over," she told a reporter in Fort Lauderdale last March, and added that she could empathize with the Cuban exile community in South Florida because her parents had also "lost everything to the Communists."

Heinz Kerry was in Fort Lauderdale to address a group of women supporters at a luxurious faux hacienda on the intercoastal waterway. It was a hot morning, and on the opposite bank, workmen building a new mansion had taken their shirts off and were gawking and gesturing, none too politely, at the ladies milling on the terrace and in the garden. Some members of the construction crew had evidently gone to the trouble of lowering a scaffold from which to spray a graffito, about ten feet high, in red paint, on the side of the bulkhead: LIBERALS RUIN U.S.A.

The guest of honor arrived late, as she tends to. Her staff tries to keep her to a tight schedule, but she says that she's "too old to be bossed around." As a speaker, she often gives more of herself than she is asked for, lingering in reception lines and becoming absorbed in an anecdote or the answer to a question. She speaks in an intent, unhurried fashion, and without notes. Her facts are hard and her command of them impressive, though her tone is whispery and caressing. Heinz Kerry describes herself as shy, and in the early months of the campaign she often hid in the corner of a stage, blushed at an introduction, covered her face, or did an awkward little pirouette of embarrassment before grabbing a mike with both hands and ad-libbing for an hour. Part of her reserve seems to be a reluctance to perform or emote on command. "My back goes up," she says. It also rises when she is asked questions that she considers demeaning, hostile, or intrusive, and she is unaware, apparently, that her provocative rebuffs encourage reporters to keep asking them. A friend in Washington who has known her well for decades sees her displays of intemperance as a function of anxiety. "When Teresa is calm and relaxed, in a small group, among supporters, or one on one, she is an utterly delightful human being: loving, funny, and kindhearted. Her friends adore her, and she's devoid of malice. But she's very spoiled, and it's not clear to her that in politics the attention—which she likes—comes with heat."

Heinz Kerry has an unlined complexion, elegant gestures that punctuate her speech, and the well-tended simmer of a retired Latin film star. Her dark eyes are widely set and, like her temper, have an emphatic flash. She dresses with expensive understatement, however. A consultant versed in the semiotics of campaign style may have suggested the bright-red ensemble that she wore to the Democratic Convention (red is said to telegraph sentimental warmth to women voters), but throughout the spring she traveled in the same three or four black, taupe, or beige designer suits. She accessorized her outfits with a misshapen straw hat; prescription sunglasses; a cardigan; Chanel boots; a large diamond ring; an Hermès satchel; a rhinestone campaign pin and a polyester scarf with a print of Kerry's initials that she helped design; and her necklace of charms. In the name of truth-telling, but also because she enjoys the incredulity of younger people when they hear that she is sixty-five, she makes a point of mentioning her age and the fact that she is married to a man five years her junior. She says that she would like to be a model for older women who feel sexually disenfranchised, and to "liberate them from the feeling that they die as women" when their youth is gone.

It should be said that Heinz Kerry is routinely cornier and more cordial than she is high-handed or inflammatory. (One of her favorite adages is "Put your arms around the problem, and it begins to get solved.") But she sometimes seems bored when others speak. On camera, her tinted reading glasses make her look aloof. At a rally one evening in Chicago's Union Station, wearing a low-cut white blouse and a black suit, she projected—while Kerry spoke—the languor of a maja. On other occasions, she took slugs from a water bottle, frowned, slumped, scribbled a note, fiddled with her rings and hair, or whispered to someone on the dais.

Heinz Kerry brightens visibly, however, when her husband sounds his call for ending America's moral, economic, and diplomatic "isolation." Kati Marton, the author of *Hidden Power*, a study of modern presidential couples (her husband, Richard Holbrooke, advises Kerry on foreign policy), believes that, whatever her liabilities as a candidate's wife, "Teresa would be an enormous asset" as the country's second foreign-born first lady. (Her only predecessor would be Mrs. John Quincy Adams, née Louisa Catherine Johnson, and in some senses she shouldn't count. Adams's mother was English, but her father was an American living in London, who became the United States consul there after the Revolution.) "At a time in American history when we have alienated so much of the world, Teresa, with her languages and her cultivation, could perform a real service as an envoy in a way that Jackie Kennedy or Hillary did," Marton says.

An envoy is a stand-in, however, and Heinz Kerry seems to prefer her own ground. She defines her role in the campaign, or the one she feels best equipped to play, as "helping people to connect the dots—that's what I like to do," she says. "For instance, during the Iowa primaries, I was talking with small farmers and environmentalists about pesticides, aquifers, the big Ag subsidies, and what they are doing. And it so happened that the WTO was meeting, and I read that the Zimbabweans had walked out, because they could no longer afford to sell their corn and compete with the American farmers subsidized by the big Ags. So I talked about it, and they got very excited to learn that what was an inequity to them was an inequity to poor people elsewhere. That is what a globalized world really does. And then I talked about AIDS and SARS, and aspects of trade or foreign policy, and I tied it up to terrorism and how you fight it—by having the best intelligence, and investing in our firefighters, our police, our CDC, and epidemiology. And maybe also in a new special force at home, but, most important, in teaching languages, knowing the countries, and forging real friendships with the world, so we can get the information ahead of trouble. You know, Americans are smart, but they only know what they see and hear. How many read op-ed pages?" She would like to make a weekly broadcast, "perhaps on C-SPAN, talking and listening and feeling part of making people's lives better."

In her eagerness to connect the dots for people, Heinz Kerry sometimes fails to appreciate that, beyond the Beltway, many voters have no idea what she means by "Kyoto," "the big Ag subsidies," "the WTO," and "the CDC," or by "Socratic dialogue" and "thinking in silos"—two of her catchphrases. The students at Bethune-Cookman College, in Daytona Beach, half of them male and most of them under twenty-one, listened politely but with glazed expressions to a digression about hormone-replacement therapy for the symptoms of menopause.

A few days before Heinz Kerry acquired a Secret Service detail, in April, she was mixing a grog for an ailing journalist (she is full of remedies and medical advice, some of it holistic or homeopathic) and lamenting the imminent end of her life "in the normal world." Despite her belief that her wealth doesn't or shouldn't define her, many Americans find it difficult to imagine that a woman as rich as Heinz Kerry lives in the normal world. They expect a grande dame in the mode of Mrs. Astor, with white gloves, if not of Alexis Carrington, with scarlet claws, and when they meet her in person, at a rally or on a rope line, they are often disarmed by her lack of affectation. "She talks too long," Jane Bell, who does market research in Des Moines, said to me after a campaign event, "and in that sense she's worse than he is. But she comes across as genuine and very bright and deeply compassionate. It's not her fault that she has all that money. I like it that she hasn't started baking cookies. And that African childhood is a terrific asset."

Maria Teresa Thierstein Simões-Ferreira Heinz Kerry was born in Lourenço Marques on October 5, 1938. She describes herself as "the dull one" of three siblings, "the easy middle one. My mom used to say I never gave them one day of worry." Her sister and brother "were supremely intelligent, particularly my sister," she says. "On the other hand, I got better grades than they did, because I applied myself." Her brother, the oldest child, earned a degree from Cambridge, and her sister—so incongruously fair in a dark family that she was nicknamed *bebé inglés*—died in a car crash at nineteen.

The Simões-Ferreira family produced some of Lisbon's most distinguished lawyers and judges (and also a poet, Heinz Kerry recalled, who was "crazy as a loon" and a friend of Sartre's), so her father's choice of a career in medicine was, from his parents' point of view, mildly heretical. He emigrated to Mozambique about the time Salazar seized power, and, having married a young woman from Lourenço Marques's cliquish British colony, set up a practice in Manjacaze, northeast of the capital—an inland village that was a center of cashew nut cultivation.

Andre Heinz describes his maternal grandmother, Irene Thierstein, as a Mediterranean matriarch of the old school. "She was sweetness incarnate," Heinz Kerry's friend Wren Wirth says, "and very firm about her faith." Thierstein was born in Mozambique to a couple who had immigrated from South Africa at the time of the Boer War. Her father was the scion of a Swiss German family living on Malta, and her mother was the half-French, half-Italian daughter of an Alexandrian shipowner who traded with Russia during the Crimean War.

When Heinz Kerry's mother was pregnant with her first child, she contracted a kidney ailment in Manjacaze and nearly died. The family returned to Europe for a few years so that she could regain her health and her husband could study a second specialty—radiology. Thereafter, they gave up the notion of living dangerously and settled in the capital, where Simões-Ferreira opened an oncology clinic. His children had a modern urban childhood that included movies, pop music, and dating. "My life was idyllic," Heinz Kerry says, "but more modern than Isak Dinesen's."

On weekends and holidays, the family stayed at a cottage overlooking the Uembje lagoon, in Bilene, a hundred miles north of the capital. There were masses of flamingos in the saline pools near the shore, and a landscape of verdant brush and white dunes. Though Heinz Kerry describes the region as "bush" (her memories of underdevelopment have a colonial flavor), it was already becoming a beach resort. But at five o'clock on Saturday mornings, her father went to work in an informal clinic under the pergola in their garden. Teresa helped him make rounds—an experience that she recounts regularly to voters. The patients were desperately poor peasants living in wattle huts, who had no other access to medical care. Infant mortality was then about 30 percent, though it often took the mothers two years, she says, to overcome their fears and bring their children for treatment. Because so few rural Africans spoke Portuguese, it was difficult to communicate. Teresa's father compiled a handwritten dictionary of Ronga, a local language, that she inherited and keeps by her bedside.

Heinz Kerry insists that even though she possesses a great fortune and its attendant perquisites, including the private jet in which she campaigns—a Gulfstream II—she could be "perfectly happy" living under a thatched roof. She also likes to say that "my Africa preserved the innocence of children." But the insouciant egotism of privilege is its own form of innocence. Though the stamp on her Portuguese identity card categorized her, she tells voters, as "a second-class citizen," her parentage entitled her to a first-class life. "There was a natural apartheid in Mozambique," she says, one that was economic and social, not legalized. "There were not that many Africans going to high school yet, or who would go to a movie, or who would do some of the things that we did, but my little school did have some mulatto girls."

When she was fourteen, Teresa was sent to a Catholic boarding school in Durban, where she was one of three foreigners and barely understood a word. Her English was still elementary, but, by working with her habitual application, she "got the hang of it." She won prizes for French and music, but she missed her own piano. "I wanted to become a concert pianist," she told me, but the music teacher crushed her hopes for a career, pointing out that her hands would always be too small to make an octave. "I felt so gypped," she said. "I never had another piano lesson."

After graduating at the top of her class, Teresa enrolled at the University of the Witwatersrand, in Johannesburg—the "Oxford of South Africa"—at a moment of heady, though not yet revolutionary, intellectual and social ferment that would shortly be suppressed. She majored in Romance languages, and she says that she especially loved seventeenth- and eighteenth-century history and French theater. She took classes in political science, which helped shape her rosy first impressions of America. Those textbook outlines of democracy were colored in by the Hollywood movies of the period. "I really admired a country that produced the Bill of Rights and *Some Like It Hot*," she often says.

In April of 1959, despite her mother's disapproval, Teresa joined her classmates and professors in an unprecedented, prominently reported demonstration of unity (the protesters wore academic robes) against a law that would extend apartheid to the few institutions of higher education that were still integrated—including their own. The legislation passed that June, nine months before the Sharpeville massacre. Some of her friends eventually went to jail, Heinz Kerry says, but the protests of 1959 were peaceful by the standards of what was to come. She left for Europe after she graduated, and enrolled at the Interpreters' School at the University of Geneva. John Heinz—the heir to the eponymous condiment fortune—was taking a year off from the Harvard Business School to work at a Swiss bank, and they met on a tennis court.

Heinz, the only child of divorced parents, had been sent to boarding school at a tender age. His old friend David Garth (who was a media strategist for Heinz's five successful runs for Congress—two for the House and three for the Senate) suggests that he suffered in his relations with an overbearing father. The Heinz patrimony traditionally helped underwrite the cultural life of Pittsburgh, where the company has its corporate headquarters in a high-rise on one side of the Allegheny River and its old factory—an industrial landmark of sooty brick, crowned by a smokestack and an enormous neon ketchup bottle—on the other. The Steelers play at Heinz Field, and a walking tour of the city's cultural district, once a combat zone of peep shows, adult bookshops, and flophouses, gives one a sense both of the family's munificence and of its mystique. According to Janet Sarbaugh, who directs the arts and culture programs at the Heinz Endowments, the formidable father-in-law of "Mrs. Heinz," as she is still known to her staff, bought up many of the derelict properties and "spearheaded their transformation." Among the benefactions that Pittsburgh owes, wholly or in part, to the dynasty of which Heinz Kerry is now what Wren Wirth calls "the Regent" are Heinz Hall, a Jazz Age movie palace restored to its period opulence; the even larger Benedum Center, home of the Pittsburgh Ballet and the Pittsburgh Opera; a modern sculpture garden with works by Dan Kiley and Louise Bourgeois; a public theater designed by Michael Graves; the handsomely landscaped riverfront; and numerous buildings at the university, including the Heinz Memorial Chapel.

"I felt sympathy for this girl from Lourenço Marques," David Garth said. He was referring to the daunting prospect of entering Pittsburgh society—a clannish oligarchy of banking and steel magnates—like the common-born upstart from a distant tropic who captivates an heir to the realm. Garth met Teresa Simões-Ferreira in New York in 1964, and was smitten with her. "John and I were a couple of bachelor jerks," he said. "And I had never heard him serious about anybody else." Garth had also never met a woman as unawed by the manly virtues and·material comforts that made Heinz "one of the ultra catches in the country," as he put it. "Teresa was not a rollover, and I liked that about her. She was very independent. When you met the two of them early on, she was the one who struck you as the natural politician. She was always concerned with issues—as a Senate wife, she took up the plight of Soviet Jewry, among other things—and she follows through. You don't make an idle remark to her and think it will be lost. She has always been—I hate the word—genuine. She doesn't watch what she says, but I've been involved with politics at what I consider a fairly high level for most of my life, and I've never seen anybody worth a damn who didn't have her attitude."

Heinz Kerry describes herself as an immigrant and makes common cause with other naturalized citizens striving toward the American dream. She spent her first year in this country living in a town-house apartment on East Eighty-first Street, near the Metropolitan Museum, deciding whether or not she could adjust to American life. Her future with Heinz hinged on the decision. The relentless pace and rudeness of New York overwhelmed her, but she had landed a job at the United Nations. She worked for the Trustee-ship Council, "which doesn't exist anymore," she noted, translating and analyzing information on colonial economic activities, and track-ing the progress of decolonialization. The job brought her into occa-sional contact with her countryman Eduardo Mondlane, the founder of FRELIMO. He worked at the Secretariat when he wasn't leading the nascent revolution in Mozambique. Mondlane encouraged her research, and they reminisced about home. She was moved to hear him say that her father had made an impression on him as a boy in Manjacaze, where he was born.

Heinz Kerry's stint at the United Nations gave her her first taste of political disillusionment. "I remember sitting in the Security Council with Mondlane, a few years before he was assassinated"—he was killed in 1969—"and they were fighting and carrying on about colonies," she recalled. He listened to the empty Cold War rhetoric for a while, then said to her, in a weary voice, "It's like watching a soccer match." She realized that "the truth was irrelevant," and "all my hard work—the facts I was searching for—meant nothing." Her experience at the UN, she told a Brazilian journalist in Fort Lau-derdale, was a *"banho"*—a bath, or, perhaps more fittingly, a bap-tismal immersion—*"de realpolitik."*

Heinz was an Episcopalian, but Catholicism, Heinz Kerry says, "is part of me, you know—part of who I am." Even in the late fifties, her piety impressed her contemporaries as anachronistic. A Heinz family member describes Teresa as "straitlaced" and uses the word "roman-ticism" to characterize her feelings for the Church: "When she was a young woman, her ideas were mystical and half-baked, but they've gotten much clearer." From the perspective of an orthodox Catholic like her mother, however, Heinz Kerry's position on reproductive rights qualifies as sinful. In her early twenties, she ended an otherwise congenial romance when her suitor admitted that if he ever had to choose between saving her life and that of an unborn child, he would, without hesitation, follow Church doctrine and let her die. She also had the courage—or impertinence, depending on one's point of view—to tell Bishop Wright of Pittsburgh, in a pastoral interview that took place shortly before he presided at her wedding, that she "wanted lots of children" but that she didn't believe in the Church's views on contraception. "You wouldn't talk about abortion in those days—you didn't think about it," she said to me. But, years later, after the birth of her three sons, she was prepared to abort a pregnancy severely compromised by high doses of a steroid medication. A miscarriage spared her from a choice that, despite her ambivalence on the subject—abortion, she says, is a "terrible thing," and anyone who treats it lightly is heartless—she feels all women should be free to make.

The wedding of John Heinz and Teresa Simões-Ferreira took place in February of 1966, at the Heinz Memorial Chapel. A blizzard had dumped five feet of snow on the city, and the bride "cried every week" thereafter through the first year of her new life. Her husband was commuting from long hours at the family company to their farmhouse on ninety acres in the fashionable suburb of Fox Chapel, and she was homesick and lonely. "But then," she told me, "you have a baby, and things start becoming a unit, and you grow up. I grew up with a guy. Who I was in love with. Who made me a woman, you know? Mother of his children. And an American."

Happy marriages seem to be as rare in contemporary politics as they are in modern fiction, though the Heinzes, according to their friends, had one. "Their closeness was something you don't see if you've done as many campaigns as I have, and seen as many disenchanted couples," Garth said. The Heinz family member noted, however, that John Heinz could be difficult and dogmatic, and that, while Teresa was always "feisty," and their tugs-of-war had a "flirtatious" tension, she lived in the shadow of his authority. "He was very tough, and he ran the show. He had the money and she didn't," a friend in Washington said. His son Chris describes him simply as "the boss."

Chris is dark, muscular, and good-natured, with his father's chiseled features. He graduated from business school three years ago and worked briefly in private banking before quitting his job to campaign for Kerry, whose steadiness, he said, supplies ballast to an "emotional family." His oldest brother, John, sanctions no intrusions into his privacy. He began working with inner-city children while he was at Boston College, and became a Buddhist. At an alternative Buddhist school that he co-founded, in Bucks County, Pennsylvania, he teaches troubled adolescents and reproduces medieval tools and armor on a blacksmith's forge. His wife is a doctor, and their daughter is Heinz Kerry's only grandchild.

Andre—a polyglot like his mother—is a consultant to businesses interested in sustainable development. He jokes that his first name destined him to be the European in the family. His coloring is Iberian, and an excellent tailor and beautiful manners that are reserved without being stiff contribute to his patrician air. When I met him at a gala in New York in April, he seemed unnerved to have been swept into his mother and stepfather's court of bodyguards, staffers, volunteers, and press. "It was all a bit surreal," he said. "We are kind of a private family." He calls Kerry his mother's "kindred spirit," though he adds that, while "John has a lot going on upstairs—he is thinking all the time, parallel processing—Mom is very intuitive. At the end of the day, she listens to her gut, and that's why she is such a conundrum."

Heinz Kerry described herself to the students in Daytona Beach as a "strict, bossy, witchy mother." Her sons were forbidden to eat junk food and were restricted to thirty minutes or, at most, an hour of television a week, after which they had to write a brief report explaining why they liked the program they had chosen. "So we spent our time figuring out how to watch TV and eat junk food," Andre said. "Mom could be terrifying," he added affectionately. "She was like concentrated juice: strong-willed, outspoken—a tour de force."

The principal reason that Heinz Kerry balked at releasing her tax returns, she says, was to protect her sons' privacy (they have complex joint trusts). John was apparently the least willing to condone the exposure. She says she initially believed that the political uproar about her taxes was just "noise from the right," but when the noise became a general uproar, she grudgingly produced a summary of her 2003 income—$5.1 million—and the effective tax she paid on it, about 11 percent.

On April 4, 1991, John Heinz and six others, including two children, died in a collision of his chartered plane with a helicopter over a schoolyard in suburban Philadelphia. Shortly before he was killed, he and his wife had been discussing ways to find financial support for an interdisciplinary research center at the Environmental Defense Fund, of which Heinz Kerry was a vice chairman. "I was in despair about it," she told me. "And he said, 'Don't worry, you are a very wise person, it will be OK.' Those were his last words, and they helped me later on. Because it wasn't something he'd ever told me—that I was wise." For a long time, she was devastated by his death, to the point of paralysis.

In addition to around half a billion dollars—which, by the most recent estimates, has since doubled—Heinz left his widow their farm, Rosemont; a brick town house in Georgetown; a fifteenth-century barn reconstructed beside a river in Sun Valley, Idaho; a beach compound on Nantucket; and one of the finest collections of sixteenth- and seventeenth-century Dutch and Flemish art in private hands. David Garth and others, including Arlen Specter, the senior senator from Pennsylvania and, like Heinz, a Republican who was willing, on occasion, to cross the aisle, urged her to run for her husband's seat, which is now filled by Rick Santorum—an outspokenly conservative politician whom Heinz Kerry once called "a Forrest Gump with attitude." Heinz Kerry was a registered Republican of the Rockefeller school until 2002, and she hasn't altered her views in any essential way. When she changed her affiliation, it wasn't for Kerry's sake, she says, but because she felt alienated by the increasingly strident, divisive rhetoric of the Republican Party. She found the tactics that the Republicans used to defeat Max Cleland, the Democratic senator from Georgia, who lost three limbs in Vietnam, "unscrupulous and disgusting." Cleland was accused of being "soft" on homeland security, and the conservative commentator Ann Coulter claimed that he had caused his own mutilations by mishandling a grenade. "What does the Republican Party need?" Heinz Kerry asked in a CBS television interview. "A fourth limb to make a person a hero?"

Having survived the abrupt and violent losses of both her husband and her sister—two "comets," as Heinz Kerry put it, whose brilliance had always eclipsed her—she felt that she had, in middle age, been given a belated chance to test her mettle and achieve her own prominence. She chose to do so in philanthropy rather than in politics. Grant Oliphant, John Heinz's former press secretary, who is now the associate director of the endowments, gave me a tour of Heinz Kerry's offices. They are laid out like a village street in some imaginary Southwestern town, and decorated with Early American folk art and artifacts, including a tattered flag with thirteen stars, a cigar-store Indian, and a statue of Uncle Sam from Coney Island. The exotic trees that supplied the wood came from sustainable plantations. In Heinz Kerry's opulently spacious private aerie, a wall of glass opens onto a terrace with sweeping views of the Pittsburgh riverfront that she has helped revitalize. What was once one of America's most polluted cities is now, according to Heinz Kerry, one of its cleanest, in part because of her environmental leadership. Like the new convention center several blocks away, for which she sponsored a design contest, the offices are so scrupulously "green" that one can, in theory, eat the carpets.

The endowments' assets—about $1.3 billion—generate between sixty and seventy million dollars a year, which, Oliphant says, "is distributed to an array of progressive, mostly environmental causes, but also to programs that are faith-based and conservative, such as charter and Catholic schools in the inner city, and organizations that teach parenting skills." Still, he says, "the endowments have been under attack for months by right-wing groups attempting to cast Teresa's philanthropy as extremist and left-wing." The attacks—which have been discredited as baseless smears by political fact-checkers at the Annenberg Public Policy Center—include assertions that Heinz Kerry helped to "launder" charitable contributions and that she gave money to a foundation with links to Hamas. (The editor whom Heinz Kerry told to "shove it" on the eve of her convention speech works for the conservative *Pittsburgh Tribune-Review*, which aired some of the accusations uncritically.) The donations in question were a decade's worth of support for the Tides Center and Foundation, and were earmarked for specific environmental projects in Pennsylvania and for youth and economic-opportunity programs. Tides also funds antiwar, civil-rights, and pro-choice organizations, but demonstrably not with any Heinz money. "It's crazy," Oliphant says, "because she isn't an ideologue—she's a pragmatist, and she thinks from the middle."

Heinz Kerry broadened the endowments' scope and changed their philanthropic style. They still provide funding for the arts, but they also support a range of experimental initiatives in toxic-waste cleanup, community mental health, early-childhood development, preventive medicine, pensions for homemakers, prescription drugs for seniors, and education. "It's the difference between old-fashioned patronage and investment," Janet Sarbaugh said. The endowments' strategically targeted grants are accompanied by tight fiscal oversight, and recipients lose their support, as the Pittsburgh public-school system did, if they don't meet high expectations of performance. "Rather than set ourselves up as white knights whose generosity and intercessions will save the world," Heinz Kerry wrote in the fall 2002 issue of *H*, the endowments' quarterly, "we need to think of ourselves as partners in the rough-and-tumble enterprise of social change."

John Kerry, like his wife, can be prickly about her immense wealth and its influence. "Yes, she has money," he told me, "but the money is irrelevant to who she is and how she defines herself." (He tends to take questions like an aggressive steeplechase rider on a testy stallion: forward in the saddle and wary of the hidden trap.) Kerry doesn't see any impropriety in a first lady funding and directing her own "policy lab." "That's the world she loves," he said, though he claims that she will also find time "to do what first ladies have done historically," which is to adopt a cause. When a reporter in Baltimore asked her what that cause might be, she answered coolly, "I don't think of my work as *causes*—I think of it as work."

Though Heinz Kerry likes to attribute what critics see as impolitic behavior to her experience of tyranny, she lived with an ambitious politician of lordly ways longer than she ever lived under a dictatorship. At the surprise party that Heinz organized for her fiftieth birthday, she, in turn, surprised the guests by telling them that she had "paid my dues and I wasn't going to put up with any more stuff I don't want to. *Finito*. It was the most liberating thing in the world."

Heinz was considering a presidential bid at the time of his death, and his wife hated the idea. She told him that he would have to run "over my dead body." I asked her why she had changed her mind this time. Two years ago, she replied, she began to have "a feeling of urgency about what's going on in the world, and at my age it seemed a little selfish" to stand in Kerry's way. She thought the matter over on a long hike and decided that "I shouldn't stop him. I should help him. And so I did."

Teresa Heinz met John Kerry in Washington, D.C., on Earth Day, 1990. He was speaking at a rally on the Mall, and she had come with her first husband, who was also scheduled to address the crowd. Both senators sat on the banking committee, and they were collegial acquaintances. While they were waiting to speak, Heinz introduced his wife to the gentleman from Massachusetts. By the time Kerry met Teresa Heinz again—in Brazil in 1992—she had been widowed. They were both delegates to the Earth Summit in Rio de Janeiro. Kerry was impressed when she took over from a Brazilian interpreter she thought was subverting the meaning of a speech. They went to Mass at the cathedral and chatted in French. (When two Americans lapse into French, it is usually for the purpose of flirting.) He had been divorced from his first wife, Julia Thorne, for four years, but they had lived separately for a decade. Their daughters, Alexandra and Vanessa, were students of eighteen and fifteen.

The adjectives that Kerry used in describing his second wife to me—"grounded, no-nonsense, down to earth, straightforward"— may not jibe with Andre's image of her as a conundrum; or with Chris's volatile, exacting Latin mother; or with the charming and "cozy" woman who, her friend in Washington says, has a tendency toward "narcissism" in times of stress. But they suggest Heinz Kerry's allure to a rootless and aloof man with a much buffeted personal life. At forty-eight, Kerry had been enjoying—or, at least from the frequency with which his name was linked with beautiful women, seeming to enjoy—the sexual prime of a powerful bachelor, but the gossip annoyed him. He just wanted "to fall in love," he told *The Boston Globe*, which had been tracking his dates, and he didn't want girlfriends attributed to him "until I'm committed and want that relationship known." Kerry's finances were unsettled, too. (His most recent disclosure lists personal assets in the range of half a million to two million dollars.) Thorne had a private income, but Kerry paid child support for his daughters. He owned a small town house in Washington with a big mortgage, and in Boston he camped out with family and friends. He struck Heinz Kerry as a "gypsy" and "a pet wolf" in need of domestication, and nesting was her forte.

Heinz and Kerry met for the third time at a dinner party in the capital, and he offered to see her home. On the way, he took her to the Vietnam Memorial. A few months later, she invited a close friend, the photojournalist Diana Walker, to lunch at her house in George-town. As Walker unlatched the back gate and walked through the high-walled garden, where brick paths define islands of roses, she was startled by a sound that presaged the announcement of a sea change in the widow's life: "Teresa whistling in the kitchen."

After a brief courtship, a short period of cohabitation, and the signing of a prenuptial agreement, the Kerrys were married in a civil ceremony on Nantucket in 1995. Heinz Kerry wore the girlish dress of a first-time bride, with a ruffled neckline and puffed sleeves, and she settled into what was, in many respects, a familiar life as the con-sort of a public man. Her second husband, perhaps even more than her first, needed her buoyance. "I think marriage is difficult," she re-flected. "When you're older, you bring a lot to the table, so it is harder work in some ways." Kerry brought two teenage daughters to the table. She believes, in retrospect, that she went about being their stepmother without enough discretion. "Because I thought, I love kids, kids love me, I'll be fine. Baloney." She says that a friend gave her some useful advice: "You have to treat stepchildren like pets. You're nice to them, but you don't get too close, or they chew you up. Well, I did it the other way." When I asked Kerry if remarriage in middle age to a woman with a history to which she still seems deeply attached was a difficult proposition, he replied, in his staccato fash-ion, "Not in the least. Why would it be hard for me? Look, she fell in love and decided to marry me."

"John makes very close friends, but few," a woman who knows him well says. "His New England austerity is compounded by his re-serve, his shyness, his politesse. He's not a glad-hander—he was trained not to be." As the son of a diplomat, who moved from school to school, "he had to be a loner to survive. What I love about John is that he's immensely curious and he never condescends. He also doesn't manipulate. But as a politician, that makes him unseductive. He leads with his head." Kerry's seductiveness may not be obvious, but the attraction of a consummately cerebral man to an irrepressibly visceral woman is. Perhaps one of the most eloquent messages that Heinz Kerry delivers to voters on her husband's behalf is that he was fearless enough to take her on.

Late in August, while the Republicans convened in New York, the Kerrys vacationed on Nantucket. They resumed campaigning on Labor Day weekend, and Heinz Kerry spent the holiday in her home state, marching with thousands of citizens in a Pittsburgh parade and speaking at a sparsely attended union picnic and rally in Philadelphia. It took place on a pier near the Benjamin Franklin Bridge, across the Delaware River from Camden, New Jersey. The audience of steamfitters, longshoremen, and janitors had come with their children and wore the T-shirts of their locals.

Heinz Kerry's hair was windblown and her cheeks rosy. Her acidgreen suit was the color of an immense tanker, the *Chemical Pioneer*, slowly steaming up the river behind the stage. "No war is worth fighting if the people in our country aren't defended by good schools, jobs, and health care," she told the audience. It was a new speech: lean of detail, punchy, brief, and delivered with the ease of a seasoned candidate. The shy whisper and distracting tics were gone. At one point, she leaned over to joke with an elderly black woman sitting on a folding chair in the front row who said that she was ninety and had plenty of opinions. There was laughter and applause. "I'm a woman of a certain age and I deserve my opinions," Heinz Kerry said to the audience. "I've earned them the old-fashioned way."

A week later, when Heinz Kerry was on her way to Pittsburgh with Wren Wirth (her close women friends take turns keeping her company on the road), I asked her what she thought about the increasingly vicious campaign and the cheap caricatures of her personal eccentricities. "It's sad that in America people have to put up with that kind of thing," she said. "It's sadder still that people like it." Her voice on the phone sounded serene—neither embattled nor tinny with false optimism. Her syntax was baroque and elegiac, perhaps with fatigue, and her sentences were curiously wonkish and poetic at the same time. "I am grateful that, being as old as I am"—she mentioned her age twice in the course of a five-minute conversation—"I have developed an interesting way to deal with it that I didn't know I had in me, which is contextualizing what is said, not reading either the puffy things which would give me an oversized head or the things which would give me a shriveled heart." She spoke of Bush's promise to reduce health-care costs, pointing out that he had just raised Medicare premiums for the elderly by 17 percent. "I never thought there would be so many lies," she said. "It's been quite amazing. But I don't dwell there, I dwell in a better house, a house of hope."

—September 27, 2004

THREE

Costume of the Country

Like many people who studiously reinvent themselves, Jacqueline Kennedy cultivated the perfect simplicity of manner that is often the grandest of affectations. She used her charm, an alloy of the gossamer and the ironic, to deflect notice from unseemly pretensions or raw appetites that her own self-scrutiny might have missed. The words commonly used to describe her beauty—"shimmering," "ethereal"— reinforce the impression of her otherworldliness. There was plenty of worldly hunger in Jackie, and steeliness, too. One sees it in her carriage. But these were sheathed, like the nails she bit to the quick, by the white gloves she wore even when she was perched atop an elephant in the heat of India, by her decorous reserve, her wifely deference, and the "feathery" voice that seemed never to utter an arrogant, vulgar, or impolitic public word. In private, though, she could be impious, even wicked. And those who knew her well also knew that, like the most absolute of queens, she was swift to punish, with implacable disfavor, the perceived crime of *lèse-majesté*.

I had the pleasure of a slight personal acquaintance with Jackie (or, rather, with Mrs. Onassis) when she was an editor at Doubleday. She had liked my first book, a biography of Isak Dinesen, and expressed interest in publishing the second, a life of Colette. We met at her office one morning early in 1990. Our interesting chat about French literature, the social history of the fin de siècle, and the Sapphic penchants of the great Belle Époque courtesans ("The touch of those ghastly old toads who kept them would have sent anyone rushing into a woman's arms") was followed, several weeks later, by one of the handwritten notes for which she was famous, expressing in the most gracious and sporting terms her disappointment that I had jilted her, so to speak, for another publisher. It was signed Jackie, and she wished me luck.

From time to time, Jackie would inquire about my progress through a mutual friend. Early in 1993—a year before her death—she invited us to "a girls' dinner," as she put it, "just the three of us," at her apartment on Fifth Avenue. My friend and I fretted about what to wear, but got it right, which is to say, we were dressed exactly as she was for a stormy winter night at home, in sweaters and slacks. A fire was burning in the library, and the wraithlike butler who kept it stoked also vigilantly refreshed our wineglasses. My memory of the conversation has both faded and been colored by sad subsequent events. We talked about books and gardens, the death of fathers and the vagaries of husbands, about pearls, Paris real estate, decorating, and the Clintons, whom she liked and pitied: they were about to discover the "horrors" of life in the White House fishbowl. We also discussed the tyranny of convention and agreed that we had all wasted our childhoods being good girls. Jackie had recently quit smoking but "approved of vice" and sympathetically offered me an ashtray. Over dinner, she recalled the tedium of formal diplomatic entertaining. "Jack," she said, "liked to complain that I always got to sit next to the fascinating men, while he got the boring wives." Mostly we spoke of love and, more especially, the love of sons. "If you play your cards right and give them their freedom," Jackie said, "they'll stay faithful to you. When you're a hideous, decrepit old woman, they'll take you to the opera."

Jackie was not fated to become an old woman, nor her son to take her to the opera as one, and nothing could have made her hideous. The proof is to be found in a new show celebrating her loveliness frozen at its peak. "Jacqueline Kennedy: The White House Years," at the Costume Institute of the Metropolitan Museum of Art, focuses on her style. That style is best summed up by a cryptic pronouncement she once made to our mutual friend: "One should always dress like a marble column." On the morning of her husband's inauguration, Mrs. Kennedy ascended the column (making sure one couldn't peek up her skirt from the base) and held her pose—like Buñuel's Simon of the Desert, though much better groomed—for a thousand days.

Her official wardrobe from that era is the drawing card of the new show—curated by Hamish Bowles, an editor at *Vogue*—which has been luxuriously installed in a suite of galleries on the second floor, rather than in the cramped basement where costumes and couture are generally shown. In addition to clothes and accessories, it includes a selection of her correspondence about fashion and decor; some of the menus and seating charts from those "tedious" official dinners (which look like they were fun); and film footage from her triumphant state visits to France and Latin America, her trip to India and Pakistan as a goodwill ambassador, and her televised tour of the Executive Mansion, which she had restored, Bowles writes in the catalog to the show (Bulfinch, 2001), "as a museum of presidential history."

The restoration was the most concrete contribution she made as first lady, although there were others, more ineffable. Unlike Diana, Princess of Wales, who so touchingly, heretically, and stupidly believed she was entitled to be an individual, Jackie acquiesced in becoming a symbol. Her aristocratic idealism was, in that respect, quite orthodox, like that of Isak Dinesen, a writer whose work had informed it. "Exactly as if a heavy weight had been tied on to her legs," Dinesen wrote (of a Somali girl on the threshold of puberty, not of Mrs. Kennedy), "she took to walking slowly, slowly; she held her eyes cast down after the best pattern . . . The Novice gave herself up gravely and proudly to all the hardships of the rite." The only writer who, to my knowledge, ever shot her own fur coats then adds that the maiden "was herself fascinated and possessed by the process of her transformation." So was Jackie.

Mrs. Kennedy had several fur coats, including one of Somali leopard, which inspired a "mad rush for the rare pelt," according to Jay Mulvaney in *Jackie: The Clothes of Camelot* (St. Martin's, 2001). It is not in the show. Nothing is in the show that might cast the slightest pall over Jackie's apotheosis as an "icon of style" who is still able to spur the sale of a million museum tickets, product spinoffs such as a line of makeup, and tie-in books—in addition to the catalog and Mulvaney's offering, there is *Jackie Style,* by Pamela Clarke Keogh (Harper-Collins, 2001)—or that might suggest her life was anything but a series of iconically happy days and iconically glamorous nights filled with iconic public service, iconic promotion of high culture, iconic travel, iconic wifehood and motherhood, iconic decorating and couture fittings, and iconic, if weird, hairdos. There is no trace of the most iconic piece of clothing Jackie ever wore, the pink Chanel suit that was besmirched with her husband's blood and brains in the motorcade at Dallas, and which she refused to change in the hours following his assassination or for the photographs of Lyndon Johnson's swearing-in, saying, "I want them to see what they have done." Also missing in action are the mourning clothes—particularly the black veil straight from a Goya that the bereft widow wore with stoic grandeur to the funeral she orchestrated so masterfully on a weekend's notice—which illustrate better than anything in the show what Bowles calls Jackie's "keen appreciation of ceremony"; the way "she rigorously oversaw her own visual presentation"; and her "understanding of the semantics of dress and of the way in which she could use her public image to help communicate the more abstract ideals that were important to her." Indeed, had one wandered into the Met on May Day after forty years in a fallout shelter, one would have had absolutely no inkling that anything terrible ever happened to this golden couple so flush with power and apparent happiness. The display of Jackie's sacred relics is maudlin enough, and it would be ghoulish if the pink suit or the black veil were part of it. But in an exhibition of her "legacy" from the White House years, they and what they represent—reality—ought to be acknowledged.

Couture, rather than reality, is Mr. Bowles's theater of expertise. He presents the clothes with a savant's reverence for their quality, construction, provenance, and metaphoric content. He writes imaginatively about the "armorial" aspect of a wardrobe that was, for the most part, cut from shiny, "rigid" fabrics with fetchingly exotic names like gazar, zibeline, Alaskine, and radzimir. He describes a shocking-pink cocktail dress by Givenchy with an elaborate bow at the back that Jackie wore to a White House Christmas party as "appropriately suggestive of a luxuriously wrapped gift." He appreciates a "liquid, columnar" evening gown of draped silk jersey—Oleg Cassini's homage to Mme. Grès—as "entirely appropriate" to Mrs. Kennedy's "dynamic modern embodiment of an ancient muse." He deconstructs an opera coat, also by Givenchy—a tribute to his mentor, Balenciaga—as "a palimpsest of historical references, suggesting by turns a Venetian domino, a Kabuki robe, and, as General de Gaulle himself remarked . . . a costume in a Watteau painting."

But the impeccable Mr. Bowles is also attached to polyester clichés like "timeless elegance." Jackie's state wardrobe wasn't timeless and wasn't all that elegant. It vacillates between the matronly and the little-girlish. The young Mrs. Kennedy was at her most chic in a riding habit or a pair of capri pants worn with a tan, sandals, a head scarf, and dark glasses. She looked most beautiful when her hair was still short and curly—before Kenneth or Alexandre pouffed and lacquered it into the modern equivalent of a court wig. With a few notable exceptions, most of them atypically "liquid" evening gowns, her endlessly copied and influential garments in their Queen Mother palette—"covered-up" dresses and suits with dirndly waists, tailored overblouses, demure bows, awkward stoles, boxy jackets cropped at the hip, and A-line shifts or skirts hemmed just below the knee—now seem dated, even mediocre. It's only on the incandescent Jackie in the old photographs (and particularly in the photographs where she's standing next to some poor frump half her height and twice her weight) that they excite desire. They repel desire, too. The "armorial" smoothness of her hair and clothes telegraphs a message of defiance: "Nothing can ruffle me."

Jacqueline Kennedy held her pose on the column—or as the column—with more aplomb than any other modern first lady or European queen. She was less provincial and better educated than most royalty and, in that respect, well endowed to rehabilitate the cultural inferiority complex of a crude frontier republic. "What a joy," John Steinbeck said at JFK's inauguration, "that literacy is no longer prima facie evidence of treason." But there was almost nothing democratic about Jackie except America's illusion, in which she briefly colluded, that she was one of us. And there was almost nothing modern about her, either. In all those photographs, whatever "simple," "crisp," or "streamlined" garment she may be wearing, Jackie projects an archaic notion of her symbolic value—of woman's value—and the exorbitance of her finery is an essential part of it. As Dinesen writes of the Somali wives on her African farm, they "cannot acquire a pair of slippers in any possible way except through a man, they cannot own themselves but must needs belong to some male . . . but they are still the one supreme prize of life. It is a surprising thing . . . what amounts of silks, gold, amber, and coral the Somali women get out of their men."

Unlike a Somali husband, Jack Kennedy was as outraged as any sitcom spouse when he found out what fabulous sums Jackie was spending on clothes (and a number of biographers have suggested that her shopping binges were revenge for his sexual ones). Mulvaney quotes the president's "frequent complaint" that "she's breaking my ass" and estimates that in 1961 Jackie's wardrobe expenditures totaled $40,000—a figure that did not include the bills from her official couturier, Oleg Cassini, which were, at the request of her father-in-law, sent directly to him. Old Joe was an archaic type himself: the tribal patriarch. As did Onassis after him, he understood what he was paying for.

Jackie's charisma, like Diana's, was a function of her status as a supreme prize, and the attributes of their official preciousness were similar: youth, beauty, class, goodness, love for their children—and marriage to an alpha mate. Perhaps when the chemistry of the brain is finally understood, we will discover that the attraction emanating from a charismatic person or thing stimulates very ancient, even atavistic circuits. The evolution of society has been away from hierarchy, but the human race is still wired for it. We seek to tame, or at least to propitiate, the powers we can't control by submitting to them, and the figures who have seized or been invested with supreme authority have learned, in the long, erratic "progress" of civilization, to make ritual gestures of obeisance to those they rule—the laying on of hands, the washing of feet, the sharing of bread—at the same time that they flaunt the emblems of their hieratic splendor: crowns, scepters, and gorgeous robes. "She took her sons to McDonald's;

they wore baseball caps; she embraced AIDS victims," people said of Diana. "She could speak to immigrants in their own language; she invited black people to the White House; she never spoiled her children," people said of Jackie. And when the charismatic figure is sincere, or seems to be, in her display of respect for those beneath her in the hierarchy, which is rare enough, she evokes a gratitude from the objects of her benevolence out of all proportion to her actual good deeds. Condescension is experienced as communion, and that is the essence—the magic trick—of charisma. For it humbles and exalts at the same time.

So does tragedy. The most intense moments of communion one had with Jackie or Diana were at funerals, and those of the president and the princess were paradoxically idyllic. What we call an idyll is a taste of wholeness—of moral or emotional unity. Idylls are often fabricated cynically for commercial and propagandistic purposes, and experience teaches us to regard them as mirages, at best—like the "unspoiled tropical paradise" offering communion with nature that is promised by the tourist brochure. A true idyll, which is unforgettable to those who experience it, is inevitably ephemeral, because the kind of passionate communality it calls for—a oneness of attention, action, feeling, purpose, and desire—is so difficult to sustain, the more so the greater the number of participants. Those two sudden and shocking violent deaths surprised us with the revelation of an everyday sense of loss: of the experience of solidarity in a fractious world.

The ersatz idyll of "Camelot" was one of Jackie's rare though egregious public lapses of taste. A week after Kennedy's assassination, she gave an interview to Theodore White in which she confided that "at night, before we'd go to sleep . . . Jack liked to play some records . . . and the song he loved most," from the Lerner and Lowe musical, ended with the line "Don't let it be forgot, that once there was a spot, for one brief, shining moment that was known as Camelot." But, according to Donald Spoto, one of the better Jackie biographers:

> Most of Jack's ardent admirers admitted, years later, that his taste in music was pretty much limited to "Bill Bailey, Won't

You Please Come Home." . . . "There was no Camelot in the
early 1960s," wrote his Secretary of State, Dean Rusk, "and
John Kennedy himself would have been the first to kick such
notions out of the window. He was too skeptical for sentimentality." Arthur Schlesinger agreed: "The Camelot idea is a kind
of mythomania."

Jackie's own mythomania was shaped by the pretensions of a family that came from the immigrant working class on both sides and invented an aristocratic history for themselves—her mother claiming to
be descended from the Lees (they were Lees but poor Irish ones) and
her grandfather Bouvier from the noble house of Fontaine (his great-
grandfather, a carpenter and cabinetmaker, had emigrated from the
south of France). It was polished at Miss Porter's and Vassar and in
the society of East Hampton and Newport. It was given depth by her
avid reading of history, and particularly the history, in French, of the
ancien régime. Jackie admired the mistresses of kings and had their
gift—which is that of Woman as supreme prize—for disarming blasé
tyrants by presenting them with the trophy of her elusive favor. She
also felt an affinity with the salonnières of the Enlightenment, and
became her own version of one. "The White House," her husband
joked, "is becoming a sort of eating place for artists. But they never
ask us out."

Jackie's passion for couture was part of her fervid romance with
all things French, beginning with her own background. There are
some droll footnotes to her Francophilia among the letters in the exhibition. In one, to Cassini, she declares, "I refuse to have Jack's administration plagued by fashion stories of a sensational nature—& to
be the Marie Antoinette or Josephine of the 1960s"—which, of
course, she was. In another she asks him to put his "brilliant mind"
to work on her wardrobe for day—ensembles for "lunch and afternoon that I would wear if Jack were President of France . . . très
Princesse de Réthy, mais jeune." Cassini, at first glance, seems like an
odd choice for court dressmaker. He was known, in the forties and
fifties, for what Bowles calls his "high-voltage" and "provocatively
form-fitting" Hollywood film costumes rather than for the original
quality of his own work. But he was a Kennedy family friend: dis-

creet, chivalrous, accommodating, wellborn—a White Russian, thus virtually French—and he liked women.

Liking women, however, was not a prerequisite for Jackie's admiration. In an essay she wrote at twenty-one, which won her *Vogue*'s 1951 Prix de Paris, she chose Baudelaire, Oscar Wilde, and Diaghilev as the three dead men she would most like to meet, and she had a fondness for the fin de siècle decadents. Decadence as an aesthetic, if not a way of life, particularly appeals to artistically inclined daughters of privilege, like Jackie, who are raised by prim mothers and neglected by glamorously wild fathers they adore, and who feel that their vital flame has been stifled by the tyranny of convention. Such wasted good girlhoods in white gloves often breed grandiosity—the fantasy of reclaiming a demonic, noble patrimony they have been denied—along with an insatiable covetousness for experience. It's not a coincidence that on a 1961 trip to Paris, when she was asked what painting she'd liked most in the Jeu de Paume, Jackie chose— scandalously—Manet's *Olympia*, the image, Wayne Koestenbaum writes in *Jackie Under My Skin*, "of a nude prostitute posed as an odalisque with a black serving girl behind her. In it, the odalisque's gaze is unashamed, direct, confrontational. It is a painting intended to *épater le bourgeois*."

A cautious woman averse to discomfort and circumscribed by fame, Jackie could engage the unashamed, the direct, and the confrontational only vicariously. She did so through literature, and through her friendships with artists. Her hunger for a woman's life rich in experience was channeled into the pursuit of a rich woman's life. But her most flamboyant fling with brazenness—the marriage to Onassis—seems to have cured her infatuation with it. After her second widowhood, it took Jackie years of serious work and quiet civilian living to reclaim the individuality she had surrendered. The world's continuing obsession with her "influence on fashion" was, as she wrote to a prospective biographer, Carl Sferrazza Anthony, an "annoyance." It's difficult to imagine that she would ever have sanctioned this exhibition.

I couldn't help measuring the distance between the wry sixty-three-year-old woman I had dined with—in a chenille sweater and a pair of slippers, with her hair down—and the fey young princess-bride doll in the film clips and photographs at the Met. One of Bowles's more delirious flights of couture scholarship arrested me. He describes a "fairy-tale" gown in "silver-spangled white synthetic tulle embroidered with rhinestones and trimmed with gray silk velvet" (which isn't quite as dreadful as it sounds), adapted by Cassini from a design by Karl Lagerfeld.

> The detailing, however, is at variance with Parisian standards. Bordering the bodice and hem, for instance, are bands of net that were embroidered before being applied to the finished garment. In a Paris couture atelier the embroidery would have been worked directly on the panels of the dress itself before it was fully assembled, thus becoming an integral part of the gown rather than an applied element. All Mrs. Kennedy required, however, was a dress that was perfectly photogenic, and Cassini's served this purpose effectively.

If the hidden seams of Jackie's character had been examined with the same meticulous regard, this perfect fashion show might have been less photogenic but more moving.

—May 14, 2001

FOUR

The Divine Marquise

Few priestesses of fashion have been better endowed for their vocation than Luisa Casati, a Milanese aristocrat who was born in 1881 to immense wealth, and who, having probably spent more money on clothes and jewels than any queen in history, died penniless in 1957. The Marchesa was exceptionally tall and cadaverous, with a head shaped like a dagger and a little, feral face that was swamped by incandescent eyes. She brightened their pupils with belladonna and blackened their contours with kohl or India ink, gluing a two-inch fringe of false lashes and strips of black velvet to the lids. Her cheekbones were vertiginous, her nose aquiline, her mouth a lurid gash. She powdered her skin a fungal white and dyed her hair to resemble a corona of flames. This alarming mask, as Cocteau observed, gave men the illusion that the woman who wore it had willfully ravaged a great beauty—a beauty she didn't, in fact, possess.

Casati's totem animal, like Medusa's, was the snake: a creature that sloughs its skin and mesmerizes with its stare. She prided herself on the freshness of the shocks her appearance delivered. Her contemporaries couldn't decide if she was a vampire, a bird of paradise, an androgyne, a goddess, an enigma, or a common lunatic. Her clothes were as esoteric as the symbols on a wizard's hat—formulas for improving on nature. Among her more memorable getups was a suit of armor pierced with hundreds of electric arrows that short-circuited and nearly fried her; an iridescent necklace of live snakes that slithered from her bare shoulders at a ball; and a headdress of peacock tail feathers accessorized, for a night at the opera, by the blood of a freshly slaughtered chicken.

The futurists and the surrealists recognized that the radical impudence of Casati's experiments with dress were kindred to their own artistic provocations (as, later, did Kerouac, who wrote, "Marchesa Casati / Is a living doll / Pinned on my Frisco / Skid row wall"). She commissioned a life-size wax mannequin of herself, with eyes of green glass and a wig purportedly made from her own hair; it sat at her dinner table dressed as her twin, and she brought it to Paris for fittings at Poiret. An emissary from Schiaparelli sent to solicit her business found her in bed in her hotel suite "covered with a rug of black ostrich feathers, eating a breakfast of fried fish and drinking straight Pernod while trying on a newspaper scarf." To a performance of the Ballets Russes, she wore a gown of egret plumes that molted in the course of the evening. For a summer of drug abuse and sorcery on Capri, in 1920, she packed a wardrobe of black dresses with cathedral trains, dyed her hair green, painted the body of her servant gold (he collapsed in the heat and was saved from suffocation by her landlord, who scraped off the gilding), and paraded through the village streets carrying a crystal ball. But when she really wanted to outdo herself, Casati wore nothing. The residents of Venice were regularly treated to the midnight apparition of their richest and thinnest neighbor strolling through St. Mark's Square perfectly nude and lunar white beneath a fur cloak, accompanied by two cheetahs on diamond-studded leashes and a majestic Negro retainer bearing torches to illuminate the scene.

The only biography of Casati in English, *Infinite Variety*, by Scot D. Ryersson and Michael Orlando Yaccarino, was published four years ago and is out of print, but it deserves to be revived. The authors are judicious historians of frivolity who capture the tone of a life that was obscenely profligate yet strangely pure. Their subject was born Luisa Annan, the daughter of a prodigiously successful, self-made Milanese textile magnate who was ennobled by his frequent houseguest King Umberto I. Both Count Annan and his wife died when their two daughters were teenagers, leaving them one of the—if not the—

greatest industrial fortunes in Italy. Luisa received a typically sketchy private education, lived in the shadow of her prettier older sister, made a decorous debut, and married the scion of an ancient family, the Marchese Casati Stampa di Soncino, a future president of the Roman Jockey Club. (They had a spunky only child, Cristina, neglected by her parents from an early age, who studied at Oxford and eloped with an English lord who was said to share her Communist sympathies.) For a few years, the young Marchesa dressed decently and lived dutifully, if opulently, as a conventional matron of her class. But at twenty-two she was seduced by Gabriele D'Annunzio, the charismatic writer, warrior, satyr, spiritualist, demagogue, and "Prince of Decadence," who was her greatest love, a man eternally on the run from his creditors, and thus ever on the prowl for an indulgent mistress. Neither he nor Casati was capable of fidelity, but she became his muse, and he helped to cultivate her horror of the mundane—a quality definitive of the fashion priestess, and one that probably originates, as it did for Casati, in repugnance for the glum and ordinary little girl in whose body and existence she was once trapped.

The Marchesa's flamboyant affair with D'Annunzio was ignored for years by her husband, and it eventually burned down to the friendship of two charming and predatory mythomaniacs who practiced black magic and communicated mostly by cryptic telegram. But once he had aroused her appetite for the poetry of excess, no extravagance could slake it. Her treasures piled up. She spent as much on the jewel-encrusted gown and headdress that Leon Bakst designed for one of her legendary masked revels as J. P. Morgan paid for his custom-fitted Rolls-Royce. Her crumbling palace on the Grand Canal (it was later owned by another priestess, Peggy Guggenheim) was decorated with rare gemstones, priceless lace, hothouse flowers, and Egyptian statuary. There, and in her Roman mansion and her Parisian villa, she installed menageries of exotic animals—not only the cheetahs but lion cubs, owls, panthers, monkeys, peacocks, a gorilla, albino blackbirds, greyhounds powdered pink and mauve, a parrot that squawked obscenities, and a boa constrictor that traveled with her everywhere in a plush-lined glass case.

It has to be said that while Casati outdid—and certainly outspent—her models, and inspired numerous imitators, though none so fantastic as she, her signature perversities weren't that original. The Princess di Belgiojoso, a man-eater much beloved of the Romantics, pioneered the macabre makeup and hair. Huysmans published *Against Nature*, which might have been her decorating manual, when the Marchesa was three. Wilde's *Salome* had its Paris premiere twelve years later. And by the height of the Belle Époque, when Casati hit her stride, it had long been fashionable for femmes fatales to keep nasty pets. The French writer Rachilde, for example, adopted two sewer rats that she named Kyrie and Eleison. When Rachilde was sentenced (in absentia) to two years in a Belgian prison for her scandalous novel *Monsieur Venus*, in which a virile noblewoman sexually enslaves a young male florist, Verlaine offered his congratulations: "Ah, my dear child, if you have invented a new vice, you are the benefactor of humanity."

Because the Marchesa Casati's gorgeous if somewhat comically ghoulish figure haunts the memoirs of her heyday (particularly those nostalgic accounts of Belle Époque and Jazz Age high life written in a drawling tone by the hardy gadabouts who never missed a well-etherized orgy), I encountered her at two separate moments in my life, fifteen years apart: first, when I was writing about Isak Dinesen, and later, doing research on Colette. Casati and Colette, both great believers in the spirit world, patronized the same fashionable mediums and frequented a circle of louche-minded grandees that included Jean Lorrain, Robert de Montesquiou, Baronne Elsie Deslandes, Baron Adelsward-Fersen, Isadora Duncan, Diaghilev, the Princesse de Polignac (née Winaretta Singer), Natalie Barney, and D'Annunzio (whose mistress, when Colette befriended him in 1915, was her second husband's rich first wife). But it would be hard to find two women better designed to loathe each other, despite a shared gift for malice and a penchant for exhibitionism. Colette was a truculently fleshy and frugal "child of nature," perennially hardworking and allergic to morbidity. Casati was a devotee of fetishism who proudly displayed the bruises and teeth marks of her love games with D'Annunzio. "Flesh," he wrote on an arresting photograph of "the Divine Marquise" by Baron de Meyer, "is merely spirit betrothed to death." Behind her back, though, the Parisians dubbed her "the Venus of Père Lachaise."

Dinesen, on the other hand, seems to have styled the witchy persona of her old age—that of Baroness Blixen—after Casati. By birth, they belonged to the same class, the nouveaux riches, and to the same generation of women who aspired to be as dangerous as their mothers had been harmless. Though I have no evidence that they met, they almost certainly crossed paths in Paris. Before and after the First World War, Casati lived there for months at a time, usually at the Ritz, taxing its staff with her tantrums and with the tiresome daily job of feeding live chickens and rabbits to the ubiquitous boa. Dinesen, who preferred the St. James and Albany, which had a Danish concierge, stopped on her way from Kenya to Copenhagen to replenish her wardrobe at Paquin and Lewis (the couture milliner), even as her coffee plantation was going bankrupt. (She brought along two African pages dressed in picturesque native regalia, who carried her parcels and slept in her bathtub.) It was an indulgence that Casati—who went bankrupt at the same time (1930–31)—would have approved. Dinesen and Casati shared a taste for pasty foundation and sooty eyes; for venerable titles acquired from complacent, much poorer husbands obsessed with blood sport; and for Oriental barbarism filtered through a gauze of ancien régime snobbery. Though the Marchesa would never have been caught dead in the fastidiously tailored gray suit that the Baroness called "Sober Truth," they both prided themselves on an emaciated figure. Dinesen held that the only dignified way for a woman to age is to become a skeleton. She, however, was naturally rather dumpy and had to battle a hearty appetite, and she didn't achieve her ideal weight (about eighty pounds) until middle age, and then only with the help of syphilis, anorexia, chain-smoking, and amphetamines. Casati seems to have enjoyed her lifelong career as a wraith without troubling to diet, though perhaps her secret was cocaine.

Unlike Colette, who was intolerant of those who let life consume them, Dinesen believed devoutly in throwing oneself away. She once told a journalist that her favorite expression in the English language was "regardless of expense" (though she was rather more reckless with other people's assets than with her own). Casati was so sublimely innocent of prudence that she spent every penny of her colossal patrimony on palaces, parties, antiques, cars, clothes, jewels, travels with a princely retinue, and art (mostly portraits of herself). By the time the Depression overtook her, she was $25 million in debt. Her last telegram to D'Annunzio begged him to wire her ten thousand lire, but the cad never replied.

"I want to be a living work of art," Casati proclaimed. Her startling appearance and peerless imagination for costume and decor promised a good play, but—as Cocteau put it bluntly—"there was none." (There was none yet. He had never attended that modern theater with which the Marchesa's inspired fashion stunts have the most affinity: the couture runway.) Her nerve never failed her, though her flesh did. "Eccentricity," the French belletrist Maurice Druon wrote, "is tolerable only in its first freshness. Cherished until it has gone stale, it becomes unbearably pathetic." He was thinking of Casati, who, in trying too hard to be unique, inevitably became a type. She was a model for the heroine of his 1954 novel, *La Volupté d'Être*, which was translated into English as *The Film of Memory* and adapted for the stage as *La Contessa*, with Vivien Leigh in the title role, and for the screen as *A Matter of Time*, starring Ingrid Bergman. Despite their illustrious leading ladies, play and film were equally wretched flops, in part, perhaps, because Casati transformed herself into a dazzling but ephemeral spectacle, like a display of fireworks, while neglecting those aspects of being—thought and feeling—that enrich a narrative. Her allure was better suited to a picture frame, and she infatuated a number of important artists (Marinetti, Van Dongen, Man Ray, Romaine Brooks, and Augustus John, among others), whose portraits capture the fever of her studied ferocity.

Casati hated getting old, but she accepted destitution with a stoical, even eerie, aplomb. This suggests that her most obvious weakness—indifference to reality—was a form of strength. After the forced liquidation of her Parisian villa, the Palais Rose, and its contents, she moved to London, where she bartered the few treasures she had managed to salvage for rent, tarot readings, and food for her Pekingese dogs. As each dog died, she had it stuffed, and forwarded the taxidermist's bill to her granddaughter. She spent her last years in a cheap bedsit, casting spells on her enemies (Cecil Beaton was one—

he betrayed her with a candid photo of her sagging chin and a dis-obliging passage in his memoirs) and compiling three volumes of a strange journal: a dreamlike assemblage of newspaper and magazine clippings. In one collage, an elegant, old-fashioned razor and two ripe peaches with suggestive lobes are juxtaposed with a Gulliverian, bejeweled Henry VIII, who dwarfs an entourage of Lilliputian fe-males, all but one with her head snipped off. Other pages featured images of Rasputin and the Duchess of Windsor: "The evident care with which they were constructed shows that this was no random amusement," her biographers write. But the minute her friends sug-gested that she mount an exhibition of her journals, if only to raise some badly needed cash, she abandoned the project. "The March-esa," Philippe Jullian observed, "seemed to have a genuine horror of money."

Perhaps, however, she had come to the conclusion, with Dinesen, who starved herself to death five years after Casati died of a cerebral hemorrhage, that there is a supreme cachet—even a nobility—in los-ing everything but one's style. Poor as she was, and increasingly ad-dled by gin and drugs, she never ceased dressing to produce a sensational effect. Jullian had seen her, he claimed, rummaging through trash bins—not for food, of course, but for scraps of velvet or lace. "When Luisa Casati walked along the streets of London," Druon wrote, "it took all of the dignity of the English not to just gawk at this phantom" with a livid face, a crooked hat, and a thread-bare black gown, half unraveled and trimmed in crackled leather or mangy fur—the finery of a madwoman. Today, of course, the hip wouldn't gawk; they would marvel at her chic. Fashion has abolished the distinction between day and evening, and nothing is more mod-ern than frayed seams, outré makeup, Goth bleakness, and cus-tomized vintage. Casati realized her most cherished ambition, though perhaps not in the form she had imagined: foretelling the future.

—September 22, 2003

· FIVE ·

Dressed for Excess

Marie Antoinette, the ex-queen of France, was thirty-seven when she was taken from her cell in the Conciergerie, the fourteenth-century fortress on the Île de la Cité, and paraded in an open oxcart to the scaffold in the place de la Révolution, a mile away. Some of the onlookers in the vast crowd lining the route that morning, on October 16, 1793, may have been among those screaming obscenities at her in 1789, when they marched with pikes on Versailles; or axed their way, in 1792, into her apartment in the Tuileries, where they spent their fury on her mirrors and closets; or waved the severed head of her friend and look-alike, the lovely Princesse de Lamballe, on a halberd outside her window. But now they observed an eerie silence.

Her husband, Louis XVI, who lost his title when the monarchy was abolished, had been guillotined nine months earlier, though he was spared the indignity of riding in a tumbrel with bound hands. The Jacobin extremists then seized her son. The eight-year-old Louis Charles—Louis XVII to royalists—had clung to her skirts and was pulled off. As part of his reeducation, his captors plied him with alcohol between beatings and taught him the "Marseillaise," which he sang with a heartbreaking swagger, wearing the red bonnet of a sans-culotte. He testified that she had molested him, and his evidence was presented at her brief show trial for treason and moral turpitude. He died two years later, alone in a dungeon.

No other queen, except perhaps Cleopatra, was more intent than

Marie Antoinette on dressing for history. While her instincts for self-display had worked more toward her undoing than her glory, they served her a last time. The mourning outfit she had worn day and night since her husband's death, in defiance of a Jacobin edict against black (a color symbolic of monarchist sympathies), had grown increasingly shabby. But, knowing that she would need to make a final and unforgettable impression—at her execution—she had managed to acquire a pristine chemise, petticoat, morning dress, and bonnet, all in white.

Early on the day of her death, Marie Antoinette arose from a few sleepless hours on her straw pallet and began her toilette. At dawn, the Jacobins' chief executioner, Citizen Sanson, arrived to cut off her hair. It had turned white in the course of a few days in June of 1791, during the captive royal family's ill-conceived flight to Varennes, which had ended with their recapture. The artist Jacques-Louis David, a radical member of the National Convention, watched the death march from a window, and what he perceived as the "arrogance" of the traitor's mien particularly incensed him. He sketched a hasty portrait of a wasted crone with a scornful grimace and a ramrod spine. Her dress looks like a shroud.

The former queen had been denied a priest of her choice (one of the dissidents who had refused to swear an oath of loyalty to the Revolution), so she mounted the scaffold alone and apologized to Sanson for stepping on his toe. After he released the blade, he exhibited the head, as was customary, and the crowd, shaken from its trance, roared, "*Vive la République!*" The remains were then taken to a cemetery off the rue d'Anjou, where the bodies of the king and of his Swiss Guard—who were butchered orgiastically at the Tuileries, with other royal retainers—had been buried, the latter in a trench. The gravediggers, as Antonia Fraser writes in her biography *Marie Antoinette: The Journey* (Nan A. Talese, 2001), were taking a lunch break, so they left the queen's head and body lying on the grass, giving a young sculptor—Marie Grosholtz, who later became Madame Tussaud—an opportunity to take a wax imprint for a death mask. In 1815, a year after the Bourbon monarchy was restored, Louis XVIII, the king's perfidious younger brother (who had married his son to Marie Antoinette's only surviving child, Marie Thérèse), exhumed the relics and had them reburied in state, at the Cathedral of St. Denis. Chateaubriand was present at the ceremony, and he claimed to have recognized the head immediately, Fraser writes, "by the special shape of the Queen's mouth, recalling that dazzling smile she had given him at Versailles." But all that was left, besides a skull, some hair, and the nostalgia of a Romantic, were two garters, in perfect condition.

Marie Antoinette is periodically disinterred in order to be reviled or celebrated or, as in recent years, to help sell clothes, as she did when she was queen. This fall, her latest avatar, Kirsten Dunst, looking dewy and regal, is ubiquitous in magazines promoting a new film biography directed by Sofia Coppola and based on Fraser's life. Coppola herself is a fashion celebrity and muse who helps to publicize the work of designer friends by wearing it with the teasing glamour of a jaded virgin playing dress-up in her mother's clothes. She has always been drawn to beautiful, trapped girls who belong to a generation too cynical to unite in rebellion and too cool to unite in conformity. You can see why she thought that the "teen queen"—a hostage to appearances—would make a good subject. But, rather than play to her forte for impiety, she and an ensemble of virtuoso technicians have produced—despite the odd postmodern wink—a sanitized, old-fashioned costume picture.

Vogue predicts that the movie "will have a considerable impact on fashion for years to come," though the shape of that impact is a bit hard to imagine, like Chateaubriand's vision of the smile. Every new runway season seems to recapitulate some version of the artificial face-off between decadent royalism and radical chic, and has done so for about twenty years. But perhaps people who live for fashion worship Marie Antoinette precisely because she represents a time when one had to take sides, and dressing not only defined them—it was a matter of survival.

Few tyrants have aroused more visceral hatred than Marie Antoinette, an ordinary woman whose life is infinitely more complex than she

was. That hatred, which is usually chalked up to the sentiments expressed in a sentence she never uttered, "Let them eat cake," has become part of her mystique. Her downfall—a cautionary tale for
politicians out of touch with their base—began almost the moment
she arrived at Versailles, as a fourteen-year-old dauphine who recklessly decided to emancipate herself from the constraints of court
protocol and, at the same time, to impress the courtiers she was offending with a display of prestige she didn't possess.

Marie Antoinette's prestige depended principally on one attribute—her fertility—and her shy, obese fifteen-year-old bridegroom
wouldn't deflower her (or at least finish the job) for seven years.
Louis XVI is, like his wife, something of a cipher, but prolonged exposure to her hectic glamour begins to make his dreariness appealing.
He spent his leisure, which was considerable, turning locks on a private forge (he had a touching faith in the virtue of useful labor),
when he wasn't hunting in the forest, and in that respect—his passion for the chase—he couldn't have been a stranger to desire. He
was less of a reactionary than many of his courtiers, including the
queen; he was, to certain modern eyes, admirable in his antiheroic
distaste for violence and martial preening; he understood that the appalling tax code needed reform; yet he was passive and befuddled.

On numerous occasions, and as tactfully as possible, Marie Antoinette brought up the subject of "living in the intimacy" required
of their vows, as did his physicians, and Louis made promises to act
that he couldn't keep. In 1777, two and a half years into his kingship, he finally managed the feat. But the bizarre impasse was resolved only when Marie Antoinette's older brother, the brusque and
plainspoken emperor Joseph II of Austria, arrived at Versailles to have
a frank talk with his sister about her spendthrift ways, and with the
bumbling dynast about his obligations. Joseph was filled with contempt at the discovery, he wrote to his cadet, Archduke Leopold, in
Vienna, that the king "has strong, perfectly satisfactory erections;
he introduces his member, stays there without moving for about
two minutes, withdraws without ejaculating but still erect, and bids
good-night." If he had been there, he swore, he would have had
Louis whipped "so that he would have come out of sheer rage like a
donkey."

Apart from the humiliation of having her bedsheets checked for blood or "emissions," and her periods reported on by ambassadors to every court in Europe, the ordeal of Marie Antoinette's prolonged virginity trapped her in a perilous limbo. As long as an annulment was possible, she had to cultivate an "appearance of credit" with the king, as she explained to her brother. Cultivating the appearance of virtue might have been a more politic strategy, but she chose, instead, to model her style and behavior on those of a royal paramour. The wives of Louis XIV and Louis XV had both been pious and obscure wallflowers, which was precisely what the French expected from a good queen. Their husbands' chief favorites, however—Mesdames de Montespan, de Pompadour, and du Barry (a ravishing former prostitute with appalling manners who was still plying her trade with the old Louis XV when Antoinette arrived at court)—were glittering cynosures whose power no one dared to ignore. So the scorned virgin began to upgrade her fictitious "credit" by acquiring the flamboyant wardrobe of a kept woman (lest the point be lost, she appeared at one of her masked balls as Gabrielle d'Estrées, the Renaissance mistress of Henri IV, wearing a cloud of silver-spangled white gauze, a diamond stomacher and girdle, and a skirt swagged with gold fringe that was pinned up by more diamonds), as well as a private real-estate portfolio of incalculable worth, including the Petit Trianon, which was built for Pompadour, and Saint-Cloud, an asset of the Crown, which she had transferred to her name.

In 1774, Louis XV, the dauphin's grandfather, died suddenly of smallpox, at sixty-four. "God help us," nineteen-year-old Louis XVI exclaimed, "for we are too young to reign." Shortly after his coronation, a year later, at which the queen made herself particularly conspicuous in an embroidered gown encrusted with sapphires and a towering ziggurat of powdered hair, she had her portrait painted for her mother. When the empress Maria Theresa received it, she was aghast. "No, this is not the portrait of a queen of France," she wrote back. "This is the portrait of an actress!"

The staggering expenses that Marie Antoinette's quixotic game plan incurred were paid for by levies on the Third Estate. Her budget overruns on an annual clothing allowance of about $3.6 million in current spending power were, in some years, more than double.

Sometimes the king made up the difference, and occasionally the queen made a propitiatory gesture of economy—she once refused a parure on the ground that the navy could use a new battleship. But her chronic debt was one source of the epithet Madame Deficit, the other being her expedience as a scapegoat for enemies on both the right and the left. The former saw her as an insidious foreign agent— *l'Autrichienne* (the epithet contains a pun on the word for "bitch," *chienne*)—and decried her corrupting influence on the countless Frenchwomen who aspired to her chic.

The republicans saw Marie Antoinette as the insatiable parasite who embodied all the evils of her regime, but one should note that the millions she funneled to her architects, gardeners, entertainers, caterers, cobblers, perfumers, decorators, coiffeurs, and—most egregiously—dressmakers wouldn't have been sufficient to compensate for the disastrous wars and centuries of corruption and inequity that were responsible for the country's bankruptcy. As a symptom, however, the inventory of her follies was hard to ignore. (Fraser asks one to forgive, if not thank, the prodigal queen for helping to create "things of great delight," and she cites the boudoir at Fontainebleau as the "supreme example.") A gown or headdress from Marie Antoinette's favorite *marchande de mode*, Rose Bertin, could easily cost twenty times what a skilled worker earned in a year, and if he wanted to see where his taxes went, he could visit the queen's wardrobe—it was open to the public.

Until the end, the ferocious hatred of the people didn't much perturb Marie Antoinette. She had told her mother, years before, that the French were "thoughtless in character but not bad; pens and tongues say many things that do not come from the heart." She seems to have thought of her own heart as pure: that of an enlightened queen who provided dowries for indigent maidens; imported peasant playmates for her children to teach them humility; adopted the orphan of a chambermaid; supported artists, like her music teacher Glück and his protégé Salieri; and paid homage to the ideals of Rousseau by building an enchanting faux-rustic village—the Hameau—where she and her ladies liked to dress in exorbitantly simple lawn frocks known as *gaulles*, set off by a ribbon sash and a straw hat.

A pure heart, however, does not entirely rule out an adulterous love affair. It isn't certain (though it seems likely, Fraser thinks) that the queen consummated her lifelong romance with Count Axel Fersen, a Swedish officer of immense charm and wealth who fought with the French forces in America, and who, in the royal triangle (if that's what it was), played Mars to Louis's Vulcan. He had met the dauphine one night by chance in the days when she and her ladies (noble age-mates who, a contemporary wrote, "loved pleasure and hated restraint; laughed at everything, even the tattle about their own reputations; and recognized no law save the necessity of spending their lives in gaiety") would throw a hooded cloak over their panniers, escape to Paris, and mingle with masked strangers of mixed estate at the opera balls. The affair probably began only once the king had managed to make Antoinette "a real wife," but it continued sporadically whenever Fersen's military and diplomatic missions brought him to Versailles. The king was fond of his gallant company, and Fersen proved his devotion, if not his competence, by helping to orchestrate the flight to Varennes.

But, apart from her profligate and imprudent greed, there was nothing vicious about Marie Antoinette. She never so much as dreamed of the atrocities, including incest and pedophilia, attributed to her as the "French Messalina" and the "Austrian whore." By the standards of Versailles (which were admittedly deplorable), she was a loyal consort, a besotted mother, and a virtuous enough wife. Nor did the French people entirely begrudge the queen her lavish toilettes. She was expected, indeed required, to make a patriotic public display of support for the luxury trades, particularly silk weaving, an important sector of the economy. But Marie Antoinette never understood that her splendor was a form of livery, and that with it came hieratic duties and sacrifices. She could not have been killed had she not first been deconsecrated, and she had unwittingly colluded in her own deconsecration by asserting her divine right to the one privilege no deified being can exercise with impunity. That, as she put it to her mother, was "to be myself."

Maria Theresa would have preferred to trade one of her older girls to France, an untested ally, but one was pockmarked and the others were married or dead. Though Antoinette, like her fiancé, was a dynastic spare (until his father and two brothers died prematurely, Louis had been fourth in line), beauty strengthened her hand. She was, according to her lady of the bedchamber and biographer, Madame Campan, a lithe and blue-eyed ash blonde "bursting with freshness," who gave the picky French little to complain of. Even her detractors admired her majestic carriage and peerless complexion. Her flat chest initially caused a disgruntled murmur, but two months before the marriage, the empress was pleased to inform the king's envoy that her daughter had "become a woman." They were both confident that once she was a wife with a busy womb, the bosom would fill out.

The "handover" (*remise*) of a dauphine was a ritual not unlike a real-estate closing, with a final inspection attended by representatives for each party to the sale. The initial report, however, had flagged some minor flaws that needed correction. So the Parisian dentist who invented braces was imported to straighten the archducal teeth; a dancing master taught Antoinette the distinctive, gliding shuffle of court ladies; and a French coiffeur, M. Larsenneur, artfully dissembled her unfashionably high forehead and the bald spots at her hairline. The rather more glaring bald spots in her culture and education were confided for repair to the worldly Abbé de Vermond, who did what he could with a lazy pupil who had been both spoiled and neglected.

Once the makeover was complete, and the frugal empress had stoically ponied up four hundred thousand livres (the yearly income of a great nobleman) for a trousseau worthy of her new in-laws, the dauphine and her entourage set off for France. Envoys of Louis XV greeted her at the border, where she entered a pavilion built for the *remise* on a riverine island that straddled the frontier of the two kingdoms. As a driving rainstorm rattled the flimsy roof, and the future queen digested the import of a tapestry that depicted Medea slaughtering her children, her Austrian retinue solemnly stripped her before all assembled and bundled up the clothes and possessions, including her pug, named Mops, that were tainted with her foreignness. Weeping and shivering, she became Crown property at the moment that her new ladies redressed her.

Marie Antoinette was twice handed over: first to produce the legitimate heir to an ossified monarchy, then to help legitimatize the fanat-
ics who abolished it. A scholar of the eighteenth century, Pierre
Saint-Amand, sums up her life between those brackets as "a series of
costumed events." That is a fair description of Coppola's film, and
also of the premise of a new biography, *Queen of Fashion: What
Marie Antoinette Wore to the Revolution* (Holt, 2006), by Caroline
Weber, a professor at Barnard. Her subtitle suggests how tempting it
is even for a serious historian to lark on her subject's principal obsession. In the gloriously witty age of *esprit*, the queen chose to—or
perhaps could only—express herself in the hyper-exclamatory prose
of (as Weber puts it) her "fashion statements." It is always gratifying
to discover how much a fashion statement can mean, and Weber's account of the transition from the ancien régime to the Republic from
a sartorial point of view is a perceptive work of scholarship that helps,
in a way, to explain the transcendent importance of fashion to French
culture.

   But was Marie Antoinette really a spirited rebel challenging "the
oppressive cultural strictures and harsh political animosities that beset
her . . . by turning her clothes and other accoutrements into defiant
expressions of autonomy and prestige"? Many of her contemporaries—and not only the libelous pamphleteers and pornographers—
wouldn't have agreed. "To be the most *à la mode* woman alive," the
Comtesse de Boigne wrote, "seemed to [the queen] to be the most
desirable thing imaginable." One might also argue that what strikes a
modern academic as proto-feminist self-"empowerment" also bears a
suspicious resemblance to the posturing of a willful teenager who
breaks the rules, ignores her mother's nagging, and does as she
pleases to be thought cool.

Sometime in the mid-1770s, a young perfumer named Jean-Louis
Fargeon, who had recently immigrated to Paris from his native
Montpellier and taken over a well-established shop on the rue du
Roule, was invited to present samples of his work to Madame du

Barry. Fargeon came from a family of artisans, and had recently grad-uated from journeyman to master. But he was also a student of the Enlightenment who had been deeply moved by Rousseau's assertion that the nose is the door to the soul. The fame of his products—not only scents and oils but cosmetics, powders, pomades, hair dyes, and such dainty novelties as a tongue-scraper—attracted the queen's at-tention. Elisabeth de Feydeau, a French professor (with a doctorate in "the history of perfume" from the Sorbonne—*Vive la France!*), tells the story of their relations in *A Scented Palace: The Secret History of Marie Antoinette's Perfumer* (Tauris, 2006), a sparely written and subtly distilled life. Fargeon's impressions of Marie Antoinette are particularly compelling, in part because of their intimacy and his keen senses, but in part because he is a witness who, despite a vocation that depended almost entirely on an aristocratic clientele, believed ar-dently in the ideals of the Revolution.

The perfumer was shocked by his first visit to the palace for some of the reasons it must also have shocked Marie Antoinette, who had grown up in a court and a family where impeccable hygiene was an article of faith. Not only did courtiers at Versailles look embalmed behind their masks of white powder and rouge, but the many who bathed only once a year smelled like corpses. The filthy halls and courtyards stank of the excrement from humans and pets; dead cats floated in stagnant water; and a butcher plied his trade—gutting and roasting pigs—at the entrance to the ministers' wing. But Fargeon was equally struck by the arcane ritual of the queen's *lever*, when, having proved himself, he was given the privilege of attending it. Madame Campan, in her memoirs, describes the bathing-and-dressing ceremony as "a masterpiece of etiquette," though the young dauphine quickly got bored and exasperated at being fetishized by a tribal cult that required her to stand naked and impassive while wait-ing for an exalted pit crew to coordinate the task of passing a shift. "It's odious! What a bother!" she had exclaimed in an outburst so sacrilegious that it became immortal. She eventually found a way around the bother: she invited Bertin to dress her, and, since her ladies-in-waiting—daughters of the Crusades—refused to share the honor with a former shop clerk, they withdrew.

Fargeon often collaborated on scented accessories with the earthy

Bertin—a genius who not only earned but invented her place in history as a political eminence whom her detractors called the Minister of Fashion. She was the architect of the famous *pouf*, and Léonard—the royal hairdresser ("the personification," de Feydeau writes, "of one of the little, beribboned marquises Molière used to make fun of")—was its engineer. This amusingly freakish coiffure became the rage all over Europe, and, like most of the queen's fashion fantasias, it proved particularly ruinous to her plebeian imitators, who, it was said, sacrificed their dowries on the altar of the Austrian's frivolity, and thus their chances of marriage, then turned to rich protectors to take up the slack, so in the end—the omega of such arguments—the French birth rate suffered.

The *pouf* was a cross between a topiary and a Christmas tree, and each creation, about a yard high, had a sentimental or political theme, depending on the wearer and the occasion. It started with a wire form that Léonard padded with wool, cloth, horsehair, and gauze, interweaving the client's tresses with fake hair. When the edifice had been well stiffened with pomade and dusted with powder (vermin were fond of both, so fashionable ladies carried long-handled head-scratchers), it was ready to be trimmed with its defining scene. Ships, barnyards, vegetables, battles, nativities, and even a husband's infidelities were some of the themes. Weber calls the *poufs* "personalized mobile billboards," and the queen wore a *pouf à l'inoculation* to publicize her triumph in persuading the king to be vaccinated against smallpox. Perched in the hairdo was a serpent in an olive tree (symbols of wisdom and Aesculapius), behind which rose the golden sun of enlightenment.

One of Fargeon's last interviews with the queen took place in the Tuileries, in 1791. She had summoned him for an urgent matter, "greeted him kindly," de Feydeau writes, "and asked him what he, as a bourgeois of Paris, thought of the events." He had the tact to parry the question, but the first thing he noticed was the scent of a perfume he had created for her in happier days. They had walked along a path outside the Trianon, and she had asked him for two essences: one for "an elegant and virile man," and the other, an elixir of the

Trianon itself, "so that she could carry it wherever she went." But now he realized with dismay that the scent of the Trianon had gone off.

Marie Antoinette was, in fact, planning her flight to Varennes, and she wanted Fargeon to restock her enormous toilet case for the journey. She had already seen to the fitting out of an impractically huge plush-lined carriage, loaded with as many amenities—a dining table, commodes, cooking equipment—as a Winnebago; and she had let herself be distracted from more salient preoccupations by fussing with Bertin over a luxurious new wardrobe, which distressed Madame Campan, because "that seemed useless and even dangerous to me, and I pointed out that the Queen of France will find chemises and dresses everywhere." But, de Feydeau continues, Marie Antoinette "could not conceive of going without her coiffeur, so Léonard was informed. He was to bring the coffer carrying the Queen's diamonds and to alert the horse relays of the approach of the fugitives." His grandiose bungling helped to betray the plot.

Fargeon had been stirred, in 1789, by the Tennis Court Oath and its promise of a new order. Though the vitriol aimed at the queen distressed him, he was more of a republican than his wife, who fainted when she heard drunks in the rue de Roule singing one of the more vile revolutionary songs. Fargeon explained the paradox of his feelings. Marie Antoinette, he said, was kind and bountiful to individuals, and nothing like her caricatures. Yet, as de Feydeau puts it, "her subjects were creatures of fiction to her." One had to distinguish between the woman and the queen, he concluded, as "every monarchy was, by nature, tyrannical." This was his paraphrase of Saint-Just's famous dictum: "No one reigns innocently." But what was true of the queen was also true of her alchemist. He recognized the humanity of Marie Antoinette but categorically despised a whole class.

I can't help thinking of Marie Antoinette as a prototype for Emma Bovary, another naïve young beauty who marries a boorish glutton, equally naïve, and lets herself be seduced by a *marchand de mode*. The Bovarys, too, were a couple with no qualities beyond the ordinary, who were doomed to an extraordinary disgrace, and both stories have a brutal ending in which no justice is served. That absence of catharsis marks the point at which tragedy loses its exaltation and becomes modern—not a tale foretold about the death of kings but the story of a futile downfall that might have been averted. And it was left to Flaubert to democratize the wisdom of Saint-Just. His works insist that no one is human innocently.

—September 25, 2006

SIX

The Queen Himself

In April 2000, a show devoted to Cleopatra opened at the British Museum. London was unseasonably cold that week, and riveted by the latest Windsor scandal: "foot in mouth disease," as the tabloids put it—the taped indiscretions of yet another garrulous royal daughter-in-law. Steak tartare appeared on the menus of patriotic pubs. The parks were emerald after a winter of deluges, and the populace, impatient for spring—for any new leaf—had, despite the chill, cast off its heavy clothes.

Dressed lightly, as usual, Cleopatra graced the cover of the London *Sunday Times Magazine*. The breaking news from the museum, the article suggested facetiously, was that she'd had rotten teeth (the English seem to be obsessed with dentistry), bad makeup, and a big nose. "Did her lovers have to hold their breath, close their eyes and think of Rome?" Was hers the "triumph of brains over beauty?" In a spectacularly vulgar illustration, the queen looked like an avatar of Leona Helmsley before plastic surgery.

Actually, there are no sensational revelations in "Cleopatra of Egypt: From History to Myth," which was curated by Susan Walker and Peter Higgs. It focuses on the historical figure and relegates the various femmes fatales, ingenues, spendthrifts, and sacred victims of millennial fantasy to the sideshow. This is refreshing. An American museum might have organized something glitzier, perhaps with film clips. The Guggenheim might even have thrown in the costumes. There are, it's true, a couple of charmingly obscene caricatures from the first century showing a Cleopatra-like figure copulating with a crocodile and having sex on a barge. There is a frieze of Hollywood queens in vulture headdresses on one wall, and a small collection—busy and gorgeous—of Old Master portraits. But numismatics is the cornerstone of Cleopatra studies, and most of the wares here are equally hard and scholarly: vitrines of coins and jewelry; mosaics, artifacts, and statuary from the Ptolemaic and Augustan periods; a recently authenticated taxation decree with a royal command—"Make it happen"—written in the queen's elegant hand; and, what is most noteworthy, seven "newly recognized" Egyptian images of Cleopatra VII, stylized and veristic, in basalt, limestone, and marble, by artists of or close to her time. These handsome relics say little and are most expressive of the distance between us and Cleopatra. Archaeology is a lesson in humility. The more we know about the past, it suggests, the more we know that we know precious little.

"Who was Cleopatra?" Walker and Higgs ask in their introduction to the catalog (Princeton, 2001), a hefty work of lively expertise and sumptuous if infuriatingly numbered illustrations. That is a difficult question to answer, at least by the standards of modern biography, because the ancient sources that so richly chronicle her life, describe her person, supply her dialogue, and analyze her motivations (a) have no footnotes, (b) conflict, (c) are almost entirely hostile, and (d) for the most part, postdate her reign. A very small body of fact has inspired a monumental edifice of speculation. So we're left not with a woman but with a character.

Yet Cleopatra is a character as Shakespeare is an artist. Her bounty is inexhaustible. Every age restyles her in its own image and invests her with its own preoccupations. "Many unpleasant things can be said of Cleopatra," A. C. Bradley wrote in 1909, "and the more that are said, the more wonderful she appears." Whoever she was, she represents a unique concentration of fabulous wealth, exalted birth, unchecked ambition, exceptional intelligence, sexual charisma, human frailty, and supreme temporal power in the fertile body of a woman who lived fast and died young. There have been other great queens, but no one of her stature.

That stature was "petite," according to the catalog—aristocratic women of the period were about five feet tall—and probably quite voluptuous. Cleopatra's great-grandfather was nicknamed Ptolemy Physkon ("Potbelly"). He thought it becoming to exhibit his monstrous (or, as he probably saw it, Dionysiac) obesity in transparent robes to a delegation of visiting Romans, who recorded this gaffe for posterity. Potbelly's grandson, Cleopatra's father, also had an epithet: Auletes, the Flute Player—an allusion both to his love of the instrument sacred to Isis and to his dissipation. The wine, women, and/or boys were subsumed by the song.

Auletes and his queen, Cleopatra V, who was also his sister, had six children. Their middle daughter, who was to become the last of the Ptolemaic pharaohs and the seventh monarch of her name, was born in Alexandria around 69 BC. She was a princess ostensibly well educated in mathematics, medicine, literature, music, philosophy, and the martial arts. She had ascended to the throne of the richest and most populous country in the Middle East by the age of eighteen. She assassinated or connived in the disappearance of two of her sibling rivals (a younger sister and the second of the two younger brothers she had married in succession), ruled by divine right for twenty-one years, and was worshipped as a living deity. She survived exile and insurrection, raised and commanded armies, shrewdly bestowed her patronage, and negotiated her foreign policy with remarkable finesse—at least as measured by her longevity as a sovereign at one of the most treacherous moments in history, the quicksand period of civil war in Rome.

As we know, the queen allied herself both strategically and sexually with Julius Caesar, who was thirty-two years her senior, then with Mark Antony, whom she seems truly to have adored. With Caesar she had a son; with Antony a pair of twins, male and female, and a younger boy. Unfortunately for future biographers, the Romans who wrote her story bothered to keep track of her only when one of her two Elvises was, so to speak, in the building. Both were respectably married, and the issue of adultery, which would have been fairly meaningless to Cleopatra—a woman to whom nothing was forbidden—has figured prominently in most later versions of these romances. Antony did leave her behind in Alexandria pregnant with the twins (Alexander Helios and Cleopatra Selene) to marry the sister of his rival Octavian, a politic union that produced two daughters. Mild, lovely, noble, virtuous, self-sacrificing Octavia—ancestress of Nero and Caligula—has always played the role of Krystle to Cleopatra's Alexis in their dynastic saga. But even those writers who have judged the queen harshly have shown a touching sympathy for her imagined humiliations as the Other Woman.

It seems improbable that the teenage Cleopatra arranged to meet the grizzled Caesar for the first time by having herself delivered to his quarters in her own palace rolled in a carpet; or that, as Pliny tells it, she challenged Antony to outspend her at dueling banquets, then, to win her bet, dissolved the world's largest pearl—one of a pair she wore as earrings—in a cruet of vinegar and drank it. But everything we know about her is improbable. She had a genius for drama (and self-dramatization), underwritten by an unlimited budget for props and extras. Her sense of stagecraft was informed by her knowledge of myth and tragedy, and by her intimate experience of murderous intrigues and of ritual veneration.

In 47 BC, Cleopatra gave birth to Caesar's son, Caesarion, and minted a coin on which she appeared as Aphrodite nursing Eros. By now she was married to her youngest brother, but he was only twelve, hardly mature enough to claim his conjugal rights. Caesar had pacified their kingdom, and the next year Cleopatra followed him to Rome, where she lived in one of his suburban villas, made an enemy of Cicero with her haughtiness, dazzled the patricians with her wit—Rome was considerably more provincial than Alexandria—and inspired a craze for things Egyptian. Caesar, in a gesture that signaled his own aspirations to divinely ordained kingship, if not his infatuation, installed a golden statue of his mistress in the temple of Venus Genetrix, divine mother of the Julian line. It became a popular attraction and was still standing in the third century. Two years later, the Senate named Caesar dictator for life, and he drew up legislation that, according to the catalog, "clearly bore [Cleopatra's] fingerprints" and would have permitted him to marry her legally, legitimatize their son, and establish a second capital for the empire at Alexandria. "The demise of this programme came with his assassination," on the ides of March in 44 BC.

As Mark Antony, Lepidus, and Octavian, who was Caesar's grand-nephew and legal heir, battled Cassius and Brutus for control of the empire, Cleopatra fled Italy and regained an Egypt gripped by famine and plague. It was a perilous moment for her, and she had no protector. Her sister Arsinoë, imprisoned in Rome, had managed to install a puppet on the throne—a boy pretending to be Ptolemy XIII, their dead brother. Once Cleopatra had deposed him and settled the disturbances in her capital, she adopted a prudent course of neutrality toward both factions in the Roman civil war, making promises of support that she delayed in keeping. Procrastination was as much the instrument of her statesmanship as seduction, and it served her well. So did a carefully nurtured alliance with the Egyptian clergy, who helped to promote her cult as the mother goddess.

After much intrigue and bloodshed, the victorious party of Antony, Lepidus, and Octavian divvied up the empire. Antony took the east and embarked on a leisurely and sybaritic grand tour to consolidate his power and collect taxes. He was greeted everywhere as a "new Dionysus," and in 41 BC, he summoned Cleopatra, his client monarch, to a meeting at Tarsus, in Cilicia (southeastern Turkey). According to Plutarch, she ignored his letters, tried his patience, and whetted his appetite. Eventually—having artfully spread the rumor that, "for the good and happiness of Asia," the goddess of love was sailing up the Cydnus River for a "festive reception" with the god of the vine—she showed up in a gilded barge with purple sails and oars of silver, wreathed in incense, attended by maids and pages dressed as sea nymphs and cupids, and arrayed as Aphrodite. She was twenty-eight, an age, according to Plutarch, "when women's beauty is most splendid, and their intellects are in full maturity." Antony was forty-one.

Already by the time of Caesar's death, and whatever she really looked like, Cleopatra's reputation as a voracious and fatal temptress was well established, and in the course of her alliance with Antony it acquired mythic proportions. Sextus Propertius claimed that she "fornicated even with her slaves." Plutarch reports that she and Antony, who tarried for a year with her in Alexandria after their summit, formed a secret society of fellow hedonists known as the Inimitables, who dedicated their lives to *methe*, drunkenness, and that this was the motto the queen engraved on her ring. Lucan—and one has to suspect that he cross-dressed in secret—thrilled to the excesses of her decor, wardrobe, and diet:

> The great door-posts [of her palace] were solid ebony, not common timber with an ebony veneer . . . Her white breasts showed through the Chinese silk which, though closely woven when imported, had been teased out by some Egyptian mercer until it became diaphanous . . . Every delicacy that extravagance, prompted not by hunger but by a mad love of ostentation, could rout out from the ends of the earth came served on golden dishes.

Plutarch sketches a temperate and beguiling character that is perhaps no more accurate than that of the Websterian virago. "Her beauty," he allows, "was not incomparable," but "the attraction of her person, joining with the charm of her conversation . . . was something bewitching."

Cleopatra's couplings may have been affairs of the heart or of the loins for the woman, but they were matters of state for the monarch. As Egypt, she went to bed with Rome.

"Nefertiti is a face without a queen," André Malraux wrote, "and Cleopatra is a queen without a face." Because her images have been so scarce, dispersed, and disputed—and certainly because she was a woman—the question of who she was has been conflated with the mystery of what she looked like. Could she really have been black?

The first Ptolemy was a Macedonian general who assumed power in 323 BC upon the death of Alexander the Great, Egypt's conqueror. All subsequent pharaohs were of Macedonian, that is to say, ethnic Greek, origin. Greek was the language of the court, the bureaucracy, and the race-proud ruling class. Cleopatra is said to have been the only member of her dynasty who bothered to learn Egyptian—in addition to perhaps as many as eight other tongues. Her gifts as a linguist would greatly facilitate her dealings with subject people and rival monarchs.

The Macedonian rulers of Egypt assimilated certain traditional pharaonic customs, though more to ingratiate themselves with the powerful native priesthood than with their subjugated people. One of these customs was royal incest. Three hundred years of strict inbreeding would seem to qualify the house for a Darwin Award. When I asked a Greek friend who is a student of the period how the Ptolemies could possibly have survived so much intermarriage between siblings, she replied, "Infanticide." Since daughters were likelier to be culled than sons, the girls who made it to puberty must have been an exceptionally clever, robust, and comely lot.

But the laws of Egypt regarding marriage, property, divorce, and inheritance, even among commoners, had long been more liberal toward women than those of Greece or Rome. Queens had been co-regents with brothers and uncles for millennia. The Ptolemies recognized the virtues of this arrangement, though occasionally one of their queens came to exercise sole power. Cleopatra I was the first to do so, and her competent if ruthless management of the kingdom for sixteen years (193–176 BC) legitimatized a precedent that her great-great-granddaughter would not forget. Certain of the Ptolemaic queens were Seleucid, which is to say Greeks from Syria. But there is at least one blank in their otherwise well-documented bloodline—the obscure consort of Cleopatra's grandfather Ptolemy IX. It is said that she was a concubine. So it is possible, though unlikely, that Cleopatra VII was of mixed descent. There is no question, however, that the figure she cut to the Romans who reviled her was as troubling and hybrid, even monstrous, as an Egyptian deity's. The nature of the monster is summed up nicely on a temple stele where Cleopatra is referred to as "the queen himself."

The curators of this show have, with diligence and tenacity, assembled under one roof every probable extant likeness of Cleopatra. Yet even the bronze and silver drachmas struck by her own mints disagree about her profile. On some she appears as a "radiant" young Greek woman with full cheeks, a small head festooned with tight braids gathered into a bun, and a finely chiseled nose. On others she has the aspect of a crone, with a taurine neck and a hawkish beak—or, better, of

THE QUEEN HIMSELF 419

"Mark Antony in a wig," as Mary Hamer puts it in her book *Signs of Cleopatra*. That, of course, was very likely the queen's intention. It was with Antony that she hoped to rule the world, and, had they not been crushed definitively by Octavian at the great naval battle of Actium in September of 31 BC, she undoubtedly would have.

Cleopatra's liaison with Antony lasted for a decade, with a three-year hiatus when he left her for Octavia. It was also frequently interrupted by his soldiering, although he sometimes took her along, at least part of the way. Wherever they traveled—Antioch, Samos, Athens, or Ephesus (and it was here that Antony is said to have plundered the great library of Pergamum to restock the shelves of Cleopatra's library at Alexandria, which had been decimated by fire)—their train was flamboyant. And whenever they converged again in her capital, their reunions were, as their first meeting at Tarsus had been, uninhibitedly bacchanalian. In 36 BC, they had a third child, Ptolemy Philadelphus. It is logical that their passion was both tempered and fueled by the mistrust, the opportunism, the ever-present sense of danger and attunement to betrayal that were natural between allies in the ancient world when so much was at stake. But in time they seem to have become something anachronistically modern: a doting couple.

Cities, provinces, and kingdoms were always Cleopatra's business, despite a coy remark, attributed to her by Plutarch, to the effect that big, strong Antony's "game" was world conquest while hers was tending the home fires. As Antony's relations with Octavian deteriorated, Cleopatra became his bulwark in the east—providing the manpower and the capital essential for his campaigns. In exchange, she demanded and received successive bequests of land—vast ones—which restored the Egyptian empire, albeit briefly, to its former glory. They invested their children with titles and dominions, and engaged them, however precociously, to the offspring of neighboring royalty—the first stage of a long-term imperial strategy. They minted the coins on which they resemble each other, with his head on the obverse and hers on the reverse. If she took on some of his attributes, he took on some of hers, appearing at her side as a fellow divinity.

At least until 32 BC, when Antony repudiated Octavia in Athens, and Octavian read Antony's will to the Senate (stipulating that he be

buried in Alexandria with Cleopatra), he enjoyed great popular support in Rome. But he never returned to rally it, leaving the political
stage to his enemy—a cavalier miscalculation that, like Caesar's,
seems to have had the queen's "fingerprints" on it. Perhaps her effect
on him was as despotic and intoxicating as the poets claimed. Rumors reached Rome that he had abandoned his toga for the Greek
chlamys; that she reviewed his troops with a bodyguard of Praetori-
ans; that he followed her litter humbly on foot (though not, as
Shakespeare would add so provocatively, that she wore his sword).

Antony's alleged response, recorded by Suetonius, when Octavian, playing the outraged brother-in-law, protested his multiple de-
sertions and sacrileges, strikes a rather too pedantically macho note:
"What has changed your mind: that I am screwing the queen? Is she
my wife? Have I just begun, or have I been doing it nine years already? And do you screw only Drusilla? . . . Does it really matter
where and in whom you get it up?" Evidently, it did. "It seemed possible," Lucan wrote, "that the world would be ruled by a woman,
and not a Roman woman, either."

Octavian finally declared war not against Antony but against the
"harlot queen" of Egypt and her "withered eunuchs." In preparation
for the inevitable showdown, Antony and Cleopatra had established a
string of military staging points along the west coast of Greece, and by
the autumn of 32 BC, they had assembled a formidable force of ships
and men. But, in the months before Actium, they seemed more intent
on revels, tourism, and staging a mammoth theater festival at Samos
than on securing their rear and their supply lines. As the Roman legions, led by the great Agrippa, inexorably bulldozed their way north-
ward from Methone, Cleopatra supposedly urged Antony to make a
final stand at sea. He may have had no choice, but most accounts of
the battle hold the queen at least partially responsible for this and a series of other strategic blunders that precipitated their catastrophe. She
was personally in command of a third of the fleet, and for obscure reasons, generally portrayed as feminine cowardice or panic, she hoisted
her purple sails and, with the outcome of the engagement still in dis-
pute, gave the order for a sudden breakout toward open water. Some
of her vessels, including the royal flagship, which was laden with her
treasury, did breach the Roman blockade and regained Alexandria. It

is said that when Antony saw her flee he abandoned his troops in order to pursue her. Octavian's chroniclers celebrated his victory as a
morally uplifting rout of a "lascivious fury" who, having unmanned a
great warrior, had aspired to corrupt a virile commonwealth.

The last Cleopatra show as comprehensive as this one may have taken
place in 29 BC, when Octavian decorated the newly refurbished ("purified" was the official term) Capitoline temples and Senate House
with the spoils from Cleopatra's tomb. The emperor had hoped to
exhibit the queen herself—no longer himself—but she had thwarted
him a year after the Battle of Actium, when he finally overran her
capital, by outwitting her guards (she was under a suicide watch) to
slip the mortal coil. Apparently, she died with more panache than
Antony, who fell upon his sword, missed his vital organs, lingered in
agony, and was finally hoisted up through a window (the doors were
barred) to breathe his last in Cleopatra's arms. Octavian had refused
her pleas for mercy and an offer to abdicate in favor of her children.
If one can credit the operatic and conflicting accounts of their final
interview (in one, she was dressed to kill; in another, she had torn
out her hair in grief, and clawed her wasted cheeks until they bled),
he also resisted her last-ditch attempt to seduce him.

However much the Romans deplored her life, they unanimously
approved her death—noble as one of their own. "No one knows the
truth about [its] manner," Plutarch admits, though supposedly two
small fang marks were found on her arm. But if the instrument of her
suicide was a snake, it was probably a cobra rather than an asp. The
venom of the latter produces lingering and unsightly suffering, the
bite of the former a swift, relatively painless petrifaction, and the cobra had as much symbolic as anesthetic value. On the basis of research done for this exhibition, scholars now authenticate Cleopatra's
portraits by the trinity of cobras she wore on her distinctive diadem.
However she died, even Octavian's famously stony heart must have
melted a little at the sight of her body. The future emperor honored
Antony's will and Cleopatra's last request: that they be buried together. Their grave site has never been found.

Historians generally agree that what we like fondly to call Western civilization was based on the "Apollonian" civic model of Augustan Rome. Octavian became Augustus in the eighth month of 27 BC, the third anniversary of his defeat of Dionysian Cleopatra. This leads Mary Hamer to suggest that our enduring fascination with her is as an "originary myth," a dark one, that punishes female desire and ambition and gives woman her place in the social order. Yet one could also argue that our fascination with Cleopatra endures precisely because she confounds the originary myth. Her desire and ambition have been rewarded with immortality; she disdains a place in the social order. And, while her coins may tarnish between polishings, her image has, for two millennia, been proof as much against Roman propaganda as against Hollywood kitsch, Orientalist fetishizing, and identity politics.

After days at the museum among crowds of restive schoolchildren on their Easter break, I spent my evenings with a friend who was closing up a Victorian row house that she had recently inherited. Its owners, a poet and his wife, of gentle birth and disposition, had, like the ancient Egyptians, been devout cat worshippers. In sixty years, they had collected much that was rare but had repaired nothing that was mundane. Their orphaned felines had been adopted, though pigeons still roosted in the leaking rafters. My friend kept finding, in this ghostly dovecote, many a curious, ancient talisman, and one night she showed me a coin that had been lodged in the floorboards beneath a ragged Persian carpet. It was worn to the shape of a waning moon and so blackened with age that we couldn't tell if the metal was bronze or silver, or read the inscription. But under a loupe we could discern the profile of a woman with handsome features and a head of tight braids banded by a diadem. It seemed familiar, even in its improbability.

"The profile," Isak Dinesen wrote, "is the true face of a king," by which she meant—as the Windsors have discovered—that when he moves out of symbolic silhouette and into the glare of secular illumination, he loses his majesty. That will never happen to Cleopatra. There's not enough light to throw.

—May 7, 2001

VII

ENVOI

Odd Jobs

Every writer I know has at one time dreamed of finding a different line of work—less solitary and solipsistic, more remunerative or athletic, something of greater immediate utility to the human race. I would have liked to be a brain surgeon.

Last week, I was inspired to rethink my alternative career plans. The 2000 census data was available for downloading, and it included lists of the thirty-one thousand professions open to census respondents. One table orders them alphabetically; another groups them into twenty-three über-categories, which are ranked according to somewhat inscrutable Darwinian criteria: "skill-level," suggested one census official, or "roughly descending socioeconomic status," according to an introduction to an older job index, or perhaps just muscle-to-fat ratio. Extrapolating somewhat recklessly, I admit, from macro to micro, from ontology through ontogeny to taxonomy via toxicology (it was happy hour), I reached the following conclusions about our new social order.

Presidents and board chairmen (but not chairpeople) are, predictably, top dogs, but so are liquor commissioners. Oil-lease operators and zoo directors share second place. Fashion stylists, along with liquidators, rate highly, at 5. Bank cashiers and bank presidents fraternize bolshevistically at 12. Farmwives, sharecroppers, and stallion keepers hover around 20, with rat and muck farmers, ahead of space physicists (170), animal and people bounty hunters (611 and 382, respectively), impregnators (881), soubrettes (270), blood donors

(465), wort extractors (896), boardinghouse keepers (34), and Web developers (111), though they may be in for a downgrade next time around; and vastly ahead of test pilots (903), blow-off workers (961), milkmen (913), goat drivers (920), and the undervalued zanjero (an assessor of water rights in the Southwest), who, at 975, is close to the bottom.

It was refreshing to think that, in someone's estimation, welfare mothers (460) rank above yacht masters (931), and that cancer researchers (165) have more prestige than tax lawyers (210)—though not, alas, more than undertakers (32). Stripteasers and bull fiddlers move and shake at 274 and 275, respectively, alongside professional athletes (272), clowns and cowboys (276), and journalists (281). Tonsorial artists are a cut above hairdressers (450 to 451), while medical doctors (in the age of HMOs) rank just 306—well behind *mohels*, at 204, and faith healers, at 206, but marginally ahead of naprapaths, at 326.

House wreckers (22) and casino managers (33) are highly prized members of society, at least by census officials. No one confessed to being a home wrecker, although, apparently, various respondents did admit to practicing the métiers of axman, bootlegger, gang leader, knockdown man, roughneck, roustabout, rabbit fancier, roving hand, slasher, skull grinder, sponger, and spooner. An unspecified number also carry out the work of baggage smasher (453). But we knew that.

It should come as no surprise that pollsters (181) rank higher than politicians (202) and political reporters (281), or that literary agents, at 50—a nose ahead of horse traders, at 51—outrank authors. However, anyone who has ever tried to put together a barbecue grill by flashlight on a buggy summer night will question the assignment of assembly-instructions writers to the top of the scribe hierarchy (284), while biographers and novelists (socioeconomically indistinguishable) must content themselves with a 285. I tarried in the book section, impressed that there was so much to do besides write: book canvasser, cleaner, coverer, cutter, finisher, jogger, mender, packer, and sewer. But I also felt an instinctive professional kinship with those who serve the public in certain other guises—as, for example, borers, bucket chuckers, carnies, impersonators, morale officers, printer's devils, puppet masters, riddlers, smoothers, smutters, snipers, snubbers, solution-makers, sourers, and perhaps also bone pullers, pickers, and crushers.

So many jobs, so little time! Briskly scrolling through the populous categories of assemblers, apprentices, assistants, officers, repairers, salespeople, and teachers, I stopped to wonder about the workday of an aging room hand, joy loader, legman, pond monkey, rabbler, rink rat, riprap man, anti-squeak worker, bad-work gatherer, skoog operator, size changer, sister superior, snake charmer, and zoogler.

I found no listing for brain surgeon as such, though there is one for brainer (781). Still, it comforted me to think that, no matter how tough times get, I can always apply—confident of my fitness—for work as a wrong-address clerk.

—April 8, 2001

Acknowledgments

I am grateful to Robert Gottlieb, who brought me to *The New Yorker* in 1986; and to David Remnick, who brought me back—or, as it now feels, home—in 1999, and promoted me to staff writer a year later.

I am grateful to *The New Yorker* staff, and, in particular, to the heroic checking department, but above all to Sharon DeLano, my editor between 1999 and 2004, and to Virginia Cannon, my current editor. Both have enriched my work immeasurably.

I am grateful to the many good friends and colleagues who have helped to give these essays focus, polish, and direction—and only they know how much.

I am grateful to my son, Will Thurman Naythons, who is now eighteen but who was ten when I took up full-time journalism again—and I don't think he can know how much.

And finally, I am grateful to my publisher and old friend Jonathan Galassi for his faith in this book. It, too, feels like a homecoming.